T0345000

Hawai‘i

Markets and Governments in Economic History

A SERIES EDITED BY PRICE FISHBACK

Also in the series:

Hawai'i

Eight Hundred Years of Political and Economic Change

SUMNER LA CROIX

THE UNIVERSITY OF CHICAGO PRESS   CHICAGO AND LONDON

The University of Chicago Press, Chicago 60637
The University of Chicago Press, Ltd., London
© 2019 by The University of Chicago
Published 2019
Printed in the United States of America

28 27 26 25 24 23 22 21 20 19   1 2 3 4 5

ISBN-13: 978-0-226-59209-1 (cloth)
ISBN-13: 978-0-226-59212-1 (e-book)
DOI: https://doi.org/10.7208/chicago/9780226592121.001.0001

Library of Congress Cataloging-in-Publication Data

Names: La Croix, Sumner J., 1954– author.
Title: Hawai'i : eight hundred years of political and economic
    change / Sumner La Croix.
Other titles: Markets and governments in economic history.
Description: Chicago ; London : The University of Chicago Press, 2019. |
Series: Markets and governments in economic history |
    Includes bibliographical references and index.
Identifiers: LCCN 2018035625 | ISBN 9780226592091 (cloth : alk. paper) |
    ISBN 9780226592121 (e-book)
Subjects: LCSH: Hawaii—History. | Hawaii—Economic conditions. |
    Hawaii—Politics and government.
Classification: LCC DU625 .L33 2019 | DDC 996.9—dc23
LC record available at https://lccn.loc.gov/2018035625

♾ This paper meets the requirements of ANSI/NISO Z39.48–1992 (Permanence of Paper).

TO THE FRIENDS AND FAMILY
WHO GAVE ME SO MUCH SUPPORT
WHEN IT MATTERED SO MUCH

Contents

Preface

My interest in Hawai'i's economic history began when I arrived at the University of Hawai'i in 1981 and picked up *Shoal of Time*, the classic work by Gavan Daws on the history of Hawai'i. His powerful and entertaining writing raised numerous questions concerning Hawai'i's economy history, and those questions led me to Ted Morgan's 1948 book, *Hawaii: A Century of Economic Change: 1778–1876*. Morgan's book is a traditional work of economic history that focuses more on documenting what happened than on trying to figure out why things happened. It raises more questions than it answers, and that opened the door for me to start my own research in the field. During the 1980s and 1990s, I worked with a team of co-authors who used the econometric and theoretical tools of the new economic history to take another look at the major issues in Hawai'i's history and economic history. Our collaboration led to numerous professional articles on a wide range of economic and political topics.

In the following decade, my research became more focused on the modern economies of Japan and China and less focused on Hawai'i's history. Beginning in 2011, I took a second look at my early research and began to think about extending its coverage to the full 750–850 years of Hawai'i history and to major events and trends not yet examined by economic historians. Maybe the delay in fleshing out the Hawai'i research was fortuitous, as extending coverage to Hawai'i's entire history was made possible only by the amazing research of the large group of archaeologists whose work over the last three decades has revolutionized what we know about Hawai'i prior to Western contact. Reading the work of Atholl Anderson, Jim Bayman, Tom Dye, Michael Graves, Robert Hommon, Terry Hunt, Thegn Lade-foged, Carl Lipo, Mark McCoy, and, in particular, Patrick Kirch and Timo-thy Earle has been inspirational and has completely changed how I think about Hawai'i's past.

My focus in this book is on how political and economic institutions co-evolved over time in Hawai'i. To carry out this work, it was important to extend the frame of history back to the discovery of Hawai'i, because the early coevolution of political institutions and the agricultural economy still casts a long shadow over today's political institutions and economic development. This is partly because political orders tend to persist and partly because the early centralization of Hawai'i's political institutions set the stage for the modern centralized political institutions that have facili-tated today's high incomes and exhibitions of rent-seeking behavior.

Each chapter has roots in the 'āina, in Hawai'i's land. That's not par-ticularly surprising for a study of an archipelago where agriculture was the major economic activity through the 1950s and whose land area is just 4.1 million acres. Land has played a central role throughout Hawai'i's politi-cal history because which persons had what types of land rights was always critical to maintaining or restoring political equilibrium. My analysis of the coevolution of political orders and land rights is facilitated by repeated ap-plication of a theoretical framework developed by Douglass North, John Wallis, and Barry Weingast to understand how different types of political orders work. In their framework, important people and their supporters agree to cooperate rather than fight with one another because they are provided with economic rents that they would lose if they decided not to cooperate. Throughout Hawai'i's history, those economic rents have been provided by allocating valuable lands to critical groups in the ruling coali-tion. When adjustments in the ruling coalition were required, land rights were reorganized or redistributed in an attempt to preempt groups from engaging in violent conflict to achieve a new political equilibrium.

A final theme that persists throughout the book is how closely changes in Hawai'i's small economy and polity have been tied to changes in the global climate, the global economy, and the global political environment. Internal changes and developments have been important, but most of the major political and economic changes in Hawai'i have been driven by its integration with world markets and its eventual absorption by the United States. It's impossible to understand Hawaiian history without placing it within the context of global economic and political history.

This book unapologetically covers just slices, albeit important slices, of Hawai'i's economic and political history. It has little to say about the specifics of the sugar plantation economy and almost nothing to say about pineapple, which grew to be as big an industry as sugar in the 1930s. It does not cover the internment of Japanese during World War II or the settlement for persons with Hansen's disease established on Moloka'i in the 1860s. It doesn't present any historical detail on the postwar Democratic Party revolution. It spends little time on the development of the tourism industry. And I have little to say about why Hawai'i's economy has grown so slowly since the early 1990s or the rise of inequality over the last 30 years. Much of the reason for these omissions is that the book is not meant to be a comprehensive economic or political history. To complete that task I would need about 700 more pages and about 10 more years.

Another, maybe more compelling, reason for leaving out these topics is that most have already received a lot of attention in wonderful works by other historians. Tom Coffman's three great books, *To Catch a Wave*, *The Nation Within*, and *The Island Edge of America* paint vivid portraits of the people involved in the transitions from monarchy to territory to statehood. The one-volume history of Hawai'i by Gavan Daws, *Shoal of Time*, is beautifully written and covers major events from the Cook voyage to the Burns governorship. James Mak's book on the rise of the tourism industry, *Waikiki: The Development of a Dream Destination*, provides a compelling and well-documented history of how Hawai'i became so rich so quickly after World War II. Jonathan Osorio's book *Dismembering Lāhui* examines closely how adoption of Western laws and institutions transformed the Hawaiian Nation in the nineteenth century. Carol MacLennan's book *Sovereign Sugar* provides a detailed history of the rise and fall of the sugar industry. Noenoe Silva's book *Aloha Betrayed* awakened me to the extent of native Hawaiian resistance to annexation. Puakea Nogelmeier's book *Mai Pa'a I Ka Leo* provides lucid insights into the many Hawaiian voices that participated in vigorous mid- to late nineteenth-century debates on Hawai'i's future but have yet to be heard today.

The book might never have been written but for a wonderful lunch in April 1999 with Michael Bordo, Hugh Rockoff, and Eugene White prior to a seminar at Rutgers University. Their encouragement was the spark that started this endless enterprise. Numerous friends and colleagues have read drafts of these chapters and the articles that preceded them over the last 30 years. John Wallis provided trenchant critiques of each chapter, and his influence is everywhere in this book. Jim Mak's knowledge of Hawai'i's history and economy helped me improve all of the main chapters. Phil Hoffman's comments on chapters 2 and 3 were absolutely vital in keeping them tied to the broader literature in economic history. I also thank Governor George Ariyoshi, Minja Choe, Alan Dye, Price Fishback, Theresa Greaney, Bruce Johnsen, Baybars Karacaovali, Lauren Moriarty, Puakea Nogelmeier, and William Richardson III for their comments on various chapters. Abraham Pi'ianai'a, Ilima Pi'ianai'a, and George Kanahele all provided encouragement and guidance when I first started doing research on Hawai'i in the 1980s. Over the last few years, numerous friends and family have repeatedly asked me, "Is the book done yet?" Believe it or not, the question always came as a bit of a shock and caused me to devote more time and reflection to the project and bring it to a conclusion. Special thanks are due to Price Fishback and Pam Slaten, who were my hosts in Tucson, Arizona, while I worked on several chapters and provided endless encouragement.

Many University of Hawai'i students have provided research assistance over the years. Special thanks are due to Thomas Yim for his careful work in compiling the data sets on Hawai'i's sugar workers. Financial assistance from the Social Science Research Institute at the University of Hawai'i was instrumental in assembling materials on the Hawaiian Homes program and in supporting my research on land reform in Hawai'i. I also thank John Barker, Jennifer Higa, Tia Reber, DeSoto Brown, Jodie Mattos, Dore Minatodani, and staff at the Hawai'i State Archives, the National Library of Australia, and the University of Hawai'i for their help finding sources and photos. Joe Jackson and David Pervin were instrumental in guiding me through the early days of this project, and Holly Smith and Jane Macdonald provided tremendous assistance and support in getting me to the finish line at the University of Chicago Press.

Some chapters have a basis in journal articles and book chapters that were previously published. All have been extensively revised, updated, and refreshed by new developments in archaeology, economics, and economic history. Thanks are due to Westview Publishers (*The Other Side of the Frontier: Economic Explorations into Native American History*, edited by Linda Barrington), *Explorations in Economic History* (April 1984, March 1989), *Journal of Economic History* (December 1990, March 1997), *Urban Studies* (June 1989, June 1995), *Research in Law and Economics* (1995), and *Advances in Agricultural Economic History* (2000). I owe huge intellectual debts to my co-authors who worked so hard and long on the articles that served as the foundations for several chapters: Jim Roumasset on chapters 4 and 5; Lou Rose on chapters 8, 10, and 11; Jim Mak on chapters 10, and 11; Chris Grandy on chapter 6; and Price Fishback on chapters 6 and 7. I enjoyed each of these collaborations immensely and can only note that the most interesting ideas in the volume surely originated from the creative and productive minds of these longtime colleagues and friends.

Sumner La Croix
Honolulu, December 2017

CHAPTER ONE

The Short History of Humans in Hawai'i

Humans have a very short history in Hawai'i. The Hawaiian archipelago was the last major land area on the planet to be settled when Polynesians traveled over 2,000 miles north to the islands about 750–850 years ago. Just 50 years ago, our understanding of the social, political, and economic changes that unfolded over the next eight centuries was limited by how little we knew about the first four to five centuries of settlement. Today, a series of snapshots of Hawai'i's early history has emerged due to extensive excavations by archaeologists, scientific advances in dating archaeological remains, and remarkable connections made between the new physical evidence and oral stories passed down across generations of Hawaiians. A series of insightful and ambitious recent studies has woven these historical snapshots into more coherent historical narratives. These synthetic narratives have, in turn, awakened us to the importance of grasping the full sweep of Hawai'i's history: knowing more about the economic and political institutions in place centuries earlier allows us to see clear linkages between those early institutions and today's institutions and outcomes.

Some linkages are obvious. When we look at the ponded taro fields at Hanalei, Kaua'i, we see not just today's taro fields but also the outlines of the irrigation systems put in place in the thirteenth and fourteenth centuries by the new immigrants from East Polynesia and their descendants. A tour of these fields quickly informs us how remarkably productive they still are today. Our new understanding of Hawaiian history allows us, however, to connect the high productivity of these fields today with their high productivity 700 years earlier. The surpluses generated by these taro fields 700 years ago allowed an economically and culturally rich society to emerge and flourish, and the rich inheritance of these ancient institutions is reflected in the productivity of today's farmers at Hanalei.

Important connections between the distant past and the present have been found in societies around the globe. Consider that one of the very best "predictors of an individual's income today is the level of riches attained by that person's ancestors hundreds of years ago."[1] Consider African tribes that captured and sold people from other tribes for the slave trade during the sixteenth, seventeenth, and eighteenth centuries. Today, the countries that encompass those societies have governments than tend to be more authoritarian and citizens who tend to be poorer and have less trust in one another than citizens of other African countries.[2] Consider the German villages where Jews were massacred during the fourteenth-century Black Death. They turn out to be the same German villages where Jews were terrorized during the 1920s and citizens voted for the Nazi Party.[3]

The linkages between the past and present in Hawai'i's political history are also quite remarkable. Archaeologists and historians now date the emergence of centralized political institutions on the island of O'ahu from sometime in the fifteenth or early sixteenth century, more than 500 years ago. Small, resource-rich chiefdoms, each supported by a state religion, merged into larger states and competed with one another for the next 350–400 years to control more territory and people within the eight major Hawaiian islands (fig. 1.1). In these well-organized states, property rights in land were well specified and enforced, and a system of post-harvest taxation facilitated risk sharing and mobilization of state resources for war. We see these well-functioning institutions mirrored in today's sophisticated political institutions and high living standards. The *maka'āinana*, the people who worked the land, had living standards with levels of nutrition and leisure that probably equaled or exceeded those of peasants in England. In 2018, the typical Hawai'i household continues to have a standard of living exceeding that of the typical English household.

Three more general features of Hawai'i's past political institutions are reflected in its twenty-first-century political institutions. First, today's political institutions reflect the centralization of those that emerged 500–600 years ago, as the state government cedes few powers to Hawai'i's four

FIGURE 1.1. *Na Mokupuni O Hawaii* [Map of the Hawaiian Islands], 1839. Drawing: Lahainaluna Prints. Source: Hawaiian Mission Children's Society Library.

county governments, and the state constitution endows the state governor with more powers than governors in other states hold. Second, ruling chiefs used land redistribution as a mechanism to form and preserve ruling political coalitions in ancient Hawai'i. Land redistribution was the lubricant that allowed a ruling chief to respond to changes in the political power of powerful chiefs and their supporters. What is striking is how land redistribution continued to be used as a mechanism to stabilize ruling coalitions when Hawai'i was unified by King Kamehameha in 1795, when King Kauikeaouli reorganized property rights and modernized the government in the 1840s, when the territorial colonial government took the crown lands in 1898, and when the new state government acted in 1967 to allow homeowners to force the sale of leased land under their homes. Today, politicians forgo explicit redistribution of land to stabilize their political coalitions, relying instead on the dual application of state and county land use laws to distribute above-normal economic returns— *economic rents*—to favored parties. Finally, Hawai'i's early political institutions reflected its origin as a society of immigrants who established independent settlements that were neither controlled by nor dependent on their home governments. It is striking that despite over 75 years of colonial rule in the late nineteenth and twentieth centuries, independent political institutions and ambitions re-emerged with the push to statehood in the 1950s, and more are emerging with the more recent push by Hawaiian sovereignty groups to achieve self-determination.

Independence is also an early theme in Hawaiian history, as the population was founded by Polynesians who embarked on long, risky voyages in hope of finding a new home. The voyages to Hawai'i are now recognized as among the last waves in a pulse of voyages and settlements of East Polynesia that happened during the eleventh, twelfth, and thirteenth centuries. It had been more than 1,500 years since Polynesians had undertaken voyages that discovered new archipelagos, but suddenly there came pulses of voyages to the north (Hawai'i), to the southwest (New Zealand), and to the southeast (Rapa Nui, also called Easter Island). From about 1200 to about 1300–1400, voyages between Hawai'i and the newly settled Marquesas Islands and Society Islands brought new immigrants, plants, technologies, culture, language, and political and economic institutions to Hawai'i (see chap. 2).[4] From the archaeological record and ancient oral traditions, the archaeologists Timothy Earle and Patrick Kirch have constructed compelling narratives of the establishment of new communities by Polynesians in their newly found islands. An emerging body of evidence suggests that the first waves of Polynesian immigrants transformed Hawai'i's environment, burning lowland forests and harnessing streams in mountain valleys to create thousands of ponded taro farms, fields of sweet potatoes and yams, and groves of breadfruit trees.

The original Polynesians carried their culture, plants, animals, technologies, and political institutions with them on their voyages to re-establish their societies when they found their new island homes.[5] They came to the islands with well-established norms of behavior and clear understandings of how governments and societies functioned on their home islands, all of which possessed natural environments not that different from those they found in Hawai'i. The immigrants were far enough separated from their homes by distance and the risks of voyaging that they surely discounted rule from the home country as a possibility. From the beginning, they must have assumed that their new settlements would be autonomous, yet surely could not have imaged how completely isolated from other societies they would become.

The Polynesians settling Hawai'i did what migrants to new lands who come from established societies always do: they re-created the societies, polities, and institutions of their homelands during their early years of settlement. There is only fragmentary evidence regarding post-discovery contacts between Hawai'i and Polynesia, but archaeologist Patrick Kirch has pointed out an array of connections that reinforce oral traditions of cultural transfer (e.g., religious traditions brought by the priest Pā'ao from Tahiti, the *pahu* drum and temple rituals brought by La'amaikahiki, and breadfruit seedlings brought by Kaha'i), technological transfer, and perhaps trade (e.g., volcanic glass adzes mined from the Mauna Kea quarry during the 1300s found in the Marquesas and an adz mined on Kaho'olawe found in the Tuamotu Archipelago).[6] With the transformation of the environment and the rapid expansion of farming and settlement came rapid population growth.[7] Archaeologists studying the first 100–150 years of settlement contend that most of the valuable lands had been claimed by 1400, setting the stage for changes in the returns to laborers and landowners and, consequently, the overall political environment.

After voyagers and their descendants re-established the political and economic orders of their homelands in Hawai'i, an unthinkable and incredibly rare event unfolded: for roughly 350–400 years, Hawaiians had no contact with the rest of Polynesia and, for that matter, the rest of the world.[8] Hawaiians are one of only a very few people in world history who have ever become isolated from other societies solely due to changes in the climate and the ocean that affected their abilities to navigate beyond the islands and other peoples' abilities to navigate to Hawai'i.[9] Perhaps the winds in the Northeastern Pacific Ocean changed, or perhaps the Polynesian peoples in the Eastern Pacific Ocean began to view long-distance voyaging as more risky or less profitable. Whatever the reasons for the end of voyaging, flows of migrants, ideas, and trade to and from Polynesia stopped completely for about three to four centuries. During these 300–400 years, the Hawai'i population grew rapidly (see chap. 3), which means that many families had large numbers of children. Losing the opportunity to migrate was a big loss for these large generations, as they were forced to compete for land in Hawai'i rather than voyage to discover and settle new archipelagos.

Closure of the migration option probably had several other important effects. It could have been important in the fifteenth century when O'ahu chiefs consolidated their control because it left O'ahu farmers with one less option to resist attempts by the chiefs who managed the land to extract more income from them. Isolation from other peoples in Polynesia meant that there were fewer ideas in circulation and no one from other societies visiting who might directly or indirectly raise questions about the increasingly exalted status of Hawai'i's chiefs (ali'i). Isolation meant that it was easier for ruling chiefs to legitimize the ideology that enshrined their exceptionally differentiated status.[10] And isolation also meant the end of trade in valuable goods, as voyaging canoes were not suited for long-distance transport of staple goods. An end in the trade for valuable goods such as volcanic glass adzes would have reduced the incomes of highly skilled craftsmen and left them more dependent on trade with high-ranking chiefs, again strengthening the chiefs' wealth and power.

The several Hawaiian states that were competing for power by the fifteenth century had evolved in a direction quite different from their Polynesian counterparts in Tahiti or the Marquesas Islands, developing more features like those seen in the states in central Mexico in the thirteenth and fourteenth centuries that consolidated into the Aztec Empire, the competing Wankan states that emerged in the upper Mantaro Valley in Peru in the fourteenth and fifteenth centuries, or even the Egyptian Pharaonic state during the Second and Third Dynasties.[11] In all of the newly consolidated states in Hawai'i, there developed a sharply differentiated elite (ali'i) whose social rank and privileges were far above those of the main body of the population (kānaka maoli). When ali'i passed through a village, kānaka maoli had to lie face down on the ground or face execution. The ali'i's divine connections were supported by a state religion and an elaborate system of genealogical mapping denied to the rest of the population.[12] These cultural developments pose a central question for the study of Hawai'i's history: What was it about isolation and internal conditions in Hawai'i that led to the development of a society with such huge gaps in status between the 1–2 percent of the population who ruled and those who worked the land?

My analysis of this question follows in the wake of a huge literature generated by a small army of archaeologists who have extensively probed the origins of archaic states in Hawai'i.[13] Chapter 3 reviews archaeologists' theories and evidence regarding the origins of archaic states in Hawai'i and considers how the widespread warfare among these states affected the institutions that evolved, and vice versa. All of the Hawaiian states were theocracies, in which religious and state officials were part of the same overall organization. A critical feature of the archaic state's architecture was its ritualized system of taxation during the New Year's festival (makahiki), which facilitated extraction of economic surplus and preparations for war. The integration of political authority with a state religion to build tens of thousands of small, medium, and monumental

FIGURE 1.2. Kalani'ōpu'u, *Mō'ī* of the island of Hawai'i, and his men paddling to Captain James Cook's ship. Drawing: John Webber, 1784. Source: Bishop Museum.

stone altars is a classic feature of the archaic states that developed in Central and South America and the Middle East. An understanding of the forces underpinning theocratic institutions is critical, as it sets the stage for understanding why Hawai'i's ruling chiefs and high priests (*kāhuna nui*) abolished the state religion four decades after Hawai'i's isolation came to a sudden end in 1778, when white-sailed British ships from the expedition led by Captain James Cook appeared off the shore of Kaua'i (fig. 1.2).

When Hawai'i re-emerged to the rest of the world in 1778, its political and social orders had evolved in directions very different from those in other Polynesian societies.[14] Small chiefdoms were gone, replaced by several larger archaic states, each ruled by a class of chiefs with status and wealth far above that of average people. Ruling chiefs were supported by specialized warriors (*koa*) and by a class of prayer specialists (*kāhuna pule*) who orchestrated ritualized ceremonies and supervised the building and maintenance of tens of thousands of small and monumental stone shrines. Societies on O'ahu, Kaua'i, and Moloka'i were richer than those on the islands of Maui and Hawai'i, in large part due to food surpluses generated by extremely productive taro farms squeezed into every corner of their fertile valleys. Population growth had been higher on Maui and Hawaiʻi than on other islands, and it was accompanied by widespread expansion of cultivation on the rain-fed volcanic slopes of Haleakala on Maui and ʻMauna Loa, Mauna Kea, Hualālai, and Kohala on Hawaiʻi. Hawaiian historians writing in the nineteenth century pointed to systems of taxation and administration that allowed competing archaic states to mobilize resources for war, with the populous states on Hawaiʻi and Maui competing to muster bigger armies and the richer states on Oʻahu and Kauaʻi using their superior resources to maintain autonomy.

Integration with foreign societies had two big contradictory consequences for Hawaiʻi's political order. In the short run, it led to further centralization of political authority with the unification of several Hawaiian states, while in the long run it undermined the chiefs' power and led to institutional change (as described in chap. 4). A ruling chief of one of the competing states on the island of Hawaiʻi, Kamehameha, combined bold strategic actions with a first-mover advantage in acquiring guns, cannons, and Western ships to bring all the islands except Kauaʻi and Niʻihau under his rule by 1795. Once unification had been achieved, Kamehameha redistributed lands on the conquered islands to five *aliʻi* from the island of Hawaiʻi who were his principal supporters. This consolidation of political power around a strong king was also accompanied by a massive decline in the Native Hawaiian population, and this decline, along with the effects of resource booms in sandalwood and whaling, would ultimately transform the relationship between *aliʻi* and *makaʻāinana*. The unification also increased the state's capacity to put down rebellions and lowered its reliance on cultural and religious beliefs and injunctions to maintain order. It was surely a factor behind the decisions by Hawaiʻi's ruling chiefs to abolish their state religion in 1819, destroying temples, burning idols, and dispersing prayer specialists.

Less than five months after the abolition of the state religion, the first wave of Protestant missionaries from New England settled in Hawaiʻi. They established churches, developed an alphabet for the Hawaiian language, printed religious and secular materials in Hawaiian, and founded a system of schools in which missionaries provided instruction in reading and writing Hawaiian. The new religious authorities also worked to suppress traditional Hawaiian religious and cultural practices, including the dancing of the hula.[15] The missionaries' influence was at least as pronounced in the political realm. They became influential advisors to high-ranking chiefs and often held cabinet posts in the government. They spread ideas about Western institutions of government and classic theories of political economy among younger and older *ali'i*, and they were the primary instructors at the Lahainaluna Seminary and the Chiefs' Children's School. The transmission of Western ideas to *ali'i* youth and elders was a major influence behind the Hawai'i government's transformation of its indigenous governance institutions. From the 1830s to the 1850s, government institutions changed to incorporate Western concepts of political representation, property, the rule of law, and individual rights. These changes served to modernize its institutions and make the transition from a basic natural state to a mature natural state. The fast transformation may well have been in response to the opportunities and dangers posed by Hawai'i's encounters with the three global naval powers, its rapid population decline, and the economic transformations induced by its sudden participation in international trade.

The political reforms coupled with the transition to private property rights provided fortuitous conditions for sugar plantations to be established, to expand, and to make increasing demands for labor to work fields and factory. Over the next three decades, the robust increases in labor demand were coupled with sharp declines in native Hawaiian labor supplies, a consequence of the more than 50 percent decline in the native Hawaiian population between the 1831–1832 census (129,814 people) and the 1866 census (62,959 people). Hawai'i's government responded to the declining labor force by passing legislation in the 1860s that allowed sugar planters to bring in contract laborers bound to serve at fixed wages for a fixed term of three to five years.[16] During the 1870s and 1880s, planters brought Chinese workers to Hawai'i. The sugar companies were disappointed with these workers, who usually left their plantation jobs at the end of their contracts. Of the roughly 14,000 Chinese workers who entered Hawai'i between 1878 and 1882, only 5,037 still worked on sugar plantations in 1882.[17] In response to this turnover and to a rising tide of anti-Chinese feeling among the populace, the planters and the government stopped bringing in Chinese workers in 1886. Beginning in 1885, a massive inflow of Japanese workers took up the slack. From 1885 to 1900, approximately 80,705 Japanese migrants came to Hawai'i.[18] The massive fall in the native Hawaiian population and the rapid growth of an indentured labor force were critical factors behind both the 1893 overthrow of the monarchy and the diminished political influence of native Hawaiians in the twentieth century under U.S. rule.

In the mid-nineteenth century, changes in property rights to land and labor and the transition to new government institutions facilitated Hawai'i's ongoing integration with the global economy. Exports of sandalwood logs and the supplying of services to whaling ships had already had been undertaken within the existing economic and political institutions, but growth of the sugar industry required large-scale investments in land, irrigation, sugar factories, port facilities, and immigrant labor. The transition to private property rights in land, immigrants working under indentured labor contracts, and Western institutions of government between the 1830s and the 1860s can also be viewed as the very changes that were demanded by a growing sugar industry with foreign ownership and by *ali'i* with interests in the land. Decisions by the king in the 1830s and 1840s to allow chiefs to enter into partnerships with foreign interests to start sugar plantations were motivated by potentially high returns to chiefs and king from exporting sugar grown on their increasingly thinly populated or abandoned lands and by a desire to raise revenues to increase government capacity. The turn to private property in the 1840s and the migration of indentured labor starting in the 1860s have similar roots.

Starting in the 1860s, the rise of large sugar interests, several of which were owned by foreigners or by Caucasian residents of Hawai'i with close ties to the United States, changed Hawai'i's political economy by linking Hawai'i's sugar exports to the U.S. market and Hawai'i's labor market to Asian and European labor markets. Integration with the U.S. sugar market came with the 1876 reciprocity treaty between Hawai'i and the United States that allowed Hawai'i sugar companies to sell in the U.S. market without paying the tariff on sugar, which varied between 20 and 40 percent of the U.S. market price. Sales under this U.S. tariff umbrella provided the sugar companies with big economic rents, but also led to a loss of local control of the sugar industry, as it provided sugar agencies and plantations with incentives to resist any changes in the political architecture that was generating their big returns. When renegotiation of the reciprocity treaty was put in jeopardy by new U.S. demands, including the right to maintain a coaling station at Pearl Bay (now Pearl Harbor), a small group of foreigners took arms to coerce King Kalākaua to sign an amended version of the treaty that included more concessions to the United States and to approve constitutional changes that had the effect of increasing the already considerable power of foreigners in the electorate and government. The 1887 Bayonet Rebellion and its accompanying coerced changes to the Hawai'i Constitution thus signaled both the ascendency of foreign interests and the inability of Hawai'i's police and military forces to prevent the use of coercion against the Hawaiian government.

The central event of Hawai'i's 800 years of history is the overthrow of the monarchy in 1893, but its foundations had already been laid in 1887 with the Bayonet Rebellion and the resulting "Bayonet Constitution." Its proximate cause was the problematic political dynamics unleashed by the renegotiation of the U.S.-Hawai'i trade reciprocity treaty, but a deeper impetus was the rise of imperial interests within the United States that favored annexation of Hawai'i (see chap. 6). The opportunistic behavior of the United States in requesting additional concessions at treaty renewal unleashed the political forces in Hawai'i that led to the Bayonet Rebellion, but it was the passage by the U.S. Congress of the McKinley Tariff in 1890 that unleashed the economic forces that would topple the monarchy. The new law's elimination of the U.S. sugar tariff eliminated the economic rents fed to the Hawai'i sugar industry and pushed it into depression. The ensuing economic crisis in Hawai'i led to immediate political crises for Queen Lili'uokalani during the first two years of her reign, as a new U.S. bounty paid to domestic producers of sugar provided increased incentives for sugar producers to support annexation proposals. In January 1893, Queen Lili'uokalani lost her throne by signaling her willingness to act to reduce the influence of foreigners in Hawai'i by restoring the constitution in effect before the Bayonet Rebellion. A small group of foreigners (the "Committee of Safety"), this time with the assistance of the U.S. minister to Hawai'i, John L. Stevens, and marines from the U.S.S. *Boston*, staged a coup d'état, with the purpose of delivering Hawai'i to the United States for annexation.

The short-lived, so-called Republic of Hawai'i (1893–1898) established after annexation was an autocracy that acted to maintain most of the effective centralized governance institutions associated with the monarchy while placing restrictions on the electorate that ensured its control of all branches of government. The queen was replaced by an unelected president, Sanford B. Dole, who was named in the republic's 1894 constitution as its first president. From its inception, this new regime confiscated lands of the government and crown, without paying any compensation to the deposed Queen Lili'uokalani for the privately owned crown lands. Two treaties of annexation between the regime and the U.S. government were opposed virtually unanimously by Hawaiians and were rejected by the U.S. Senate. Even with the outbreak of the Spanish-American War in April 1898, a two-thirds vote of the Senate could not be obtained for annexation. Imperial interests in the U.S. government found a mechanism for annexation, which proceeded on July 7, 1898, via a resolution approved by a majority vote of both the U.S. Senate and House of Representatives—the same quasi-constitutional method by which the United States annexed the Republic of Texas in 1845.

In 1900, Congress passed the Organic Act, which established a territorial government for its new colony. Its power was concentrated in the U.S. president, who appointed the territorial governor as well as the three territorial Supreme Court justices (see chap. 7). The new colonial government retained extensive executive powers, which for almost six decades were used to create economic rents and distribute them to a dominant political coalition consisting of the U.S. military, the Big Five sugar corporations, and a coalition of Hawaiian and Caucasian voters. However, the stability of the dominant coalition was threatened during the 1910s by the declining welfare of the native Hawaiian population (see chap. 8). During this decade, native Hawaiians began to organize more effectively to demand that the territorial and federal governments take action to address their situation by returning some of the best government-owned agricultural lands to them for settlement. In 1921, the U.S. Congress responded by passing the Hawaiian Homes Commission Act (HHCA), the goal of which was to lease federal government lands to Native Hawaiians for use as ranches, farms, and house lots.[19] Chapter 8 analyzes why this program has struggled to fulfill its goals throughout its existence. Modern econometric techniques are used to test hypotheses that executive and legislative support for the program was driven by the power of Hawaiians at the ballot box and by the changing value of the lands dedicated by the HHCA to the program.

With the power of the territorial government located in Washington, D.C., some groups in Hawai'i advocated for statehood (see chap. 9), as this would establish a sovereign state government and allow a transition from a limited-access colonial political order to an open-access political order, albeit set within the U.S. economic and political union. In 1921, Hawai'i's territorial representative to Congress, Prince Jonah Kūhiō Kalaniana'ole, introduced a bill to admit Hawai'i as a U.S. state, but neither house of Congress would pass a statehood bill until 1950. In the 1940s and 1950s, there was strong support for statehood among Hawai'i residents, probably due to their still-fresh memories of absolute rule by the U.S. military in Hawai'i during World War II and to their longer memories of the poor performance of the territorial government in providing public goods to Hawai'i's emerging middle class. At the national level, statehood was approved because there was a softening of opposition from Southern senators, a lessening of fears that communists had undue influence within Hawai'i labor unions, and a desire by President Eisenhower to provide a Republican counterweight in Congress to the admission of Democratic Party–dominated Alaska as a state.

The popular election of Hawai'i's governor, the appointment of Hawai'i's judiciary by the elected governor, the removal of the U.S. Congress and the U.S. president as an absolute check on passage of laws by the Hawai'i legislature, and the election of two senators and one representative to the U.S. Congress marked a swift and sudden transition in the formal institutions of government from a limited-access to an open-access political order. The policy changes that were enacted over the next 15 years were equally dramatic: a program mandating employer-paid health insurance for full-time (i.e., working more than 20 hours per week) public and private employees, additional money to K–12 education, a massive expansion and transformation of the University of Hawai'i, a strict program of state antitrust legislation and enforcement, and increased investment in infrastructure encompassing new highways, ports, and airports.

Hawai'i's transition to an open-access political order was marred by incorporation in the state constitution of three aspects of the colonial era: highly centralized formal institutions of government; state ownership of the illegally confiscated crown lands; and the provisions of the Hawaiian Homes program. The earlier declaration by the federal government in 1898 that the crown lands were the property of the U.S. federal government was continued by section 5(b) of the Hawaii Admission Act, which turned over 1.4 million acres of public lands, including crown lands, to the new state government.[20] The Admission Act included a nod to native Hawaiian rights in and claims to the crown lands with its establishment in section 5(f) of a trust in the public lands, a requirement not seen in other congressional acts admitting territories as states. Revenues from the public land trust were dedicated to five purposes: "for the support of the public schools and other public educational institutions, for the betterment of the conditions of native Hawaiians, as defined in the Hawaiian Homes Commission Act, 1920, as amended, for the development of farm and home ownership on as widespread a basis as possible, for the making of public improvements, and the provision of lands for public use."

With the distribution of revenues among these five purposes left unspecified, it was to be expected that this poorly constructed constitutional provision would generate endless litigation over both the distribution of revenues and the use of the public land trust. The 1978 constitutional convention tried to resolve these issues by adding more specificity to the revenue distribution requirements, but despite the changes, the crown lands became a symbol for many Hawaiians of how property rights to their lands had been lost or deeply attenuated by the colonial political order imposed by the United States when it absorbed the previously independent kingdom as a territory.

Other land issues besides the crown lands have played a central role in Hawai'i politics since statehood. One was the decision by large landed estates during both the territorial years and the first two decades of statehood to lease land for new housing development rather than to sell it with the home to new homeowners. In chapters 10 and 11, I analyze the origins and effects of a state law, the Land Reform Act (LRA) of 1967, that reorganized property rights for homeowners who leased the lands under their homes. One of many major policy initiatives enacted in the decade after statehood, the LRA was highly controversial when it passed, when it was challenged in state and federal court, and when it was finally implemented. The act allowed owners of single-family homes to petition the state government to use its powers of eminent domain to force the sale of the leased land on which their homes stood. Chapter 10 focuses on why Hawai'i landowners chose to develop so much housing on leased land in the first place and why homeowners demanded the right to buy the land under their homes. Chapter 11 shows that the LRA's reorganization of property rights in leased residential land failed to achieve its stated purpose, a reduction in Honolulu's high land and housing prices. The act's ineffectiveness was not surprising, as three other factors are the main sources of Honolulu's high land and housing prices: natural and cultural amenities, a limited natural supply of developable land, and state and county land use regulations. These factors were responsible for the high land and housing prices in Honolulu in 1960, and they are still responsible for even higher land and housing prices in 2018.[21]

Chapter 12 concludes by examining why Hawai'i has been able to overcome some aspects of its colonial legacy, but not others. Hawai'i escaped some of the deeper problems of colonialism because of its early and long experience with centralized government, its avoidance of slave labor, and the relatively short duration of U.S. colonial rule. During its 60 years of statehood, Hawai'i has, however, been only partly successful in devising mechanisms to redress issues of uncompensated land transfers and suppression of Hawaiian cultural practices and the Hawaiian language. Hawai'i's future as a multicultural open society depends on whether native Hawaiians, the Hawai'i state government, and the U.S. federal government can cooperate to find new mechanisms to redress uncompensated land transfers and the lost sovereignty of native Hawaiians.

CHAPTER TWO

Voyaging and Settlement

The discovery and settlement of Hawai'i by Polynesian voyagers is one of the two signal events of Hawaiian history. Despite its importance, we knew very little about it until recently, partly because the first settlers, Polynesians from the Marquesas Islands and the Society Islands, did not have a written language and thus left no written records. Archaeologists have not found a "first canoe," or, for that matter, any canoe, and it is uncertain where Polynesians first landed in Hawai'i, where the first settlements were located, and how fast they expanded. Nor do we know much about the frequency of return trips to and from the Polynesian homeland or how long they continued. The *mo'oelo*, oral stories of the past, provide glimpses of how discovery and settlement proceeded, but our main source of knowledge is Hawai'i's expanding archaeological record, which has increased dramatically in size and quality since the 1950s, when radiocarbon dating revolutionized the field of archaeology. Over the last 50 years, a flood of excavations by a growing number of archaeologists (often conducting state-mandated archaeological surveys prior to land development) has vastly increased our knowledge and understanding of Hawai'i's prehistory. Multidisciplinary research over the last 25 years has also been crucial, as analyses of ancient tree trunks, sediment cores from ponds, skeletal remains of birds and rats, and tree pollen have provided evidence of significant events that occurred in the first century of settlement. Demographic analysis also provides strong hints that population growth was quite rapid over the first 200–250 years of settlement.

Understanding Hawai'i's discovery, initial settlement, and ensuing rapid population growth are important for understanding the full sweep of Hawaiian history, as the effects of initial events, trends, and institutions often persist far into a society's future. Understanding Hawai'i's discovery requires that three somewhat existential questions be addressed: When did Polynesians voyage to the central Eastern Pacific and then to Hawai'i? Why did those Polynesians voyage? And why did they voyage to Hawai'i, far to the north of the Polynesian heartland? My analysis provides ingredients for tentative answers to these questions by bringing together material from pioneering studies of Hawaiian history recently undertaken by an array of teams of archaeologists and other social scientists. The same teams have also provided new glimpses into how the initial settlement of Hawai'i proceeded, and once again, I use their materials, as well as insights gathered from other initial colonial settlements around the globe, to provide a rough and somewhat speculative sketch of Hawaiian polities and economies after 150–200 years of settlement.

When Did Polynesians Voyage to East Polynesia and Hawai'i?

East Polynesia, with its 15 major archipelagos, was the last area on earth to be reached by human settlement. It encompasses an enormous, roughly triangular expanse of ocean, stretching from the northern tip of the Hawaiian archipelago—1,500 miles north of the island of Hawai'i—to Rapa Nui—4,650 miles southeast of the island of Hawai'i—to the southern tip of New Zealand—5,300 miles to the southwest of the island of Hawai'i (fig. 2.1). The big question that naturally arises is how these archipelagos, scattered over such a huge expanse of the Pacific Ocean, were settled.

In the journal of his first exploratory voyage to the Pacific Ocean, Captain James Cook proposed the idea that Polynesia was settled by

people sail[ing] in those Seas from Island to Island for several hundred Leagues, the Sun serving them for a Compass by day and the Moon and Stars by night. When this comes to be proved, we shall be no longer at a loss to know how the Islands lying in those seas came to be peopled, for if the inhabitants of Uleitea [Raiatea'a in the Society Islands] have been at Islands laying 2 or 300 Leagues

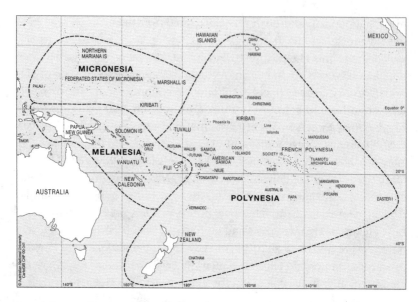

FIGURE 2.1. The Polynesian triangle. Source: CartoGIS Services, College of Asia and the Pacific, the Australian National University.

to the Westward of them, it cannot be doubted but that the inhabitants of those Western Islands may have been at others as far to Westward of them, and so we may trace them from Island to Island quite to the East Indies.[1]

In the journal of his third voyage, Cook also noted the case of the Tahitian people whose canoes had been blown 1,000 miles off course, leaving them stranded on the island of Aitu. Cook's hypothesis that some islands may have been settled by this type of accidental drifting was generalized by historian Andrew Sharp in the 1950s who directly questioned the idea that purposeful long-distance Polynesian voyaging had ever been successful.[2] Two computer simulations helped to kill Sharpe's drift hypothesis.[3] In one study, over 100,000 simulated canoes were set randomly adrift to face an array of simulated weather conditions. The results? Drifting canoes could not account for settlement at distant locations. In the 1970s and 1980s, the successful voyages of the *Hōkūle'a*, a recreation of a traditional Hawaiian voyaging canoe (but for the use of stronger modern materials), also proved instrumental in discrediting the accidental drift hypothesis, as the navigators of the *Hōkūle'a* sailed several times from Hawai'i to Tahiti relying only on traditional Pacific island navigation techniques based on observations of the stars, the sun, the wind, the tides, and seabirds. Both the computer simulations and the modern ocean voyages point to organized voyaging and settlement of Polynesia rather than accidental dispersion.

Recent advances in the science of radiocarbon dating and the application of advanced statistical techniques to materials from archaeological sites have allowed scientists to estimate more accurately when voyagers from West Polynesia first arrived in different parts of Central and East Polynesia.[4] Consider these four central findings from the recent literature on first settlement of Polynesian archipelagos. First, in their seminal survey of radiocarbon dates of initial human colonization in East and Central Polynesia, archaeologists Janet Wilmshurst, Terry Hunt, Carl Lipo, and Atholl Anderson estimated that the initial settlement of West Polynesia—Fiji, Tonga, and Samoa—proceeded over a 1,500-year period between 2300 BC and 800 BC.[5] After these settlements, no major new Polynesian discoveries and settlements occurred for at least 1,800 years, an extraordinary period known as the "Long Pause."[6]

Second, studies by this same team of researchers moved estimates for the dates of first settlements of East Polynesia forward several centuries, placing the arrival of the first canoes in the Society Islands between 1025 and 1120 and in the Marquesas Islands between 1200 and 1277.[7] Because first voyages to Hawai'i probably originated from the Society Islands via the Tuamotu Archipelago or from the Marquesas Islands, the team concluded that the twelfth century was the earliest possible period for Polynesian voyaging to and settlement of Hawai'i.

Third, the new settlement dates for the Hawai'i archipelago were further narrowed in a 2011 study by archaeologists Timothy Rieth, Terry Hunt, Carl Lipo, and Janet Wilmshurst.[8] They conducted a meta-survey of 926 radiocarbon dates from the island of Hawai'i and concluded that "the current best estimate for the Polynesian colonization of this island [is] between AD 1220 and 1261." A 2014 study by archaeologists J. Stephen Athens, Timothy M. Rieth, and Thomas S. Dye uses a different statistical methodology to review radiocarbon data and concludes that the time frame for Hawai'i settlement falls within the wider range of 1000–1210.[9] Together, the new estimates from these radiocarbon studies provide bounds for the settlement of Hawai'i between 1000 and 1260, with the weight of the evidence falling toward the upper end of the range.

Fourth, the Polynesians who colonized the Society Islands and Marquesas Islands during the eleventh or twelfth century engaged in a "pulse" of clustered exploratory voyages during the thirteenth century that reached all three vertices of the Polynesian triangle: the northern vertex (Hawai'i) between 1200 and 1261, the eastern vertex (Rapa Nui) between 1200 and 1253,[10] and the southern vertex (New Zealand) between 1230 and 1282. This pulse of clustered voyages of discovery signals to historians and social scientists that voyages to any one of the triangle's corners need to be understood not just as singular events, but as parts of a "pulse of discovery" during the twelfth or thirteenth century that spread from the Society Islands in every conceivable direction.

The new evidence points to settlement of all island groups in East Polynesia sometime between 1000 and 1260, with the weight of the evidence for Hawai'i pointing toward the upper range of these bounds. These new findings are a big shock to anyone interested in Hawaiian history because only 20 to 40 years ago, many social scientists and historians (including this author) studying Hawai'i accepted discovery dates in a range from the first to the seventh century.[11] By pushing the settlement of all East Polynesian archipelagos to sometime between the eleventh and thirteenth centuries, scholars have also had to consider that they were studying much younger Polynesian societies than they thought. The prehistory of East Polynesia is compressed to just 500–700 years, rather than 1,000–1,500 years. This more compact prehistory forces social scientists to reconsider the circumstances under which Hawai'i was settled, how fast its population grew, and how rapidly political, social, and economic change happened.[12]

Now that we have a better idea of *when* Hawai'i was settled, we can better consider the question of *why and under what circumstances* Hawai'i was settled. Why did small groups of Polynesian voyagers choose to leave their villages in the Marquesas and Society Islands in the twelfth and thirteen centuries and sail and row voyaging canoes (*vaca moana*) into the unknown Northern Pacific, where they found Hawai'i; into the Southeastern Pacific, where they found Rapa Nui; and into the Southwestern Pacific, where they found New Zealand? Archaeologists who have written extensively on this topic have typically applied "push-pull" migration theories to explain why a young Polynesian couple might decide to join a voyage or why a group might organize a voyage.[13] The "pull" factor emphasizes voyagers' expectations of the probability of discovering new habitable islands as well as the extent and quality of the environments found in those islands. The "push" factor considers characteristics of the voyager societies that would constrain voyagers' opportunities at home and open them to the possibility of undertaking a risky migratory voyage. Push and pull factors could include the homeland's and the unknown destination's social organization, languages, returns to labor, availability of arable lands to claim and settle, natural resource endowments such as fresh water, forests, fish, and animals, environmental characteristics, voyage distance and difficulty, and the probability of surviving the voyage and establishing a viable new society.

Archaeologists have focused on four "push-pull" factors potentially affecting a group's decision to undertake a voyage. A first pull factor, the risk of perishing on voyages into unknown parts of the Pacific, must have been clear to Polynesian voyagers. Hurricanes, rogue ocean waves, the wind's vicissitudes, faulty canoe construction, accidents, and poor judgment by the navigator were all factors that could end a voyage on the open seas. Voyages also faced the simple risk of a slower than expected voyage, on which food and water became exhausted and no immediate source of resupply was available.[14] Canoes did, however, have capacity to bring foods with them, such as fermented breadfruit paste and giant swamp taro, that would last for months. Given that a fully outfitted canoe could travel roughly 100 miles per day, even a risk-averse voyager might choose an expedition reaching more than a thousand miles from home.[15]

Archaeologists have argued that more than three millennia of voyaging allowed Polynesians to accumulate a massive stock of practical and navigational knowledge that enabled them to progressively reduce the risks associated with voyaging. They have emphasized the rapid expansion of voyaging in the roughly 80 to 130 years during which the Society Islands and the Marquesas Islands were settled and trade networks established with polities in Central Polynesia. These researchers have reasonably argued that the quickened pace of voyaging should have led to more rapid accumulation of navigational skills, advances in voyaging canoe architecture, better knowledge of wind patterns, and a higher confidence by participants in the likelihood of survival and success of these voyages of unknown length and circumstances. Or, to put it more succinctly, more knowledge from more voyages should have reduced the cost of voyaging, leading to even more voyages and a higher probability of new discoveries.

One example of Polynesian voyagers making choices to reduce voyaging risk is their design of exploratory voyages to reduce their chance of being stranded at sea, far from home and running short on food and water. They designed the course of voyages to increase their chance of returning home when they were far at sea and new habitable islands had not been found. Anthropologist Ben Finney and numerous social scientists who have carefully studied the capabilities of different types of Polynesian voyaging canoes have concluded that the maritime technology (e.g., sails, boom, masts) during the pulse of discovery voyages into the Eastern Pacific Ocean (1000–1260) made windward sailing difficult and downwind sailing relatively easy.[16] In addition, they provide considerable evidence that most exploring expeditions were made against the wind. While this voyaging strategy made it difficult to discover new islands, it also enabled voyagers to return home relatively easily if they had failed to discover new islands and food supplies were running low because they were sailing downwind on their return voyage.

Such a cautious approach to ocean exploration raises an obvious question: How was it that far-flung places like Rapa Nui and Hawai'i were ever discovered? In 1985, Ben Finney raised the idea that prolonged El Niño episodes in the Eastern Pacific may have reversed the direction of prevailing winds for prolonged periods. He argued that these "anomalous westerlies" facilitated exploratory voyages to the Northern Pacific and the Southern Pacific because the outbound journey was now downwind, and this allowed voyaging canoes to journey much farther, thereby raising the probability that habitable land would be found.[17] Finney's hypothesis became much more actively discussed by researchers during the first decade of the twenty-first century as evidence accumulated that between 900 and 1350, the climate in the Eastern and Central Pacific Ocean substantially changed.

A second pull factor is the geographic configuration of an archipelago's islands.[18] The height of unknown islands is likely to affect when they are discovered. Islands with tall volcanoes, which can be viewed from 50–150 miles away—think the island of Hawai'i, with two volcanoes over 13,600 feet (fig. 2.2), and the island of Maui, with a volcano over 10,000 feet—are far more likely to be discovered by voyagers than coral atolls, whose highest point is often only 10–25 feet above sea level. Voyagers might not even notice an atoll until they were a few miles away and perceived changes in seabird presence or in ocean currents and waves, or until their canoes were almost directly upon them. The groups of islands from which Hawai'i was colonized both had tall volcanoes: Mount Oave, on the island of Ua Pou in the Marquesas Islands, rises 4,040 feet above the ocean, and Mou'a 'Orohena, on the island of Tahiti in the Society Islands, rises to 7,352 feet. These volcanic peaks and others in East and Central Polynesia suggested that other undiscovered islands might also have tall volcanoes, thereby raising the probability of their discovery on a series of voyages.

FIGURE 2.2. Hawaiian voyaging canoe sighting Mauna Kea. Painting by Herb Kane. Source: Herb Kane Foundation.

Increases in the probability of discovering new islands raised the expected value of voyages of discovery and should have led to more canoes being launched to claim these valuable prizes.

A second geographic feature that could have acted as a pull factor and affected discovery is the geographic orientation of archipelagos in Central and East Polynesia. They generally have a northwest to southeast orientation, a feature stemming from their formation by the drift of the Pacific plate, on which the archipelago is embedded, to the northwest over a volcanic hotspot. If Polynesian voyagers recognized these orientation patterns and made the assumption that other Eastern Pacific archipelagos would have the same northwest-southeast orientation (a BIG if!), then they could have devised voyaging strategies to increase the likelihood of discovery.[19]

A third pull factor might have been provided by the presence of migratory birds.[20] A voyage to the north might have seemed quite risky to its participants, as travel by celestial navigation to the east or slightly north had been the standard path by which other discoveries had been made. So why risk a voyage to the north? The seasonal migration of a small bird—the golden plover, know as *tōrea* in the Marquesan language and *kolea* in the Hawaiian language—could have provided an important signal to voyagers. The plover flies seasonally to the north to feed during the summer and then returns south to winter on the same plot of land on the same tropical island from which the bird started. Potential voyagers might have surmised from the healthy condition and annual return of the plovers that they were coming from lands to the north that offered sufficient nourishment for the flocks to survive their return flight. Their presence and voyager inferences about the course of their journeys raised not just the expectation that a new place might be discovered, but also the chance that it might have sufficient resources to sustain human life.

A fourth pull factor less discussed by archaeologists is the expectation probably formed by voyagers that any newly discovered archipelago would be uninhabited. Such an expectation would be reasonable because every other Polynesian voyage of discovery had found uninhabited lands. Voyages over the previous 250 years from Central Polynesia to the Society Islands, the Marquesas Islands, and the Tuamotu Archipelago had reached islands previously untouched by human settlement, and thereby provided more evidence to reinforce what Polynesians already knew from their previous discoveries of uninhabited islands in Central Polynesia, now more than 1,800 years behind them.

Polynesian colonists did not encounter first peoples in Hawai'i. There is no archaeological evidence pointing to earlier human settlement.[21] By contrast, virtually all of the lands colonized by the English, French, Portuguese, Spanish, Dutch, and Russians after 1492 were inhabited. The absence of first peoples living in Hawai'i affected how settlement unfolded. An obvious point is that settlers did not have to devote resources to countering resistance from native peoples or resolving conflicts among settlers. Land in Hawai'i capable of being cultivated in taro was abundant, with more than enough not only for the few hundred people who made the initial voyage, but also for several more waves of voyagers. With no external enemy to fight and no reason to fight among themselves, the colonists could devote less of their time and resources to preparations for war and more to investments such as clearing and burning forests for new farms, building simple irrigation works, constructing canoes for fishing, mining volcanic glass and basalt, making fishhooks, and other productive activities.

The absence of first peoples also implies that Polynesian immigrants did not face additional disease burdens from human sources and that they probably had morbidity and mortality rates that were similar to those experienced in their homelands in East Polynesia.[22] The lack of competition for land from first peoples also meant that the new arrivals were free to select the best geographic locations to colonize first. In an economy centered around agriculture, this meant land with superior access to water sources. The best of the lands suitable for ponded taro production were on Oʻahu and Kauaʻi, and this provides us with a hint that these two islands may have been the first to be settled.

A fifth pull factor, again less discussed by archaeologists, is the expectation by colonists that if they made a discovery of a new island or archipelago, it would be rich in resources. Most potential voyagers would have known that Polynesians had already discovered and settled numerous resource-rich islands and archipelagos during their first 3,500 years of voyaging: Tonga, Fiji, Samoa, and the Society Islands, among others.[23] With this spectacular record of success in both discovery and settlement, why not attempt other risky, yet potentially highly rewarding, voyages of discovery and settlement? The expectation would be that a new place would be discovered and that the voyage would pay off—that is, that if the *vaca moana* and its human and animal passengers actually arrived at some destination, that place would be capable of supporting human life upon landing and of sustaining it in the longer run. Some of these voyages of discovery—for example, to Samoa—had taken place more than 2,000 years earlier, and were probably a bit too distant in the oral histories and traditions to directly influence the decisions of groups of potential voyagers. But other successful voyages of discovery—to the Society Islands, the Marquesas Islands, and the Tuamotu Archipelago, all uninhabited places—had taken place only within the previous two centuries and were surely more prominent in the oral histories. Some voyagers may even have been the children, grandchildren, or great-grandchildren of explorers— that is, they may have actually known people who had contact with earlier voyagers, or had themselves been voyagers.

Anthropologists and archaeologists studying oceanic migration have also considered whether push factors, characteristics of voyagers' societies that constrain the opportunities of some potential migrants, were important factors behind the pulses of migration in the Eastern Pacific. Environmental disruption, such as devastation from hurricanes, tsunamis, earthquakes, or drought, could have been one push factor. I am unable to evaluate this hypothesis, as there exists little information regarding the frequency or extent of disasters in the Eastern Pacific between 1000 and 1300.

Historians and social scientists studying migration have long hypoth-esized that hierarchical societies might be a second push factor for emi-gration. Some members of younger generations would have few oppor-tunities given their relative place in the family's and society's hierarchy and might be open to seeking new opportunities in a freshly established society. A growing population could amplify this effect, as bigger families would leave more younger sons without land or with smaller subdivided parcels. In England, which until the twentieth century restricted inheri-tance of land to the oldest son (primogeniture), a growing population in the eighteenth and nineteenth centuries pushed younger sons to join the military or emigrate.

Could a fast-growing population in either the Marquesas or Society Islands have led more individuals to voyage because Polynesian social hi-erarchies were limiting their wealth and status?[24] Consider first the 2015 study by the interdisciplinary research team of anthropologists Geoffrey Irwin and Adrian Bell, ecologist Thomas Currie, and geologist Christo-pher Bradbury. They used statistical models to "assess competing coloni-zation theories of Near and Remote Oceania," including the influence of "oppressive social hierarchical societies" and "the allure of becoming a founder." They note that "in such societies, dominant figures assume des-potic roles, taxing the people for expensive ceremonial displays, requiring corvée labor, and so forth."[25] The team created statistical models in which several variables—land area, class stratification, numbers of levels of ju-risdiction beyond the local level, and information on the hierarchy of an-cestral societies contained in its language (phylogenetic relationships)—are used as proxies for hierarchy in the home society. Results indicate good performance (i.e., correspondence with known migration patterns) for a model incorporating how tall islands were and their northwest to southeast orientation; little support for a model using distance between islands; strong support for risk models allowing for a safe return home from voyaging; and little support for the effects of hierarchy variables, partly because of insufficient variation in some variables, such as land area, to adequately test the hierarchy model.

Of course, none of the islands in the Eastern Pacific are very large, with the exception of the North and South Islands of New Zealand. Even relatively large islands, such as O'ahu in Hawai'i, might fill with settlers relatively quickly and face tensions regarding how to accommodate new settlers or natural increases in population. Without specific information on how uninhabited islands in Polynesia were settled, we might consider the settlement of an almost uninhabited island in the Atlantic Ocean: Iceland. Vikings settled Iceland sometime in the ninth or tenth century,[26] and Viking histories written within two or three centuries of the initial settlement relate that rules emerged to govern how much land each family could claim. Rules were necessary because, as one history, the *Landnámabók* (*The Book of the Settlements*), relates, "Iceland was fully settled in sixty years, so there was no more settlement after that."[27] It tells us that "the Southern Quarter which has the best quality land in the whole of Iceland" was settled first and that "the land between Hornafiord and Reykianes was the last to be fully occupied." Some settlers were dissatisfied with the land they were able to claim, complaining that they had left good land in Norway for barren land in Iceland. The *Landnámabók* then goes on to tell us how the rule governing the size of land claims was established: "The men who came here later thought the earlier settlers had taken too extensive estates. Then Harold Finehair [the King of Norway] made this regulation, that nobody should take over land broader than he and his crew could bear fire across in a single day."[28] The rule was designed to limit the size of estates claimed by earlier settlers, many of whom were opponents of Finehair, and to accommodate newer settlers.

We don't know whether Finehair's rule became the norm determining the extent of property claims in Iceland, but this case neatly illustrates the type of challenge offered by coalitions of new arrivals and some settlers seeking more land to large initial land claims made by the first waves of settlers. Large initial land claims and grants are typical of new settlements, and challenges to them are inevitable. Modern examples include the mid-Atlantic colonies in the United States during the late eighteenth century and New South Wales, Australia, from the 1830s to the 1870s.

How do states and large landholders respond to these challenges? One option is for the state and landowners to defend their claims vigorously and put additional private and public resources into their enforcement. Results from stronger enforcement vary, with the rights of the owners of large tracts solidifying in some cases (England) and with violence emerging in others. Economic historians Lee Alston, Gary Libecap, and Bernardo Mueller document how conflict between owners of large tracts of land in the Brazilian Amazon and squatters (new claimants occupying the land) led to violence during the 1970s and 1980s.[29] A second option is for the owner of the land or other natural resource to yield somewhat to the new claimants. Two economic historians, John Umbeck and Gary Libecap, showed in pioneering studies of property rights in California gold fields and Nevada silver mines in the mid- to late nineteenth century how rules for claiming property rights were adjusted to accommodate changes in the power of alternative coalitions of claimants.[30] A third option for challengers was to forgo legal and physical conflict and instead establish new claims on land not yet claimed. My colleagues, economic historians Lee Alston, Bernardo Mueller, Edwyna Harris, Alan Dye, and I, in our studies of the settlement of New South Wales in the 1830s and 1840s, concluded this is what happened when vast tracts of land were being claimed to use for grazing sheep.[31] Rather than challenging existing claimants, new settlers continued walking with their flocks of sheep until they reached unclaimed lands suitable for grazing.[32] A fourth option for challengers was particularly compelling for those living in the newly settled archipelagos of the Eastern Pacific: migrate to a less populated island in the archipelago or become part of a voyage searching for new uninhabited archipelagos. Why fight with entrenched, powerful chiefs or accept marginal lands on the fringe of a settlement when new, highly productive lands might be just a few hundred or a few thousand miles over the horizon?[33] Given the short time, perhaps just 50–100 years, between the settlement of the Marquesas and Society Islands and the pulse of voyaging to Hawai'i, this push factor could have put settlers on canoes in search of new places to settle as the best lands in the Marquesas and the Society Islands had already been taken.

Settlement

The first voyagers to arrive in Hawai'i were surely stunned when the gentle summits of the Big Island's two 13,600-foot volcanoes appeared on the horizon, and when eight environmentally rich, unsettled, subtropical islands were revealed to them. That said, most of the islands' lands were unsuitable for cultivation due to steep slopes, high elevation, or lack of water. There were no indigenous plants that could serve as staple crops for even a moderately large population. Some of the islands—Ni'ihau, Kaho'olawe, and Lāna'i—were relatively small, had little rainfall, and could not support substantial populations. The other islands—O'ahu, Hawai'i, Kaua'i, Maui, and Moloka'i—had arid leeward coasts and wet windward coasts.[34] It is likely that the first settlements were concentrated on the windward coasts of O'ahu and Kaua'i, as their environments were particularly suited to the development of small ponded taro farms.[35] These

TABLE 2.1. **Arable Land in Hawai'i by Island and Type of Land**

Island	Land with high potential for irrigation-fed cultivation (km²)	Land with high potential for dryland cultivation (km²)	Total island area (km²)
Hawai'i	14.3	556.6	10,433
O'ahu	83.3	34.1	1,546
Kaua'i	57.6	0.0	1,430
Moloka'i	8.7	7.5	673
Maui	25.7	139.4	1,884

Source: Kirch (2010) using data from Ladefoged et al. (2009).

two islands were older geologically, and constant trade winds and rain had carved deep valleys into these aging volcanic land masses. The windward valleys were natural collectors of the rainfall, and these small valleys' sizable but manageable streams could, with some investment of labor by the settlers, be diverted through carefully constructed ponded taro terraces at higher elevations and carefully delineated taro ponds on the valley floor. Both islands were also enveloped by coral reefs, which harbored incredibly varied populations of reef fish, mollusks, algae, sponges, and other marine life. Most communities were concentrated on the shoreline, as reef and ocean fish were able to provide much of the protein for the islands' *kānaka maoli*.

The islands of Maui and Hawai'i were younger geologically, and when the first Polynesian voyagers landed, their still active volcanoes had not yet had time to subside into the earth's crust or to be eroded as substantially as O'ahu or Kaua'i.[36] Although these two islands were both rich in a variety of land and marine resources, neither had the profusion of valleys and streams that settlers used to build irrigation-fed taro farms on the more elderly neighbor islands. Maui (1,884 km²) and Hawai'i (10,433 km²) were the two largest islands, but they had less acreage suitable for irrigation-fed cultivation than the smaller O'ahu (1,546 km²) or Kaua'i (1,430 km²) (table 2.1, first column). Each of these two younger islands, however, had much more land on the slopes of its volcanoes that could be used for dryland cultivation than the other three islands combined (table 2.1, second column). Successful cultivation on these upper slopes depended on sufficient rainfall, and we know from oral traditions and religious rituals that annual rainfall in these areas of prehistoric Hawai'i varied substantially. Historical rainfall data from the nineteenth and twentieth centuries provide quantitative evidence for such variation, albeit for a potentially different climate period. It is, therefore, not surprising that settlers initially invested in clearing upland valley lands that could support irrigated taro production and only later started cultivation of sweet potatoes on rain-fed lands. We know these settlement patterns because of the creative contributions of archaeologists, geneticists, biologists, palynologists, and social scientists who analyzed pollen and plant residues in Oʻahu's marshes and ponds, fossils from Oʻahu's flightless geese and ducks, and bones from the Polynesian rat.

Palynology—the science of plant pollen, spores, microscopic plankton, and their fossils—has made a particularly important contribution to our understanding of how and when the first generations of Oʻahu people transformed their environment as they settled the island.[37] In the early 1990s, an archaeologist, Stephen Athens, drilled sediment cores from the floors of ancient fish ponds near Haleiwa on Oʻahu's north shore and from Kawainui marsh in Kailua, Oʻahu. Jerome Ward, a palynologist, conducted radiocarbon dating on the cores' pollen layers and found that in the period prior to AD 922–1152 on the north shore and in the period prior to AD 1219–1403 in Kailua, a large percentage of the plant pollen came from one particular type of palm tree: the *loulu*, a 30-foot-tall tree with edible nuts and long fronds. After these periods, the percentage of *loulu* pollen rapidly decreased. Researchers identified three more plants represented by less and less pollen in the cores' pollen layers over time: the *koa*, a hardwood tree famous today for the durability, beauty, and price of its wood, and two shrubs, the *ʻaʻaliʻi* and the *kanaloa*. Patrick Kirch paints a picture of thirteenth-century windward Oʻahu coastal areas covered by "dryland forests towered over by tall *loulu* palms, interspersed with *koa* and other hardwood trees, [that] had shaded lower spreading shrubs, such as the *ʻaʻaliʻi* and the now nearly extinct *Kanaloa*."[38] The falling proportions of pollen indicate that these native palms, trees, and shrubs were disappearing. A natural suspect in the disappearance of these forests is the newly arrived settlers, who needed to clear them to establish what would become tens of thousands of small taro farms.

The decline in native forests coincided with precipitous population declines for several varieties of native snails that coexisted with these forests.[39] Fossil evidence shows that populations of flightless geese and ducks on Oʻahu crashed in the twelfth and thirteenth centuries. The *Thambetochen* ("astonishing goose"), the *Cherlychlynechen* ("turtle-jawed goose"), and the *Ptaiochen* ("stumbling goose") all found their food on the forest floor, and the concentration of their bones in the fossil record dropped after settlers began to enter the area. Given the lack of natural predators on lumbering flightless birds in Hawai'i, one can speculate that it was the new settlers who were mostly responsible for their demise, as the settlers not only harvested them for sustenance, but also burned and cleared their habitats as they established farms.

Archaeologists Terry Hunt and Carl Lipo have identified another migrant from Central Polynesia that also played a big role in the rapid decline of Hawai'i's *loulu* palm forests: the Polynesian rat (*Rattus exulans*).[40] Radiocarbon dating of rat bones from sinkholes on the 'Ewa plain of O'ahu has traced them to the same (but broader) time period when the first settlers arrived. Hitchhiking on the Polynesians' voyaging canoes, the rats would have found the *loulu* palm nuts to be a fine food source. As they multiplied and fed, they contributed to the ongoing intentional human deforestation of O'ahu and quickened the subsequent transition of its vast forested lands into taro farms.

The contributions of archaeologists, palynologists, linguists, anthropologists, and the nineteenth-century compilers of the *mo'oelo* have brought us to the point where we understand better when Hawai'i was first settled and the process by which the forested lowlands of O'ahu were first cleared and converted by settlers into small taro farms. Economists, political scientists, and economic historians, however, have paid little attention to the early settlement of Hawai'i, although they have extensively studied initial settlement and colonization in other parts of the world. Over the last two decades, social scientists have been far from silent regarding the topic of settlement and colonization, and the post-1492 institutional origins of colonized "neo-Europes" are now at the epicenter of an expanding debate over how much European and Asian colonialism is to blame for the great gap between rich and poor countries that we see today. Several competing teams of economic historians, development economists, and political scientists have recently offered new models of colonial settlement to explain the different types of institutions initially adopted by settlers and changes in those institutions over time. So what could these models, and empirical findings related to them, contribute to our understanding of early settlement in Hawai'i?

Consider first the sweeping theory put together by economic historians Stanley Engerman and Kenneth Sokoloff to explain why institutions established at the start of colonization or settlement so often persist and determine the path and conditions of these societies several centuries into the future. Engerman and Sokoloff argued that a society's endowments of human capital, land, and natural resources—known by economists as "factor endowments"—point to answers to two important questions about how the society is organized: Is production based on coerced or free labor?[41] And do government institutions favor the interests of settler/colonial elites or a broader base of the population? The two economic historians analyzed European colonial settlements in the Americas from the 1500s and found two very striking patterns. In sparsely inhabited temperate lands, such as New England and the mid-Atlantic colonies, governments were set up with political institutions that facilitated use of free labor. Farmers produced a mix of livestock and grains, including wheat, barley, and oats, all of which are crops that can be produced most efficiently on small farms. Farmers' incomes were relatively homogeneous and there were not big wealth differentials among them. Engerman and Sokoloff argued "that great equality or homogeneity among the population led, over time, to more democratic political institutions, to more investment in public goods and infrastructure, and to institutions that offered relatively broad access to economic opportunities."[42]

Conversely, colonial governments were more likely to allow colonists to use coerced labor—first peoples or imported slaves—when geographic conditions favored production of crops that could be produced at least cost with coerced labor. Engerman and Sokoloff argued that some colonies, such as those "established in the Caribbean or Brazil, enjoyed a climate and soil conditions that were extremely well suited for growing crops, such as sugar, that were highly valued on world markets and most efficiently produced on large slave plantations. Their populations came to be dominated by large numbers of slaves obtained through the international slave market, and they quickly generated vastly unequal distributions of wealth, human capital, and political power."[43] Engerman and Sokoloff argued that extreme inequality during the first decades of initial settlement meant that "political institutions were less democratic, investments in public goods and infrastructure were more limited, and the institutions that evolved tended to provide highly unbalanced access to economic opportunities and thereby greatly advantaged the elite."[44]

Now consider how this sweeping theory would play out if it were to be used to infer what types of institutions would be established in Hawai'i as initial settlement proceeded. Engerman and Sokoloff's theory points to the establishment of a more egalitarian type of society during the first 100–150 years of settlement because the main crops that could be cultivated in thirteenth- and fourteenth-century Hawai'i—sweet potatoes, yams, taro, breadfruit, bananas—could all be cultivated at least cost by individual farmers and their families independently working small plots of land. They do not include any crops that could be cultivated at lower cost using coerced labor operating in gangs. Moreover, taro (*kalo*) the primary staple food of ancient Hawai'i, was cultivated by small farmers. Taro fields were concentrated in valleys with streams that could be diverted into small-scale irrigation systems. Such small-scale independent irrigation systems are often well managed today by small cooperatives of 5–15 farms. Even 700 years ago, these farms would not have benefited much from more centralized and bureaucratized management and governance.[45]

What type of political institutions would the Engerman-Sokoloff framework infer for Hawai'i? Consider first that, unlike European countries that established colonies in the Americas after Columbus, chiefdoms in Eastern Pacific homelands were unable to maintain political control over the new settlements in Hawai'i. This was probably due to a number of factors: voyages were dangerous and long, voyaging canoes had very limited capacity, and the newly established Eastern Pacific chiefdoms were not sufficiently centralized to organize large military expeditions. My hypothesis is that the lack of colonial political ties was important for the development of Hawai'i, as it meant that new chiefdoms in Hawai'i were likely to be more focused on achieving their own objectives than on ones set by chiefs in the Polynesian homelands. Given that chiefdoms emerged in the context of thousands of small, productive taro farms, chiefs would have been constrained in how much they attempted to take from the typical farmer, at least until settlement had filled all of the lowlands in Hawai'i's productive mountain valleys.[46]

Now consider another model, developed by economic historians Douglass North and William Summerhill and political scientist Barry Weingast, that examines choices made by settlers among different types of political institutions and considers why the basic structure of these institutions sometimes persisted and sometimes changed over time.[47] This research team found that European colonies in North America, Australia, and South Africa in the sixteenth, seventeenth, and eighteenth centuries initially tended to adopt political and economic institutions that mirrored those in the colonists' home country. Some of these institutions, developed within the context of the more land-scarce and labor-abundant European continent, performed poorly and in many instances changed to reflect the realities of the colonial environment, where land was more abundant and labor was relatively scarce.[48]

What implications does this theoretical framework have for an understanding of Polynesian settlement of Hawai'i? The North-Summerhill-Weingast theory implies that chiefdoms established in Hawai'i would mirror the chiefdoms newly established in the Society Islands and Marquesas Islands in the century before voyagers sailed to Hawai'i. There are two complementary reasons to believe that their political institutions would also work in Hawai'i. One is that factor endowments across the Eastern Pacific archipelagos were broadly similar. All three island groups had abundant land, scarce labor, and tropical climates. The second is that during the first 150 years of settlement, tens of thousands of small farmers produced the staple crop (taro) in each of the three island groups. A more stratified hierarchical political system would have been more suited for a society with a concentrated rather than a widespread distribution of wealth.

Rapid Population Growth

Estimates by historians and social scientists of Hawai'i's population dynamics between settlement in AD 1260 and contact with the Cook expedition in AD 1778 are now much improved by the development of better estimates of the settlement date (1260) and the 1778 population (at least 400,000 people).[49] Patrick Kirch's survey of the literature on population growth in pre-contact Hawai'i also identifies AD 1500 as the approximate date when rapid population growth in Hawai'i slowed to a crawl.[50] Backcasting a population growth rate of 0.25 percent to AD 1500 yields a population of 200,000 people. Suppose now that the initial wave of canoes brought 200 migrants to Hawai'i and additional waves of canoes never arrived.[51] To grow to 200,000 people over the next 240 years would require a 2.88 percent increase in population each and every year for the full 240-year period. This growth implies a net total fertility rate of more than four births for every female reaching adulthood, with the mean age of the mother equal to 25.[52] This high rate would have to be sustained through the droughts, tsunamis, hurricanes, earthquakes, and warfare that regularly punctuated Hawai'i's natural and political environments. Is this type of population growth possible?

One test of the plausibility of such high growth rates is whether we can identify other historical settler populations with comparable rates of population growth that persisted for two and a half centuries. The French population of Quebec provides one well-documented example of a settler population that grew exceptionally fast, increasing from "12,000 in 1684 to 132,000 in 1784, with an average annual growth rate of 2.4 percent, almost entirely owing to natural increase."[53] Estimated population growth in Hawai'i, however, is more than 18 percent higher per year (2.88 percent vs. 2.4 percent), and this higher rate of growth would have had to persist in Hawai'i for an additional 140 years. For such an exceptional growth rate to persist for such a long time is without historical precedent and is therefore highly unlikely. But this test forces a closer look at the assumptions underlying the estimate.[54]

An annual population growth rate of 2.88 percent over 240 years that relied only on natural increases (i.e., increases in population without any inward or outward migration) seems highly unlikely, yet might be more plausible if the natural increases in population were augmented initially by new waves of migrants from East Polynesia.[55] Consider, then, an alternative scenario in which additional waves of canoes with new migrants regularly arrived until, say, 1350, when the climate in the Eastern Pacific Ocean changed and made voyaging more difficult.[56] A migration-assisted annual increase in population of 5.57 percent between 1260 and 1350 would bring the population in 1350 to 30,000 people, which is very close to archaeologist Robert Hommon's estimate of 29,535 people in 1350.[57] Once immigration stopped in the decades around 1350, population would then have to grow at 1.26 percent annually for the next 150 years to reach 200,000 people in 1500.[58] By modern standards, a population growth rate of 1.26 percent sustained over 150 years is unexceptional, but by the global standards of AD 1260–1500, it still would have been an exceptionally high rate. Consider that annual increases in global and continental populations between 1200 and 1500 were very small, with the global population increasing by an average annual rate of 0.05 percent, the population of Africa increasing by an average annual rate of 0.20 percent, and the population of the Americas increasing by an average annual rate of 0.16 percent.[59]

Another way to test the plausibility of such high population growth rates is to consider whether environmental and social conditions in Hawai'i over the thirteenth through the fifteenth centuries were favorable to population growth. The initial conditions encountered by settlers, the rapid transition to an agricultural sector, and the high productivity of ponded taro farms signal that Hawai'i could have supported rapid population growth. First, initial conditions were highly favorable for survival of the first wave(s) of settlers. When the first Polynesians voyagers arrived in Hawai'i, they encountered an environment in which they could cheaply and productively forage for food to survive the initial years of settlement. Fresh water was abundant. Fishing within and beyond the islands' protective coral reefs for a variety of ocean fish, reef fish, and mollusks could have provided one immediate source of protein, while a large stock of the flightless birds discussed earlier in this chapter could have provided a second easy source. Along with some edible plant products, such as coconuts, the large stocks of birds, fish, and mollusks would have provided sustenance for the new arrivals until newly cleared and irrigated agricultural lands yielded adequate supplies of the standard staple foods (taro, yams, and sweet potatoes) in the Polynesian diet.[60] Moreover, because the migrants arrived on an uninhabited archipelago, they faced neither additional disease burden nor attacks from first peoples.

The fast transition to a farm economy was a second factor that could have supported high population growth. The initial transition probably took only two to three decades, as many of the small streams flowing through fertile mountain valleys on the windward coasts of O'ahu, Kaua'i, and Moloka'i could be quickly harnessed to grow taro in irrigated ponds. Abundant rainfall on the windward sides of the island chain and a tropical environment at sea level that allowed multiple growing seasons completed the formula for a rapid scaling up of farm production.

High farm productivity was a third factor that could have supported high population growth. The ponded taro farms put in place over the first 100–150 years of settlement were established on the best lands. Because the first migrants were also the first people to inhabit Hawai'i, these soils had not previously been exploited for cultivation. In the absence of natural disasters—in particular, hurricanes and tsunamis—and major conflicts among settlers, the new taro farms should have been extremely productive, yielding an agricultural surplus—additional food beyond that required to feed the farmers and their families. In their 1992 study, archaeologists Matthew Spriggs and Patrick Kirch looked at archaeological and historical evidence on yields for several ponded taro systems on O'ahu and concluded that the average output per worker allowed substantial agricultural surpluses of 30–70 percent.[61] A 2009 study by a large team of archaeologists—Thegn Ladefoged, Patrick Kirch, Samuel Gon III, Oliver Chadwick, Anthony Hartshorn, and Peter Vitousek—examined yields on rain-fed fields and irrigated fields on Kaua'i, O'ahu, Hawai'i, Moloka'i, and Maui. They found that a worker on a rain-fed field produced enough output to support the worker and dependents and yield some surplus in a year with average rainfall. In contrast, a worker on an irrigated field produced more than 10 times as much output, and thus a massive agricultural surplus that could be used to regularly feed nonagricultural workers and elites.[62]

To sum up, Hawai'i's initial conditions, its fast transition to a farm economy, and the high yield from ponded taro farms all point to the potential for relatively high population growth over its first 250 years of settlement. This is good news for a social scientist studying Hawai'i's population growth, as the recent shortening of Hawai'i's prehistory (from roughly 1,300 years to just a little more than 500 years) requires high population growth rates to reach a 1778 population of over 400,000 people.

Conclusion

Waves of exploratory voyages from the Central Pacific led Polynesians to discover and settle new islands and archipelagos in the Eastern Pacific. The new discoveries stretched thousands of miles in every direction, from the Society Islands and Marquesas Islands to the east, Hawai'i to the north, Rapa Nui to the southeast, and New Zealand to the southwest. The Eastern Pacific was the last major region on earth to be discovered and settled, and seven decades of research on Polynesian voyaging has found that the voyagers used intentional, rational strategies to guide their journeys. Recent research conducted by archaeologists Janet Wilmshurst, Terry Hunt, Carl Lipo, and Atholl Anderson has changed the field of study dramatically, as their results move the dates of voyages of discovery in the Eastern Pacific forward by 400 to 900 years. The later discovery of the Society Islands and Marquesas Islands means that Polynesian voyagers were coming to Hawai'i in the twelfth and thirteenth centuries from islands that had been settled less than 100–150 years earlier. This dramatic shortening of Hawai'i's prehistory has big consequences for our understanding of population dynamics during that period, as population growth rates would have to have been exceptionally high by historical standards to achieve a population of over 400,000 by 1778. This chapter's analysis conjectures that the natural growth rates required in the population would be historically more plausible—that is, much lower—if there was a prolonged period of voyaging and migration after the discovery of Hawai'i. My somewhat speculative analysis of population growth between

1260 and 1778 clearly cannot establish specific population numbers for specific dates or specific population growth rates within this period. The analysis is, however, clearly anchored around a few solid benchmarks that allow me to conclude that the population grew rapidly from 1260 to about 1350, that rates of population growth declined substantially between 1350 and 1500, and that they declined substantially again between 1500 and 1778.

The remarkable natural growth rate of Hawai'i's population ranks among the highest on earth, yet seems plausible given the favorable conditions faced by the new arrivals. Population growth can induce big changes in political and economic organization in any society, but is much less likely to do so when new, high-quality land remains available and existing societies can replicate in new locations. My somewhat speculative conclusion is that the chiefdoms that emerged in Hawai'i in the thirteenth and fourteenth centuries were relatively egalitarian, given the combination of large surpluses from ponded taro production and the availability of unsettled lands where farmers receiving too small a share of output could relocate. When those lands fill, as they did in Hawai'i in the fifteenth century, population expansion is likely to lead to changes in economic organization as people grasp enhanced opportunities for labor specialization as well as changes in political organization due to changing age structure dynamics and the presence of surplus agricultural production.

CHAPTER THREE

The Rise of Competing
Hawaiian States

Hawai'i was first settled sometime in the twelfth or thirteenth century, with 1260 being the best estimate of the settlement date. As the settlers transformed the natural environment into intensely productive networks of farms, Hawai'i's population surged, due to high birth rates and perhaps due to new waves of migrants. Rather than fighting over rights to already developed taro farms, new arrivals and young adults had strong incentives to move to and develop other rich island valleys. If settlement of the Hawaiian islands proceeded like that on other uninhabited islands—say, Iceland in the tenth century—one would expect the best lands to be taken within 120 to 150 years after Hawai'i's discovery, sometime around 1400.[1]

Archaeologists who have pieced together sketches of early societies in Hawai'i from physical evidence and oral traditions (mo'oelo) are united in characterizing these societies as chiefdoms. Hawaiian settlers did what other global voyagers typically did: they established societies that were microcosms of their home societies, and their home societies, the Marquesas Islands and the Society Islands, were organized as chiefdoms when voyagers sailed to Hawai'i. Archaeologist Timothy Earle characterizes early Hawai'i chiefdoms as simple political organizations "in which chiefs led local landholding descent groups."[2] Earle argues that chiefs most likely derived their authority from early "Proto-Polynesian principles of rank and leadership." An individual's rank was "based on the measured distance from a senior line, whereby the highest-ranked individual is the eldest son in the direct line of eldest sons."[3] While genealogy mattered, distinctions between chiefs (*ali'i*) and people working the land (*maka'āinana*) were not very large. This could have been due to the landholdings of extended *maka'āinana* families or to the potential for those families to move to unoccupied high-quality lands in another district if *ali'i* tried to exercise power to extract additional income.

The economists Douglass North and John Wallis and the political scientist Barry Weingast have more formally characterized chiefdoms (and the archaic states that followed them) as "natural states," polities in which a dominant coalition of powerful elites and their networks forms in an attempt to control one of the fundamental problems encountered by all societies: the use of violence.[4] Members of the dominant coalition possess special privileges, and the control of violence follows from "members agreeing to respect each other's privileges, including property rights and access to resources and activities. By limiting access to these privileges to members of the dominant coalition, elites create credible commitments to cooperate rather than fight among themselves."[5] They do so because the special privileges provide members with a stream of above-normal economic returns—economic rents—that they would lose by fighting among themselves. The distribution of rents is heavily influenced by groups' and individuals' violence potential and by established networks of unique personal, family, and group relationships.

In the North-Wallis-Weingast framework, chiefdoms are best characterized as "fragile natural states." These authors note that in a fragile natural state, "commitments within the dominant coalition are fluid and unstable, often shifting rapidly, and dependent on the individual identity and personality of the coalition members. The coalition is fragile in the sense that small changes in the situation of the coalition members ... can upset the coalition."[6] Members of the coalition typically cannot commit fully to obeying rules when "pervasive uncertainty about outcomes" provides frequent situations in which it is not in their interest to keep the rules. The laws that develop tend to be public laws "that govern the relationships among individuals based on social identity and stipulate a set of rules that patrons can use to make decisions."[7]

Simple chiefdoms are often found in societies that are not too far from subsistence, and the form of government, if not the particular chief or family line, tends to persist because the society is unable to generate sufficient resources to support a more complex type of political organization. Societies engaged in slash-and-burn agriculture, such as Hawai'i settlements during their first few decades, clearly fit into this mold. In Hawai'i, however, the viability of simple chiefdoms changed as settlers completed construction of irrigation works in mountain valleys that allowed them to grow taro, the staple food of Polynesia and Hawai'i. The massive increase in output from these productive fields created an environment in which a skilled chief and supporters could establish a new political order and profitably reorganize rights to land and systems of production so as to increase both output and their own wealth.

In his 1997 classic *How Chiefs Came to Power*, the archaeologist Timothy Earle paints a picture of fourteenth- and fifteenth-century Hawai'i in which many farmers produced much more food than they needed for themselves and their dependents. The amount of extra food—known as "agricultural surplus"—varied both across and within islands, and only farmers with access to certain types of land produced surpluses.[8] The lands capable of producing the largest agricultural surpluses were located in mountain valleys on both the windward and leeward sides of Kaua'i and O'ahu. All were fed by streams that could be diverted and used to irrigate taro farms. A typical ponded taro farm in the Anahulu district of O'ahu could generate an agricultural surplus equal to 50 percent of output.[9] To put the magnitude of these surpluses in perspective, the surplus from an O'ahu farmer in the late fifteenth century outstripped agricultural surpluses from most farmers in the United States, France, and England in the early nineteenth century or even in Pharaonic Egypt.[10] The existence of agricultural surpluses is a necessary, though not a sufficient, condition for a state to emerge because ruling elites and the people who facilitate their rule must be fed. The surpluses from ponded taro agriculture were large enough to satisfy this necessary condition and facilitated formation of states throughout Hawai'i during the fifteenth and early sixteenth centuries, when both populations and surpluses were expanding. O'ahu unified under a single ruling chief (*ali'i nui*) sometime in the mid- to late fifteenth century, partly because it enjoyed large food surpluses due to its thousands of small, irrigation-fed, ponded taro farms. In the midst of this abundance and population pressure, it is not surprising that a ruling chief undertook a fundamental reorganization of the island's economic institutions and the system of rights to land. The new system not only allowed for better land management, but also facilitated a redistribution of property toward the core supporters in the chief's ruling coalition.

At the heart of the political orders established in Hawai'i during the five centuries after first settlement stood the use and control of violence by competing groups. Despite the mechanisms embedded in chiefdoms and archaic states to control violence, the use of violence to gain power and resources was pervasive. Ruling chiefs were regularly overthrown by other chiefs from within their coalition or by members of their close and extended families. Within a state, civil wars between competing chiefs were common. And those same states competed to take control of highly productive lands under the control of other states. Oral histories inform us that interisland conflicts occurred as early as the fifteenth century.

In this chapter, I set forth the case that Hawai'i had the necessary food surpluses to form complex states, then compare several theories developed to explain state formation in Hawai'i during the fifteenth and sixteenth centuries. A central question considered is why Hawaiian states were simultaneously fragile enough to have frequent usurpation while durable enough to support military invasions across the ocean channels separating the Hawaiian islands.[11] The chapter concludes by briefly considering advantages that states on the islands of Maui and Hawai'i had been accumulating in the 100–150 years prior to the late eighteenth-century European voyages that brought foreigners, diseases, trade, and Western ideas to Hawai'i.

Hawai'i's Agricultural Surpluses

Were agricultural surpluses sufficient to support formation of states in Hawai'i in the fifteenth and sixteenth centuries? Agricultural surpluses are necessary to support ruling elites as well as skilled craftsmen, artists, prayer specialists, canoe makers, home builders, warriors, and genealogical specialists. One line of evidence supporting the presence of agricultural surpluses relies on the high productivity of irrigated taro farms, which generated an agricultural surplus of about 50 percent of output in the nineteenth century. The underlying assumption is that farmers could have had similar yields centuries earlier using about the same technology. A second, more indirect line of evidence considers the central role in Hawaiian societies of an array of activities that could only be possible if the societies generated substantial agricultural surpluses. At the time of the Cook expedition, there is abundant evidence that agricultural surpluses in Hawai'i were large enough to allow artisan specialists to produce elaborate, spectacular feathered capes and helmets; to support numerous sports played by *maka'āinana, ali'i,* or both groups; and to support the construction of tens of thousands of small and medium-sized stone altars and hundreds of monumental temples.

FIGURE 3.1. Boxing matches during the *makahiki* festival on the island of Hawai'i. Engraving: John Webber, 1779. Source: Bishop Museum.

One signal that Hawai'i produced large agricultural surpluses was the amount of resources devoted to producing densely feathered capes (*ahu'ula*) and feathered helmets (*mahiole*) for high-ranking chiefs, many of which contained several million feathers.[12] Agricultural surpluses meant that the bird catchers who harvested feathers from the *O'o* and other birds and the artisan specialists who used the feathers to craft the capes and helmets could be fed. The mid-nineteenth-century Hawaiian historian David Malo noted that the *ali'i nui* provided strong incentives for districts to devote substantial labor to gathering feathers: "Feathers were an immense tribute offering (mea auhau nui ia) in the districts ('āina) during the makahiki (*annual tribute*). Feathers were given (ho'okupu) to the makahiki god. If a district had no feathers to offer, then the land was released to others (hemo). Feathers were the pālālā (*birth gift*) of the ali'i. They were greatly desired."[13]

A second signal that some Hawai'i farmers generated big agricultural surpluses was that they had considerable leisure time and activities. Consider that sports were at the heart of the second of three phases of the makahiki New Year's festival (fig. 3.1). The *makahiki* god of sports (*akua pā'ani*) "stood at the 'aha mokomoko (*boxing rings*) and at other sporting activities" such as *no'a* (guess where a pebble is hidden in bundles of bark cloth), *he'e hōlua* (sledding on a packed earth track down a hill), *pahe'e*

FIGURE 3.2. *Pi'ilanihale heiau* near Hana, Maui. Photograph by Sumner La Croix.

(sliding a stick over a smooth surface), *maika* (a form of lawn bowling), *kūkini* (foot races), and *hākōkō* (wrestling).[14] During this phase of the *makahiki*, work in the fields or fisheries, war, and religious rites were all forbidden (*kapu*). A society without agricultural surpluses could not afford such a lengthy festival.

A third signal of substantial agricultural surpluses was that each of the main islands was covered with several thousand small stone temples and shrines (*heiau*) constructed over the first 550–650 years of settlement. Hawaiians also built numerous monumental temples, each of which required tens of thousands of man-hours to build.[15] Consider two *heiau*: the *Pu'ukoholā heiau*, built near Kawaihae, Hawai'i in 1790–1791 in preparation for Kamehameha's war of conquest, and the *Pi'ilanihale heiau* (fig. 3.2), built near Hana, Maui, in the fourteenth century and then expanded in the sixteenth century after the ruling chief of West Maui, Pi'ilani, conquered the Hana district to unify the island. Both are huge structures. They cover, respectively, 22,400 square feet and 141,515 square feet. Thousands of people were mobilized for months to form human chains to hand-carry stones from distant areas to the sites of these *heiau*, a construction process that could not possibly be accomplished if the population lived close to subsistence.[16]

Changes in the Pace of Population Growth

My analysis of population in prehistoric Hawai'i relies on four population benchmarks: 200 people arriving in Hawai'i in 1260, two big declines in population growth rates in 1350 and in 1500, and at least 400,000 people in 1778. My qualitative analysis of the impact of population change in Hawai'i is little affected by modest changes in the precise timing or specific sizes of these benchmarks—for example, if we were to move the original settlement date back to 1200, or allow migration to continue through 1400, or move the date by which the population grew to 200,000 forward to 1550, or increase the 1778 population to 500,000 people.[17] We would still observe high initial rates of population growth from 1260 to 1350/1400, lower rates of population growth from 1350 to 1500/1550, and still lower rates of (positive) population growth from 1500/1550 to 1778.

The first 250 years of Hawaiian history (AD 1260–1510) saw not just the establishment of a rich society, but of one with a population that expanded more rapidly than that of any other (reasonably sized) human society between 1000 and 1500. The natural increase in population in Hawai'i had to be exceptionally high—2.88 percent annually—for the overall population to increase from 200 people in 1260 to roughly 200,000 people by 1500. The alternative population scenario presented in chapter 2 accounts for annual waves of migrants from Polynesia over the 1260–1350 window, and this helps to reduce the growth rate in population from natural increases required to reach 200,000 people in 1500. Even with a migration-assisted annual rate of 5.57 percent between 1260 and 1350, the rate of natural increase required to reach a population of 200,000 in 1500, 1.26 percent, would still be exceptionally high by contemporary standards.[18]

How does a fast rate of population growth affect a society? It can be beneficial because it allows for greater specialization among workers and therefore lowers costs of production. More people can generate more ideas and innovations, and their application can generate benefits that, ideally, can be fully shared among the larger population. But more people can also result in the overburdening of finite shared public and natural resources, and this can impose costs on the overall population. For Hawai'i in the fourteenth and fifteenth centuries, its growing population had two big and straightforward consequences: massive expansion in the extent of land under cultivation and a population tilted toward younger age groups.

In the 1950s, Robert Solow, a Nobel laureate in economics, developed a simple yet powerful model of economic growth that showed, among other things, how changes in a society's population growth rate would affect the growth rate of its output. Solow's analysis starts by pointing out that a growing population also implies a growing labor force. For new young workers to be as productive as the average worker, they need to be outfitted with at least as much capital and land as the average worker already has. That means that a big share of total output needs to be devoted to investment—that is, production of new capital goods and preparation of new lands to be used by new workers. In the context of Hawai'i's fourteenth-century economy, this meant that a substantial portion of the labor force had to be dedicated to such investment activities as clearing land for more farms, building more irrigation works, making more boundary walls and paths, and manufacturing more canoes for more fishermen.

Consider now the scenario in which Hawai'i's population grew at a migration-assisted annual rate of 5.57 percent between 1260 and 1350 and by 1.26 percent between 1350 and 1500. When a population and a workforce grow at 5.57 percent annually, they double in size every 12.57 years. Thus, the Hawai'i labor force would have roughly quadrupled in size between 1260 and 1285, increased by about a factor of 21 by 1315, and increased by about a factor of 49 by 1330.[19] Because the population in 1330 in this scenario would amount to just 9,852 people, it implies that high-quality lands would have still been available for settlement and development by both migrants and young Hawaiian adults. In this case, the Solow theory predicts that between 1260 and 1350, the Hawai'i economy would have expanded annually at the rate of population growth, 5.57 percent, by rapidly bringing new high-quality land into production, and then by an annual rate of 1.26 percent over the next 150 years. Annual output growth rates would have been lower if the growing workforce could be matched only with low-quality land or smaller amounts of high-quality land, and they would have been higher if a larger economy facilitated additional specialization and trade, such as feather gathering, feathered cape and helmet production, canoe building, and manufacture of bark cloth (*tapa*).[20]

A rapidly growing population also implies that the society's population has skewed shares of children and young adults. In our context, a larger proportion of children affects how a society develops because more of its agricultural surplus must be used to feed those children. With less food remaining to feed elites and nonagricultural workers who provide services to the state (such as prayer specialists, bird catchers, canoe builders, and warriors), fewer nonagricultural workers can be supported.

Over long periods, it is very likely that average population growth rates substantially declined in prehistoric Hawai'i. In the alternative population scenario discussed in chapter 2, Hawai'i's population grew by a factor of 150 in the 90 years from 1260 to 1350, then increased by a factor of 6.67 between 1350 and 1500. By contrast, the population merely doubled between 1500 and 1778. The backcast annual population growth rate of just 0.25 percent during that period is much lower than the 1.26 percent natural increase estimated between 1350 and 1500 and more in accord with the global population growth rate between 1500 and 1750, which averaged 0.21 percent annually. One reason for the fall in population growth in the decades around 1500 may have been that the new lands opening for cultivation were marginal agricultural lands, located primarily on the rain-fed volcanic slopes of the islands of Hawai'i and Maui.[21]

The transition from a higher to a lower population growth rate is a phenomenon that social scientists have studied extensively for both developing and developed countries in the nineteenth and twentieth centuries.[22] In most of these countries, this "demographic transition" was driven by declines in birth and death rates. The causes of Hawai'i's demographic transition are unknown, but it seems unlikely that changes in mortality rates played a large part. There is no evidence of changes in mortality due to new hygienic practices or medical treatments or additional deaths stemming from war and insurrection. It is much more plausible that a decline in birth rates drove the lower population growth rates. In this case, the decline in population growth would have reduced the share of younger people in the population and increased the share of older people.

The transition to a somewhat older population would have increased the potential for state formation in two important ways. First, a gradual decline in the fertility rate over three to four decades would have led to slower growth in the population of dependents for several decades. Because less of the agricultural surplus would need to be devoted to the support of a smaller group of young dependents, this change would have allowed food to be provided to more workers who provided services to *maka'āinana* and to the rulers of an emerging archaic state. Second, a decline in the fertility rate would have led to an increase in the share of the population in the workforce. A larger workforce can generate more output, and the resulting increase in output has the potential to generate the additional tax revenues necessary for a new state to be formed.[23]

Hawaiʻi's transition from rapid population growth in the fifteenth century to slow population growth in the sixteenth century facilitated the formation of competing states because it led to increases in agricultural surpluses and in adult manpower for the armies of ruling chiefs. Demography, however, is not the only driver, or even the main driver, of state formation. In the next section, I consider other forces that could have influenced state formation in Hawaiʻi, such as geography, the presence of large irrigation systems, and agricultural innovations.

Why Did Hawaiian States Develop?

Agricultural surpluses set the stage in the fifteenth century for transitions from chiefdoms to archaic states. *Archaic states* are distinguished from other types of political orders by their extensive reliance on distinctive institutions, such as investments in monumental architecture, ritual, and redistributive taxation, to sustain their legitimacy and efficacy. Within the North-Wallis-Weingast framework characterizing political orders, an archaic state is categorized as a "basic natural state." This type of state is distinguished from a "fragile natural state" by the emergence of a more "durable and stable organizational structure for the state." Public institutions emerge that "provide standardized solutions to recurring problems such as succession of the leader, succession of elites, determination of tax and tribute rates, and division of spoils of conquest."[24] Public institutions, such as a state religion, also allow for a "widening [of] the set of commonly held beliefs among elites," and this "broadens the range of credible commitments that a dominant coalition can sustain."[25] Expansion in the number and scope of these credible commitments allows for skilled specialists and higher levels of income and wealth to jointly emerge.

Development economists, such as Dale Jorgenson, and archaeologists, such as Patrick Kirch, have emphasized that the skilled specialists needed to support the machinery of the basic natural state can be fed only if the society is generating agricultural surpluses.[26] Moderately large agricultural surpluses are, however, a necessary but not sufficient condition for a basic natural state to emerge. This is because a basic natural state also needs to have sufficient institutional capacity to tax away some of the farmers' surpluses in order to support the skilled specialists who play vital roles in sustaining the basic natural state. Timothy Earle identifies three specific types of specialists who played vital roles in Hawai'i's basic natural state: warriors (*koa*), workers who support the ruling chief's household, and land managers (*konohiki*); prayer specialists (*kāhuna pule*) who provide ideological and cosmological support for the state's mission; and artists and skilled craftsmen, including sculptors (*kāhuna kālei*) who produce high-quality goods for high-ranking chiefs that are designed to illustrate the power and legitimacy of the ruling chiefs.

Suppose that a society generates agricultural surpluses that are large enough to allow a basic natural state to emerge. Is it preordained that a basic natural state will emerge, or might another outcome dominate—say, emergence of roving bandits who prey on the productive areas?[27] The ethnologist Robert Carneiro has argued that a state is most likely to develop in geographic areas with particular characteristics that facilitate monitoring of both agricultural production and migration of the population. Carneiro conjectured that all archaic states "have one thing in common: *they are all areas of circumscribed agricultural land*. Each of them is set off by mountains, seas, or deserts, and these environmental features sharply delimit the area that simple farming peoples could occupy and cultivate."[28]

It is very unlikely that these conditions held over the first 150 years (1260–1410) of settlement in Hawai'i. Attempts by one group to violently appropriate more than a competitive amount of land rent at the expense of others would rarely occur for the simple reason that labor was so scarce relative to land. If a chief tried to exact more than competitive rent, many farmers had a better option available than violent confrontation: walk, row, or sail to a different part of the island (or even to another island) and make claims to land in an unsettled or sparsely settled valley.[29] On O'ahu and Kaua'i, the mountain valleys were not so geographically circumscribed or distant from each other as to raise prohibitively the cost of migration.

Consider now the situation in the fifteenth century, particularly on O'ahu: the population was rapidly growing, the good lands in O'ahu's rich valleys were already taken and densely settled, and irrigated fields were generating big agricultural surpluses. Now suppose that significant costs would have to be borne by a group of *maka'āinana* who migrated to another island. In this case, there would be incentives for a coalition of chiefs, or a ruling chief acting for the entire island, to impose higher rents on their tenants and prevent unchecked movement between O'ahu's districts. In addition, as each of the valleys became more fully settled, their economies would have become more alike, and this would have made it easier for their chiefs to form a coalition.[30] Thus, there might be a grain of truth in Carneiro's geographic circumscription theory, not because of barriers to mobility imposed by Hawai'i's mountains, but rather because of geographic and information barriers imposed by the Pacific Ocean.

Historians and archaeologists have proposed several other theories to explain why archaic states formed in Hawai'i. Writing in the 1950s, the historian Karl Wittfogel pointed to the irrigation works shared by ponded taro farms as the main reason for the rise of Hawaiian states. Wittfogel suggested that building, maintaining, and running irrigation works required close cooperation among chiefs and the development of specialized administrative skills by land managers (*konohiki*). Chiefs and *konohiki* could then transfer those skills to establishing and running a state that enveloped numerous valleys with irrigation works. As evidence for his theories, he pointed to the early rise of despotic, centralized states with major irrigation works, including Somalia, China, Egypt, and Mesopotamia as well as Hawai'i.[31] Scholars have criticized Wittfogel's applications of his theories to particular states, arguing that they were neither despotic nor centralized. Timothy Earle has questioned the applicability of Wittfogel's theory to Hawai'i because irrigation works in Hawai'i were very small: they encompassed just a few hectares of land, served an average of five farmers, and employed relatively straightforward technologies. Neither their construction nor their maintenance required the specialized managerial or tax-collection machinery typically provided by a centralized state.[32]

Some scholars have argued that centralized states can arise when rulers of smaller chiefdoms have chances to observe how institutions of a nearby centralized state work and then to imitate them. Ancient Egypt provides a good example, as prior to the rise of Egypt's centralized state in the fourth millennium BC, Egyptians traded with Sumerian city-states and were well acquainted with their institutional machinery.[33] Could the main features of Hawai'i's archaic states have been borrowed from another Polynesian society with which Hawaiian chiefs had contacts? A recent comparative study of Polynesian societies by the archaeologist Robert Hommon finds little evidence that archaic states were emerging during the fourteenth century in either the Society Islands or the Marquesas Islands, the two most likely destinations for return voyaging from Hawai'i.[34] There is some evidence that the institutions of the ancient Tongan state were in place by the fourteenth or fifteenth century, but no particularly compelling evidence for direct linkages between Hawai'i and Tonga.[35]

One argument supporting the role of outside influences on state formation comes from stories from the *mo'oelo* about how particular individuals from Tahiti affected religious and political institutions—which, in a fragile natural state such as fourteenth-century Hawai'i, are one and the same. Abraham Fornander, the Swedish immigrant to Hawai'i who compiled *mo'oelo* in the late nineteenth century, tells the story of La'amaikahiki, the son of the O'ahu ruling chief (Mo'ikeha), who grew up in Tahiti. After his father made a return voyage to Tahiti and brought him back to Hawai'i, La'amaikahiki introduced *pahu* temple drums from Tahiti into Hawaiian religious ceremonies. The Hawaiian historian David Malo relates the story of a Tahitian priest named Pā'ao who had migrated to Hawai'i and "settled in Kohala until the time Hawai'i('s) chiefs begun (sic) to live wrongly (i hewa ai). Then Pā'ao [went to and] got a chief in Kahiki [so to restore the blood lines]. Pili was the name of that chief in Kahiki and the name of that chief who sailed with Pā'ao. He was established (ho'onoho) in the chiefly lineage of the Hawaiian Islands."[36] Fornander has a slightly different rendition. He adds that upon his return to Hawai'i, Pā'ao also introduced religious practices that became canonical elements in the Hawai'i state religion, including the cult of Kū—the god of war, human sacrifice, and the building of walled temples.[37] Fornander argued that these new elements sanctioned and strengthened the idea that the *ali'i* had divine origins and *maka'āinana* did not, thereby allowing the *ali'i* to enforce institutional arrangements that simultaneously generated more wealth for the entire society and extracted more wealth from *maka'āinana*.

Both Fornander and Malo emphasized imitation of foreign institutions, but it may have been imitation of domestic institutions that played a crucial role in the rise of archaic states on the islands of Maui and Hawai'i. During the late fifteenth century, *ali'i nui* from other islands visited the ruler of O'ahu at his Waikiki headquarters and were awed by his power and O'ahu's wealth. They were surely cognizant that the newly evolving machinery of O'ahu's more centralized state could be used to organize armies to conquer or exact tribute from the other islands. In this situation, groups of chiefs on the other main islands had incentives to cooperate and to adopt their own centralized institutions as a defensive response to increased external threats.[38] Robert Hommon has argued that authority in Polynesian societies was most likely to have consolidated during a crisis.[39] Economic historian Philip Hoffman has made similar arguments for Europe. France, for example, got its first substantial permanent taxation during the Hundred Years' War, when marauding soldiers wreaked havoc throughout the country. King Charles V essentially promised to guarantee security in return for a permanent flow of taxation that also served to consolidate authority within the emerging national state.[40]

Consider the crisis in Oʻahu in the late fifteenth century prior to consolidation, when three different chiefs ruled over the island's four districts. The *Mōʻī* (king) of the island of Hawaiʻi, Kalanuiohua, who had already defeated and captured ruling chiefs on Molokaʻi and Maui, invaded Oʻahu and defeated and captured Huapouleilei, the ruling chief of the Waiʻanae and ʻEwa districts, and brought him to Kauaʻi, which he invaded next.[41] In the midst of, or perhaps after, this turmoil, one chief, Haka, gained some degree of authority over all of Oʻahu's districts. Fornander tells us that Haka's rule was viewed as tyrannical by both *aliʻi* and *makaʻāinana*.[42] Haka was subsequently killed in a rebellion, and the council of Oʻahu chiefs (*ʻaha aliʻi*) chose an *aliʻi* from a different family (the Maweke-Moika line), Māʻilikūkahi, as Haka's successor. Māʻilikūkahi had already served as the administrator of the government. Samuel Kamakau, a nineteenth-century native Hawaiian historian, tells us that when Māʻilikūkahi assumed power, "the land divisions were in a state of confusion," with the various units (*moku, ahupuaʻa*, etc.) "not clearly defined."[43] Māʻilikūkahi ordered his chiefs to divide Oʻahu into *moku* (districts), *ahupuaʻa* (mountain-to-sea slices of land), and smaller divisions of land, and assigned six chiefs (*aliʻi nui ai moku*) to head each of the *moku*, other high-ranking chiefs (*aliʻi ai ahupuaʻa*) to head each *ahupuaʻa*, and lesser chiefs (*kaukau aliʻi*) to head smaller land units. Lands within these units "were given to the *makaʻāinana* all over Oahu" who farmed them as private plots.[44] There are no reports regarding how or to whom Māʻilikūkahi made the assignments, but his land allocations represent the first reported redistribution of land by a Hawaiʻi ruling chief to bolster his support among powerful chiefs in his coalition. Kamakau also tells us that in Maui and Lānaʻi, the ruling chief, Kakaʻalaneo, implemented the same administrative land system, and, in so doing, again probably redistributed lands to bolster his coalition.[45] On Kauaʻi, the ruling chief, Manokalanipō, played a similar role, as he centralized island governance and "executed long and difficult works of irrigation and brought fields of wilderness under cultivation."[46]

What is remarkable is that the system of property rights in land implemented by Māʻilikūkahi and Kakaʻalaneo in the mid-fifteenth century would endure for roughly 400 years, until the *Māhele* land reforms of the 1840s and 1850s. One obvious factor underpinning the change to the new system was the more than threefold increase in population between 1350 and 1450. In an agricultural economy, the value of land is fundamentally determined by its scarcity relative to labor. During the fourteenth century, Oʻahuʻs population was relatively small, and some valuable lands in mountain valleys had not yet been claimed or were only sparsely settled. Land could not command a rent under these circumstances. However, once the most productive lands (those suitable for ponded taro cultivation) had been developed and the only lands available for new settlement were much less productive lands (those suitable for rain-fed sweet potato, yam, or taro cultivation), new farmers had incentives to pay a rent up to the difference in productivity to gain access to the better lands. Willingness by users to pay rent would increase the value of the land to elites with political power and provide them with incentives to specify property rights in the land more precisely—that is, to delineate boundaries, to specify which parties have the rights to income streams from the land, and to specify which parties have the power to make decisions about land use.

The system of land management specified a wedge-shaped unit of land, the *ahupuaʻa*, as the geographic area within which managers (*konohiki*) appointed by the ranking chief (*aliʻi ai ahupuaʻa*) would coordinate production decisions. Stretching from mountain slopes through valleys to the sea, the *ahupuaʻa* contained a variety of resources that allowed for self-sufficient production of a full array of staple agricultural products as well as goods and services produced by a variety of specialists.[47] The centralized coordination of production made sense in light of the large agricultural surpluses generated by most *ahupuaʻa* and the inability of decentralized market institutions to function properly in the absence of a written language and effective institutions to enforce agreements among chiefs.

Another reason for the implementation of a centralized system of land administration was that some resources within specific *ahupuaʻa* were in demand throughout the islands. Goods exchanged among islands included high-quality adzes manufactured from Mauna Kea volcanic glass, *koa* logs from Kona used to make canoes, *wiliwili* wood from Kaʻū used to make canoe outriggers, *tapa*s from specific communities on various islands, and spears from Kauaʻi.[48] Some of these goods were natural resources with finite supplies. In the absence of defined property rights to these resources, current users would have incentives to harvest too much of a resource due to insecure rights to its harvest in future years. Trade across different polities would raise the price of the resource and exacerbate problems with overharvesting.[49] A ruling chief with forward-looking expectations would specify and enforce property rights to *ahupuaʻa* to limit harvesting. Even if finite resources were not in jeopardy, well-specified and well-enforced property rights to those resources would serve to limit supply and keep the barter exchange price high. An early nineteenth-century example is provided by King Kamehameha's realization that pearls harvested from Pearl Bay (today's Pearl Harbor) were highly valued by visiting American and European ships. Kamehameha then acted to establish a royal monopoly on their sale by placing a sacred prohibition (*kapu*) on their harvest without his permission.[50]

I have argued that the ability of land to command a rent provided the incentive for a state to form and its ruling coalition to appropriate these rents. An event or sequence of events, such as the decision by the Oʻahu council of chiefs to choose Māʻilikūkahi to be *Mōʻī* after their successful rebellion against the tyrannical ruler Haka, can provide a rationale for chiefs to take action to realize these potential benefits. This conclusion leads me to consider whether war also led to formation of polities on other islands. To answer that question, we first need to consider how common war was in ancient Hawaiʻi and understand its implications for the state.

War between Hawaiian States

War rarely took a long break during the three to four centuries when the Hawaiian islands were isolated from the Polynesian homelands and the rest of the world. Robert Hommon writes that "the traditional histories of ancient Hawaiʻi are filled with accounts of usurpation, insurrection, and warfare between sovereign kingdoms."[51] Officers on American and European ships visiting Hawaiʻi in the late eighteenth century saw a ruling chief on the island of Hawaiʻi, the soon-to-be King Kamehameha, mobilize 1,200 double-hulled and outrigger canoes to transport an army of more than 15,000 chiefs, *makaʻāinana*, and professional warriors across ocean straits to invade Maui, Molokaʻi, and Oʻahu.[52] Samuel Kamakau wrote that the winners took away pigs, mats, canoes, feather cloaks, and bark cloth (*tapa*).[53] The winners sometimes occupied productive areas, with chiefs and warriors establishing themselves on developed and newly opened lands.[54] Other times, armies would leave a trail of fallen breadfruit trees, ruined irrigation works, and wrecked fish ponds.[55]

Perhaps war was prevalent in ancient Hawaiʻi because young chiefs were trained in the art of war. They learned boxing, wrestling, spear-thrusting, and the Hawaiian martial art *lua*, "the art of breaking bones."[56] The Hawaiian historian David Malo tells us that "it was the policy of the government to place the chiefs who were destined to rule, while they were still young, with wise persons, that they might be instructed by skilled teachers in the principles of government, be taught the art of war, and be made to acquire personal skill and bravery."[57]

Late medieval and early modern Europe provides a useful comparison with Hawai'i because Europe had three centuries of pervasive war during the same time frame, 1450–1750. Small and large states in Europe spent most of their budgets on war, and the princes who ruled European states were fixated on war. Philip Hoffman concludes that the reasons for this fixation

> were not hard to understand. The kings and princes had been raised to fight one another, with toy soldiers, pikes, and firearms as children and actual training in their youth. Advisors like [Niccolò] Machiavelli might tell them that princes "ought to have no object, thought, or profession but war." Their own fathers would teach them that war was a path to glory, a means "to distinguish [kings] . . . and then fulfill the great expectations . . . inspired in the public" in the words of Louis XIV's instructions for his son. For the fighting had gone beyond the needs of defense and become, in the words of Galileo, a "royal sport."[58]

In some ways, war in Europe, and in Hawai'i, was a royal sport, and in other ways it obviously amounted to much more. Success in war provided glory for the European prince, a sign that his rule was founded in divine origins or inspired by divine guidance. Hoffman argues that if a prince won a war, he basked in the glory of the victory and won the lion's share of the benefits. If he lost, his subjects bore the brunt of the costs. With this kind of calculus, it did not pay for leaders to reach agreements to avoid war, because without war, there can be no glory:

> Glory could not be divvied up. In fact it simply vanished if there were no fighting, making the peaceful exchange of resources potentially more expensive than fighting.
>
> Peace brings little glory. Dividing up a commercial opportunity may bring increases in welfare to both sides, but it does not inspire subjects to believe that your rule is divinely inspired. Glory required a successful war; and for either prince to find it, they had to fight.[59]

Analogies between prehistoric Hawai'i and pre-modern Europe are never exact, and should not be pushed too far, but are often suggestive. European kings may have been seeking a path to glory, but Hawai'i's elites, both *ali'i* and *kāhuna*, were also preoccupied with seeking a path to control *mana*, the "manifestation of [the gods'] power in the world of humans."[60] War and victory in war were essential for an *ali'i nui* to achieve *mana*. This is because the power manifested by the gods cannot be divvied up so that each chief achieves 50 percent of it. Nor can Lono, the god of the clouds and fertilizing rain, be incarnated in two *ali'i nui*—just one.[61] An *ali'i nui*'s decision to start a war was also governed by the celestial cycle as embodied in the *makahiki*. Whether resources would be available to the *ali'i nui* to carry out a war would become more apparent after the *ho'okupu* tax collections, which were made in the course of the *makahiki* festival (described later in this chapter). On the islands of Hawai'i and Maui, the amount collected would be closely related to the amount of rain that had fallen during the growing season, which would influence the size of harvests ripe for taxation.

Glory and *mana* aside, perhaps the best choice for a prince or a chief was to stay on the sidelines and avoid the dissipation of resources associated with war: the pestilence, destruction, and death that usually devastated one or more sides in a conflict, whether it took place in Europe, Asia, or Polynesia. And yet, somewhat contrary to this idea, new research on European wars over the fifteenth to nineteenth century shows a positive association between the frequency of a country's wars and its wealth. Economic historians Nico Voigtländer and Hans-Joachim Voth have shown how persistent war in Europe allowed its participants to break the famous "Malthusian" wage cycle and earn wages that allowed them to live well above subsistence.

Here's how the Malthusian wage cycle works. The Reverend Thomas Malthus, one of Britain's famed classical economists, argued that when wages are above subsistence levels, they provide a variety of incentives for people to marry rather than remain single, to marry at an earlier age, and to have more children. The result? An increase in population growth. The surge in population then generates a feedback loop, as within a few decades it leads to an increase in the supply of labor. In the absence of accompanying technological or organizational innovations, the surge in labor supply pushes wages down until, at the limit, they reach subsistence levels.[62] At the lower wages, people decide to remain single more often, to marry later, and to have fewer children. Eventually, the lower supply of labor leads to increases in wages, and the Malthusian cycle repeats.

Voigtländer and Voth argued that frequent warfare in Europe short-circuited the Malthusian cycle by its effects on population growth. This happened because invading foreign armies and home armies returning from abroad spread disease and thereby reduced populations. Paradoxically, this negative check of war and disease on a country's population, while far from desirable, regularly reduced its labor supply, thereby increasing wages and allowing its population to live above subsistence.

Could this kind of short-circuiting of the Malthusian feedback loop also have occurred in Hawai'i, which experienced round after round of internal warfare starting in the late fifteenth century? At first glance, the answer would seem to be no, as Hawai'i's isolation had kept out the viruses and bacteria frequently spread by invaders in Europe and Asia.[63] Nonetheless, we know from the record of warfare in Hawai'i between 1778 and 1825 that invading armies often left behind other ravages of war that could reduce populations: devastated landscapes, plundered villages, flooded irrigation works, and slaughtered families. If agricultural recovery came relatively fast, then the Voigtländer-Voth model of short-circuiting the Malthusian cycle could have worked in Hawai'i. But if recovery from war came slowly, then a more traditional Malthusian cycle could have been operating.

The bottom line is that we have just one good observation to evaluate Voigtländer and Voth's Malthusian explanation, and that one comes from 1778, the year that the Cook expedition first saw Kaua'i and Ni'ihau. After centuries of warfare, these Europeans nonetheless encountered a well-fed population that clearly lived well above subsistence, had considerable leisure time, and had enough agricultural surplus to allow the building of monumental stone temples and the creation of royal Hawaiian featherwork (nā hulu ali'i).

Could there be, however, another factor underlying the high living standards found in Hawai'i in 1778 besides the effects of periodic wars in depleting populations? The archaeologists Mark McCoy and Michael Graves provide an answer that is often brushed aside by modern Malthusians: widespread and prolonged innovation by Hawai'i farmers.[64] Consider that the population increase from roughly 200,000 people in 1500 to over 400,000 people in 1778 was primarily accommodated by a big expansion of cultivation on the lower-quality rain-fed volcanic slopes of Haleakala on Maui and of Mauna Loa, Mauna Kea, and Kohala on the island of Hawai'i. Expansion into these more marginal lands should have reduced the marginal product of labor in agriculture, and competition among labor should have pushed labor compensation closer to subsistence levels. Consider now how McCoy and Graves trace out the situation faced by migrants when they first encountered the island of Hawai'i:

> Polynesian farmers had for generations settled geologically old islands with deep-set valleys and had never before encountered a high volcanic island as geologically young and large as Hawai'i Island . . . The island's first farmers would have been surprised to find that on this massive island with a land mass greater than all the other Hawaiian Islands combined, they found little arable land for irrigating—only a single large valley, a few mid-sized valleys and networks of gulches. These valleys and gulches account for less than 8 percent of the land in the archipelago naturally suited for pondfield agriculture.[65]

How did the island's farmers deal with this new environment? McCoy and Graves argued that they developed two production techniques not previously observed in Polynesia. First, farmers locating on tablelands (land located in between gulches) "used terraced fields in narrow gulches, some using simple flooding barrage terraces and water diversion channels to take irrigation water from gulches to otherwise un-watered adjacent tablelands." Second, farmers locating on west- and south-facing slopes "built permanent rock and earthen alignments . . . that served as windbreaks, retained soil moisture, and lessened erosion."[66] McCoy and Graves concluded that these innovations made marginal lands more productive and had the effect of at least partially offsetting Malthusian forces pushing down labor earnings.[67]

Expansion of population and area under cultivation on Maui and Hawai'i during the seventeenth and eighteenth centuries changed the incentives for ruling chiefs.[68] A larger population would have allowed the state to raise and train a larger force of warriors. If a larger army had a higher probability of prevailing in battles, the ruling chief would have had increased incentives to start a war. Other ruling chiefs would have been limited in how they could respond. They could take steps to bolster their own defenses or to increase their own populations and thus the potential size of their armies. Their ability to increase their populations would have been limited, however, by the supply of marginal arable land that could be put into production and by the time required for such policies to show results.[69]

There were, however, two big consequences to bringing larger areas of less productive volcanic lands on Maui and Hawai'i into production. The first was the possibility of famines. The cultivation of yams and sweet

potatoes on these marginal lands was rain-fed, and annual rainfall varied over time and within islands. Therefore, the farmers–part-time warriors populating the volcanic slopes struggled to survive during drought
years. Imperial China faced similar problems with drought, and its central government developed a network of state-financed granaries for rice
and wheat to ensure that farmers on marginal lands survived short and
long droughts.[70] The lack of an island-wide government on the island of
Hawai'i, however, meant that even intra-island risk sharing could not be
effectively accomplished. Moreover, yams, sweet potatoes, and taro can
be stored for only about six months, so a network of granaries could have
resolved only short-term starvation risks. Inability to store staples also
made it difficult to solve famine problems by trade. During good years,
a portion of crops could be stored as animal protein in the form of pigs,
chickens, and dogs, and fish could be salted and dried. These are, however, costly forms of storage that are incapable of providing insurance
against several years of drought. In the absence of some type of redistribution in bad years, famines were possible.

A second drawback to expanding cultivation of marginal lands was
that a succession of bad harvests could lead to rebellions against ruling
chiefs. Such rebellions were difficult to prevent, as they could be triggered
by any of the three groups receiving a share of agricultural output from
these lands: *konohiki*, *ali'i*, or *maka'āinana*. Native Hawaiian historian
David Malo provides a partial chronicle of revolts against ruling chiefs on
the island of Hawai'i:

> It was proper for the ali'i nui to protect and care for his own maka'āinana be-
> cause they were the full body of the chiefdom. There were many ali'i who were
> killed by the maka'āinana because they were oppressed.
>
> These were the ali'i who were killed by the maka'āinana because they op-
> pressed them. Ko'ihala was killed because he overburdened the maka'āinana
> in Ka'ū . . .
>
> Ko'ihalalani was an ali'i who was killed in Ka'ū. Hala'ea was another ali'i
> who was killed in Ka'ū. 'Ehunuikaimalino was an ali'i who was secretly killed
> by the lawai'a [fishermen] at Keahuolū in the Kona [district on the island of
> Hawai'i]. Kamai'ole was another ali'i killed by Kalapana at 'Anaeho'omalu in
> the district of Kona.
>
> Hākau was the ali'i killed by 'Umi at Waipi'o [Valley] in the Hāmākua [dis-
> trict] on the island of Hawai'i. Lonoikamakahiki was presumed to be expelled
> in Kona and 'Umiokalani was another ali'i who was expelled in Kona.

Therefore several of the traditional or old ali'i feared the maka'āinana but the maka'āinana faced death when the ali'i was pono (*moral, proper, or fair*).[71]

How could ruling chiefs prevent conditions ripe for rebellion from developing? And once such conditions developed, how could the burdens associated with them be lightened? One path allowing progress toward both objectives would be to signal that the burden of taxation would be reduced during poor harvest years, and then to actually reduce them during those years. Consider how three primary types of taxation used by *ali'i nui* might be adjusted. The first type is corvée labor, whereby farmers have obligations to work one day per week in the fields of the *ali'i ai ahupua'a* and on public projects in the *ahupua'a*. These obligations were unlikely to vary, as the fields of the *ali'i* would have experienced the same conditions as the fields farmed by *maka'āinana*. The second type was consumption by a ruling chief and his extended household of an *ahupua'a*'s food supplies when they travelled through the *ahupua'a* or moved to a new location. A ruling chief could have reduced taxation of an *ahupua'a* particularly hard-hit by drought by avoiding it entirely, by walking through it at night en route to another settlement, or by stopping and eating its food supplies for fewer days. Consider the results in 1779 when the *Mō'ī* of the island of Hawai'i, Kalaniopu'u, seized "all the products of the cultivated areas [in Kona] . . . even those which were the people's property" while his court was in residence in Kona. The seizures occurred during a famine, and Kamakau tells us that "people wept bitterly over this seizure of their property, and life in Kona became so uncomfortable" that the *Mō'ī* and his court had to leave Kona.[72]

The third form of taxation was the *ho'okupu* demanded by tax agents of the ruling chief during the New Year's *makahiki* festival. On the islands of Hawai'i and Maui, there was an annual three- to four-month-long set of religious rituals tied to the lunar cycle that served to redistribute income, prepare for war, and worship Lono, the god of the clouds and fertilizing rain. The appearance on the horizon of the Pleiades[73] marked the start of the New Year's festival. In 1500, the constellation would have appeared in the morning sky on November 11. The festival began during the last month of the dry cycle and continued through the first three months of the wet cycle in the islands, the time when sweet potatoes are planted on the rain-fed volcanic slopes of Hawai'i and Maui. The *ho'okupu* tribute was collected by tax collectors and warriors who were accompanied by a "long" image of the *makahiki* god (*akua loa*). It made a long tour of the ruling chief's entire kingdom, and a "short" image of the *makahiki* god (*akua poko*) made a short tour of each of the districts (six districts per island) controlled by the ruling chief. David Malo relates that tribute paid to the *makahiki* god included

> Ō'ō feathers, Mamo feathers, and 'I'iwi feathers, Pua'a (pigs), kapa and pa'i'ai *(hard pounded but undiluted taro)*, for the carrier of the akua [idol] (ke amo akua). The assessment of tribute for the larger districts was much larger than those for the smaller districts. If the assessment was deficient, then the district was discharged [from the konohiki] to the luna auhau(s) [tax collector]. It was at this place, where the tribute that the konohiki(s) had first prepared were gathered from the districts and ahupua'a(s). It was piled up and left there for the makahiki. . . .
>
> When the akua arrived and was erected in a pile [of rocks] (ahu) at the boundary of this ahupua'a, there was someone else who went ahead of the akua with two sticks. Ālia was the name for these two sticks.
>
> This person set up the sticks in the ground, and then the akua was erected behind the ālia sticks. The area inside of the ālia sticks was made kapu. The area outside was noa *(free from kapu)*. There the konohiki(s) would present the tribute and they could be criticized [for the amount of tribute given] by the luna auhau(s) who came with the akua makahiki.
>
> When the wealth of this district [given] was sufficient, then the kahuna came to pray to free the district [from the kapu]. The name of this pule *(prayer)* was hainaki. [This was a prayer to remove the kapu on the land after the tribute had been collected.][74]

Malo's description of *makahiki* tax collections is complemented by another from Kamakau, who emphasized the severe penalties that would be imposed on the people of the *ahupua'a* if the tax collector's demands were not met: "If any district did not contribute properly on any occasion, the gods would complain. They were not laid down, and the end of it was that the section, whatever it was, was given over to be plundered."[75] Nowhere in these or other passages is there any sign that tax burdens were fixed. Malo makes reference to "delinquent taxpayers," but this implies only that negotiations might allow landholders to pay some tax in the following year, not that taxes were generally fixed. In the early 1830s (when practices were already in flux), the missionary William Ellis observed that rents and taxes were "regulated entirely by the caprices or necessity of their rulers."[76]

One way for taxes to be reduced during years of poor harvests would be for a ruling chief and the *kāhuna* associated with Kū, the god of war, to initiate wars mainly during years with good harvests. War was an expensive undertaking that required the building of a large stone temple (*luakini*) and attendant human sacrifices; extensive preparations, including canoe building, weapons making, and accumulation of stores of food; and mobilization of adult male farmers (who would otherwise work in the fields) to serve as warriors. Less expenditure by the state on these activities in years with bad harvests would have allowed the chief's tax collectors to accept a smaller tribute from an *ahupua'a* with a bad harvest due to drought. In addition, the absence of war would have allowed adult male farmers to spend more time working in the fields, which could have increased output somewhat during less severe drought years. Concern for the welfare of farmers was surely not the only factor underlying decisions by the *ali'i nui* and *kāhuna nui* to forgo extensive preparations for a war of conquest during a year of bad harvests. A reduced agricultural surplus would also directly reduce the capacity of a state to wage war.

What Changed after 1600?

Archaeologists studying Hawai'i generally agree that after 1600, Hawai'i's population (slowly) increased, new lands were prepared for cultivation, most existing lands were farmed more intensively, and competition between states intensified.[77] On the timing and extent of these changes and the forces driving them, there is considerable disagreement. I provide a brief review of the controversies and use economic theory to try to shed new light on these relationships.

Expansion into new lands was probably not driven by declining productivity on ponded taro farms. Chiefdoms transitioned to states in the late fifteenth and sixteenth centuries primarily because ponded taro cultivation—a form of production in which farmers made large capital investments in their lands—produced the big agricultural surpluses necessary to feed the skilled specialists who provided services in support of the state. After over three centuries of cultivation (1260–1600), it is worth considering whether these productive lands were still capable of yielding big surpluses. Mark McCoy and a team of archaeologists investigated whether soil qualities in ponded taro farms in the North Kohala district of the island of Hawai'i declined over six centuries of cultivation. They found "no clear evidence that . . . soils show signs of having been artificially depleted of nutrients by farming and the harvesting of taro." There was, however, some evidence that overall soil quality had marginally declined due to "influx and accumulation of deposits" from upland areas. They concluded that ponded taro cultivation was still incredibly productive, and that it continued to provide "a remarkably sustainable, low investment, high return crop ideal for creating a surplus" to pursue or maintain political power.[78] If McCoy et al.'s results for North Kohala are indicative of how the productivity of ponded taro fields on other islands evolved, then one can infer that expansion of staple production via new rain-fed fields was not driven by declining productivity on more established fields, but rather by other factors.

Since stable ponded taro surpluses are more likely to have reinforced the status quo than to have been a source of change, archaeologists have instead focused on considering whether the development of riskier rain-fed agricultural fields might be the key to understanding the growing political competition that occurred in the seventeenth and eighteenth centuries. Archaeologists studying the period between 1600 and 1778 on the island of Hawai'i are divided as to when the development, expansion, and intensification of rain-fed field systems happened.[79] Patrick Kirch has concluded that Hawai'i's population reached its maximum (400,000–500,000) sometime during the 1600s, and that on the island of Hawai'i, "a final phase of intensification, typically marked by highly formalized garden plots and territorial boundaries, commenced about AD 1600 to 1650, and continued until the early post-contact period."[80] Plots were subdivided, new walls built, new crop dividers planted, and new fields opened. Thegn Ladefoged and Michael Graves have identified considerable evidence that the process of developing, expanding, and intensifying production on rain-fed fields was initiated in the fourteenth century, with the most productive of these fields developed on Hawai'i, Maui, Moloka'i, and O'ahu. A second phase took place in the seventeenth and eighteenth centuries, characterized by "a more rapid expansion into and more limited intensification of areas associated with greater costs or risks."[81] James Bayman and Thomas Dye concluded that the timing of this development was somewhat later, presenting evidence that large portions of the sprawling agricultural complexes on the volcanic slopes of Maui and Hawai'i were not built until the late seventeenth century or the eighteenth century, or even until after Western contact.[82]

Archaeologists have offered several explanations for the timing and extent of development of rain-fed fields, all primarily focused on incentives for ruling chiefs and their retainers to expand the supply of land for agriculture. The most common and most likely explanation is that past, current, or expected future expansion of working-age populations provided chiefs with incentives to open new lands. Some researchers have articulated the idea that development of the rain-fed volcanic fields was a technique used by ruling chiefs to more effectively spread the burden of providing for elites over a larger land area. The idea is that any additional land that generated some surplus would add to the overall pool of surplus available to feed *ali'i* and their families as well as to support specialists providing services to them.[83] Evidence for state-driven intensification of production comes from walls that span several land parcels. Because their construction would have had to be coordinated with parcel users, they imply that the chief's land manager (*konohiki*) organized this community effort. Thegn Ladefoged and Michael Graves, and others, have suggested a number of other potential causes, including expansion of a district's population, relocation of people from other areas with growing populations, changes in the environment that altered rainfall and land productivity, territorial expansion of the state, and consolidation of the state's power.[84]

The explanations offered by archaeologists are carefully developed and plausible in a variety of circumstances found in Hawai'i. That said, they are also incomplete, as they focus primarily on incentives for the *konohiki* and *ali'i* who controlled land use and less on competition among *maka'āinana* who farmed the land. The economist Steven N. S. Cheung, in his classic book *The Theory of Share Tenancy*, argued that the extent of competition for land among farmers affects plot size, land rent, and hours of work from the farmer and family.[85] One factor that triggers increased competition among farmers is natural population growth, and as we have seen, Hawai'i probably experienced very high population growth over the first 200–250 years of settlement. Population pressure would have been the key factor that drove expansion of land area under cultivation as wave after wave of people demanded the opportunity to farm new lands during this period. High-quality land was probably still available for development, however, so the large, rapid increases in population could be accommodated without changes in plot size, taxes, land rent (including tribute), or hours of work by farmers.

But then the demographic environment radically changed. From 1500 to 1778, the population grew at an average annual rate of just 0.25 percent. This lower growth rate would still have had big consequences as it doubled the population, from about 200,000 people in 1500 to 400,000 in 1778. On an archipelago with a limited amount of land (4.1 million acres) and much less potentially arable land, the supply of quality-adjusted land brought into production would have had to double by 1778 to keep per capita agricultural surpluses constant. High-quality lands had already been taken by 1450–1550, and the quality of new lands opened for production diminished as they were located at higher altitudes and on steeper slopes, had less fertile soils, and were more distant from coastal settlements and canoe landings.[86] Because the newly opened lands were less productive than existing ponded taro and rain-fed fields, competition among *maka'āinana* to gain access to high-quality rather than low-quality lands would have emerged. The effects of this competition could be expressed in a number of ways: a farmer could accept a smaller plot of high-quality land to farm or signal willingness to pay more tribute. But this strategy raises a critical question: How does a farmer pay more tribute with a smaller plot? One option would have been to work more hours, which would have increased output.[87] Since Hawaiians generally had living standards well above subsistence and had considerable leisure time, working a smaller plot and longer hours would have depressed their welfare, but would not have pushed them below starvation in most years.

It is also important to recognize that increases in competition among *maka'āinana* for land would have generated other effects beyond adjustments in tenant rent, plot size, and work hours. An increase in demand for land increases its value, and this increase provides incentives for those who control land use—the *konohiki*—both to use it more intensively and to develop more land. To use land more intensively and more efficiently, *konohiki* and *maka'āinana* would have gained from making additional capital investments in the land and in implements used to work the land. Numerous scholars have documented the additional trails, walls within plots, and cultivated plant species that were implemented in major dryland systems, including Kalaupapa on Moloka'i and North Kohala on the island of Hawai'i.[88] The agricultural innovation on the island of Hawai'i identified by McCoy and Graves could also have been triggered by an increase in the value of land due to persistent increases in population. The bottom line is that the intensification and expansion of agriculture from 1500 through 1778 were not independent processes, but were both driven by population growth, which increased the value of all agricultural lands, thereby providing incentives for both intensification and expansion.

Conclusion

The existence of agricultural surpluses is a necessary condition for state formation, and the surpluses from ponded taro agriculture facilitated rapid formation of states in Hawai'i, only two centuries after a few hundred people first migrated from the Society Islands and the Marquesas Islands. Both home societies were chiefdoms, and migrants to Hawai'i brought knowledge of how their home institutions worked with them. The new finding that Hawai'i was first settled only in the twelfth or thirteenth century is at the heart of this chapter's analysis, as reducing the span of Hawai'i's prehistory from fourteen centuries to just five or six centuries increases dramatically the rates of population growth needed for Hawai'i's population to increase from just a few hundred people in 1260 to over 400,000 people in 1778. If one is willing to start their historical analysis assuming 1260 as the initial date of settlement, 30,000 inhabitants in 1350, and a population of 400,000 in 1778, then population growth necessarily emerges as the main driver of land settlement, state formation, and the evolving political economy of Hawai'i's competing states.

Polynesian voyagers were fortunate to find the Hawaiian archipelago, as the sizes of the six largest islands, the variety of natural resources, and the farming and governance experience of the voyagers combined on O'ahu and Kaua'i to produce an exceptional prosperity once eight to ten generations had fully developed thousands of small, incredibly productive ponded taro farms. By the mid- to late 1400s, all lands on O'ahu suitable for ponded taro cultivation had very likely been taken, so rents from land should have become more important in building political coalitions. The change in the value of land set the stage for O'ahu's ruling chief to use a crisis to undertake a fundamental reorganization of the island's economic administration, implement a new system of property rights to land, and carry out a redistribution of property toward the core supporters of his ruling coalition.

The rise of the Hawaiian state on O'ahu probably stimulated the formation of archaic states on the islands of Hawai'i and Maui. These states are notable because of their extensive reliance on distinctive institutions such as investments in monumental stone architecture, ritualistic human sacrifice, and redistributive taxation (*ho'okipu*) during the *makahiki* festival months to sustain their legitimacy and efficacy. Their reliance on a set of more severe incentives is not fully understood; it could have originated from the more severe environment encountered on the island of Hawai'i, or it could have been due to a lack of outside political competition between 1450 and 1778, when Hawai'i was totally isolated from Polynesian homelands and the rest of the world.

The development of states in Hawai'i was facilitated by the network of farms that had already been put in place by chiefdoms. The ongoing increases in population and state formation must, at some point, have collided with the limited extent of the islands' arable lands and led to smaller plot sizes, rent increases, and longer work hours. Demands by *ali'i* for additional tribute sometimes led, as they did in Europe, China, and the Middle East, to rebellions against state authority, although the *mo'oelo* do not allow explicit tracing of most rebellions to concerns about food shortages or starvation.

The archaic states that formed in Hawai'i from the late 1400s struggled to control violence, the primary function of any state. Usurpation, rebellion, and wars of conquest remained common. In some ways, the early political economy of chiefdoms based on ponded taro production seems stable compared with that of the seventeenth and eighteenth centuries, when the development of large rain-fed fields on volcanic slopes of the islands of Hawai'i and Maui allowed their populations to swell. Competition between states intensified during the seventeenth and eighteenth centuries. Intra- and interisland wars were fought, although scholars disagree as to their frequency and severity. Occasionally, larger political units emerged, only to break apart after a short time.[89] The ocean seems to have provided a barrier to maintaining interisland states for substantial periods.[90] In general, states arose around particular islands (O'ahu and Kaua'i) or productive agricultural areas that were more contiguous (East Maui and West Maui). On the island of Hawai'i, the presence of several large volcanos and the distances between the five main areas of agricultural production and settlement made it more costly for a unified island state to emerge and, when it did, to persist. Despite the differences between islands, Robert Hommon has carefully documented how the pattern of partition-unification-partition also extended to states on other islands.[91] All of this would change forever when the ships of the Cook expedition entered Hawai'i's world in 1778.

CHAPTER FOUR

Guns, Germs, and Sandalwood

Maloko o Kekuiapoiwa
O ka Mano nui kapu lalakea
O ke alii o ka pali nui kiekie
O Malu ka lani, he kaha na Awini
E hii ana ia kalani nui mehameha

Me he hulu nenu la ka haki manawa
From within Kekuiapoiwa
A great, sacred, white-finned shark
A chief of the great, tall cliff
Sheltered was the heavenly one at the land of Awini
There the great chief Kamehameha was borne in the arms
Like the feather of a goose

—*Mele* celebrating Kamehameha's birth[1]

Contact with the world outside Hawai'i disrupted and changed virtually every aspect of life in the islands. The outside world brought guns, germs, new technologies, and trade to Hawai'i.[2] Guns disrupted the balance of power between *ali'i nui* (ruling chiefs) and led to the consolidation of competing polities in a single state that would endure for nearly a century. Germs massively reduced the Hawaiian population and transformed Hawai'i's economy by forever changing the relationship between the people and the land. Technology transfers led to the development and widespread use of a written Hawaiian language, introduction of new production techniques and products, and dissemination of new information,

ideas, and knowledge. Trade with other countries, particularly in sandalwood, changed the value of resources and was an important factor leading
to institutional changes that altered the islands' fabric of life forever.

This chapter uses models of resource booms and political orders to
provide a framework for understanding the massive changes in Hawai'i's
economy and political order that occurred during the first 50 years after
Western contact. It shows why the interaction of three events—the discovery and opening of trade in sandalwood, the big decline in the Native
Hawaiian population, and the consolidation of political power under King
Kamehameha—led, between 1795 and 1830, to a decline in traditional
agriculture, big changes in land rents and wages, and changes in the power
of the *Mō'ī* (king) and *ali'i*. It then explains how the resource boom in
sandalwood and the increased power of high-ranking chiefs led to a weak-
ening of property rights in sandalwood during the 1819 transition to a
new king.[3]

Three major findings emerge from this chapter's analysis. One is that
wages fell during the sandalwood resource boom (1815–1831) and rose
during the whaling resource boom (1825–1870). This finding is a bit of a
puzzle, as the expansion of a labor-intensive resource sector should have
combined with the big decline in the Hawaiian population to push up
wages during *both* resource booms. During the sandalwood boom, evidence points to falling wages, as increases in the political power of chiefs
allowed them to extract more income from *maka'āinana* labor as well as
to coerce additional hours. During the whaling boom, evidence points to
increasing wages, as upward pressure on wages from the resource boom
and population decline was reinforced by several new opportunities for
maka'āinana to escape the chiefs' tight control of rural labor supplies. A
second finding is that the abandoned farms observed during the 1810s and
1820s were the result of both the population decline and the mobilization
of *maka'āinana* labor by chiefs to harvest sandalwood at distant locations.
Large declines in population in Europe, Asia, and North America have
typically been associated with large-scale abandonment of farms, and labor movement out of agriculture and into sandalwood harvesting reinforced this tendency in Hawai'i, leaving even more fields untended and
the population closer to subsistence levels of nutrition. A third finding
is that the changes in property rights to sandalwood that occurred in the
middle of the resource boom were instituted to enable the king's supporters to realize a larger share of the economic rents from harvesting sandalwood and thereby stabilize the ruling coalition of *Mō'ī* and *ali'i*.

Guns, Disease, and Political Consolidation after 1778

Western contact triggered the consolidation of Hawai'i's competing states. There had been frequent wars between Hawai'i's states in the decades before 1778, and contact with Westerners fundamentally changed the nature of warfare in Hawai'i. States competed to add Western arms, ships, and military strategies to their arsenals. With the help of two British military advisors (Isaac Davis and John Young), a fortuitous eruption of Kīlauea (which asphyxiated warriors in a retreating army), and a first-mover advantage in arming his warriors with modern weapons, Kamehameha, the ruling chief of one of the archaic states on the island of Hawai'i (fig. 4.1), conquered all but two islands (Kaua'i and Ni'ihau) in 1795. Thousands of O'ahu warriors and high-ranking chiefs lost their lives in the final battles, and others found refuge in Kaua'i. Several thousand of Kamehameha's warriors were resettled on O'ahu, primarily in the Anahulu district on O'ahu's north shore.[4]

To maintain his newly won position as king and reduce the possibility of a rebellion, Kamehameha had to devise a method to effectively integrate the conquered chiefs into his ruling coalition. Each chief in his ruling council received the right to administer large areas of land. Those land areas were not consolidated on a single island, however, but consisted of relatively small strips of land (*ahupua'a*) on several islands. Although a rebellious chief might gain lands on one island, he would surely be stripped of his holdings on other islands remaining under Kamehameha's control. A revolt thus became more costly to conduct and still more costly if it failed.[5] Because the chiefs earned economic rents (i.e., returns above normal returns) from their participation in the coalition, and because the cost of rebellion had increased, Kamehameha's redistribution of lands increased the stability of his coalition and of the new unified state.

Consider now four more implications of Kamehameha's redistribution of island lands. First, although monitoring of production by the chiefs became more costly, the land was divided such that each of the mountain-to-coast land units known as *ahupua'a* remained under the control of a single chief. As a result, technical efficiency within the *ahupua'a* was not disturbed by the division of lands.

Second, the redistribution reduced the Mō'ī's cost of monitoring his chiefs. If a particular *ali'i* with jurisdiction over Maui happened to produce fewer tax revenues this year, the *ali'i* could claim that poor local

FIGURE 4.1. King Kamehameha. Etching: Lahainaluna Prints. Source: Hawaiian Mission Children's Society Library.

weather or other local circumstances reduced crop yields and thus taxes paid. If, however, multiple *ali'i* were responsible for different strips of land on Maui, the *Mō'ī* would be able to compare tax revenues from many *ali'i* to evaluate the validity of such a claim.

Third, the redistribution was also designed to reduce variation in income among high-ranking *ali'i* with large landholdings. If a chief's landholdings were concentrated on one island, island-specific variations in weather could lead to sharp variations in crop yields and incomes. The *Mō'ī*'s decision to allocate lands on several islands to his core supporters would allow the impacts of island-specific weather shocks to be less concentrated on a single supporter. Reduced income variability would be important to the stability of the dominant political coalition if members were more likely to rebel when they had a bad year or sequence of bad years.

Finally, decision making in the chiefs' council would become less costly. Consider that the interests of Kaua'i are different from the interests of O'ahu. If a single chief had jurisdiction over each island, the council's decisions could reflect the interests of a dominant coalition of just a few islands. With each chief owning a portion of each island, the interests of all islands would more likely be reflected in their decisions.

Kamehameha twice assembled large fleets and forces on O'ahu to attempt a conquest of Kaua'i. In spring 1796, over 10,000 warriors, some with rifles, and more than 1,200 canoes left O'ahu to invade Kaua'i, but bad weather sank canoes and drowned warriors, forcing the rest of the fleet to return to O'ahu. In May 1804, Kamehameha assembled a second heavily armed force of roughly 7,000 Hawaiian men and 50 Europeans.[6] The expedition never sailed, as an epidemic on O'ahu's windward coast— the *oku'u*—decimated the warriors. Recent research tentatively identifies the culprit as bacillary dysentery caused by shigella bacteria. The epidemic led to thousands of deaths, with heavy tolls exacted from *ali'i* with long ties to Kamehameha.[7]

Incentives for Kaua'i to cooperate with O'ahu changed in 1804 with the opening of the sandalwood trade. The shipment of small but growing amounts of sandalwood over the next six years increased the chiefs' awareness of the potential for large gains from expansion of the trade as well as from increased cooperation. Competition between Kaua'i and O'ahu chiefs could either have directed more profits to the foreign shipping intermediaries or led to interisland war, which would have interrupted the trade and reduced the chiefs' profits. The potential gains from a trade monopoly were growing during the first decade of the 1800s, as an increasing number of ships in the fur and sandalwood trade were stopping at the islands for provisions and sandalwood.[8] In 1810, a visiting trader, Captain Nathan Winship, persuaded Kaumuali'i, the *ali'i nui* of Kaua'i, to visit Kamehameha on O'ahu. Winship's first mate was left on Kaua'i to guarantee Kamehameha's good faith.[9] Both parties agreed that Kaua'i should be a tributary kingdom, that Kaumuali'i would continue to govern the island, and that Kaua'i chiefs would receive a share of the sandalwood revenue.[10]

The 1810 agreement was made against the backdrop of continued distrust between the two parties. While most of the chiefs defeated by Kamehameha in the 1795 invasion of O'ahu and Maui had been killed, some had fled to Kaua'i and had been welcomed by Kaumuali'i. Any change in the two parties' potential to wage war could have prompted either party to end the agreement. That change came in 1815, when Russian traders arrived in Hawai'i and searched for ways to gain a share of its trade with China and to establish a colonial presence.[11] The agreement ended in 1816, when a trader (Georg Schäffer) working for the Russian-American Company reached agreement with Kaumuali'i to be the exclusive agent for the island's sandalwood trade and to lead an army of Kaua'i warriors in a conquest of O'ahu. Kamehameha's response was to build a large fort at Honolulu Harbor and to purchase more arms.

Political consolidation and trade were accompanied by a massive decline in the native Hawaiian population over the next 50 years. The decline is undisputed, but its exact size is still subject to debate. Hawai'i's first official census counted 129,814 Hawaiians in 1831–1832, but estimates of the population at contact by people visiting Hawai'i before 1800 and by recent scholars have ranged from just 150,000 to more than 800,000 people.[12] Thegn Ladefoged, Patrick Kirch, Samuel Gon III and colleagues' 2009 study provides a new benchmark for this literature by presenting archaeological evidence consistent with roughly 243,800 people working in agriculture in 1778.[13] Patrick Kirch has suggested that this estimate is consistent with an overall population estimate of over 400,000 people, given the large agricultural surplus that Hawai'i's lands generated.[14] My conclusion is that the Kirch-Ladefoged-Gon estimates are the best available because they take into account the full array of evidence bearing on the matter, combining earlier demographic analysis, quantitative evidence from recent archaeological work on the extent of dry and wet cultivation in eighteenth-century Hawai'i, and qualitative evidence presented by late eighteenth-century visitors to Hawai'i. The extent of Hawai'i's population decline is an important unresolved historical question, but for our purposes it is enough to know that its extent between 1778 and 1831 was massive, perhaps as much as 75–80 percent of the 1778 population.

How the Sandalwood Trade and Population Decline Transformed Hawai'i's Economy

Journals from Cook's expeditions were published in 1785, and their vivid depictions of resource abundance in the Pacific Northwest, particularly beavers and otters, caught the attention of British and American traders. It took only a few years for them to start a robust trade in furs between the Pacific Northwest and Canton, China.[15] From the 1790s onward, traders found it advantageous to stop in Hawai'i for provisions, buying pigs, chickens, yams, fruits, vegetables, water, firewood, and salt for curing the furs. In return, the Hawaiian chiefs who supplied these provisions received a variety of Western consumer goods as well as tools, utensils, guns, and ammunition. After his conquests of 1795, King Kamehameha took action to establish a monopoly on supplying provisions to visiting ships, usually by imposing a *kapu* on places that could supply provisions.[16]

China's demand for sandalwood (*'iliahi*) changed Hawai'i's economy when chiefs and traders became aware of the large stocks of sandalwood growing on the mountains throughout the islands. Sandalwood is "a tolerably heavy and solid wood, and after the sap, or part next to the bark is taken off, is of a light yellow or brown color, containing a quantity of aromatic oil."[17] Sandalwood trees take about 40 years to reach maturity and can grow 25 feet tall. They have a gray trunk, small, shiny leaves, and heartwood that contains the famous fragrant oil. Sandalwood had many traditional uses in Hawai'i, including medical applications, perfume, firewood, and musical instruments.[18] Most of it was located in areas more than 1,500 feet above sea level. Digging the tree up by its roots and stripping all wood and branches allowed the heartwood, the most valuable part of the tree, to be harvested. Sandalwood was brought from the mountains to the beach in pieces ranging from 12–18 inches in diameter and 6–8 feet long to small sticks not more than 1 inch thick and 18 inches long.[19] The entire process of production—locating the trees, harvesting, and moving the sandalwood to the beach—was highly labor intensive.

Sandalwood from Hawai'i was sold at the port of Canton, China, which had been at the center of the Asia-Pacific trade in sandalwood since at least the sixth century, when China first imported sandalwood from India and the East Indies. Chinese craftsmen used sandalwood to make boxes, fans, ornaments, perfumes, cosmetics, and medicines, and the fragrant smoke from sandalwood was essential to important religious and cultural ceremonies.[20] An increase in European and American trading ships in the Eastern Pacific Ocean during the late eighteenth and early nineteenth centuries led to the discovery and harvest of sandalwood in Fiji (1800–1816), the Marquesas Islands (1811–1814), Hawai'i (1804–1845), the southwestern Melanesian islands (1827–1865), Australia, and New Zealand. Hawai'i's sandalwood trade spanned roughly 40 years, with most sales concentrated over a 23-year period (1811–1833).

The sandalwood trade between Canton and Hawai'i started poorly. Two American ship captains brought shipments of Hawai'i sandalwood to Canton in 1794, only to discover that the wood was actually another variety (a "false sandalwood") and that their cargoes had no value in Canton.[21] A decade later, in 1804–1805, Canton customs statistics recorded the first imports of sandalwood from American traders, 900 piculs in total.[22] Between 1804 and 1810, the annual Hawai'i-Canton sandalwood trade fluctuated between 476 and 4,800 piculs. The first large cargo of sandalwood (11,261 piculs) left the islands in 1811.[23]

In the early years of the trade, various American ship captains made deals with Kamehameha and other *ali'i*. In 1812, Kamehameha signed a deal with three American traders (the Winship brothers and W. H. Davis) providing them with exclusive rights to the trade.[24] Only one shipment was sent to China under the exclusive contract before the War of 1812 between the United State and Great Britain interrupted the trade. Armed British and American ships drove traders to seek shelter in safe ports.[25] When trade resumed after the war, Kamehameha sold sandalwood to a number of American traders.[26] The first large shipment of sandalwood that left Hawai'i after the end of the War of 1812 arrived in Canton in 1816–1817.

How did the opening of trade in sandalwood affect Hawai'i's economy? To answer this question properly, I first introduce a simple general equilibrium model that shows how a boom in tradable resources affects returns to labor and land, use of labor in agriculture, and outputs in different economic sectors. The model is a variant of the classic model developed by the economist Max Corden of a three-sector economy undergoing a resource boom.[27] The economy has a booming tradable resource sector (sandalwood), a tradable agriculture sector (food in demand by ships), and a nontradable sector (consumer services), "nontradable" meaning that the good or service cannot be imported but must be produced in Hawai'i. Each sector's products require two inputs: labor, which is mobile across sectors, and a second input that is used only by that sector. For the Hawai'i economy, sandalwood was the unique input used by the booming resource sector, and land was the unique input used by the agriculture sector.

Corden's model identifies two central effects generated by a resource boom in a small open economy: a *spending effect* and a *resource movement effect*. The spending effect occurs when some of the extra income from trade in the booming sector is spent on goods in the nontraded sector, thereby driving up their prices relative to the prices of the goods produced in the other two sectors. From 1804 to 1819, when Kamehameha controlled the trade, the spending effect was muted, as Kamehameha's income from this barter trade consisted of imported armaments, ships, and consumer goods. Corden's second effect, the resource movement effect, occurs when a higher marginal product of labor in the booming sector pulls in labor from the other two sectors. Less labor in the agriculture sector means that it shrinks, a phenomenon known as *direct de-agriculturalisation*.[28] Each of these effects should have pushed up wages and lowered land rents in Hawai'i's booming sandalwood economy of the 1810s and 1820s.

The changes in wages and rents should have been magnified by the extreme population crisis that Hawai'i encountered during the sandalwood boom. Hawai'i's population crisis was bigger than the fourteenth-century Black Death population crisis in Europe. In England, for example, the population declined from 4.81 million in 1348 to 2.50 million in 1377, a reduction of 48 percent. Careful research by leading economic historians has established that England's large population decline was accompanied by large wage increases, with average wages of skilled and unskilled workers more than doubling (105 percent) from the 1340s to the first decade of the 1400s.[29] The decline in England's population also led to widespread abandonment of fields for months and years afterward. Between 1350 and 1380, landlords responded by converting lands formerly farmed by serfs into contractual tenancies, eliminating work requirements and other feudal obligations, and according tenants increased status.[30]

With the decline of Hawai'i's population by 50–75 percent between 1778 and 1833, there were many fewer people working in the agricultural sector, and those workers remaining should have experienced big increases in their wages, with chiefs competing for labor to farm their lands. The upward pressure on agricultural wages from the decline in population should have been intensified by competition for labor from the booming sandalwood sector.[31] As more labor was drawn from agriculture to sandalwood harvesting, the smaller labor supply in agriculture should have commanded even higher wages.

The historical record in Hawai'i clearly shows a reallocation of labor from agriculture to sandalwood harvesting as fields were abandoned throughout the islands. In fact, reports of untended fields in Hawai'i were first made at the resumption of the sandalwood trade after the end of the War of 1812. The Hawaiian historian Samuel Kamakau identified the cause of an 1815 famine as a "rush of labor to the mountains" to harvest sandalwood, which "brought about a scarcity of cultivated food throughout the whole [island] group."[32] In March 1821, Lieutenant Boyle from the Russian sloop *Otkrytie* noted in a report he compiled on Hawai'i that because the common people had to gather sandalwood, "the fields often remain unattended and uncultivated for a long time." The leader of a Russian expedition in the Pacific, Lieutenant-Commander M. N. Vasilyev, stated that in April 1821, Liholiho brought 5,000 men from Maui "for felling and pulling down from the mountains the sandalwood unmindful as to how they should maintain themselves." Lieutenant Lazarev from the same Russian expedition noted in December 1821 that "a multitude of people were sent for felling and storing up sandalwood" and that "the fields about the harbour became deserted."[33] Two English missionaries, Daniel Tyerman and George Bennett, reported "nearly 2,000 persons . . . wearied with their unpaid labor" carrying sandalwood to royal storehouses in Kailua in 1822.[34]

The second prediction coming from the resource boom model is that wages should have increased as the population declined and the new sandalwood sector competed for scarce *maka'āinana* labor. To the contrary, the economist James Roumasset and I, as well as the anthropologist Marshall Sahlins, found considerable evidence that wages fell after Kamehameha's 1795 unification of the islands.[35] In his detailed discussion of the sandalwood trade, Sahlins emphasized that the chiefs exacted more labor from *maka'āinana* during the sandalwood trade era.[36] Sahlins attributed the increased exaction to Kamehameha's practice of placing more chiefs on the productive lands on O'ahu, Maui, and Moloka'i after the 1795 conquests and compared it to the medieval European practice of "subinfeudation." He argued that more chiefs for a given parcel of land meant more taxation of *maka'āinana*. Given the burdens placed on Hawai'i's rural labor force by subinfeudation, it is unsurprising that workers in agriculture looked to urban areas and foreign ships for exit opportunities.

James Roumasset and I examined corvée labor exactions by *ali'i* by focusing on *why* exactions occurred, an analysis complementing that of Sahlins, who focused on *which groups* of chiefs engaged in this practice.[37] We identified three major reasons underlying the exactions.[38] First, after unification, there were fewer exit options for *maka'āinana* who were unhappy with their situation. In the pre-unification period, Hawaiian states competed for labor because of its implication for military advantage as well as agricultural production. They would usually accept *kānaka* migrants from other states. Second, labor was becoming a more valuable factor as the labor-intensive sandalwood sector expanded and population declined. Rulers had greater incentives to establish property rights in the most valuable goods, including labor, as there were more rents to extract. Third, in the unification era, the possibility of an overthrow of the ruling chief of a localized state as a safety value for preventing too many labor exactions disappeared. The strong military forces of the king would be sent to punish the perpetrators who killed or defied his supporter. An incident in Waialua (on Oʻahu) illustrates the stark choices that *makaʻāinana* faced if they refused orders by the chief to join sandalwood expeditions:

> Cox [the chief who had been granted rights to the *ahupuaʻa* of Waialua] had given orders to some hundreds of his people to repair to the woods by an appointed day to cut sandal-wood. The whole obeyed except one man, who had the folly and hardihood to refuse. Upon this, his house was set fire to, and burnt to the ground on the very next day; still he refused to go. The next process was to seize his possessions and turn his wife and family off the estate; which would have been done . . . had he not made a timely submission to prevent this extremity.[39]

To find the circumstances of labor deteriorating during a time of population crisis is rather extraordinary. Theoretical models predict, and historical experience with other large population declines confirms, increases rather than decreases in wages. In Hawaiʻi, however, contact with Western ships after 1778 caused not just a decline in population, but also a change in the institutions governing competition among chiefs for labor. While population decline should have led to more competition among chiefs for labor, the simultaneous unification of competing states led to less competition in rural markets. Once institutional change is considered, the Malthusian paradox can be at least partly resolved.

Property Rights in Sandalwood under Kamehameha

Political tensions within the Kamehameha regime, as well as the transition to a new king, are best observed in the changing property rights to sandalwood in the 1810s and 1820s. Samuel Kamakau stated that Kamehameha reserved sandalwood for the king after a severe famine in 1815 brought on by "the rush of labor to the mountains."[40] In response, Kamehameha

"declared all sandalwood to be the property of the government and ordered the people to devote only part of their time to its cutting and to
return to the cultivation of the land." Louis de Freycinet, the captain of a
French ship visiting in May 1819, tells us that Kamehameha ordered the
chiefs to supervise collection of the wood, and took for himself "all of
the profits from the sale of this wood to the foreigner," while allowing no
chief "to receive any part whatsoever of the European merchandise that
had been accumulated in the King's stores." De Freycinet speculated that
Kamehameha's behavior stemmed from "fear on his part that in increasing the resources of these men [high-ranking chiefs], whom he held under
control only by force, he might be furnishing them the means of emanci-
pating themselves."[41]

Kamehamaha's decision to tighten control of sandalwood harvesting reflected the insecure nature of property rights in Hawai'i, even under the reign of a strong *Mō'ī*, in a limited-access political order. In a
political order in which property rights to land and resources were secure and in which rules of enforcement were impersonal (i.e., enforcement of property rights is independent of the identity of the individuals
holding the rights), annual sandalwood harvests would not depend on
whether control of harvesting was consolidated in one property owner
or dispersed among several property owners.[42] Chiefs who were secure
in their property rights and who were profit maximizers, aware of global
market conditions, and knowledgeable about the rate at which sandalwood matures—four big assumptions—would have followed optimal
harvesting rules and sold the tree's heartwood to traders when the present value of rents from the harvest was maximized. That their property
rights were insecure is further indicated by the story told by Kamakau
about restrictions that Kamehameha (and earlier ruling chiefs) placed on
the harvesting of very young sandalwood: "[Kamehameha] ordered the
sandalwood cutters to spare the young trees and not to let the felled trees
fall on the saplings. 'Who are to have the young trees now that you are
getting old?' he was asked and he answered, 'When I die my chief and
my children will inherit them.' He gave similar orders to bird catchers,
canoe makers, weavers of feather capes, wood carvers, and fishermen.
These are the acts of a wise and Christian king who has regard for the
future of his children, but the old rulers of Hawaii did the same."[43] Sheldon Dibble, a missionary who came to Hawai'i in the early 1830s, tells a
similar but more detailed story about Kamehameha's rules for harvesting
sandalwood:

Kamehameha was a wise and considerate man. He looked well to his own ways, and especially to the welfare of his kingdom. He was anxious to transmit his dominions in good condition to his sons when called himself to leave them.

The following circumstances evince his thoughtfulness in this particular. When the men were collecting sandalwood, they cut the young sticks and brought them to the shore, which when Kamehameha perceived, he inquired, "Why do you bring the small wood hither?" They replied, "You are an old man and will soon die, and we know not whose will be the sandalwood hereafter." Kamehameha replied, "Is it indeed that you do not know my sons! To them young sandalwood belongs."

He instructed his bird catchers as follows: "When you have a bird, do not strangle it, but having plucked the few feathers for which it is sought, set it free that others may grow in their place." They inquired, "Who will possess the bird set free? You are an old man." He added, "My sons will possess the bird hereafter."[44]

Rapid harvesting of young wood signals that even under the rule of a strong *Mō ʻī*, rights to the land and its resources were insecure and possibly subject to redistribution.

Why might property rights have been insecure under a strong *Mō ʻī*? First, and most generally, property rights are never secure in a natural state, as members of the dominant ruling coalition know that a ruling chief will redistribute rights among supporters whenever he needs to do so to stay in power. Kamakau and David Malo related repeated episodes of *aliʻi nui* being overthrown by conquest, by brothers, by other close relatives, and by unrelated *aliʻi*.[45] Patrick Kirch, Lilikalā Kameʻeleihiwa, and Robert Hommon have each provided detailed accounts of property rights redistributions in pre- and post-contact Hawaiʻi in which rights to land rents from productive agricultural lands were directly redistributed to a group of high-ranking chiefs who could constitute a stable core of support for a *Mō ʻī* who had recently assumed power.[46] Abraham Fornander related that "it has been the custom since the days of Keawenui-a-Umi on the death of a Moi (King) and the accession of a new one, to redivide and distribute the land of the island between the chiefs and favorites of the new monarch."[47] Following this ancient practice, King Kamehameha extensively redistributed rights in land on Oʻahu, Molokaʻi, and Maui to a group of chiefs from the island of Hawaiʻi and their warriors who fought with him throughout his unification campaigns. This redistribution of lands occurred after elaborate inquiries and ceremonies conducted by *kāhuna nui*, prayer specialists in the state religion.

Second, the age of the *Mō'ī* enforcing property rights matters when supporters expect that property rights will be redistributed at the chief's death. King Kamehameha was at least 57 years old (and probably older) when sandalwood sales resumed in 1815.[48] High-ranking chiefs understood that a transition to a new *Mō'ī* would probably occur within the next few years and that Kamehameha's successor would redistribute valuable lands to his supporters.[49] Even if their rights to use the property were secure at the moment, given the looming transition to a new *Mō'ī*, chiefs with sandalwood on their lands had incentives to harvest it more quickly given the possibility that they would be on the losing side of the redistribution of rights by the new *Mō'ī*.

The Sandalwood Trade under Liholiho

After the death of Kamehameha in May 1819, the structure of property rights evolved to reflect fundamental shifts in the underlying power structure. At Kamehameha's death, his heir was his son, Liholiho (fig. 4.2), who had been designated for this role as a young child in 1802. The 21-year-old king shared power with one of Kamehameha's favorite and most powerful wives, Ka'ahumanu (fig. 4.3), who Kamehameha had appointed as *kuhina nui*, a cross between a prime minister and a regent. A transfer of power is one of the most serious situations to be faced in a natural state, as the transition to a new leader immediately raises questions about which aspects of the system of rights and privileges supporting the current order will survive and which aspects will change to reflect new sources of support for the new ruler and changes in the underlying ability of various factions in the coalition to harm one another.[50]

Just a few months after Kamehameha's death, Liholiho and Ka'ahumanu faced a revolt from another high-ranking chief, Kekauaokalani, the son of Kamehameha's brother. Kamehameha had designated Kekauaokalani to be the guardian to the statue of the war god Kūkā'ilimoku. This was the same position from which Kamehameha had risen to power on the island of Hawai'i. While Kekauaokalani was following the traditional Hawaiian path of attaining *mana* by winning battlefield victories, he also mounted his rebellion as the defender of the traditional state religion. This role was important because Ka'ahumanu and Liholiho and their immediate

FIGURE 4.2. King Kamehameha II (Liholiho). Lithograph: John Hayter. Source: Bishop Museum.

entourages had taken actions shortly after Kamehameha's death to dismantle the cultural and physical manifestations of the state religion. The
introduction of Western military technology to the islands rendered the
support offered by the existing religious and political order less important, and the resources used to maintain the network of temples and the
voluminous sacrifices to the Hawaiian gods loomed as more of a burden
on the state.[51] The dismantling of the state religion can be traced to decisions made by the new *Mō ʻī* and his family. Violations by the monarch, his
family, and ranking chiefs of key religious rules mandating that males and
females eat separately provided a signal to *aliʻi* and *kānaka maoli* alike
that the king no longer considered the state religion to be a key element
in the political, economic, and cultural mechanisms that supported his
dominant coalition. Within a few weeks, Hawaiians reacted to the news

by burning the wooden temple statues (*akua*) and plundering the archipelago's vast network of large and small stone temples (*heiau*). This religious vacuum would prove fortuitous for the Protestant missionaries from New England, who arrived in Hawai'i in March 1820 with a new religion to support the monarch's rule.

Liholiho's victory at the Battle of Kuamo'o over his rival, Kekauaokalani, came about because he had taken necessary measures to solidify his own support and because Kamehameha had used sandalwood revenues to purchase arms for the government's forces in case they had to wage a civil war. Both Kekauaokalani's army and Liholiho's army (led by Kalanimoku) had rifles, but a cannon used by the government forces proved a

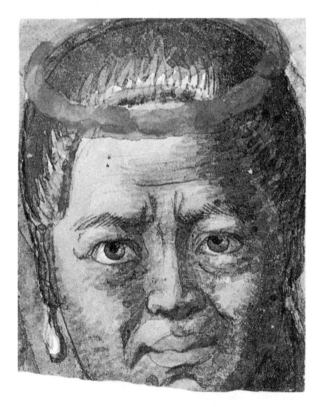

FIGURE 4.3. Queen Ka'ahumanu, Woman of the Sandwich Islands. Lithograph: Painting by Louis Choris. Source: Wikimedia Commons, https://commons.wikimedia.org/wiki/Category: Louis_Choris#/media/File:Louis_Choris_%27Kaahumanu,_Woman_of_the_Sandwich _Islands%27.jpg.

decisive factor.[52] To consolidate his power base among the lesser chiefs, Liholiho opened up the sandalwood trade to their independent participation, enabling them to make their own deals with foreign traders.[53] In effect, the king maintained his share of the sandalwood revenues, but lost his ability to set restrictions on the total quantity sold per period.[54]

Despite the short-term glue that the deal provided to the existing coalition by raising the rents received by leading chiefs with big sandalwood endowments, the underlying problem of *ali'i* having insecure property rights was the same one that Kamehameha faced in 1815: ensuring that the coalition is stable today does not remove future problems of unstable rights due to coming leadership transitions. Given the insecurity of their property rights and their higher shares of the proceeds, the chiefs had incentives to harvest any sandalwood tree on their lands that would justify the marginal cost of harvesting, regardless of how immature the tree was. The incentives to harvest more sandalwood quickly were reflected in the sales of sandalwood by American traders in Canton. Canton imports tripled, from 16,078 piculs in 1819 and 1820 to 47,475 piculs in 1821 and 1822 (table 4.1, third column).[55]

Historians have carefully documented how, during Liholiho's reign, access to independent trading in sandalwood and the resultant accumulation of individual wealth led to lavish spending by chiefs on Western consumer goods. In his insightful treatment of the sandalwood trading era in Hawai'i, the anthropologist Marshall Sahlins pointed out major differences between Kamehameha's use of sandalwood revenues received between 1815 and 1819 and the chiefs' use of their sandalwood revenues when they acquired the ability to trade independently in 1819.[56] Kamehameha used his revenues to acquire military equipment, ammunition, and ships that could be used to ferry warriors to islands where revolts were taking place or chiefs were not paying their required share of revenues from trade or from the land. In addition, the new revenues from sandalwood and other resources enabled the king to open a royal shipyard in Kailua-Kona that made both Western ships and Hawaiian canoes. Kamehameha also used his revenues from the sandalwood trade to purchase and commission the building of approximately 20 large ships. While many of the ships he purchased were old and rotting, they nonetheless enhanced his short-term ability to move warriors. Revenues accruing to the king from sales of sandalwood and provisions were also used to construct a large fort at Honolulu Harbor, armed with 54 cannon, in response to the increased threat from Kaua'i in 1815–1816. By contrast, Liholiho's

TABLE 4.1. **Sandalwood Sales and Prices at the Port of Canton**

Year	U.S. exports (U.S.$)	Quantity (pounds)	China imports (piculs)	Price per picul (U.S.$)
1804		119,997	900	
1805		213,328	1,600	
1806		359,991	2,700	
1807		266,660	2,000	
1808		266,660	4,800	
1809		241,994	1,815	
1810		66,132	496	
1811		1,501,429	11,261	
1812		2,538,070	19,036	
1813		0	550	
1814		0	550	
1815		333,325	2,500	
1816		986,642	7,400	
1817	174,075	2,109,947	15,825	11.00
1818	91,368	1,983,150	14,874	6.14
1819	101,228	1,343,033	10,073	10.05
1820	67,133	800,647	6,005	11.18
1821	269,320	3,576,177	26,822	10.04
1822	139,408	2,753,664	20,653	6.75
1823	67,232	1,120,505	8,404	8.00
1824	66,942	991,709	7,438	9.00
1825	32,518	412,923	3,097	10.50
1826	83,500	890,644	6,680	12.50
1827	211,070	1,768,622	13,265	15.91
1828	127,442	2,427,406	18,206	7.00
1829	43,228		10,807	
1830	39,000		9,750	
1831	7,000		1,400	
1832	28,000		5,600	

Sources: Chinese import data for sandalwood (in piculs) are from Gützlaff (1834, vol. 2). All other data are from Fontenoy (1997, tables 1 and 2).

supporters primarily spent their sandalwood revenues on imported luxury goods, ranging from Western houses to fine cloth, Chinese arts, jewelry, and furniture.

Marshall Sahlins attributed the chiefs' behavior to their desire to replace a ritual system of tribute that had waned under Western influence and the abolition of the state religion.[57] The accumulation of stocks of novel luxury goods enabled them to differentiate themselves from one another as well as from the newly arrived New England missionaries and lower-ranking *ali'i*. An alternative and complementary explanation for the differences is that the existing military strength of Liholiho, Ka'ahumanu, and their supporters lowered returns to other chiefs from investing in arms. Their main competitor, Kekauaokalani, had been defeated at the Battle of Kuamoʻo in 1819, and the military threat from Kauaʻi had diminished in 1821, after the ruler of Kauaʻi, Kaumualiʻi, was tricked into coming to Oʻahu in October 1821, thereby losing his ability to govern Kauaʻi. Upon his death in Honolulu in May 1824, Prime Minister Kalanimoku traveled to Kauaʻi to convey Kaumualiʻiʻs declaration that lands not be redistributed after his death and his commitment to uphold those wishes. Unrest arose among chiefs in Kauaʻi who were expecting a redistribution of lands at the death of Kaumualiʻi. Kalanimoku quelled an initial uprising and, with reinforcements from Oʻahu, crushed the remaining rebels.[58]

I have argued above that the depletion of sandalwood in Hawaiʻi started when Liholiho lost control over the total amount of sandalwood that chiefs could harvest, and chiefs responded to the new incentives and insecurity of property rights by over-harvesting sandalwood. James Roumasset and I used a similar line of reasoning to explain why the chiefs borrowed heavily from American ship captains in the early 1820s against future sandalwood sales.[59] For example, Boki, the governor of Oʻahu in the 1820s, borrowed heavily against future sandalwood shipments to purchase "whole bolts of cloth and boxes of dry goods."[60] An individual chief could gain by trading an uncertain future income stream for a certain stream of current consumption. Each chief had little incentive to take into account the strategic externality that he was imposing on the Hawaiian Kingdom by incurring personal debts, although mounting aggregate debts to foreigners could jeopardize Hawaiʻiʻs independence. Because each chiefʻs contribution to the overall debt was small, each rationally ignored that contribution. Collectively, the result was a large debt for which foreigners would ultimately hold Hawaiʻiʻs *Mō ʻī* and *ali ʻi* responsible. An effective, far-sighted government would have controlled total borrowing, but a weaker government, such as Liholihoʻs, would be reluctant to impose such a ceiling for fear of angering important supporters.

Conclusion

The unification of all but two of the Hawaiian islands in 1795 allowed the dominant coalition of chiefs to extract more income from the *maka ʻāinana*, as they no longer faced significant competition. This situation would last only about 25–35 years, however, as a large decline in population placed upward pressure on agricultural wages. This pressure was reinforced by the growth of a labor-intensive industry, sandalwood harvesting, that also took labor supplies away from the agricultural sector and acted to push up *maka'āinana* incomes.

The decline of Hawai'i's sandalwood stocks and harvests starting in the mid-1820s should have taken some of the pressure off of agricultural wages, but the decline of sandalwood harvesting was accompanied by the rise of a new labor-intensive sector that supplied services to American and European whaling ships working the Northern Pacific whale fisheries. The replacement of one labor-intensive industry with another, coupled with continued deep population declines after 1825, meant that upward pressure on wages persisted. The next chapter considers how these changes in rents and wages combined with the integration of Hawai'i into international product markets to drive transformative institutional change in Hawai'i at mid-century.

Globalization and the Emergence of a Mature Natural State

From first canoe to 1850, Hawai'i underwent two big transitions in government and property rights regimes. The first settlers were politically organized as small chiefdoms that were built around layers of extended family ties. These chiefdoms lasted for roughly 150–300 years, until a wave of consolidations of political power led to the emergence of larger political units that controlled entire islands or large portions of an island. The new political units were "basic natural states" in which a ruling chief (*ali'i nui*) controlled the land and distributed lands to high-ranking chiefs (*ali'i*). Chiefs and their land managers (*konohiki*) had traditional rights in the land that allowed them to collect taxes from the people farming the land (*maka'āinana*), who also retained restricted rights of occupancy and use of the land. The second transition in government began when new military technology introduced after Western contact in 1778 changed the calculus of battles between warring Hawaiian states and led to Kamehameha's conquest in 1795 of all islands except Kaua'i and Ni'ihau. This consolidation of state power, combined with the rapid decline of the Native Hawaiian population after 1778, produced conditions that allowed the king (*Mō'ī*) and *ali'i* to reach agreement in the 1830s and 1840s to institute new forms of government and to reorganize land rights as (mostly) private property.

Why did the *Mō'ī* and *ali'i* make the changes that transformed the basic natural state of 1795 into the mature natural state of 1850? Historians have pointed to a number of factors: the influence of Western ideas on Hawai'i's *ali'i*; the pressure exerted by Western governments on the *Mō'ī*, Kauikeaouli, to allow foreigners to own property; and beliefs held by the *Mō'ī* and important *ali'i* that annexation by France, Britain, or the United States would be less likely if Hawai'i adopted Western institutions. In this chapter, I suggest that two other factors were particularly important: the big decline in Hawai'i's population and the integration of Hawai'i's economy with global markets. Both fundamentally changed the political economy of Hawai'i by providing strong incentives for wealth-maximizing elites to adopt new forms of government and property rights.

Economic historians who have studied transitions in property rights to land have often identified population pressure as the major force behind such transitions. They have suggested that more people competing for a fixed amount of land bid up annual land rents and thus land prices. Whenever an asset, such as land, becomes more valuable, both owners and users of the asset have incentives to define property rights to it more precisely.[1] Economic historians Douglass North and Robert Paul Thomas concluded that this was precisely what happened to property rights in land in England in the seventeenth and eighteenth centuries, when the country made the transition from a system of nonexclusive property rights ("open fields") to a system of exclusive, transferable property rights in agricultural land. As England's expanding population competed for a fixed amount of land, they drove up land rents. As the value of land increased, so did the additional value that could be gained by switching from traditional communal management of agricultural lands to private management. With big gains available to landowners who worked with Parliament to reorganize land rights into bundles of more exclusive, transferable rights, landowners and members of Parliament became more willing to incur the substantial political and economic costs necessary to enact and implement a new system of exclusive, transferable private property rights to land.[2]

Economic historians have found extensive support for population growth as the driver of changes in land rights in a wide variety of countries and time periods. Economic historian David Feeny, who studied the development of property rights in land in Thailand, Burma, India, and the Philippines, concluded that "the growth of population [and the increase in the terms of trade] were indeed associated with a rise in real land prices" and that land scarcity induced changes in the institutions governing its use.[3] Economic historians Lee Alston, Edwyna Harris, and Bernardo

Mueller, who studied formation of property rights to land in Brazil, the United States, and Australia in the mid- to late nineteenth century, concluded that expanding populations led to political pressures to accommodate groups who had not acquired land and to define de jure property rights in land more precisely.[4]

So is Hawai'i another case study that reinforces the received wisdom among economic historians regarding property rights changing due to population pressures? Not exactly. In Hawai'i, private property rights in land emerged in the middle of a 125-year period of *drastic population decline*. If Hawai'i wages and land rents had followed the course predicted by a simple macroeconomic model, its drastic drop in population should have raised wages relative to land rents (as labor had become more scarce) and thereby diminished incentives to specify and enforce more precise property rights in less valuable land.[5] The puzzle to consider is why property rights to land moved in the opposite direction, becoming more defined as land values fell.

The answer to the puzzle stems from Hawai'i's integration with global markets during the first half of the nineteenth century. Integration with global markets increased the potential value of Hawai'i lands if they could be used to grow crops highly valued in world markets. But that potential value could be realized only if governance institutions did not place impediments on transfer of resources to expanding industries. Economic historians Dan Bogart and Gary Richardson document such impediments in Britain in the seventeenth century, showing how "Britain's preindustrial property rights regime" prevented landowners from putting resources into more productive, newly discovered uses. The old property rights regime prevented landowners from "trying to reallocate resources toward more productive uses, particularly opportunities arising from technologies unanticipated in the distant past. Holders of equitable estates could neither mortgage, nor lease, nor sell much of the land under their control. Holders under many types of tenures could transfer property only to particular persons or members of a local community. Residents in common-field villages often had to keep land in traditional uses. Residents could neither utilize resources in new ways, nor improve infrastructure, nor repackage rights."[6] To put it simply, property rights that had persisted for centuries in Britain prevented deployment of the new technologies of the Industrial Revolution to their best use on lands that had been traditionally dedicated to other uses. Bogart and Richardson argue that the British Parliament eventually responded to the logjam by enacting bills of enclosure that allowed landowners to consolidate and reorganize ownership of groups of land parcels.

My explanation for why Hawai'i reorganized property rights to land is closely related to the Bogart-Richardson argument. It is that the integration of Hawai'i's economy with global markets increased the profitability of deploying rapidly evolving technologies of sugar production on fertile Hawai'i lands.[7] Another, more technical way to say this is that Hawai'i's rapid integration into the global economy gave it a comparative advantage in sugar production, as the development of U.S. West Coast markets in the 1840s increased the price of sugar for Hawai'i producers vis-à-vis prices for yams, sweet potatoes, and taro, the traditional goods produced by Hawai'i farmers. Globalization did for the Hawai'i economy what it does for all small economies that become closely linked to the global economy: changes in rents and wages lose their direct ties to changes in the country's population and become more closely tied to changes in the prices of goods bought and sold in global markets.[8] My analysis of these changes begins with a reexamination of other arguments previously offered by historians for the emergence in Hawai'i of a mature natural state and private property rights in land.

The Pervasive Influence of the New England Missionaries

In the 1810s, several native Hawaiian youths were educated at Protestant schools in Connecticut, and their stories of life in Hawai'i prompted the American Board of Commissioners for Foreign Missions to fund a large-scale project designed to convert native Hawaiians to the Protestant religion. In March 1820, missionaries from New England arrived in Hawai'i and moved quickly to seek permission to settle permanently and to preach their Presbyterian, Congregationalist, and Dutch Reformist doctrines. After receiving permission from the king to settle, they gradually set up churches and mission schools throughout the islands. The missionaries' influence extended far beyond the realm of church services and teaching youth. They acted to suppress expressions of traditional Hawaiian culture (such as hula dancing and chanting, marriage between close relatives, and infanticide), spread ideas about Western economic and political theories to chiefs and their children, and served as advisors to the king.

Perhaps the most notable of the missionaries' activities was the development of a system of writing for the Hawaiian language and the introduction and dissemination of a printed Bible and other religious and secular texts in that language. Numerous scholars have noted the speed with which high-ranking *ali'i* learned to read and write and how rapidly the general population became more literate. Missionary schools established during the 1820s drew large numbers of *kānaka maoli* adults and children to their classrooms. While these schools were scaled back somewhat in the 1840s and 1850s, by the 1850s and 1860s a majority of Hawaiian adults knew how to read and write in Hawaiian, an astonishing change for a society that in 1820 did not have a written language. An elite college, Lahainaluna Seminary, established in 1831 to serve children of high-ranking *ali'i*, graduated prominent Native Hawaiian scholars, such as David Malo and Samuel Kamakau, and notable politicians, such as Jonah Kapena and Timothy Ha'alilo. John Papa 'Ī'ī, from a family whose members traditionally served as *kahu* (caretaker/guardian) to chiefs, took that role at the Chiefs' Children's School in 1840, a position from which he fostered the education of many prominent Hawaiians and contributed to the preservation of knowledge about Hawaiian history.[9] The Hawaiian studies scholar Puakea Nogelmeier has argued that widespread literacy facilitated the development of numerous Hawaiian-language newspapers from 1834 onward and that those newspapers then spawned a rich dialogue among Hawaiians about contemporary issues, documented family genealogies, and recorded important events, people, and cultural practices from Hawai'i's history.[10]

Why did literacy spread so rapidly in Hawai'i? The most important reason is that the mission schools quickly gained the support of Ka'ahumanu, the regent for the young king Kauikeauoli, and in the 1830s, the support of Kauikeaouli himself. The effect of their support was amplified by the more centralized government put in place after the 1795 unification, as it allowed mission schools to be implemented both in the new urban centers and in villages throughout Hawai'i. Probing one level deeper, one might ask why both Ka'ahumanu and Kauikeaouli so strongly fostered the development of broad literacy among both *ali'i* and *kānaka maoli*. Fostering literacy has potential dangers for any government, as an educated public has an ability to analyze government policies and the performance of their leaders more clearly and critically as well as to read and discuss religious and political tracts and newspaper stories. Widespread literacy also generates many well-known benefits for both the public and government, such as allowing people to be more productive at work and at home, to participate more fully in governance and other civic activities, and to monitor the government and its leaders more effectively.

Recent work by economic historians Jeremiah Dittmar and Ralf Meisenzahl, who examined how the Protestant Reformation changed sixteenth-century Germany, provides important insights into potential channels by which adoption of the Protestant religion may have affected Hawai'i in the first half of the nineteenth century.[11] They suggest that the Reformation was a factor in the development of new political institutions in German cities that resulted in increased state capacity to provide public goods, such as education, that were more economically inclusive.[12] Implementation of these reforms occurred during a population crisis in some cities that were hit by outbreaks of plague. The epidemics led to the deaths of people in the wealthy elites and a decline in their overall political power.[13] Dittmar and Meisenzahl provide evidence that these political changes facilitated implementation of economically inclusive education reforms that ultimately led to an increase in literacy.

These same forces—a religious upheaval and adoption of the Protestant religion, a series of epidemics, and changes in the power of rulers—were also present in Hawai'i in the early 1820s, albeit manifesting differently. The main difference is that in Hawai'i, the elite, the high-ranking *ali'i*, consolidated their position after the death of Kamehameha in three different ways. First, the overthrow of the state religion in 1819 expelled the large group of religious specialists from the dominant coalition and thereby reduced the state's resource requirements. Second, in 1819, at the Battle of Kuamo'o, the king's forces defeated an uprising led by a high-ranking *ali'i*, Kekauaokalani, who was advocating a return to the traditional state religion (see chap. 4). Third, Ka'ahumanu's forces quickly and decisively crushed another revolt on Kaua'i in 1825, again demonstrating the power of the central government throughout the islands.

Despite its strong position in the mid-1820s, the ruling coalition faced daunting external and internal challenges. The central external challenge came from the presence of military forces of the United States, France, and Great Britain in the Pacific. Each was sufficiently powerful to impose a colonial government on the kingdom if it so desired. Failure to pay debts in the sandalwood trade in the mid-1820s had already led to the bombardment of Lahaina by a U.S. naval ship. The central internal challenge came from the punctuated population declines among Hawai'i's ruling elite and their children, as they threatened the present and future ability of the elites to govern and maintain a stable ruling coalition.

The Rush to Integrate Western Institutions into the Monarchy

Social and demographic changes also contributed to the transition in land rights and government institutions. Three large villages—Honolulu on Oʻahu, Lahaina on Maui (fig. 5.1), and Hilo on Hawaiʻi—arose in the 1820s and 1830s despite the big decline in population over the previous 50–60 years.[14] The combination of a declining overall population and concentration of the surviving population in Honolulu, Hilo, and Lahaina implies an even bigger decline in the rural population. This population shift had two important repercussions. First, the movement to urban areas disrupted the relationship between *aliʻi* and *makaʻāinana*, prompting the rapid development of new governance institutions. Second, the decline in the rural population stimulated competition among the chiefs' *konohiki* for tenants and led to tenants receiving better terms for farming lands.

The exodus from rural areas changed Hawaiʻi's political economy by making traditional systems of governance based on the hierarchy of *aliʻi* and *makaʻāinana* less viable. In the late 1820s, as more common people pursued activities outside the traditional economy, and as divisions among *aliʻi* over the development of a new code of law grew, enforcement of the law by local *aliʻi* began to break down. When the regent, Kaʻahumanu, died in 1832, the new *Mōʻī* and his Council of Chiefs responded to the confusion over law enforcement by promulgating new laws designed to protect public order and settle private disputes. District courts had already been established informally in 1829 and were formally instituted in 1840. The existence of a rudimentary court system was important for the

FIGURE 5.1. Lahaina, Maui, as seen from Lahainaluna Seminary. Etching: Lahainaluna Prints. Source: Hawaiian Mission Children's Society Library.

subsequent land reform, as it provided a new mechanism for enforcement of rights and dispute resolution, thereby lowering the transaction costs associated with the transition to the new property rights.[15]

The *Mō'ī*, Kauikeaouli, with the approval of Hawai'i's important chiefs and with the assistance of a missionary advisor, William Richards, promulgated the "Declaration of Rights and the Laws of 1839," which defined and secured certain rights for the people, including protection of property. Government by the king and his ministers was formalized by the establishment of a constitution in 1840. While most existing institutional arrangements were retained, a house of representatives chosen by the people was established as one house of a two-house legislature that included the existing Council of Chiefs.

These changes indicate that Hawai'i was making the transition, at least in its formal institutions, from a basic to a mature natural state. A mature natural state is characterized by "durable institutional structures for the state and the ability to support elite organizations outside the immediate framework of the state."[16] A body of law emerged in the 1850s that provided individuals with guidance regarding the types of contracts that would be enforced and the types of organizations that would be recognized by the law (e.g., different types of estates, trusts, corporations, and partnerships). Organizations were recognized as persons for contracting purposes. Recognition by a state of a wider variety of organizations allows for more opportunities to be realized independently by elites and provides them with more power and potentially more leverage over the state. In Hawai'i, the public law that emerged partly balanced such concerns. It specified public offices (king, cabinet, legislature, judiciary, etc.) and provided for methods of "resolving conflicts within the state and, by extension, within the dominant coalition."[17] As public institutions became more durable and private organizations emerged, the *Mō'ī* and *ali'i* also had more incentives to define their rights vis-à-vis one another, particularly with respect to their rights in land.

The *Māhele*

The *Māhele* (division) refers to the massive reorganization of rights to Hawai'i lands that occurred during the 1840s and early 1850s. In a narrower sense, it also refers to the division of Hawai'i lands, recorded in the *Buke Māhele* (Book of the *Māhele*), between the king, the chiefs, the government, and a bit later, the people farming the lands. The *Māhele's* proximate origins can be traced to an 1845 proposal by Hawai'i's interior minister, Gerrit P. Judd, to convert customary rights in land into private property rights. Judd called for a law permitting the sale of land "as freehold property forever" to Hawaiian subjects.[18] Later that year, the legislature passed a law establishing a board of commissioners that would award title to various tracts of land. A valid claimant would receive a "Land Commission Award," which could be exchanged for a title upon payment to the government of one-third of the value of the unimproved land. But how was the Land Commission to divide land among the three parties (king, landlord, and tenant) holding interests in it? After several meetings of the Privy Council (an advisory body to the King) in December 1847, the council adopted a set of rules to facilitate the land division. They are aptly summarized by John Chinen:

(1) The King was to retain all of his private lands as his own individual property, subject only to the rights of the tenants. (2) One third of the remaining lands was to be for the Hawaiian Government; one third for the chiefs and the konohikis [chiefs who were land managers]; and one third to be set aside for the tenants, the actual possessors and cultivators of the soil. (3) The division between the chiefs and konohikis and their tenants under Rule 2 was to take place whenever any chief, konohiki, or tenant desired such a division, subject only to confirmation by the king in privy council. (4) The tenants of the King's private lands were entitled to a fee simple title to one third of the lands possessed and cultivated by them, which was to be set off for the tenants in fee, whenever the king or any of the tenants desired such a division. (5) The divisions prescribed in the foregoing rules were not to interfere with any lands that may have been granted in fee simple by the king or his predecessors. (6) The Chiefs and konohikis were authorized to satisfy the commutation by either the setting aside of one third of their lands to the government or by the payments of one third of the unimproved value of their lands. (7) The lands of King Kamehameha III were to be recorded in the same book as all other allodial titles, and the only separate book was to be that listing the government lands. It was Kamehameha III who insisted upon the seventh rule, as a means of protecting his private lands in the event of an invasion by a foreign power.[19]

On January 27, 1848, "245 landlords came forward to arrange their lands and divide with the King."[20] By March 7, 1848, the *Māhele* was complete. The next day, the king divided his lands into government lands and crown lands, the latter and smaller portion to be his private lands. The process of division between the king and his landlords ended in the summer of 1850. The historian Ralph Kuykendall observed that "many of the chiefs surrendered to the government portions of their land, which were accepted by the privy council as full commutation of the government's interest, and fee simple titles were accordingly given to those chiefs for the lands which remained to them."[21]

The Privy Council resolutions of December 21, 1849, specified procedures for tenants, the people who farmed the land, to claim land shares. These resolutions provided for "fee simple titles free of commutation, [to] be granted to all native tenants for the lands occupied and improved by them, but not including houselots in Honolulu, Lahaina and Hilo. . . . The resolutions further provided that some government land on each island should be set aside to be sold in fee simple in lots of from one to fifty acres to such natives as were not otherwise furnished with sufficient lands at a minimum price of 50 cents per acre."[22] The house lots carried a commutation fee of one-fourth their unimproved value. In 1855, the completed division of lands was roughly as follows: crown lands, 984,000 acres; chiefs' lands, 1,619,000 acres; government lands, 1,495,000 acres; and *kuleana*s, the land grants to commoners, 28,600 acres.

The final division of lands was affected by numerous factors, including political maneuvering by stakeholders, the lack of surveying expertise in the kingdom, the division of units of land by their traditional names, and reluctance on the part of many *ali'i* and *maka'āinana* to file claims for their lands with the Land Commission. When the legislature approved the division of lands between king, government, and *ali'i* on June 7, 1848, the division was still subject to claims by *maka'āinana*. The division recorded in the *Buke Māhele* referred only to the traditional name of the *ahupua'a* (or smaller land unit assigned to some *ali'i*) rather than to a surveyed land unit or to land demarcated by metes-and-bounds markers, such as a large stone, a stream, a path, or a prominent tree.[23] The division was done in this way because there was one—yes, just one—trained, experienced surveyor in the islands: Theophilus Metcalf. Surveying the lands they received in the 1848 division was critical for both the chiefs and the government, as their lands could not be "patented"—that is, their clear title could not be established—until they had been surveyed. To fill the gap, the government would hire 30 more surveyors, some of whom were just teenagers. Curtis Lyons (age 17) and Henry Lyman (age 16) were both hired directly from Punahou School and, remarkably, were generally thought to have done excellent work. Other very young surveyors received less glowing evaluations, including Asa Thurston ("work was fair"), W. H. Pease ("One of the more careless and unreliable surveyors of that time"), and John T. Gower ("A very careless surveyor").[24]

This haphazard surveying would prove disastrous for some *maka'āinana*. While the *Māhele* principles provided for *maka'āinana* to receive one-third of the lands they occupied, issues regarding land in "fallow" (i.e., left uncultivated in order to revive its fertility) left surveyors confused and many *maka'āinana* shortchanged. The young surveyor Curtis Lyons related the following story:

> Well, responsibility came again—how much land to give the natives in cases where they planted now here, now there, so as to rest the soil from year to year. Some agents gave only the particular patches then under cultivation—stingy they—while others, too generous, gave from twenty to forty acres. The rule was to give what the natives improved. I multiplied the average cultivation by the number of years of fallow, or rest—three acres by three—and decided upon ten acres as a fair number, so the Hāmākua natives have an average of ten acres to the kuleana. It was of no use to wait for orders from headquarters, so I acted for myself, and was approved.[25]

Other factors limited *kuleana* claims. Commutation fees ($6–$12) charged by the government to patent the land often exceeded its value and thus sharply reduced incentives to patent. Some *maka'āinana* were unaware of the *Māhele* process, did not understand how to file claims, or did not understand which of the lands they worked could be claimed. Many did not receive awards or actually applied for fewer plots than they cultivated. To the matter of incorrect applications, Lyons asked, "What [should be done] when a man has more patches under cultivation than are written down, as is sometimes the case?"[26] Furthermore, claims by *maka'āinana* for *kuleana* land grants came from allocations previously made to *ali'i*, and this created a natural source of conflict between the two groups. Lyons again commented, "Waipio Valley, with its crowded native population and its infinity of taro patches held me three long, laborious months. The chiefs' men fought the kuleana system as hard as they could."[27]

Disputes were common on *kōʻele* lands and *kuakua* lands. *Kōʻele* lands—also known as *pōʻalima* lands—were those controlled by an *aliʻi* and on which *makaʻāinana* in the *ahupuaʻa* were obliged to work one day per week, often on Friday (*pōʻalima*).[28] *Kuakua* lands were strips of land between taro or sweet potato fields that were often planted in sugarcane or bananas to demarcate various stakeholders' rights and to provide windbreaks.[29] Disputes over boundary fences are a staple of modern property law, so it is unsurprising that such lands would be subject to vigorous dispute at the time of de jure rights specification and surveying. Consider this letter sent by surveyor Curtis Lynham to George Robertson, a member of the Land Commission: "There is a hau grove on the land claimed by one of the natives, & which is claimed as having been planted by his father (or uncle). The konohiki at first claimed it as his, because, as he said, some one of the people told him that it was a *koele* grove. The people all denying that it had ever been worked by the koele labor until this day, he then proposed to divide it. The claimant would not consent."[30]

In 1847, the legislature passed an act allowing foreigners to keep lands they possessed, but limiting sale of those lands only to native subjects. Foreigners were not allowed to acquire new lands. Kuykendall argued that the boom in the demand for Hawaiʻi's agricultural products between 1848 and 1850 prompted a reconsideration of this earlier position regarding foreign land ownership. The editors of the *Polynesian*, the major weekly newspaper of the missionaries, supported plans to allow foreign acquisition and conveyance of land to attract foreign capital and enterprise to agriculture. Legislation allowing foreigners to hold and convey land was, however, rejected in 1848.

The chief justice of the Hawaiʻi Supreme Court, 29-year-old William Little Lee, wrote the legislation to allow foreigners to own land. Widespread foreign ownership of land was opposed by Gerrit P. Judd, now the influential minister of finance, but he was overseas when the legislation was proposed in July 1850. The proposed law was approved by the Privy Council and then was sent to the Legislative Council (composed of the house of representatives and council of nobles); it gained unanimous support from the *aliʻi* but was strongly opposed by all six *kānaka maoli* members of the house of representatives. Their argument was straightforward and prescient: "They were afraid the foreigners who were not naturalized would own all the lands and some day there would be trouble."[31] Despite the vigorous *kānaka maoli* opposition, the *Mōʻī* approved the act on July 10, 1850.[32]

Institutional Change: Traditional Explanations

The traditional explanations offered by Hawai'i's historians for the mid-century reorganization and redistribution of property rights are all founded in Hawai'i's sudden plunge into globalization after 1778. Historians Ralph Kuykendall and Gavan Daws emphasized that ideas regarding the economy and governance transmitted by Western visitors and missionaries after 1822 were important both to the transition to constitutional government and to the reorganization of land rights.[33] The proposal for the *Māhele* came from then–Interior Minister Judd, formerly an American medical missionary. William Richards, an American missionary living in Lahaina since 1823, became the king's teacher and advisor in 1838 and was an important influence on the transition to constitutional government. He delivered regular lectures to the king and chiefs on government and political economy, emphasizing the advantages of free trade. American missionaries at the Lahainaluna Seminary taught children of *ali'i* who would later become advisors to kings on political philosophy, political economy, and history. Visiting ship captains regularly advised the king to adopt liberal economic policies, including the establishment of secure rights to property.[34] Virtually all missionaries taught either elementary or secondary school, and in so doing emphasized Western rather than Hawaiian values.

Political pressure by the British, French, and American consuls to institute fee simple titles for foreigners' building lots and farms sparked several diplomatic crises for the king. Perhaps the most important was the conflict with British consul Richard Charlton, which led Kauikeaouli to cede Hawai'i to Great Britain on February 25, 1843, provisionally pending the outcome of the dispute. On July 31, 1843, Admiral Thomas of the British Navy brought his ship into Honolulu Harbor with the news that Britain was returning the islands to the king. This perilous episode left an indelible impression on king, chiefs, and *kānaka maoli*: they now realized that their sovereign rule could disappear with virtually no warning as the casualty of a single dispute with France, Britain, or the United States.

The annexation crisis with Britain, and other dangerous episodes with the United States and France, led to a charged atmosphere in the 1840s, as the *Mō'ī* and *ali'i* remained aware that a small diplomatic incident could easily escalate to annexation.[35] This realization undoubtedly increased the *Mō'ī*'s desire to secure his landholdings as private property. If Hawai'i were to be annexed by a foreign power, government lands would be taken by the new authorities, and the *Mō'ī* would have lost his main source of income—land rent. Holding his crown lands as his private property increased the chance that the *Mō'ī* would have a legitimate case to retain them after annexation.

Robert Wyllie, a Scottish physician who immigrated to Hawai'i in 1844 and became Hawai'i minister of foreign relations, posed 116 questions to 12 missionaries in 1847–1848 regarding the situation of Hawaiians in the districts where those missionaries were stationed.[36] Many of the responses were critical of the burdens imposed on *maka'āinana* to work on *kō'ele* lands and the restrictions imposed on transporting agricultural products to markets. All responses were supportive of providing *maka'āinana* with private property rights to the plots they worked. Some rationalized that an influx of foreign capital could not be expected until transferable ownership rights to land were secured, while others observed that establishment of private property rights in land would be an incentive motivating Hawaiians to work their lands more effectively. Many worried that the Hawaiian people would not survive the cumulative impact of globalization, disease, and the presence of foreigners in Hawai'i.

Institutional Change: Economic and Demographic Explanations

While the traditional explanations all have some relevance, most of them concentrate on outside cultural and political influences and fail to examine how economic and demographic forces could have played a role in transforming Hawai'i's institutions. Between 1778 and 1857, structural change in Hawai'i's economy was driven by two overarching forces: integration with global markets and persistent population decline. Both forces affected factor prices and product prices, which, in turn, can be drivers of institutional change.[37] I consider each force in turn.

Exposure to Western diseases after 1778 led to a massive decline in the native Hawaiian population, from 400,000–500,000 in 1778 to just 129,814 people in 1831–1832, when the first missionary census was conducted (see chap. 4). Over the next two decades, rapid population decline continued, punctuated by a series of epidemics of newly introduced diseases. A net population loss of 22,000 between 1832 and 1836 has been attributed to epidemics of whooping cough and measles.[38] In 1839, an epidemic of mumps spread through the islands, and in 1848, measles and whooping cough outbreaks were followed by epidemics of diarrhea and influenza.

Contemporary observers believed that "ten thousand would be a low estimate for 1848 and 1849 which those epidemics took away."[39] Another factor behind the population decline was the decrease in the crude birth rate, starting perhaps in 1778 from first contact with Westerners carrying venereal diseases. The demographer Robert Schmitt argued that "crude birth rates must have remained below 30 per 1000 most of the time and may have fallen to as low as 15 per 1000. Specific factors included sterility (caused by gonorrhea), a high proportion of fetal deaths (from syphilis), and induced abortion."[40] High death rates and low birth rates combined to drag down the Hawaiian population in the 1850 census to just 82,035 full Hawaiians and 558 part-Hawaiians.[41]

Chapter 4 contains a brief discussion of how massive population decline in England during the fourteenth-century Black Death led to big increases in wages and decreases in land rents. In Hawai'i, the much larger decline in population also led to an increase in wages, which was reinforced by the effects of the boom in sandalwood harvesting (running from 1811 to 1833) as it drew labor out of agriculture and into the labor-intensive sandalwood harvesting sector. But even before the sandalwood boom ended in the 1830s, the whaling boom had begun. By the end of the 1820s, Hawai'i had become the base for the North-Central Pacific whaling trade. The impetus for the new trade was the 1818 discovery of the "Off-shore Ground" west of Peru and the 1820 discovery of rich sperm whale grounds off the coast of Japan. The first whaling ship visited the Hawaiian islands in 1820, and by the late 1820s, over 150 whaling ships were stopping in Hawai'i annually. Although the number of whaling ships visiting Lahaina and Honolulu fell from over 200 in 1832 to fewer than 90 in 1840, by 1843, over 350 whaling ships visited both ports annually, and these high numbers continued (with some fluctuations) until the beginning of the U.S. Civil War in 1861.

Providing services to the ships and their crews was a labor-intensive activity that drew farm labor to the growing population centers of Lahaina, Hilo, and Honolulu. Foreign traders and entrepreneurs, mostly from the United States, competed with the chiefs for labor to outfit, repair, and supply ships as well to provide labor in bars, restaurants, hotels, stores, and other businesses providing services to ships' crews spending extended time in Hawai'i. The continuing decline in population, the gradual collapse of the *ali'i* labor cartel over the 1820–1850 period, and the replacement of one labor-intensive traded good (harvested sandalwood) with another labor-intensive traded good (services to whaling and merchant ships) points to increasing wages for Hawaiian workers. Competition from whaling ships for labor was yet another force acting to push up wages. The sociologist Romanzo Adams estimated that in 1850, roughly 12 percent of the male Hawaiian population over the age of 18 were either employed as sailors on whaling ships or absent from the islands.[42] In the agricultural sector, the decline in population reduced product demand, which coupled with increased competition for labor, should have led to a decrease in land rents.[43]

The decline in the Hawaiian population, the movement of *maka'āinana* from rural farms to urban areas to provide services to visiting ships and their crews, and the employment of Hawaiians as ship crew provide qualitative evidence that through the 1830s and 1840s the incomes of the *Mō'ī* and *ali'i* were falling, while the wages of rural workers and urban migrants were improving.[44] In the decade leading up to the *Māhele*, the *ali'i* faced declining incomes, rural lands without tenants, a low and uncertain personal life expectancy, and the loss of many of their highest-ranking members in the epidemics of the 1830s and 1840s. In the early 1840s, many *ali'i* responded to their circumstances by considering new commercial ventures that would use abandoned lands and their new access to global markets to increase their incomes.

The first major attempt to grow sugar commercially in Hawai'i was made by the American mercantile firm of Ladd & Company in 1835. That attempt cannot be judged a success, as it lasted only until 1844, but it succeeded in stimulating interest in sugar production. Population increases in Oregon and California also pointed to potentially large markets in future years for Hawai'i sugar. Numerous other small sugar mills were started between 1835 and 1840 by missionaries and *ali'i*. Sugar grown by *kānaka maoli* labor on land controlled by *ali'i* was milled by these new establishments for a share of the output.

While the Hawaiian government and the missionaries were adamantly against foreign land ownership throughout the 1830s and 1840s, vigorous discussion took place over the necessity of stimulating the interest of the *maka'āinana* in commercial agriculture. Considerable capital investment was required to mill and manufacture sugar. Changes in the methods of milling and manufacture came rapidly in the early nineteenth century, and the historian J. H. Galloway concluded that the new technology "created larger mills and factories than the industry had known before and they demanded a more extensive hinterland of cane-pieces."[45] Without alienable land, it could be difficult for a chief to assemble enough land to enable the new mills to operate near capacity. *Maka'āinana*, who had traditional use rights in the lands they occupied, could not be compensated for the loss of these rights, as they were inalienable. Moreover, chiefs who did not have the skills to produce sugar themselves or to organize sugar milling and manufacture could not capitalize their rights in the land. Given the declining income of chiefs during this period, the opportunity to move their lands into more valuable uses gave additional impetus to the movement to define alienable land rights. Even without such rights, eleven mills for the manufacture of sugar had been established by 1846: two on Kaua'i, six on Maui, and three on the island of Hawai'i.[46]

Demand for agricultural products in Hawai'i had been declining throughout the early 1840s due to the massive decline in its population. The situation changed in the late 1840s due to the sudden appearance of a market for agricultural products in California during the 1849–1851 gold rush.[47] After 1851, California's agricultural production increased, and Hawai'i's agricultural exports to California dropped. This fall in demand for Hawai'i crops was followed by a return to declining land prices in Hawai'i during the 1850s. Letters written by prominent residents of Hawai'i to Joel Turrill, U.S. consul in Hawai'i from 1846 to 1850, provide convincing evidence that land prices (and by implication, land rents) fell from 1851 to 1858.[48] Prospects for export of commercial crops, including sugar, dwindled in the 1850s.

In her comprehensive and insightful study of Hawai'i's sugar industry (*Sovereign Sugar*), the anthropologist Carol MacLennan found that the form of ownership in the sugar industry changed rapidly. When the initial sugar plantations formed in the 1830s under the institutions of the fragile natural state, most plantations were organized as partnerships, "established through agreement between investors and owners and licensed under kingdom law."[49] In a fragile natural state, elite organizations can only be formed if they have tight connections with the state, and MacLennan finds that "the earliest partnerships required cooperation with Hawaiian landowners and chiefs. The king and *ali'i* frequently collaborated with foreigners to release the land and labor from traditional obligations. In return, they shared in profits and losses."[50] In the late 1840s and 1850s, Hawai'i made the transition to governance institutions associated with a mature natural state, and this meant that elite organizations without close ties to the state could be allowed to flourish without their presence being a threat to the survival of the state. This was fortuitous for foreign and Hawaiian investors in the industry, as the technological changes that were increasing the scale of the mills needed to grind sugar for export markets mandated larger capital expenditures than the partnership model could support. The limited liability corporation, which had few ties to the state beyond registration and rudimentary regulation, "first appeared on the larger plantations at Ha'ikū (Maui), Kohala (Hawai'i), and Līhu'e (Kaua'i) on the three missionary plantations started during the Civil War boom era."[51]

With the end of the Civil War, a new form of organization, the agency, emerged to supply plantations, arrange for interisland and foreign transport of sugar and supplies, and provide loans in an environment without fully developed commercial banking services. Merchant houses that had previously served the whaling industry evolved to fill the agency (or "factor") role for the sugar industry, and by the 1870s, they were purchasing and managing some plantations and providing managerial services to others for which they served as agent. By the late nineteenth century, "key decisions about new equipment, planting schedules, and plantation store policy and inventories, as well as about new land leases and purchases all required approval of the agent." The transition to this new system, under which numerous plantations were partly managed by an umbrella firm providing a wide variety of complementary services, was accomplished because of the transition, just 10–15 years earlier, to a mature natural state that could accommodate flexible forms of organizations with limited ties to the state. Despite their use of independent limited liability corporations, the plantations and agencies were not without close ties to the state, as they leased lands from king and chiefs and relied on the state's cooperation to bring contract labor from Asia and Europe to Hawai'i from the 1850s onward.

Emergence of the Mature Natural State and Increased Government Capacity

Establishment of the rule of law in urban areas and the rise of constitutional government reduced the power of the *ali'i* over *maka'āinana*. Tenants who were dissatisfied with their role in the traditional economy could now migrate to urban areas. The resulting decline in rural land rents reduced government revenues. Taxes collected by the king were directly tied to the number of people working in agriculture, as those people were also obligated to work one day per week in the king's fields. The combination of increased competition from the whaling services sector for labor and a declining total population put pressure on the chiefs to adjust the traditional obligations and taxes paid by tenants. A failure to do so would have jeopardized their ability to retain tenants.

In response to the declining productivity of traditional taxes, the Hawaiian government made two important changes in its system of taxation. First, the Laws of 1839, proclaimed by the *Mō'ī* with assent from high-ranking chiefs, codified the taxes owed by various individuals while (partially) converting most taxes from in-kind obligations to monetary payments. Taxes and land rents were collected in several ways: commoners usually worked 52 days on the king's lands (taxes), worked 52 days on the land manager's lands (rents), and paid additional harvest taxes from their own parcels. Economic historians Douglass North and Robert Thomas have argued that the growth of labor and commodity markets is usually the reason for a shift from in-kind to monetary taxation.[52] Rulers could more efficiently collect money taxes and then use the proceeds to purchase the goods and services they needed as markets became better developed than in the earlier period, in which taxes in kind were used to minimize the transaction costs of revenue collection. Given the absence of such markets in Hawai'i prior to the sandalwood trade and their subsequent development in the 1820s and 1830s, North and Thomas's analysis is consistent with the timing of this shift in taxation methods.

With the promulgation of a constitution in 1840, a series of laws were enacted between 1840 and 1843 that together are known as the "Laws of 1842." Their provisions reduced the overall amount of taxes owed by rural agricultural families and increased the overall amount owed by urban families. From 52 days owed to the landlord and an equal number to the king, the Laws of 1842 reduced the required number of days to 36 for the king and 36 for the landlord.[53] The effect of the laws was to reduce a tenant's rental and tax payments by equal amounts, thereby increasing real wages in agriculture. These changes provide corroborating evidence for the earlier inference in this chapter of rising real wages during this period.

The establishment of a poll tax in the Declaration of Rights and the Laws of 1839, and its continuing presence in the Laws of 1842, reflect this migration of workers from their traditional residences in the fertile mountain valleys to the growing villages of Hilo, Honolulu, and Lahaina.[54] The new tax was supported by the Council of Chiefs as a measure to maintain land rents and taxes (as migrants to the new urban areas did not owe the in-kind taxes) by stemming the flow of migration from rural areas. Other provisions in the Laws of 1842 reinforce this goal by prohibiting tenants from leaving the land without cause.[55] These somewhat futile attempts by the king and chiefs to ameliorate problems stemming from rising wages and declining land rents are mirrored in measures taken by other societies facing severe population declines. Similar laws were common in Europe in the late fourteenth century, when wages increased and land rents fell after the Black Death epidemic had swept away 25–50 percent of its populations in the mid-fourteenth century.[56] Such laws are consistent with earlier inferences that, starting in the 1830s, wages rose and land rents fell as Hawai'i's population declined and competition for labor from the whaling services sector increased.

Another provision of the Laws of 1842 provided a total exemption from taxes for families with more than three children.[57] A reduction in the cost of raising additional children would have stimulated population growth (or reduced the rate of population decline) and would have tended to ameliorate the medium-term upward pressure on wages and relieve the downward pressure on rents, thereby improving the future lot of the chiefs.

The adjustments in traditional tenant obligations reduced in-kind labor services to chiefs and king and left the government without substantial additional revenues. In 1842, revenue collected amounted to only $41,000. To increase revenues, the legislature approved an ad valorem duty of 3 percent on all imports, effective at the beginning of 1843. Tax revenue increased to $50,000 in 1843, while government expenditures increased to $80,000. Although a bond issue was floated to cover the shortfall, a debt of this magnitude could not be regularly financed by the government unless it wished to compromise its independence from foreign powers. Other taxes were subsequently imposed. A tax on whaling activities was collected by arresting sailors from whaling ships for no apparent reason and then releasing them upon payment of a fine. The general tariff was raised from 3 percent to 5 percent in 1845, and in 1855 some imported articles had duties of 10 and 15 percent imposed on them, with heavier charges imposed on wines and spirits. Chattel taxes on horses, mares, cattle, dogs, and cats were imposed in 1846.

The reorganization of land rights via the *Māhele* added two new sources of revenue for the Hawaiian government. First, the *Māhele* enabled the government to sell a large proportion of its lands. Royal Surveyor-General W. D. Alexander stated that "between the years 1850 and 1860, nearly all the desirable Government land was sold, generally to natives."[58] The historian Ralph Kuykendall supports this view, noting that evidence of active

TABLE 5.1. **Government Land Sales, September 1846–December 1857**

Year	O'ahu	Hawai'i	Maui	Kauai	Others	Total
			Acres			
1846	851	10	0	0	0	861
1847	172	764	1,365	0	0	2,301
1848	488	14	213	202	0	917
1849	2,022	233	4,868	8	0	7,131
1850	15,331	1,859	6,989	1,029	1,371	26,579
1851	5,568	5,285	6,570	2,634	92	20,149
1852	7,939	20,791	2,599	302	358	31,989
1853	1,447	3,261	6,143	834	316	12,001
1854	1,610	3,976	16,931	710	0	23,227
1855	3,842	15,753	3,616	3,961	646	27,818
1856	1,890	14,427	3,330	120	332	20,099
1857	478	8,116	320	44	2	8,960
Total	41,638	74,489	52,944	9,844	3,117	182,032
			Revenue (U.S.$)			
1846	526	50	0	0	0	576
1847	2,208	752	1,839	0	0	4,799
1848	1,782	50	208	367	0	2,407
1849	12,936	303	4,597	18	0	17,854
1850	17,626	4,216	11,166	3,243	489	36,740
1851	6,934	5,568	11,101	3,005	165	26,773
1852	7,765	19,076	4,402	274	1,128	32,645
1853	3,739	2,624	6,468	552	579	13,962
1854	8,181	2,595	18,885	428	0	30,089
1855	4,840	8,571	6,243	1,058	1,062	21,774
1856	5,368	6,112	3,746	390	365	15,981
1857	6,725	4,421	515	154	2	11,817
Total	78,630	54,338	69,170	9,489	3,790	215,417

Source: Hawaii, Department of the Interior (1858).

sales of public land was documented in "official records and in the newspapers, letters, and other contemporary writings."[59] These anecdotal reports are corroborated by more direct, quantitative evidence found in an 1886 private compilation of government land sales (also known as "royal patent grants") and in the 1858 *Report of the Minister of the Interior*.[60] The 1886 survey indicates that 654,622 acres, or 44 percent of the original 1,495,000 acres awarded to the government, were sold between 1841 and 1886.[61] The bulk of the sales activity occurred between 1846 and 1861, when the government sold 470,781.76 acres, approximately 31 percent of its total holdings. The 1858 interior minister's report contains annual data on acreage sold and revenue received from sales on each island (table 5.1). A comparison of land sales revenue with total government revenues (table 5.2) indicates that a significant proportion of government revenues during this period was derived from land sales.

Second, the creation of private property rights in land allowed the king and chiefs to make changes in how they managed their lands and which crops they grew. Some lands were leased to new sugar plantations (to be discussed in chap. 6), and others were switched from traditional crops to cash crops to be exported to Northern California.

Governments seldom encounter such favorable revenue opportunities when they undertake institutional reforms. The economic historian Douglass North examined whether establishing property rights in land or any other type of property would typically allow governments to raise additional revenue.[62] He concluded that "the property rights structure that will maximize rents to the ruler (or the ruling class) is in conflict with that that would produce economic growth."[63] North observed that declining land rents and increasing wages tend to generate a budget deficit in agrarian societies where property taxes are an important component of state revenue and state expenditures are labor intensive. He cited several instances of factor price–induced deficits, such as the fiscal crisis faced by European kings in the fourteenth century in the wake of Europe's

TABLE 5.2. **Government Revenue, 1846–1857**

Year	Government revenue (U.S.$)	Land sales revenue (U.S.$)	Land commission, net revenue (U.S.$)	Land sales as share of government revenue (%)
1846	75,000	576		0.77
1847	127,000	4,799		3.78
1848	155,000	2,407		1.55
1849	166,000	17,853		10.75
1850	194,000	36,690		18.91
1851	284,000	27,772		9.78
1852[a]	278,934	32,645	−3,232	0.54
1853[b]	326,620	13,962	523	4.43
1854	323,393	30,090	−214	9.24
1855	419,228	21,773	3,454	6.02
1856	319,521	15,981		5.00
1857	319,521	11,816		3.70

Sources: Government revenue is from Hawai'i, Department of Finance (various years, 1847–1860). Other data are from Hawai'i, Department of the Interior (various years, 1847–1860).

[a]Government revenue for 1852 was calculated by adding one-fourth of the revenue from the March 1851–March 1852 revenue to the reported data for the period March–December 1852.

[b]Figures for 1853–1857 should be interpreted cautiously. In 1856, the government halted the sale of large tracts of land. It adopted a policy of leasing the remaining lands in response to the lower land prices prevailing during this period. Land sales reported for 1855 and 1857 were actually made in 1854 and 1855, but are reported in later years due to a delay in the issuance of royal patent grants.

declining population. He concluded that tax revenues "were . . . declining during the fourteenth and fifteenth centuries as a result of the fall in land rents due to a declining population—at precisely the time when more revenue was required for survival."[64]

In Hawai'i, the fiscal crisis of the king and state in the 1830s was also due, at least in part, to a fall in in-kind land rents collected from the declining population. However, the crisis also coincided with an integration of Hawai'i with world markets that rendered alienable property rights in land more attractive. The revenue from land sales and tax revenue from an expanding agricultural economy enabled the government to finance its increased expenditures without resorting to the instruments of mercantilism. This contrasts with the European case, in which monarchs did not face the same favorable opportunities encountered by the Hawaiian monarch. Instead, they sold licenses, monopoly rights, and other restrictions on commerce to raise revenue, thereby sacrificing economic growth for the maintenance of the state.[65] In these cases, the monarch's maximization of tax revenues was generally in conflict with efficient incentives for private economic activity. The Hawaiian case provides an interesting counterexample wherein the revenue-seeking interests of the monarch had a positive effect on overall private investment and economic growth.

Conclusion

Pursuit of self-interest by the Mō'ī and ali'i accelerated the transition from a complex system of traditional use rights to a system of exclusive, transferable property rights in land during the 1840s and 1850s. Many gained from the transition. The Mō'ī was able to increase his chance of retaining his privatized landholdings in the event of a foreign takeover. The government was able to raise more revenue via the sales of government lands and make the necessary expenditures to run a government capable of fending off foreign takeover plots. The ali'i were able to lease or sell unused lands to plantations raising sugarcane. Missionaries were able to find new commercial ventures to operate as American support for their operations wound down in the 1850s and stopped in 1863. Maka'āinana, who were often unfairly treated by surveyors and by their chiefs in assignment of their kuleana land claims, gained the option of leasing, mortgaging, or selling their properties to sugar plantations, ranches, and Japanese and Chinese farmers growing rice.

These economic gains came, however, with growing political risks, as growth of the sugar industry was driven by foreign investments from German, British, and U.S. investors and corporations. The initial investments in the sugar industry were made in the form of partnerships with the king and *ali'i*, as, in the context of a basic natural state, it would have been too risky for the king and powerful elites to allow new organizations to form that might challenge the way the state operated. Autonomous organizations might grow to be powerful enough to compete with the dominant coalition for rents, or ask for a big share of the coalition's rents, or decide that they should coordinate the dominant coalition—that is, that they should become or control the government. Hawaiian elites could have reasonably judged the situation to be stable in 1850, as partnerships with king and *ali'i* limited the autonomy of new sugar firms, the government's capacity to function well was being bolstered by its revenue from sales of government lands, and the global market for sugar from Hawai'i was limited by tariffs and colonial preferences (see chap. 6). The chance that the new, partially foreign-owned sugar plantations would become large enough to dominate the economy and be able to impose considerable political pressure on the government seemed small.

The three factors underlying this supposed stability would all change over the course of the next 20 years, however. As the "minimum efficient scale" of a firm (i.e., the size at which it minimized its average total costs) increased, it became necessary for ventures to raise additional capital from more investors, and such ventures with passive equity investors were best organized as limited liability corporations. As these corporations replaced partnerships in the 1860s, the role of the king and *ali'i* became more limited, in many cases restricted to their leasing of crown and *ali'i* lands to plantations and agencies. Additional revenue from land sales bolstered the capacity of king and cabinet to run a capable government, but revenues were never sufficient to fund a standing army that the government could call on in a crisis. In fact, in a crisis, foreign firms were able to call on U.S. and other foreign warships in Honolulu Harbor to support them. Finally, any presumption that the market for sugar was limited was upset by the U.S. Civil War, as California, Oregon, and Washington massively increased their purchases of Hawai'i sugar after their supply sources in the Confederacy were cut off. Expansion of production and profits during the early 1860s showed the way to what might be achieved if access to the U.S. market could be secured by full or partial exemption from its tariff.[66]

Treaties, Powerful Elites, and the Overthrow

B eginning in 1826, when a visiting U.S. warship demanded that Hawaiian chiefs pay debts owed to U.S. ship captains, the Hawaiian government accommodated major U.S. interests in Hawai'i. The importance of Hawai'i to the United States was underlined in December 1842 by U.S. President Tyler's special message to Congress that brought Hawai'i into the groups of nations covered by the Monroe Doctrine. Tyler stated that there would be "dissatisfaction on the part of the United States at any attempt by another power . . . to take possession of the islands, colonize them, and subvert the native government."[1] Trade between the two countries had grown rapidly in the 1830s and 1840s, with the U.S. share of Hawai'i's imports reaching over 50 percent by the late 1840s. The two governments twice (in 1855 and 1867) negotiated treaties eliminating tariffs on most trade between Hawai'i and the United States, but the U.S. Senate failed to ratify both treaties. Approval of a third free-trade treaty in 1876 became the trigger for massive growth over the next decade in the scope and scale of the Hawai'i-owned and foreign-owned sugar firms known as the Big Five.[2] At the treaty's renegotiation in 1887, Hawai'i's dependence on the U.S. as a market for its sugar led the U.S. government to demand more favorable terms. During the resulting political chaos, a small group of foreigners staged a coup d'état and forced a new constitution upon King Kalākaua that increased the voting power of foreigners and restricted the king's power to take unilateral actions to transform property rights or alter the constitution.

In January 1893, a small group of Caucasian residents overthrew the Hawaiian monarchy and set into motion a complicated political dance that just five years later culminated in the U.S. annexation of Hawai'i. The overthrow and annexation are the defining political events in Hawai'i's modern history. The overthrow ended the Hawaiian monarchy and resulted in the establishment of a new government in which the influence of native Hawaiians was small. More than 90 percent of native Hawaiians signed petitions opposing annexation and the loss of over 650 years of sovereignty. Annexation meant the establishment of a colonial government dominated by presidential appointments, concentrated foreign sugar interests (the Big Five corporations and affiliates), and a Republican party supported by a coalition of Hawaiian and Caucasian voters. Beyond stripping sovereign power from Hawaiian elites, annexation forever changed the pattern of land ownership in Hawai'i and generated controversies over land and native Hawaiian rights that remain at the heart of Hawai'i politics in the twenty-first century.

Historians have extensively discussed many of the factors that led to the overthrow and annexation. After the 1893 overthrow, U.S. newspapers focused on the desire of sugar interests to secure the two-cent-per-pound bounty on U.S. sugar production provided by the McKinley Tariff of 1890.[3] Numerous historians have challenged this view. Julius Pratt argued instead that the overthrow was a racially charged bid to secure a more stable government. William Russ, Jr., also took up this theme, suggesting that the immigration of Asian labor to work the sugar plantations threatened the white elite.[4] Merze Tate indicated that the source of the overthrow was the goal of the foreign economic elite to secure property from the threat of excessive taxation.[5] Ralph Kuykendall noted the opposition of native Hawaiians to the overthrow and annexation, and Noenoe Silva discovered the original petitions opposing annexation, signed by the vast majority of adult Hawaiians, that were delivered to the congressional leadership during debates over annexation treaties.[6] Tom Coffman emphasized the singular role of Vice President Theodore Roosevelt in forcing annexation on sometimes reluctant U.S. politicians.[7]

This chapter focuses on another, less discussed factor behind the overthrow and annexation: the preferential trading relationship between Hawai'i and the United States.[8] The 1876 reciprocity treaty, which eliminated Hawai'i tariffs on most U.S. manufactured goods and U.S. tariffs on Hawai'i sugar and rice, led to a big expansion of trade between the two countries. However, the treaty also generated strategic problems for the Hawaiian government that were manifested in two ways. First, the large foreign investments made in the sugar industry increased Hawai'i's wealth as its sugar exports to the United States increased, but at the same time they gradually worsened Hawai'i's bargaining position vis-à-vis the United States. This allowed the U.S. government to extract better terms when the treaty expired in 1883. Second, the treaty transformed Hawai'i's internal politics by massively increasing the wealth of the Hawai'i, British, American, and German owners of the Big Five corporations as well as those chiefs who leased large tracts of land to these corporations and affiliated plantations. At this time, the Hawaiian monarchy was a mature natural state—an advanced limited-access political order—and the rise of a new powerful group within the state posed a stark dilemma: how to make adjustments in the dominant coalition to provide the new foreign players with a sufficient share of the economic rents generated by the state's architecture without providing them with enough leverage to ultimately displace domestic interests in key decision-making roles.

This chapter builds on the well-documented political history of the overthrow by assembling economic evidence and using economic theory to show how the U.S.-Hawai'i reciprocity treaty ultimately led to annexation. First, the U.S.-Hawai'i treaty is the most vivid illustration of how a preferential trading agreement between a large and a small country can unleash forces that increase the small country's wealth while decreasing its bargaining position vis-à-vis the large country.[9] If the treaty has a limited term (or can be canceled by either country), then renegotiation will occur in an environment that has been altered by the structural changes induced by the treaty. The large country's bargaining position will have improved, as the preferential trade treaty will have expanded the small country's exports and redirected them toward the large country, thereby creating assets specific to the trade with the large country. When the treaty expires and is due for renegotiation, the large country will be able to demand better terms. The diminished position of the small country combined with the heightened demands of the large country has the potential to spark a political crisis in the small country.[10]

Second, the U.S.-Hawai'i treaty illustrates how a preferential trade treaty between a large and a small country can transform the domestic politics of the small country. Corporations producing the now tariff-free export good(s) become wealthier as sales and profits both increase. In an advanced natural state such as Hawai'i, the question for the groups in the dominant political coalition is how to accommodate these newly powerful players. Because the wealth of the owners of the foreign corporations and of affiliated domestic firms critically depends on the continuation of the preferential trading relationship between the two countries, these players on the edge of the dominant coalition have strong incentives to take political action to ensure that the preferential trade relationship continues in force.

To sum up, this chapter suggests that preferential trade treaties between Hawai'i and the United States not only changed the structure of Hawai'i's economy, but also changed the nature and course of Hawai'i politics. The preferential trade treaty facilitated expansion of the Hawai'i sugar industry and allowed plantation owners to accumulate great wealth. The increased reliance by some Hawai'i interest groups on treaty benefits weakened the negotiating position of Hawai'i, allowed the United States to extract better terms when the treaty was renewed in 1887, and set the stage for Congress to act opportunistically when it revised U.S. tariff law in 1890. The greater wealth provided by the reciprocity treaty to sugar interests also raised the question of how they would be accommodated within the dominant coalition. My conclusion is that strategic problems unleashed by the U.S.-Hawai'i reciprocity treaty played a central role in the overthrow of the Hawaiian monarchy by creating a powerful group of foreign sugar firms that could not be easily accommodated within the dominant coalition.

Hawaiian Political Economy before Reciprocity

In chapters 4 and 5, I discussed how Hawai'i's economy and politics were fundamentally transformed by the massive decline in Hawai'i's population, the unification of competing Hawaiian states, and two resource booms (in sandalwood and whaling) tied to trade with U.S. companies. I argued that many high-ranking *ali'i* who survived the late eighteenth-century wars between the Hawaiian states initially gained from the unification of Hawai'i under Kamehameha, as they were able to extract more surplus from commoners whose options to leave rural agricultural work had shrunk. The new equilibrium between commoners and *ali'i* did not last long, however, as the sandalwood boom (1815–1832) and the persistent, massive decline in the Hawaiian population both had the effect of raising returns to labor. The sandalwood boom was short-lived but was followed by the whaling boom, which employed Hawaiian labor as sailors on whaling ships and workers in newly rising urban areas servicing those ships. From the perspective of *ali'i* who owned large tracts of rural lands, returns from traditional agriculture were falling, and earning robust future returns from their land depended on finding new uses for it.

The American firm of Ladd & Company established the first commercially viable sugar plantation on Kaua'i in 1835, but sugar played a relatively small role in the Hawaiian economy for the next 25 years.[11] Andrew Lind reported that by 1840, sugar exports ($25,000) had increased to a point where they were just below exports of hides and skins ($28,000) at a time when the value of imports ranged between $218,000 and $455,000.[12] Supplying the whaling vessels that visited the ports of Lahaina and Honolulu for the spring and autumn whaling seasons provided the main source of income for many Hawai'i businesses in the 1840s and 1850s.[13] By 1853, sugar was being grown on 2,750 acres but was far from the leading crop, with taro grown on 4,000 acres.[14]

Trade sparked the interest of foreigners in Hawai'i, and Britain, France, and the United States jockeyed to influence the island nation throughout most of the nineteenth century. America quickly established its influence with its 1820s and 1830s gunboat diplomacy to force payments of Hawaiian debts to U.S. traders. When Britain and France each threatened Hawaiian sovereignty in the 1840s, American diplomacy helped maintain Hawai'i's independence in both episodes. Indeed, in response to the French crisis, King Kamehameha III secretly ceded the islands to the United States, though Secretary of State Daniel Webster instructed his minister to return the deed of cession to avoid antagonizing France.[15]

Over this period, several Americans played prominent roles in the Hawaiian government. With the formation of the first government under the constitution of 1840, power was concentrated on an American missionary physician, Gerrit P. Judd, who consecutively held the offices of minister of foreign affairs, minister of interior, and minister of finance. Two other Americans with law backgrounds held top positions in the government: John Ricord as attorney general and William Little Lee as chief justice of the Hawai'i Supreme Court. The unusual number of foreigners holding top posts signaled the king's and other high-ranking *ali'i*'s interest in adopting Western governance institutions and in fostering good relations with Washington, D.C., and other foreign powers. It also reflected a concept of citizenship that was broad enough to encompass not just race and ethnicity, but also loyalty to the government.

The share of Hawaiian imports coming from the United States (fig. 6.1) provides another measure of the two countries' interdependence. From

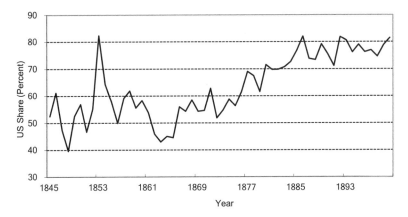

FIGURE 6.1. U.S. share of Hawai'i merchandise imports, 1845–1901. U.S. import data include California, Oregon, and Washington prior to their annexation and Vancouver Island in 1851. Source: Schmitt (1977, 541–542).

1845 to 1865, the average U.S. share of Hawaiian imports averaged more than 50 percent, with spikes up to 70–80 percent occurring during the early years of the California gold rush, when demand for food soared and a local supply had not yet been developed.

The growing U.S. West Coast market presented export opportunities for Hawai'i, but sugar farmers in Hawai'i found their sales restricted by the high U.S. tariff on sugar. Between 1850 and 1870, the population of California increased sixfold, to 560,247, and the combined populations of Washington, Oregon, and California reached 675,125.[16] The U.S. tariff on raw sugar (fig. 6.2) posed a major obstacle to expanding sugar production and trading with the United States. Sugar tariffs varied from 20 percent to 42 percent between 1850 and 1870 and can be viewed as a tax on the sale of sugar to the United States.[17]

Negotiations between the two governments twice resulted in reciprocity agreements. Both the 1855 and 1867 agreements permitted duty-free access for a specified list of Hawaiian goods—most importantly, raw sugar—to the United States market in exchange for similar access to the Hawaiian market for a specified list of American goods.[18] The U.S. Senate rejected both treaties, with Louisiana's sugar growers leading the opposition to the 1855 treaty. The U.S. Civil War saw the ascendance of Hawai'i sugar production, as Hawai'i sugar exports soared in response to the loss by Union states of sugar imports from Confederate states (fig. 6.3). But the end of the Civil War meant the end of the boom in Hawaiian sugar.

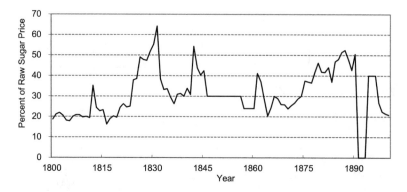

FIGURE 6.2. U.S. sugar tariff as a percentage of U.S. raw sugar price, 1800–1900. Sources: 1800–1859: wholesale raw sugar prices from Carter et al. (2006, vol. 3, Series Cc205–266, 3–202–203); 1860–1879: raw sugar prices from Taylor (1935, 167–168); 1880–1900: 96 degree sugar prices from U.S. Tariff Commission (1920, 17). U.S. sugar tariffs are compiled from U.S. Senate (1894, 19–36), Taussig (1914, 313), and Wright (1924, 93).

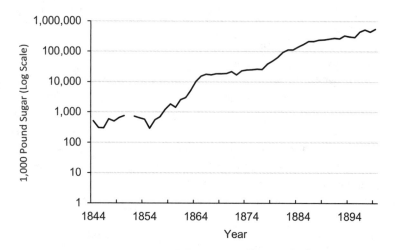

FIGURE 6.3. Hawai'i sugar exports, 1844–1899. Source: Schmitt (1977, table 21.6).

A second reciprocity treaty was negotiated in 1867, and it was rapidly approved by the Hawaiian government, but once again, the U.S. Senate failed to ratify it. The historian Chalfant Robinson argued that the high U.S. government debt after the Civil War was the main reason for the defeat: a loss of revenue from any source, including the sugar tariff, would have conflicted with the U.S. government's postwar goal of paying down its record-high debt.[19] The historian Merze Tate emphasized a different reason for the treaty's defeat: its potential impact on U.S. sugar production.[20] The Louisiana sugar industry had not yet recovered from the devastation of the Civil War, and Tate argued that imports from Hawai'i could have slowed its revival.

Some American proponents of annexation worked to defeat the 1867 reciprocity treaty because they thought it would interfere with the larger goal of annexation.[21] Proponents of the treaty responded that reciprocity was a prelude to annexation and would be more easily shepherded through the U.S. Senate. Many Hawaiians agreed with this view and opposed the treaty on those grounds.[22]

The negotiation and then rejection of annexation and reciprocity treaties during the 1850s and 1860s came during a period when the American political and economic presence in Hawai'i continued to increase. President Tyler had brought Hawai'i under the Monroe Doctrine in 1842, and U.S. Secretary of State John Clayton reiterated in 1850 that the United States "could never with indifference allow [Hawai'i] to pass under the dominion or exclusive control of any other power."[23] And much of the sugar's industry growth in the 1850s and early 1860s was tied to investors from the United States and to the first- and second-generation Americans and Europeans living in Hawai'i. The stage was set for a transformation of the economic and political ties between Hawai'i and the United States.

The 1876 Reciprocity Treaty

The U.S. government favored a reciprocity treaty with Hawai'i as an inducement for the two countries to form closer political ties and to exclude foreign governments from using the islands for strategic advantage. In 1872, U.S. Generals Schofield and Alexander had traveled to Hawai'i on a government mission to evaluate the strategic value of Hawai'i's ports and had submitted a secret report emphasizing the value of Pearl Bay as a harbor for U.S. ships.[24] As early as 1873, the Hawaiian government offered exclusive use of Pearl Bay to the United States in exchange for a reciprocity treaty, but subsequent opposition by the Native Hawaiian public forced the government to withdraw the offer.[25]

Sugar interests helped elect David Kalākaua to the throne over the British-leaning Queen Emma[26] in February 1874 (as described in chap. 7), and the new king immediately renewed the quest for a reciprocal trade agreement. Later that year, the two countries concluded a reciprocity treaty that did not mention Pearl Bay.[27] During its debate on the treaty, the U.S. Senate inserted a clause that prevented the king from leasing or disposing of any "port, harbor, or other territory in his dominions" to any foreign government for the life of the treaty. The Senate ratified the amended treaty in March 1875 by a vote of 51 to 12. Because reciprocity affected tariff revenue, a separate bill implementing the treaty had to originate in the U.S. House of Representatives. The House passed that bill on May 8, 1876, by a vote of 115 to 101, and the Senate approved it on August 14, 1876, by a vote of 29 to 12. King Kalākaua proclaimed the treaty on June 17, 1876, and the Hawai'i legislature passed an act carrying it into effect on June 23, 1876.[28]

U.S. congressional debate over the treaty focused on a few critical issues that supporters and opponents of the treaty evaluated very differently. Supporters of the treaty emphasized the strategic value of Hawai'i to the United States and soft-pedaled the loss of U.S. tariff revenue. For example, the majority report of the House Committee on Ways and Means asserted that

> the slight loss of [tariff] revenue is of small value as compared with the many higher and more important interests to be subserved.
>
> The Pacific Ocean is an American ocean, destined to hold a far higher place in the future history of the world than the Atlantic. It is the future great highway between ourselves and the hundreds of millions of Asiatics who look to us for commerce, civilization, and Christianity. These islands rest midway between us and them as the necessary point provided by the Great Ruler of the universe as points of observation, rest, supply, military strategy, and command, to enable each other to unite in protecting both hemispheres from European assault, aggression, and avarice.[29]

By contrast, the minority report feared enormous tariff revenue losses and emphasized the lack of benefits to U.S. consumers of sugar:

> Should we, therefore, secure the whole trade of the islands by this treaty, it would cost us a dollar [in tariff revenue] for the privilege of selling goods of the value of another, and during the seven years' continuance of the treaty, should it be ratified, it will cost us at least $10,000,000.
>
> Neither would this give us cheap sugar; the quantity imported is only one per cent of our consumption, nor can it exceed (for natural causes, such as the

limited quantity of arable lands) five or six per cent of our consumption; and this cannot reduce the prices in our market.[30]

The minority also noted the strategic importance of the islands, but distinguished between excluding European powers and obtaining a "foothold" in the islands via treaty concessions:

> Much stress is laid by the report of the majority upon the importance to the United States of obtaining a foot-hold upon these islands in the safety of our Pacific commerce with the continent of Asia, and of our safety in case of future wars with any great naval power.
>
> The undersigned are not insensible to these considerations . . . but it is one thing to decide that no other nation shall take hold upon the islands, and quite another to determine we will not do so ourselves. The policy of annexing the islands to the United States is one full of difficulty. It would entail upon us enormous expense, and would make it as important to extend our domain beyond them to protect our possession in them as it is now plausibly argued the possession of them is essential to the security of our Pacific seaboard.[31]

The debates in the House and Senate, as well as Hawai'i's acceptance of the "port and harbor" leasing clause in the final treaty, can be fruitfully analyzed using well-developed economic theories of the impact of international trade restrictions.[32] My analysis is based on two central assumptions: that the United States was a price taker in the world sugar market and that Hawai'i was a price taker in the U.S. sugar market. For the United States, which imported over 90 percent of its sugar in 1875, being a price taker in the world sugar market meant that small changes in its sugar imports would not affect the world price of sugar. For Hawai'i, which supplied less than 2 percent of U.S. sugar imports, being a price taker in the U.S. sugar market meant that changes in its sugar exports would not affect the price of sugar in the U.S. market.

Through the first 90 years of the nineteenth century, the price paid for sugar by U.S. consumers was above the world price of sugar because the United States imposed a tariff—a tax on sales of sugar imported from abroad. The price paid by U.S. consumers (P_{US}) and the price received by U.S. sugar producers was roughly equal to the world price of sugar (P_w) plus the U.S. tariff T. Foreign sugar producers exporting sugar to the United States received P_w. The U.S. sugar tariff had three important effects on the U.S. sugar market: it raised the price of sugar paid by U.S.

consumers, thereby reducing U.S. sugar consumption; it increased U.S. production of sugar by providing U.S. producers with a price higher than the global price; and it reduced U.S. sugar imports by pushing down the net price received by foreign producers.

How did the U.S.-Hawai'i reciprocity agreement, which lowered the U.S. tariff on sugar only for Hawai'i sugar producers, affect Hawai'i and U.S. sugar producers and U.S. consumers? Its biggest effect was to increase the price received by Hawaiian sugar producers by the amount of the U.S. tariff—resulting in a big 20–40 percent premium for those producers (depending on the particular year and the world sugar price). The higher price received by Hawaiian sugar producers gave them incentives to expand output substantially in order to export more to the U.S. market. Because the extra supply of sugar from Hawai'i was extremely small relative to the overall size of the U.S. sugar market, that additional supply would not have changed the price of sugar paid by U.S. consumers or the amount of sugar they consumed. The reason why sugar consumption was unchanged is that the expansion of Hawaiian exports to the United States was offset by an equal contraction in supply from other exporters. In the economics literature on preferential tariff reductions, this diversion of supply from a lower-cost exporter—in this case, Cuba—to a higher-cost exporter—in this case, Hawai'i—is known by economists as the *trade diversion effect*.[33]

The U.S. government lost all tariff revenues on Hawaiian sugar sold in the U.S. market and on foreign sugar diverted from the U.S. market.[34] Part of the lost tariff revenue was transferred to Hawaiian sugar producers and workers, and part of it was dissipated in the form of higher costs of producing sugar in Hawai'i rather than in Cuba.[35]

How did the elimination of Hawai'i's tariffs on U.S. exports of manufactured goods affect the market for manufactured goods in Hawai'i? The very small size of the Hawai'i market relative to the size of the U.S. market implies that additional supply to Hawai'i from U.S. industries could have been accommodated without an increase in marginal cost or industry price in the United States. In other words, U.S. firms should have been able to accommodate the increased demand for U.S. manufactures with a very small increase in output that would not put any upward pressure on prices of U.S. manufactures. Competition among U.S. firms for the Hawai'i market would push down prices of manufactures in Hawai'i from the world price plus the Hawai'i tariff to the world price.[36] The lower U.S. price would result in *trade creation* for U.S. manufactures and *trade diversion* for manufactures from other countries.[37]

To sum up, the economic theory of preferential trade agreements indicates that no U.S. interests would have gained from the U.S.-Hawai'i reciprocity treaty, that the U.S. government would have lost tariff revenue on the import of Hawai'i sugar, and that the United States would have experienced a reduction in its economic welfare due to the trade treaty.

It is notable that both proponents and opponents of the treaty in Congress correctly recognized that its commercial provisions would not produce gains for either U.S. interests or the government. Instead, the debate in Congress focused on *how big* the loss in tariff revenue would be. The size of the loss in tariff revenue would have depended critically on the export elasticity[38] of Hawai'i sugar as well as the size of the U.S. sugar tariff. Because the U.S. tariff on sugar amounted to about 30 percent of the price of sugar in 1874, the stage was set for potentially large U.S. tariff losses if the export elasticity of Hawai'i sugar proved to be large.

This analysis suggests that in terms of direct economic benefits, only Hawai'i sugar producers and sugar workers stood to gain much from the treaty. This is the key to understanding why the U.S. government demanded compensation for entering into the reciprocity treaty. While some U.S. legislators might have been satisfied with the implicit promise of enhanced influence (so-called soft power) over Hawai'i, inclusion of a treaty provision more clearly advancing U.S. interests, such as the restriction on foreign access to Pearl Bay, surely made the treaty more palatable to a somewhat skeptical Congress.

Interestingly, the U.S.-Hawai'i treaty provisions were consistent with what economists know about "equilibrium" tariff rates between large and small countries. An *equilibrium tariff rate* is one that would be best for Hawai'i given the U.S. tariff rate, and would be best for the United States given the Hawai'i tariff rate. From the economic theory of equilibrium tariff rates comes a fascinating result that stands at the heart of this chapter's analysis: for two countries of sufficiently different size, a zero-tariff rate instituted by a "free-trade" treaty cannot be an equilibrium tariff rate for the large country.[39] Given the small country's zero tariff, the large country can gain by imposing a positive tariff on imports from the small country.[40] Building on this analysis, trade economist John McLaren showed that the large country requires compensation from the small country in order to accept a free-trade treaty that imposes zero tariffs on both countries.[41] In the United States-Hawai'i case, the compensation was the U.S. Senate's amendment restricting the Hawaiian government from leasing or disposing of any "port, harbor, or other territory" to any foreign government for the life of the treaty.[42]

Viewed in this light, the House and Senate debates over the 1876 treaty make considerable sense. Supporters and opponents of the treaty clashed mainly over their evaluations of the size of the economic losses to U.S. interests that would result from the treaty. The Senate's amendment to the treaty had the effect of adding a side payment from the Hawaiian government, thereby allowing the treaty to gain support from U.S. legislators who doubted the economic value of the treaty and yet highly valued the political implications of its restrictions on British or French military presence in Hawai'i.

Expansion of the Sugar Industry

The rapid expansion of Hawai'i's sugar industry quickly settled the U.S. congressional debate over the extent to which the treaty would increase sugar exports from Hawai'i in favor of the treaty's opponents. Sugar exports to the United States rose from 21 million pounds in 1876 to 114 million pounds in 1883 and to 224.5 million pounds in 1890.[43] Acreage devoted to sugar production increased from 8,500 in 1870 to 26,019 in 1880 and to 87,016 in 1890: a more than 10-fold increase over 20 years![44] Sugar plantations expanded their acreage by purchasing private and government lands and by leasing crown lands.[45]

This phenomenal increase in sugar production was fueled by enormous investments in capital. These investments took the form of large-scale irrigation projects, projects tapping water from newly discovered aquifers, and adoption of the most recent advances in sugar processing technology and equipment. Expanded use of fertilizer was also important. The value of capital in Hawaiian sugar (1910–1914 dollars, excluding land) rose from $1.4 million in 1870 to $4.5 million in 1880 and to $14.7 million in 1890, a 10-fold increase over 20 years.[46]

Reciprocity also radically altered the demographic composition of the islands and laid the groundwork for later political concerns on the part of both native Hawaiians and the white elite. Expansion of sugar production sharply increased the plantations' demand for labor. Plantation employment rose from 3,921 in 1872 to 10,243 in 1882 and to 20,536 in 1892.[47] This increase was accompanied by a drop in the number of Hawaiians and part-Hawaiians employed on sugar plantations, from 3,299 in 1872 to 2,575 in 1882 and to 1,717 in 1892. This amounted to an absolute decline of 48 percent over the 20-year period.[48] While the 21 percent decline in the

TABLE 6.1. **Hawaiian and Part-Hawaiian Populations, 1853–1896**

Year	Hawaiian		Part-Hawaiian		Combined	
	Population	Change (%)	Population	Change (%)	Population	Change (%)
1853	70,036	. . .	983	. . .	71,019	. . .
1860	65,647	−6.3	1,337	36.0	66,984	−5.7
1866	57,125	−13.0	1,640	22.7	58,765	−12.3
1872	49,044	−14.1	2,487	51.6	51,531	−12.3
1878	44,088	−10.1	3,420	37.5	47,508	−7.8
1884	40,014	−9.2	4,218	23.3	44,232	−6.9
1890	34,436	−13.9	6,186	46.7	40,622	−8.2
1896	31,019	−9.9	8,485	37.2	39,504	−2.7

Source: Schmitt (1977, 25).

native Hawaiian population during this period (table 6.1) might account for roughly 50 percent of this decline, the remaining 50 percent represents Hawaiian workers moving to other sectors of the economy.

The enormous increase in the plantation workforce consisted of first Chinese, then Japanese laborers who came to Hawai'i after the reciprocity treaty under three-year contracts.[49] As table 6.2 indicates, this large flow of immigrants dramatically changed Hawai'i's demographic picture. As their three-year labor contracts with plantations expired, many workers did not renew them and instead moved to urban areas, where they competed with both whites and native Hawaiians in retail and labor markets.[50] Both of those groups expressed concerns about the economic and potential political threats to the status quo posed by competition from the relocated immigrant workers.[51]

Renewal of the Treaty

By 1883, groups were organizing in the United States to abrogate or modify the 1876 reciprocity treaty. Reports from U.S. congressional committees on a bill to terminate the treaty let loose a barrage of criticism. The majority report of the House Committee on Foreign Affairs asserted that "the relative advantages to the people of the two countries appear to have essentially changed since the treaty went into effect. The change of these relations has been chiefly effected by the very large increase in the production of sugar . . . which [has] been exported therefrom to the United

TABLE 6.2. **Hawai'i's Population by Place of Birth, 1872–1900**

	Hawai'i		U.S.		China		Japan		Portugal	
Year	Population	% of total	Population	% of total	Population	% of total	Population	% of total	Population	% of total
1872	52,380	92.0	889	1.6	1,938	3.4	...	...	395	0.7
1878	48,455	84.0	1,276	2.2	5,916	10.2	...	...	436	0.7
1884	46,272	57.0	2,066	2.6	17,939	22.0	116	0.1	9,377	11.6
1890	48,117	53.5	1,928	2.1	15,301	17.0	12,360	14.0	8,602	9.6
1896	53,237	49.0	2,266	2.1	19,382	18.0	22,329	20.5	8,232	7.5
1900	58,931	38.0	4,238	2.7	21,741	14.0	56,234	36.5	6,512	4.2

Source: Schmitt (1977, 90).

TABLE 6.3. **U.S. Losses from the 1876 Reciprocity Treaty (U.S.$)**

Year	Tariff revenue lost on Hawaiian sugar	Sugar duties to American-owned sugar firms	Net U.S. losses
1877	986,475	246,619	739,856
1878	989,602	247,401	742,201
1879	1,266,555	316,639	949,916
1880	1,881,563	470,391	1,411,172
1881	2,427,778	606,945	1,820,833
1882	3,314,939	828,735	2,486,204

Sources: Laughlin and Willis (1903, 86) and Searle (1886, 9).

States under the treaty in question."[52] The committee noted that "this result is entirely without the intent of the contracting parties when the treaty was made." Despite these adverse results, the committee recommended renewing the treaty with modifications, as "it would be folly to take any step which might lose to us the most important key to the commercial and naval situation [in the Pacific]."[53] The majority report of the Senate Committee on Finance echoed these themes, but had a completely different view of the strategic importance of the islands. Noting that the country with the most powerful navy would always control Hawai'i, the committee stated that "it cannot concern us who the rulers of these islands may be, as they can never be formidable for aggressions, being over two thousand miles distant from the Pacific coast."[54] The Senate committee recommended abrogation of the treaty, possibly as a "first step" to its ultimate modification.

My rough calculations (table 6.3) of the money losses to the U.S. government during the treaty's initial seven years provide considerable support to the arguments of treaty opponents.[55] U.S. losses consisted of forgone tariff revenue on sugar, reduced by the share of American-owned sugar production in Hawai'i. This calculation uses John Searle's estimate of the American share in Hawai'i sugar plantation capital, roughly 25 percent.[56] Using Searle's estimate, my lower-bound estimates of these annual tariff losses grows from roughly $740,000 in 1877 to $2.5 million in 1882, a more than threefold increase over the initial years of the treaty. Large losses for the U.S. government remain even if the American share in Hawai'i sugar plantation capital is pushed up to 50 percent or 75 percent. Let me also note that this calculation underestimates U.S. tariff losses because it does not include U.S. losses on other Hawaiian goods exported duty-free to the United States—notably rice.[57]

In spite of congressional concerns over renewal, the two governments agreed on a seven-year extension of the treaty in December 1884. In a move reminiscent of its decision to attach an amendment to the 1876 treaty, the U.S. Senate attached an amendment to the extension agreement, demanding a critical concession from Hawai'i: "His Majesty . . . grants to the Government of the United States the *exclusive* right to enter the harbor of Pearl River, in the island of O'ahu, and to establish and maintain there a coaling and repair station for the use of vessels of the United States, and to that end the United States may improve the entrance to said harbor and do all other things needful to the purpose aforesaid" (emphasis added).[58] With this amendment, the Senate approved the treaty by a vote of 43 to 11 in January 1887.

Four factors allowed the United States government to calculate that it could squeeze more out of Hawai'i at treaty renegotiation. The first was the unexpectedly large gains accruing to Hawai'i planters and workers from the rapid expansion of the sugar industry and the accompanying transfer of tariff revenue from the U.S. government. Because the economic losses to the United States had exceeded expectations and could have reasonably been expected to grow during the course of the treaty extension, the United States could demand a larger compensating side payment—in this case, in the form of an exclusive right to the use of Pearl Harbor.

Second, Hawai'i's bargaining position had deteriorated due to the expansion of its sugar industry and its plantations' investment in specific capital—that is, capital that has lower (or negligible) value in other uses. Most of the investments in large-scale irrigation projects and other land improvements were specific to the sugar industry because crops of similar value could not be produced on most sugarcane lands. Dependence on exporting to a large country hampers a small country's bargaining power. The economist John McLaren has shown that when small-country investment in specific, export-sector capital is coupled with future trade negotiations with the large country, the small country becomes vulnerable to opportunistic behavior by the large country. In fact, McLaren found that whenever exports insufficiently substitute for imports, negotiated free trade is worse than no trade for the small country because it ultimately has the effect of transferring the value of the specific capital in the small country's export industry to the large country.[59] Put another way, the large country gains the capacity to expropriate a portion of the returns from the small country's capital stock devoted to producing exports for the large country.

Why was this deterioration in Hawai'i's terms of trade not taken into account when Hawai'i planters decided whether to expand their sugar production? The reason is that each decision by an individual sugar planter to invest in specific capital to expand production contributed only a very small amount to the deterioration in Hawai'i's terms of trade. Each firm found it rational to ignore its contributions to the decline in Hawai'i's negotiating position.[60] Taken together, however, the individual decisions of many firms to expand added up to a big decline in Hawai'i's overall bargaining position.

A theoretical model of bilateral trade talks and trade wars developed by trade economists Gene Grossman and Elhanan Helpman is also relevant for analysis of the Hawai'i-U.S. reciprocity treaty. Their model shows that trade agreements tend to reflect the relative strengths of interests groups in both countries.[61] In this context, the huge increase in the wealth of Hawai'i's sugar planters conferred a negotiating advantage on the United States, as the bulk of the sugar planters' wealth depended on the continuation of the treaty. The Big Five firms had little reason to object to Hawai'i's additional concessions of territorial rights as long as the sugar produced on their plantations continued to enter the United States free of duty and their wealth continued to climb.

Hawai'i's government officials clearly understood the risks associated with expanding sugar production and becoming dependent on the U.S. market. During negotiations over the 1867 reciprocity treaty (which the U.S. Senate failed to ratify), Charles de Varigny, the foreign minister of the Hawaiian Kingdom, had warned King Kamehameha V of future problems associated with a limited-term reciprocity treaty with the United States. He noted that a reciprocity treaty would immediately benefit Hawai'i's "agricultural interests," but would also expose Hawai'i to "appalling dangers" at the treaty's renewal:

> Suppose the tariff were in effect for a period of seven years ... and thus assured us a remarkable prosperity for this period of time. What if, at the expiration of this term, the United States government should exert the right to annul the treaty and impose on our sugar a tariff rate of fifteen centimes per pound, as it was already doing at that moment? Would not such a shift in future policy result in a terrible commercial crisis? Threatened by imminent ruin, would not our planters all rally round the notion of annexation to the United States, if only that nation would assuage the planters' fears of the future by permanently abolishing the tariff on sugar? Such circumstances would be a formidable test of our political autonomy. How would Hawaii survive it?[62]

De Varigny's commentary raises a difficult question: Why would Hawai'i enter into an agreement that had a substantial chance of reducing its over-all welfare at treaty renewal? De Varigny provided a partial answer to his own question:

> But was it feasible to reject the overtures of the United States and, out of fear of possible danger to Hawaii, ignore the present and very positive economic ad-vantages contributing at exactly the right moment to the success of our political program for Hawaii? Even if I had sought to refuse the proposed agreement, I could not have succeeded . . . The King shared my hesitation and arrived at the same conclusion as mine . . . Furthermore, seven years would give us time to establish our sugar production on a solid basis. Above all, we would have an opportunity to open up other markets that would compensate us for the loss of California, in the event that our gloomiest forecasts would be fulfilled.[63]

De Varigny's comments point out that potential competition from other large countries for a small country's political favor could limit the ability of a large country to extract better treaty terms in the negotiations to ex-tend the term of a treaty. In Hawai'i's case, such competition would take the form of other countries providing preferential access to Hawai'i sugar exports.

Third, despite de Varigny's hope of developing other markets for Hawai'i's sugar, alternatives to a treaty with the United States evaporated in the de-cade after the treaty was implemented in 1876. Hawai'i had considered reci-procity treaties with Great Britain, Canada, or Australia in 1874, but these options were much less promising in 1883. Great Britain had repealed its tariff on sugar in 1874 and therefore could not offer Hawai'i duty-free access to its sugar market; all nations, including Hawai'i, already had duty-free ac-cess. Among the Australian colonies, Queensland's sugar output had grown rapidly during the 1870s, and it was exporting raw sugar as early as 1880.[64] In 1883, the tariff on raw sugar in New South Wales was just 20 percent of the U.S. tariff on raw sugar, and in Victoria, just 35 percent. Australia's market for sugar was also very small, as its population in 1880 was only 4.4 percent of the U.S. population. Its low tariffs and small population meant that a reci-procity treaty with Australia would have generated less than 5 percent of the benefits from the U.S. reciprocity treaty. Canada remained a potential treaty partner in 1883, and it had a substantial tariff—roughly 25 percent—on raw sugar. But its population was only 8.8 percent as large as that of the United States, so a reciprocity treaty with Canada would have generated less than

10 percent of the benefits from the U.S. reciprocity treaty.[65] As Hawai'i's opportunities to enter treaties with other countries fell by the wayside during the first seven years of the reciprocity treaty, the negotiating position of the United States improved, allowing it to demand more from Hawai'i at renegotiation.

Finally, the 10-fold expansion of Hawai'i sugar production between the 1876 treaty and the 1883 renegotiation greatly increased the wealth of Hawai'i sugar planters and widened the divergence of interests among Hawai'i residents. The planters had big incentives to expend resources and to take actions to ensure the successful renegotiation of the treaty, including its concession of Pearl Harbor rights. By contrast, most native Hawaiians were adamantly opposed to this concession. Sugar planters favored the additional concession, as they cemented Hawai'i's ties with the United States and in many ways increased the security of their property rights. From the perspective of the United States, the increased prominence of an interest group within Hawai'i favoring this concession increased its bargaining position vis-à-vis Hawai'i, as that group would make it more difficult for Hawai'i's government to muster domestic support for resisting U.S. pressure for this concession. From the perspective of native Hawaiians, the concession of Pearl Harbor's sovereignty represented a significant loss that was not matched by any added gains to Hawaiians in the renegotiated treaty. Given the increased stake of the sugar planters in maintaining reciprocity, the higher demands set forth by the United States government, and the opposition of native Hawaiians to the additional concession, the stage was set for confrontation.

King Kalākaua, who opposed early proposals to cede Pearl Harbor to the United States, vowed never to sign the new treaty, and thereby jeopardized his throne.[66] The king's opposition to the treaty came against a background of rising Hawaiian and foreign resident opposition to a number of his other policies, including those relating to government finance. The sugar boom dramatically raised the revenues available to the Hawaiian government. As table 6.4 reveals, total receipts grew at an annual rate of almost 9 percent between the biennium ending in 1874 and the one ending in 1886. Customs receipts, which financed 30–40 percent of the kingdom's budget in this period, grew at a 7.5 percent rate between 1874 and 1886. Receipts from internal taxation rose at a faster 10 percent annual rate, thereby pushing up their share of total receipts. Further, the share of receipts from real and personal property taxation jumped from 11.1 percent in 1874 to 19.7 percent in 1884 before declining to 17.6 percent in 1886.[67] Over this twelve-year period, real

TABLE 6.4. Hawai'i Government Fisc, 1874–1898

Year[a]	Total receipts	Customs duties		Total internal taxes	% of total	Internal taxes				Expenditures	Bonded debt
		Receipts	% of total			Real estate	Personal property	Total property	% of Total		
1874	867,124	350,135	40.4	206,723	23.8	53,892	42,708	96,600	11.1	1,055,806	340,200
1876	877,792	346,909	39.5	213,930	24.4	58,645	47,988	106,633	12.1	894,357	445,600
1878	1,064,513	360,790	33.9	331,163	31.1	94,584	94,378	188,962	17.8	944,081	444,800
1880	1,679,857	582,018	34.6	465,252	27.7	143,716	155,945	299,661	17.8	1,347,187	388,900
1882	2,070,260	718,427	34.7	596,615	28.8	187,929	208,096	396,025	19.1	2,126,181	299,200
1884	2,423,185	943,844	39.0	680,397	28.1	223,100	254,286	477,386	19.7	3,097,464	898,800
1886	2,779,155	858,094	30.9	696,869	25.1	227,195	262,307	489,502	17.6	3,088,564	1,065,600
1888	2,680,843	931,268	34.7	766,422	28.6	252,362	299,974	552,336	20.6	4,246,237	1,936,500
1890	2,926,636	932,951	31.9	901,803	30.8	339,390	329,908	669,298	22.9	2,932,519	1,934,000
1892	3,254,320	1,204,305	37.0	963,496	29.6	358,745	341,206	699,951	21.5	3,425,732	2,314,000
1894	3,014,106	856,048	28.4	987,414	32.8	338,894	313,126	652,020	21.6	2,673,622	2,693,700
1894[b]	1,302,652	306,126	23.5	523,831	40.2	167,083	151,580	318,663	24.5	1,099,656	2,833,800
1895	1,798,065	430,530	23.9	592,692	33.0	196,608	164,272	360,880	20.1	1,822,494	3,005,300
1896	1,975,322	511,758	25.9	706,542	35.8	240,971	210,194	451,165	22.8	2,092,109	3,330,200
1897[c]	2,188,828	563,798	25.8	752,006	34.4	246,829	242,719	489,548	22.4	2,445,044	3,679,700
1898	2,568,489	730,875	28.5	811,819	31.6	268,203	266,621	534,824	20.8	2,102,059	3,785,500

Source: Hawai'i, Department of Finance (various years, 1874–1898).

Note: All values are given in U.S. dollars.

[a] Biennium ending March 31 until 1894 from which fiscal year and calendar year coincide.

[b] For nine months ending December 31, 1894.

[c] Customs duties and internal tax receipts reported for the biennium 1896–1897. The 1897 data were obtained by subtracting the 1896 data.

and personal property tax receipts grew at an annual rate of 13.5 percent. The government's appetite for revenue quickly exceeded even these resources, however, sowing the seeds of discontent in the business community. Expenditures more than kept pace with the growth in receipts, forcing the kingdom to resort to debt financing of the resulting deficits. Its bonded debt rose over the period from $340,000 in 1874 to just over $1 million in 1886. In the next biennium, the debt would almost double. Planters were less concerned about the resort to debt financing than about the insufficient proportion of the additional expenditures that had been devoted to infrastructure complementary to sugar production. They charged that the Hawaiian government had "shamefully neglected roads, harbors, and other public works" and that there had been "misapplication[s] of funds contrary to statutory requirements."[68]

Other issues besides reciprocity and taxation contributed to the king's unstable position. An ill-fated diplomatic mission to Samoa, rumors that bribery was a factor in awarding an opium concession, charges of extravagant spending by the king, and a dispute with Claus Spreckels (the leading sugar planter) over a large loan to the Hawai'i government from London brokers had all increased opposition to the Kalākaua government. Thus, while there were several complaints against the king and government, the king's threatened rejection of the amended reciprocity treaty was the key reason behind the revolt against him that followed.

The McKinley Tariff and the Bayonet Constitution

In July 1887, backed by a small armed force consisting mostly of Caucasians, government opponents forced the king to accept a new cabinet and constitution.[69] The "Bayonet Constitution" weakened the king's veto power by allowing an override on a two-thirds vote of the legislature and requiring a cabinet member's signature to make any royal act effective.[70] The new constitution also changed the franchise from "subjects" to "residents . . . of Hawaiian, American, or European birth or descent," thereby removing the franchise from Asians.[71] A special election in September 1887 brought a pro-American government to power. After an exchange of notes that limited U.S. rights to Pearl Harbor to the life of the treaty extension, King Kalākaua signed the amended extension of reciprocity in October.[72]

Thus, in little more than a decade since 1876, Hawai'i had seen its economic and political situation change dramatically. It had established a formal reciprocity treaty with the United States that had vastly expanded its sugar industry and raised the wealth of the Big Five corporations and their affiliated firms. On two occasions, the U.S. Senate had added provisions to the trade treaties that made clear the U.S. interest in acquiring control of the future Pearl Harbor. The effect of the treaty within Hawai'i was to lay bare the division of political interests: the native Hawaiian population became opposed to more concessions, while planters and merchants, who had reaped big increases in wealth under the treaty, were willing to trade part of Hawai'i's sovereignty for continued access to the U.S. sugar market.

For the Hawaiian government, the problem was clear: the reciprocity treaty had allowed new independent organizations, the sugar plantations and sugar factors, to reap enormous rents and become independent centers of power that were beyond the control of the state. What this meant for the government of Hawai'i, a mature natural state, was that it had lost control of the process of rent creation and rent distribution. For it to have continued to be an effective government in this type of environment, it would have needed to bolster its capacity to resist violent attempts to overthrow its institutions and overturn its policies. The corporate interests who had invested in Hawai'i to reap rents under the tariff umbrella had interests that were closely aligned with those of the United States, and this alignment of interests allowed them to call on the U.S. government and military to support their cause.[73] For the Hawaiian government, a buildup of state capacity to enforce its policies was necessary, yet ultimately it could never succeed in confronting U.S. forces. It is not surprising that the Hawaiian government was reluctant to choose that path. Its inability to threaten force against those interests opposing its policies would ultimately lead not just to a new constitution, but to its untimely end.

The McKinley Tariff, enacted by the U.S. Congress in 1890, provided a second major shock to the prevailing trade arrangements between Hawai'i and the United States. The new U.S. tariff law had generally raised tariff rates, and it was expected that the increased tariff revenues would produce a large, politically unpopular budget surplus for the federal government. Congress dealt with the problem by cutting the tariff on raw sugar to zero and replacing it with a 2-cent-per-pound bounty on domestic sugar output.[74] By replacing tariff revenues from sugar imports with bounties paid to domestic sugar producers, Congress was able to maintain protection for domestic sugar producers, increase protection for other manufacturing interests, and reduce its unpopular budget surplus.

One of the classic results of modern international trade theory is that a subsidy paid to domestic producers can provide the same protection for their product as a tariff on foreign producers. The effect on foreign producers depends, however, on whether they are exporting under a reciprocity treaty.[75] For producers in Hawai'i exporting under a reciprocity treaty, the elimination of the U.S. tariff on raw sugar would *reduce* the price received by Hawai'i sugar producers by close to the full amount of the rescinded tariff. In any case, the overall effect of the McKinley Tariff on Hawai'i sugar producers was to erase the price premium that reciprocity had provided to them relative to other foreign sugar producers selling in the U.S. market.

During its debates over the McKinley Tariff, the U.S. House of Representatives considered the effect of the U.S.-Hawai'i reciprocity treaty on the price of sugar in California.[76] Several representatives noted that the price of sugar on the West Coast still retained a tariff premium despite the waiver of the tariff for Hawai'i sugar imports. They argued that if the main effect of the reciprocity treaty was to transfer tariff revenue to Hawai'i sugar producers without benefiting U.S. consumers, then sugar should be placed on the free list to end such unnecessary gifts. Discussion in the U.S. Senate on September 2, 1890, focused on the high price of obtaining political influence in Hawai'i with a reciprocity treaty. Senator Joseph Dolph observed that "if the treaty stands five years more we will have given to the sugar kings of the Sandwich Islands and the sugar kings of San Francisco enough money to construct and put into operation the Nicaraguan canal."[77]

The congressional debates over the McKinley Tariff provide a strong basis for concluding that its provisions on sugar constituted opportunistic behavior by the United States.[78] The United States retained all privileges granted to it under the reciprocity treaty, while the elimination of the U.S. tariff on sugar effectively removed the most important privilege enjoyed by Hawai'i under the treaty.[79] Until the treaty expired in 1895, the small island kingdom had little recourse but to allow the now patently one-sided treaty to continue in operation.

The effect of the McKinley Tariff was to plunge Hawai'i into depression and again threaten the value of investments in specific capital on lands devoted to sugar production. Sugar prices fell 38 percent on the day the sugar tariff was removed.[80] The value of Hawaiian merchandise exports (including sugar) plunged from $13 million in 1890 to $10 million in 1891, and then to a low point of $8 million in 1892.[81] The decline in the price of raw sugar received by Hawai'i producers meant that the specific capital invested in the sugar industry lost much of its value, despite redeployment of some land and capital to other agricultural crops, such as coffee and pineapple.[82] Fifteen years of reciprocity had made Hawaiian incomes dependent on sugar exports to the U.S. market and on the U.S. government maintaining a high tariff on raw sugar imports.[83]

In sum, on the eve of the overthrow of the Hawaiian monarchy in January 1893, Hawai'i's economy had suffered a dramatic reversal of fortune primarily attributable to the McKinley Tariff's elimination of the U.S. sugar tariff. One could legitimately speculate whether the 1850s debate over reciprocity versus annexation was beginning to be resolved in favor of annexation due to the failure of the United States to carry out its commitment to reciprocity.

The Overthrow

During 1891, the United States and Hawai'i considered revising the reciprocity treaty to extend preferential trade benefits to all Hawaiian goods. The reasoning was that preferential access for new Hawai'i exports to the U.S. market would partially make up for the loss of preferential access to the U.S. sugar market. In exchange, the Hawaiian government would extend the Pearl Harbor concession to the United States indefinitely. In late fall 1891, Secretary of State James Blaine and the Hawai'i minister of finance, John Mott-Smith, completed a draft treaty, but President Harrison decided early in 1892 that he could not submit the treaty to the U.S. Senate. With prospects for an expanded preferential treaty looking bleak, planters and others indirectly deriving income from the sugar industry had incentives to take actions designed to incorporate Hawai'i into the United States in order to eliminate the rising uncertainty associated with reciprocity and to claim the two-cent-per-pound bounty offered to U.S. sugar producers.

The incentives for planters to move closer to the United States were coupled with important changes in Hawai'i's domestic politics. King Kalākaua died in January 1891, and his sister, Lydia Kamakaeha Lili'uokalani, succeeded him (fig. 6.4). The queen regretted Kalākaua's acceptance of the 1887 Bayonet Constitution and adamantly opposed the concession of rights to Pearl Harbor under the renewed reciprocity agreement.[84] Under article 41 of the 1887 constitution, the legislature could reject the crown's

FIGURE 6.4. Queen Liliʻuokalani, 1891 photograph. Source: Hawaiʻi State Archives.

cabinet with a no-confidence vote. Over the late summer and autumn of 1892, the queen repeatedly formed cabinets and the legislature repeatedly rejected them.[85] Liliʻuokalani later reported receiving several petitions from native Hawaiians requesting a new constitution at the same time.[86]

The constitution the queen considered would have reversed the Bayonet Constitution and was perceived by foreign residents as a threat.[87] It would have restored the franchise qualifications of the pre-1887 constitution, requiring voters to be subjects and removing any reference to ethnicity.[88] The power to override a royal veto of legislation would also have been muddied.[89] Perhaps most threatening to the forces opposing the crown, the promulgation of a new constitution would have revived the possibility of promulgation itself. Declaring a new constitution would have undermined

FIGURE 6.5. U.S. Marine Guards from the U.S.S. *Boston* with the American flag that was flown briefly over Aliʻiolani Hale, Honolulu, Hawaiʻi. Photo: Unknown photographer. Source: Bishop Museum.

constraints on the monarch's power.[90] From the white elite's perspective, the diminished benefits from the reciprocity treaty paled beside this threat.

With the eager assistance of John L. Stevens, the U.S. minister to Hawaiʻi, a small but prominent group of white residents used the new constitution as the precipitating event for the overthrow.[91] For some months prior to January 1893, they prepared for their opportunity.[92] On January 14, 1893, the queen sought cabinet approval (as required by the 1887 constitution) to promulgate the new constitution. The cabinet ministers declined, and the queen postponed her announcement. News of these events reached the small Caucasian group, who decided its time had come. The leaders formed themselves into a 13-member Committee of Safety, dominated by Americans and Hawaiian citizens originally from the United States.[93] They solicited and received support from the U.S. minister. On

January 16, 1893, the U.S. minister commanded the U.S.S. *Boston* to land troops to "protect American lives and property" (fig. 6.5). The next day, the Committee of Safety occupied the nearly empty government building, the Aliʻiolani Hale, and the U.S. minister recognized the newly formed provisional government.[94] Under protest, Queen Liliʻuokalani yielded the throne.

Conclusion

The overthrow of the Hawaiian monarchy came about because of a complex interaction between U.S. strategic goals and Hawaiʻi's internal political economy. As described above, the passage of the reciprocity treaty in 1876 put in place incentives for the sugar industry to expand, and Hawaiʻi sugar planters responded by making big investments in specific capital. Those investments made the now more politically powerful planters particularly eager to continue the preferential trading relationship, thereby providing the United States with an improved bargaining position in treaty renewal negotiations in 1884. The U.S. Senate's Pearl Harbor amendment to the reciprocity treaty then significantly altered Hawaiʻi's domestic political economy. By making treaty renewal unacceptable to native Hawaiians concerned about protecting Hawaiʻi's sovereignty, but all the more compelling to sugar planters, the amendment provided the planters with incentives to take action to protect their massively increased wealth. The reluctance of King Kalākaua to renew the treaty with a new clause ceding Pearl Harbor added another major grievance against him to their already large stack and helped to precipitate the 1887 revolt and the Bayonet Constitution. When the shock of the McKinley Tariff in 1890 deprived the sugar planters and the white professional elite of big economic rents, attempts to integrate Hawaiʻi more closely with the United States were predictable.

The reciprocity treaty was, of course, far from the only factor leading to the overthrow. Conventional explanations of the overthrow still have considerable merit. The immigration of Chinese and Japanese laborers facilitated the rapid accumulation of planter wealth, but subsequent pressure by the Japanese government to grant citizenship and voting rights to Japanese immigrants was perceived by planters as raising the likelihood of increased taxation of their economic rents. Gains by Hawaiian political parties in the mid-1880s and Queen Liliʻuokalani's attempt to promulgate a new constitution in January 1893 raised the planters' fears for the security of their property rights and rents and provided the immediate trigger for the overthrow. And the scheming actions of the rabidly pro-annexation U.S. minister to Hawai'i, John L. Stevens, also greatly increased the rebels' chances of success.

All that said, the U.S.-Hawai'i reciprocity treaty is particularly important for understanding the overthrow and annexation. The phenomenal structural change in Hawai'i's economy induced by the treaty—the massive expansion of the sugar industry—reduced Hawai'i's bargaining position when the treaty was up for renewal and unleashed a wave of political change that ultimately led to the overthrow of the monarchy and the U.S. annexation of Hawai'i. Economists usually extol the benefits of trade, and indeed, increased specialization and trade can benefit all nations. Preferential trade is, however, another matter and should be viewed with caution given the political changes that it can unleash, particularly in smaller countries.

CHAPTER SEVEN

Colonial Political Economy

Hawai'i as a U.S. Territory

Why can not we be honest in our utterances touching the territories we have recently acquired? Really it would save time and trouble, to say nothing of life and treasure, to come out frankly with the announcement that we have annexed these possessions in cold blood and that we intend to utilize them to our profit and advantage.—Editorial in the *Washington Post*, January 21, 1900

In 1885, Hawai'i was a mature natural state. The constitutions of 1840, 1852, and 1864 clearly set out major positions and agencies of the government; delineated their responsibilities and powers; specified a rule of law that formally encompassed both *ali'i* and *kānaka maoli*; mandated regular elections for a two-house legislature; placed limitations on the king's authority; and allowed certain types of organizations without direct ties to the government. Actual practice provided some hints of aspects of an open-access political order. Most importantly, there was effective competition for places in the house of representatives, and this political competition was facilitated by economic and political competition between large numbers of Hawaiian newspapers with differing views.

The political institutions of 1885 were, however, inadequate to accommodate the two big changes in the political and economic environment that occurred after 1850. They could not accommodate the interests of foreign corporations, whose presence had expanded enormously after the 1876 reciprocity treaty, or the ambition of the rising military power in the

Pacific Ocean, the United States, to affect political decisions in Hawai'i. Hawai'i's military forces were almost nonexistent, consisting mainly of the king's household guard. By contrast, foreign corporations had the option to call on the United States to use soft or hard power to protect their interests in Hawai'i. Consider that U.S. power had already directly affected the election of a new king in 1874. Two high-ranking *ali'i*, Emma Kalanikaumaka'amano Kaleleonālani Na'ea Rooke and David La'amea Kalākaua, faced each other in a legislative election to succeed King William Lunaliho, who had died without a successor. Emma lost the election, and her supporters rioted to protest the vote and perhaps force her selection. Soldiers from a U.S. naval vessel in Honolulu Harbor were landed to put down the riots and ensure that Kalākaua, the candidate favored by the U.S. government and foreign sugar interests, became king.[1]

In June 1900, Hawai'i became a colony of the United States. Its new territorial government was established by the U.S. Congress, without any vote by the Hawaiian population or consent from their representatives. The new colonial government remained a mature natural state in which government acted to create economic rents and distribute them to important interest groups. The big change was that the source of most government power had shifted to the U.S. president and U.S. Congress. Previously, a prime minister and cabinet appointed by the king would take actions to effect rent creation and distribution, but now this process was coordinated by a governor appointed by the U.S. president and enforced by judges also appointed by the U.S. president.

In this chapter, I show that the big winners from the change to U.S. colonial rule were the U.S. government, which moved quickly to establish a network of military bases within Hawai'i to serve as the focus of its projection of power in the Pacific Ocean, and the sugar plantations and Big Five agencies, whose influence in government deepened and whose property rights in plantation land became more secure. Native Hawaiians were the big losers: although they continued to be a part of the dominant coalition, the share of economic rents they received was much reduced. This reduction was due to elimination of the institution of the monarch within government; the transfer of sovereignty and most important decision-making powers to Washington, D.C.; the loss of the monarch's vast crown lands; increased competition in labor markets with foreign contract laborers (who were freed from their contracts at annexation); and big influxes of U.S. and Asian immigrants.

Asians living permanently or temporarily in Hawai'i were mostly excluded from gaining access to economic rents created and distributed by the dominant coalition until after World War II, when the International Longshore and Warehouse Union (ILWU) negotiated higher wages for sugar plantation workers. Asian immigrants were the majority of the population throughout the territorial era, but had little political power because U.S. law did not allow their naturalization and thus barred their participation in territorial elections.

The Organic Act, which established a territorial government for the new U.S. colony, contained some provisions more characteristic of an open-access political order than a mature natural state. Most importantly, the act extended the protection of the U.S. Constitution to Hawai'i residents who were designated as U.S. citizens: a group that included Hawaiians, most Caucasians, and the children of Asian-Americans born in Hawai'i. They had the protections of the U.S. Constitution's Bill of Rights and were free to form new political and social organizations, establish religious schools, and publish newspapers, among other things. Their inclusion in the institutional mix was debated heatedly in the U.S. Congress, as opponents and support-ers both recognized that their inclusion provided several mechanisms that would facilitate Hawai'i's eventual transition from a colony to the open-access order of a U.S. state. Groups left out of the dominant coalition or dissatisfied with their shares of economic rents now had pathways by which they could compete away a portion of the dominant coalition's economic rents, thereby loosening the adherence of coalition participants to the co-lonial regime, and participate in political action to change the status of Hawai'i within the United States. I conclude by arguing that martial law during World War II and changing voter demographics provided the shocks that would trigger the change to statehood in 1959.

From Annexation to the Organic Act

On July 7, 1898, a joint resolution (the "Newlands Resolution") of the U.S. Senate and the U.S. House of Representatives was enacted to accept the offer of the Republic of Hawai'i to cede Hawai'i to the United States (fig. 7.1):

> Whereas the Government of the Republic of Hawaii having, in due form, signi-fied its consent, in the manner provided by its constitution, to cede absolutely and without reserve to the United States of America all rights of sovereignty of whatsoever kind in and over the Hawaiian Islands and their dependencies, and

FIGURE 7.1. Lowering the Hawaiian flag at the U.S. annexation ceremony at ʻIolani Palace, August 12, 1898. Photo: Unknown photographer. Source: Bishop Museum.

also to cede and transfer to the United States the absolute fee and ownership of all public, Government, or Crown lands, public buildings or edifices, ports, harbors, military equipment, and all other public property of every kind and description belonging to the Government of the Hawaiian Islands, together with every right and appurtenance thereunto appertaining; Therefore

Resolved by the Senate and House of Representatives of the United States of America in Congress Assembled, That said cession is accepted, ratified, and confirmed, and that the said Hawaiian Islands and their dependencies be, and they are hereby, annexed as a part of the territory of the United States and are subject to the sovereign dominion thereof, and that all and singular the property and rights hereinbefore mentioned are vested in the United States of America.[2]

The Newlands Resolution provided for the appointment by the U.S. president of a five-member commission to recommend legislation to Congress to establish a territorial government for Hawaiʻi. President McKinley did not appoint any native Hawaiian members, but rather chose three Caucasian members of the U.S. Congress—Chair Shelby Cullom, Republican U.S. senator from Illinois; John Morgan, Democratic U.S. senator from Alabama; and Robert Hitt, Republican U.S. representative from Illinois—and two Caucasian members of the government of the Republic of Hawai'i—Sanford B. Dole, president of the Republic of Hawai'i; and Walter Frear, a justice of the Supreme Court of the Republic of Hawai'i. The Hawaiian Commission held an organizational meeting in Washington, D.C., on July 18, 1898, and then, starting August 18, 1898, held regular daily sessions in Honolulu and on the other islands. On November 9, 1898, it issued a final report to Congress with recommendations on legislation.[3]

Debates over legislation (H.R. 2972 and S. 222) to organize a government in Hawai'i took place in both the Senate and the House between December 1899 and April 1900.[4] Members of Congress were particularly concerned that the legislation, which was based on the Hawaiian Commission's report, gave too much power to the foreign corporations and Caucasian elites who had taken power after the overthrow and too little power to Congress and the U.S. president. They argued that the proposed legislation perpetuated the system of bound contract labor, concentrated too much power in the governor of Hawai'i (who appointed Supreme Court justices for life terms), and disenfranchised native Hawaiians in elections for the territorial senate by imposing income and property requirements to vote. In the absence of these requirements, native Hawaiians would constitute more than two-thirds of the electorate; with the requirements, just a few thousand Caucasian voters would have the majority. In response to these concerns, Congress amended the original legislation to void and prohibit bound labor contracts, to transfer some powers from the territorial governor to the U.S. president, and to eliminate income and property requirements for voters in territorial senate elections. Elimination of the property and income requirements opened the door to control of both houses of the territorial legislature by Hawaiian voters. The next section presents an overview of the formal political institutions that Congress set forth in the Organic Act, which was enacted on April 30, 1900, and put into effect on June 14, 1900.[5]

Hawai'i's Formal Political Institutions as a U.S. Territory

Unlike the territories acquired by the United States in the Spanish-American War, Congress provided for Hawai'i to become an organized, incorporated territory. "Organized" meant that a civil government was authorized by Congress. "Incorporated" meant that citizens of the Republic of Hawai'i became citizens of the United States and possessed all of the rights granted in the Bill of Rights of the U.S. Constitution.[6] It also meant that the Territory of Hawai'i was allowed to form a government with institutions bearing a surface resemblance to those found in the governments of other U.S. states. Hawai'i's government, however, was not sovereign in any way, as the Organic Act was subject to amendment by Congress at any time. The territorial executive and judiciary branches both derived their power from the U.S. president, while the power to legislate was tightly controlled by the U.S. Congress. The Organic Act centralized government functions and powers in the territorial government rather than in county governments. This was done to ensure that the U.S. federal government could more easily monitor and control actions of the Hawaiian government. Consider now the structure and source of authority for the executive, legislative, and judicial branches, county governments, and the delegate to the U.S. House of Representatives.

THE EXECUTIVE POWER. Executive power was essentially delegated to and controlled by the president of the United States. The Organic Act empowered the president to appoint the governor of Hawai'i, subject to advice and consent of the U.S. Senate,[7] and to remove the governor at any time during his four-year term. The governor was required to be a resident of Hawai'i. Unlike those of U.S. states, the legislature was not provided with the power to impeach either the governor or judges, regardless of the nature of their misconduct. The governor had the power to suspend habeas corpus and declare martial law. All other territorial officials were appointees of the governor, subject to advice and consent of the Hawai'i territorial senate. The combination of the president's power to appoint and to remove and the legislature's inability to impeach meant that the governor and his appointees had strong incentives and lots of latitude to implement the president's policies on legislation, appointments, and executive actions.

THE JUDICIARY. The Organic Act provided the U.S. president with the power to appoint all members of the Hawai'i judiciary—the chief justice and two associate justices of the Hawai'i Supreme Court and all circuit court judges—subject to advice and consent of the U.S. Senate.[8] Each Supreme Court justice served a term of seven years, and each circuit court judge a term of six years.[9] The Organic Act also provided the president with the power to remove a justice or judge at any time during his term. The combination of the power to appoint and to remove (whether exercised or not) and the limited term of each judge gave the president effective mechanisms to shape the general direction of judicial rulings.[10] Perhaps the biggest check against the president's power over the Hawai'i judiciary was the right of litigants, in some types of cases, to appeal their case to the U.S. Ninth Circuit Court of Appeals or the U.S. Supreme Court.

THE LEGISLATURE. The Organic Act specified a two-house legislature elected by male voters age 21 and over who could read and write either English or Hawaiian. Legislation required majority approval of both houses, and the legislature had the power to override the governor's veto of legislation with a two-thirds vote of each chamber. While the legislature's cooperation in passing legislation was needed for the executive to govern effectively, its power was tightly constrained by checks over its legislative authority vested in the U.S. Congress. Congress retained the power to enact legislation that applied only to Hawai'i. It could, by majority vote of each house of Congress, override territorial legislation. And it retained exclusive authority to amend the Organic Act.[11] By retaining the authority to impose legislation, veto legislation, and amend the constitutional framework, Congress tightly limited the frame for independent action by the territorial legislature. Congress had, however, neither the need nor the will to take on the detailed job of legislating for the territory. Some power would need to be delegated to the territorial legislature to reflect its better knowledge of people, circumstances, and places in the territory.

COUNTY GOVERNMENTS. During the first five years of the territory's existence, the territorial government was the only government in Hawai'i. There were no county governments. It was not until 1905 that an amendment to the Organic Act established Hawai'i's three counties (Maui, Hawai'i, and Kaua'i) and the City and County of Honolulu. The first elections for mayors and boards of supervisors were held in 1907. The territorial legislature delegated only a few functions of government to the new county governments, with the territorial government continuing to finance, provide, and regulate education, welfare, agriculture, forestry, fish and game conservation, labor, airports, and harbors. Some responsibilities, such as provision of roads and business regulation, which in the rest of the United States were usually the province of local governments, were shared in Hawai'i by the counties and the territorial government.[12] Local governments financed and provided public elementary and secondary schools throughout the United States, but in Hawai'i the territorial government kept this responsibility.

Why was the organization of territorial and local government in Hawai'i so different from the organization of state and local government in U.S. states? In his classic study of state government in Hawai'i, the political scientist Norman Meller provided an efficiency explanation. Meller emphasized that "the plantation, characterized by its system of private government, obviated the necessity in the rural areas for most municipal services normally performed by local government."[13] Meller's reasoning applies particularly to Maui, Kaua'i, and Hawai'i Counties, in which plantation agriculture dominated the economy and employed most of the workers. Plantations often provided rudimentary medical care, worker housing, general stores, transportation inside the plantation, water, and other services usually purchased from private firms or supplied by local governments.

Meller also suggested that the limited powers provided to county government may have been a mechanism for enforcing policies of the dominant coalition. The delegation of so few functions of government to the counties made it easier for the territorial governor and the U.S. president to monitor how the territorial government was dispersing economic rents to the interests that constituted the dominant coalition. Powerful independent county governments would also have had the potential to set up services that competed with services provided by the territorial government, which had been structured to create rents and distribute them to the dominant coalition. Competition to provide such services would have dissipated the territorial government's rents and eroded the basis for effective government in a mature natural state: creating and distributing a pool of rents to members of a dominant coalition.

FEDERAL REPRESENTATION. The Organic Act did not allow for any formal or informal representation of Hawai'i's citizens in the U.S. Senate. Section 85 provided for Hawai'i's citizens to elect a delegate to the United States House of Representatives who was allowed to participate in debates, but not to vote.[14] Hawai'i citizens were not allowed to cast a vote for president, and Hawai'i had no representation in the electoral college that elects the U.S. president. Thus, most Hawai'i citizens had little electoral influence over the federal government. While Hawaiian voters did not have voting representation in Washington, D.C., Hawai'i's large corporations and its longtime nonvoting delegate to the U.S. House of Representatives, Prince Jonah Kūhiō Kalaniana'ole, pursued other channels of influence. Kūhiō entertained U.S. representatives, senators, and government officials frequently and elaborately. He was able to communicate effectively the views and requests of Hawai'i interests and corporations to Congress, the president, and other federal agencies. Hawai'i firms and powerful individuals frequently made campaign contributions to senators and representatives who served on important congressional committees that wrote legislation affecting the territory. Thus, Hawai'i was not without some representation in the federal government, but it was skewed toward representation of groups sufficiently wealthy and organized to lobby in the nation's capital.

Confiscation of Crown Lands

The confiscation of crown lands by the Republic of Hawai'i was ratified by the federal government when it passed the Organic Act. Confiscating the crown lands was essential for a territorial government that was focused on distributing economic rents to the interests in the dominant coalition and wanted to defuse effective opposition to its rule.

Hawai'i's kings had long been aware of the danger that after a rebellion or coup d'état, their lands could be confiscated. To protect against this possibility, Kauikeaouli, the *Mō'ī* from 1825 to 1854, took steps to ensure that the crown lands were his private property. As chapter 5 describes, titled, fee simple property was first established in Hawai'i during the *Māhele* in the late 1840s. The islands' lands were divided among four claimants: chiefs (*ali'i* and *konohiki*), the king (*Mō'ī*), the government, and the common people (*maka'āinana*). One of the motivations of Kauikeaouli in bringing Western property institutions to Hawai'i was to establish certain landholdings as his personal private property rather than the property of the government. The background for this action was the demands made by foreigners in the late 1830s to own land in Hawai'i. The demands culminated in February 1843, when Kauikeaouli temporarily ceded Hawai'i to Great Britain in response to threats regarding payment of outstanding debts made by the commander of a British warship visiting Honolulu. In July 1843, British Admiral Richard Thomas settled the debt disputes and reaffirmed the king's sovereignty.

Historians Gavan Daws, Lilikalā Kame'eleihiwa, and Ralph Kuykendall have all argued that Kauikeaouli moved quickly to start the process of establishing private property rights in land to protect his own holdings from being taken in a future foreign intervention or annexation. If the lands were the *Mō'ī's* private property rather than the government's property, it would be more difficult for a foreign power to justify their confiscation after it assumed control of the government. Standing against this argument is the extent of the crown lands, which represented a substantial portion of Hawai'i's landed wealth and thereby provided a foreign power with strong incentives to take them in order to disable any resistance from an overthrown *Mō 'ī* after the takeover. In 1894, the crown lands amounted to 971,463 acres—a little under 24 percent of the islands' total.

Consider first the initial taking of the crown lands by the government of the Republic of Hawai'i 14 months after a small band of insurrectionists overthrew Queen Lili'uokalani. The Republic of Hawai'i convened a constitutional convention on May 30, 1894. President Sanford Dole appointed 19 of the 37 delegates, thereby ensuring that supporters of the overthrow would have a majority. The remainder of the delegates were elected under voter eligibility rules that disenfranchised most native Hawaiians.[15] The new constitution was proclaimed on July 4, 1894. Article 95 proclaimed that the crown lands are "now to be, the property of the Hawaiian government, and to be now free and clear from any trust of or concerning the same, and from all claim of any nature whatsoever, upon the rents, issues and profits thereof."

Now consider how the U.S. government treated the matter of the crown lands when it accepted the offer of the Republic of Hawai'i to cede the Hawaiian Islands to the United States. The Newlands Resolution—the July 1898 Joint Resolution of the U.S. Congress used to annex Hawai'i—began by stating that the Republic of Hawai'i "cede[s] absolutely and without reserve to the United States of America all rights of sovereignty of whatsoever kind in and over the Hawaiian Islands and their dependencies, and also to cede and transfer to the United States the absolute fee and ownership of all public, Government, or Crown lands, public buildings or edifices, ports, harbors, military equipment, and all other public property of every kind and description belonging to the Government of the Hawaiian Islands, together with every right and appurtenance thereunto appertaining."[16]

The resolution then goes on to give the new public lands in Hawai'i (which included the crown lands) special status for the purposes of management: "The existing laws of the United States relative to public lands shall not apply to such lands in the Hawaiian Islands, but the Congress of the United States shall enact special laws for their management and disposition."[17]

The crown lands were also specifically addressed in the provisions of the Organic Act. In section 99, which borrows its language from article 95 of the short-lived (1893–1898) Republic of Hawai'i's constitution, the crown lands are declared to be the property of the U.S. government. Congressional debates on S. 222, the bill amended to become the Organic Act, contain explicit discussion of the queen's claims to crown lands as well as a proposed amendment to the bill that would have awarded $250,000 to her in compensation for loss of those lands. In the debates, some congressmen argued that the crown lands were the queen's private property, while others argued against this idea.[18]

Over the next decade, Queen Lili'uokalani made a series of complaints to the federal government and made several trips to Washington, D.C., to press her arguments regarding both annexation and the U.S. taking of crown lands. She asked that her private lands be returned, and that if that could not be accomplished, she be awarded some compensation for their loss. These requests proved unsuccessful, and in 1910, she filed a case in the U.S. Court of Claims to recover a "vested equitable life interest" in the crown lands. The court dismissed her claim, finding that as a deposed monarch, "she held no vested rights in the crown lands."[19] The second part of her claim, that the taking of the crown lands was unlawful, was never heard by a U.S. court.

The decisions by the U.S. Congress to include the crown lands as part of the public lands of the new territory in both the 1898 Newlands Resolution and the 1900 Organic Act established the willingness of the federal government to redistribute private property to bolster its political position in Hawai'i. Its decision to take the crown lands without compensation set the precedent for uncompensated use of the territorial government's lands by the U.S. military and for uncompensated federal use of lands assigned to the Hawaiian Homes program (described in chap. 8).

The matter of Hawai'i's crown lands provides a striking example of how, in a limited-access political order, government will redistribute rights to private lands both to bolster the ruling coalition and to harm its opponents. In a limited-access political order, property rights to land are never really secure. They are always subject to redistribution by the governing authorities to bolster the ruling coalition when the distribution of power among groups within the coalition changes or a new coalition is formed. In an organized U.S. territory like Hawai'i, the rights granted by the Constitution apply to U.S. citizens, and one might think that the protections to private property afforded by the fifth and fourteenth amendments would restrict the taking of crown lands. In this case, the protections were never tested in the courts, perhaps because of the clear treatment of crown lands in the Organic Act.

Economic Rents to The Hawaiian Electorate

From 1900 to 1954, the Republican Party dominated the territorial legislature. The party's dominance was the result of a coalition between native
Hawaiians and Caucasian immigrants from the U.S. mainland, who in the
pre-World War II period together constituted a majority of the electorate.
Asian migrants and their children had coalesced around the Democratic
Party but, despite being a majority of the population, were a much smaller
proportion of the electorate. Until a series of federal laws passed in the
1940s and 1950s changed their status, Chinese, Japanese, and Filipino immigrants to Hawai'i—a majority of Hawai'i's voting-age population between 1900 and 1920—were ineligible to become U.S. citizens and thus
ineligible to vote in territorial elections.

Hawaiians held the majority of the seats in both the house and the
senate through the mid-1930s. Most Caucasian voters were aligned with
the interests of the federal government and the plantations, but Hawaiian
voters were not. Legislation enacted during this period was generally directed toward the interests of the sugar and pineapple plantations. Given
the ethnic composition of the legislature, how did the sugar and pineapple
corporations and federal interests generally get their way?

Native Hawaiians were offered three types of political consideration
to be part of the dominant political party. First, many patronage appointments were reserved for native Hawaiians, and they dominated some public professions, serving as judges, lawyers, and police.[20] Second, nonciti-
zens were excluded from hiring on federal projects. This was a substantial
consideration during the 1920s and 1930s, when construction of harbor
facilities and a shipyard at Pearl Harbor and an Army base at Schofield
Barracks were under way. Third, Congress's establishment of the joint
state-federal Hawaiian Homes Program provided some Hawaiians with
virtually free ($1 per annum) leases on urban house lots and rural farm
and ranch lands.

The Republican Party's control of the legislature was also facilitated
by the failure of the territorial government to reapportion legislative districts as the population moved from rural to urban areas. The same legislative districts used in the first territorial election in 1900 were also used in
the last territorial election held in 1958. In 1900, only a small proportion
of citizens lived in the state's urban areas. A majority of residents were
sugar plantation workers who were born in Asia and under U.S. law could
not become citizens. As the native-born sons and daughters of immigrants

moved to urban, already Democratic districts in the 1920s and 1930s, rural, reliably Republican districts with increasingly smaller shares of the electorate dominated state legislative elections. The Republican control of the legislature lasted for over five decades, coming to a spectacular end with the decisive victories in the 1954 election that brought big Democratic majorities to both chambers.

How Rents Were Distributed to the Big Five Corporations

Caucasian voters were a key element in the dominant political coalition due to their large share in the electorate during the territory's first 40 years. The payoffs to these voters for participating in the coalition were indirect ones, stemming primarily from the benefits provided to five key corporations for which Caucasians were employed as skilled workers, managers, and owners. C. Brewer & Co., Theo H. Davies & Co., Castle & Cooke, Inc., H. Hackfeld & Co., and Alexander & Baldwin, Ltd., were together known as the "Big Five." Along with a string of affiliated corporations, they dominated the Hawai'i economy from the overthrow of the monarchy to the early years of statehood.[21] By the late nineteenth century, their primary role was to serve as agencies for Hawai'i's 60 or more sugar plantations, providing shipping, supplies, financing, wholesaling, and other critical management services.

Three of the Big Five companies were owned and controlled by foreigners. They began their Hawai'i businesses by facilitating trade and shipping between Hawai'i and China, North America, and Europe. As these firms evolved to provide finance and agency services to sugar plantations, their headquarters in Bremen, Boston, or Liverpool served as sources of capital for Hawai'i sugar plantations. The first entrant, C. Brewer and Company, was founded by New Englanders. Their Hawai'i business was founded on trade, including exporting Hawai'i sandalwood to China and importing U.S. manufactured goods from Boston. The second company, Theo H. Davies & Co., was founded by a British trading firm based in Liverpool that had already established branches in San Francisco and Victoria, British Columbia. The third company, Hackfeld & Co., was a branch of a German trading firm based in Bremen that started its Hawai'i business by exporting whale oil and bone to Germany and importing European goods to Hawai'i. All of the Big Five firms expanded their activities to provide services to sugar plantations after the conclusion of the U.S.-Hawai'i reciprocity treaty in 1876, but Hackfeld & Co. was by far the most successful, working with 18 of the 60 sugar plantations in 1879.

The fourth company, Castle & Cooke, Inc., was founded by two immigrants from New England, the ministers Samuel Northrup Castle and Amos Starr Cooke. The American Board of Commissioners for Foreign Missions (ABCFM) originally sent them to Hawai'i to manage trade between missionaries stationed in Hawai'i and New England firms. ABCFM's withdrawal of support for Hawai'i missions in 1849 prompted Castle and Cooke to start their own wholesale and retail trade business. They began financing new and existing sugar plantations in the late 1850s, and that became the main focus of their business by the 1870s.

The last Big Five company, Alexander & Baldwin, Ltd., was formed by two sons of missionaries, Samuel T. Alexander and Henry P. Baldwin. During the 1870s, their business focused on developing sugar plantations on Maui and on building big irrigation projects (the most prominent being the Hāmākua Ditch) designed to bring water from windward areas with high rainfall to sugar plantations in leeward areas. Castle and Cooke provided agency services for Alexander & Baldwin through the 1880s, but by 1900 the latter firm had expanded into providing finance and agency services for 10 or more plantations.

Each of the agencies supported King Kalākaua's efforts in the mid-1870s to negotiate a reciprocity treaty with the United States, as relief from the high U.S. sugar tariff would allow an enormous expansion of the sugar industry and generate big increases in economic rents for the Big Five firms and their affiliates. With the signing of the treaty in 1876, each of these firms grew enormously as Hawai'i exports of unrefined sugar expanded by a factor of 50 between 1876 and 1910.[22]

During the critical period of the 1890s, the Big Five firms and the sugar plantations were united around the objective of retaining their waiver from U.S. tariffs on imports of raw sugar, but often differed as to the best strategy and tactics. Most were in favor of the U.S.-supported overthrow of the monarchy, but some, including "Sugar King" Claus Spreckels, were strong supporters of Queen Lili'uokalani and lobbied for her restoration in Washington, D.C., during the 1890s. Spreckels thought that continued flows of contract labor to the sugar industry were most likely under the monarchy. Others in the sugar industry were against annexation, fearing that the shower of rents conferred on them by the U.S.-Hawai'i reciprocity treaty might be lost once Hawai'i was properly incorporated into the United States. They argued that Hawai'i would lose its bargaining position as a vital security asset that might otherwise come under the influence of foreign powers. Many plantation owners and some Big Five executives argued that annexation was the best way to maintain the enormous flow of rents to the sugar industry, as it would enable Hawai'i interests better access to U.S. government representatives and officials.[23]

The incorporation of Hawai'i as a U.S. territory in 1900 ultimately led to expansion of the three Big Five firms with American owners. In 1897, Hackfeld & Co., owned by the Hackfeld family of Bremen, Germany, and German corporate executives such as Paul Isenberg, marketed sugar from 12 plantations, and Theo H. Davies & Co., owned by the Davies family of Great Britain, marketed sugar from 6 plantations.[24] Suspicions during World War I about the activities of its German owners led the U.S. federal government to confiscate Hackfeld's assets in Hawai'i and sell them to the three American-owned sugar agencies.[25] Renamed American Factors, the resulting new firm managed 11 sugar plantations and marketed 29 percent of the sugar crop in 1920. The same families and agencies who gained control over American Factors made loans to Theo H. Davies in the 1920s and accumulated more than one-third of its shares, thereby gaining some influence over its operations.

The Big Five firms competed to supply agency services to sugar plantations but cooperated in numerous other areas, including overseas labor recruiting, establishing a jointly owned sugar refinery, maintaining forest watersheds, and collecting and evaluating information on sugar cultivation and manufacturing technologies.[26] Tormented for years by the market power of the American Sugar Refining Company in the U.S. sugar refining market, the Big Five companies established the California and Hawaiian (C&H) Sugar Company in 1906 to refine Hawai'i cane sugar at their own refinery in Crockett, California.[27] The C&H Board of Directors was composed of the five agency presidents, a situation that presented its members with additional opportunities for collaboration. Collaboration between agencies and plantations also occurred via the Planters' Labor and Supply (PL&S) Company.[28] Historian Carol MacLennan argues that PL&S trustees worked "to secure their economic and political interests in Honolulu and Washington" while a string of committees worked on topics "ranging from cultivation techniques to sugar machinery to experience with imported labor to forest decline to irrigation," among others.[29] PL&S's successor, the Hawaiian Sugar Planters' Association (HSPA), continued and expanded the extensive cooperation within the industry, undertaking scientific research regarding control of pests, problems with soil exhaustion, and maintenance of forest watersheds.

The contractual integration of agencies and plantations that marked

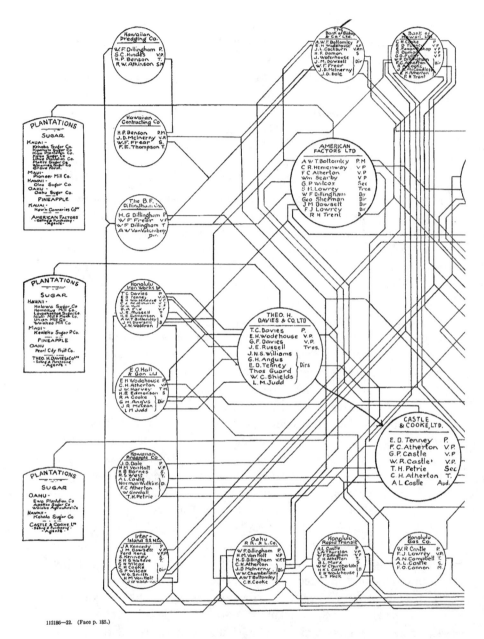

112186—32. (Face p. 185.)

FIGURE 7.2. Diagram showing interlocking directorates in Hawai'i, 1931. Source: U.S. Department of Justice (1932).

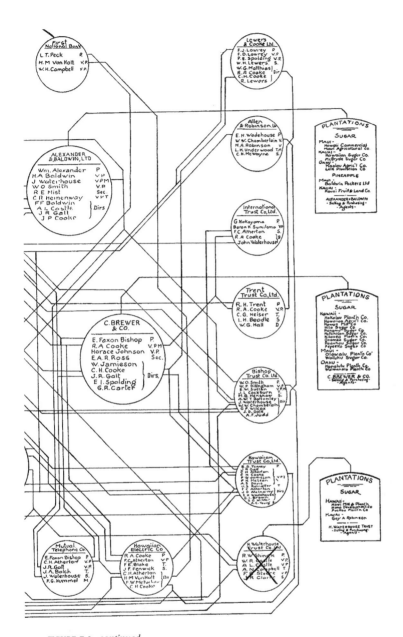

FIGURE 7.2. *continued*

Hawai'i's sugar industry in the 1890s gave way to more explicit vertical integration during the first three decades of territorial rule as agencies acquired more plantations to run directly. The trend toward vertical integration accelerated during the Great Depression, as many plantations owed significant sums to agencies and were forced to default on loans due to the low sugar prices of 1929–1933. The defaults allowed Big Five firms to become outright owners or controlling stockholders in more than 20 plantations.

Interlocking directorates—that is, boards of directors with overlapping membership from a common group of elites—fostered relationships among trust companies, the Big Five firms, and affiliated companies. They facilitated exchange of information among firms as well as coordination of their business and political activities. The 1932 Richardson report, compiled by the U.S. Department of Justice after an investigation of crime in Hawai'i, contains a Rube Goldberg–like diagram detailing the extent of interlocking directorates, which clearly shows the scope of these relationships (fig. 7.2).[30]

Vertical integration, interlocking directorates, and extensive lobbying in Washington, D.C., allowed the Big Five to dominate not just the sugar and pineapple sectors of the economy, but also shipping, retail, and finance. They worked with the territorial government to impose barriers to entry for rival firms. The Matson Navigation Company held a monopoly that made it difficult for other industries potentially competing for the use of Hawai'i resources to ship their exports. Property tax breaks awarded to agricultural firms in particular industries also served to reserve resources for the Big Five firms. As the Big Five consolidated their power, two other groups, the International Longshore and Warehouse Union and the U.S. military, were also consolidating their positions to claim economic rents generated by the colonial political order.

The Military and the Dominant Coalition

Economic historians Douglass North and John Wallis and political scientist Barry Weingast have argued that one of the hallmarks of an open-access order is that "consolidated organization of military and police forces is subject to control of the political system."[31] In territorial Hawai'i, this control would seem to be unquestioned, as the military was under the control of the U.S. president, the commander in chief. Never was there a doubt that the president controlled the military. However, in territorial Hawai'i, the military was also a key part of the dominant coalition that ruled the islands. After annexation, various U.S. military services built a network of army bases, airfields, and the large Pearl Harbor naval base, most of which were located on the densely populated island of O'ahu. With 45 percent of Hawai'i lands owned by the federal government, most land acquisition for the military came either via an order of the governor to reserve a tract of federal land or by purchases from large estates under the threat of eminent domain. It was always in the interest of the military to keep good relations with island residents as it expanded. Residents' voices in federal affairs were extremely limited, however, as they did not vote in U.S. presidential elections or send voting representatives to either the U.S. House or Senate, and this provided military leadership in Hawai'i with space to pay less attention to the views of the islands' people.

The place of the military in the dominant political coalition is best understood by the military's involvement in the infamous Massie rape case of 1931–1932.[32] Best known for the racial tensions that permeated it, it also exposed the attitudes of the U.S. military toward the territorial government. On September 12, 1931, Thalia Massie, a 20-year-old Caucasian woman who was the wife of a U.S. Navy submarine lieutenant based in Pearl Harbor, reported that she had been raped by six local young men. Their highly publicized trial ended with a hung jury, and the Massie family and their Navy friends decided to take matters into their own hands. After kidnapping, interrogating, and murdering Joseph Kahahawai—one of the six people acquitted—Thalia Massie's mother, Grace Fortescue, was arrested after a car chase when Kahahawai's body was discovered in the car's back seat. Indicted with three others for second-degree murder, Fortescue hired Clarence Darrow, perhaps the best-known criminal defense attorney in the United States. Darrow's bombastic efforts in the courtroom were initially not enough, as the jury convicted all four defendants on manslaughter charges, and the judge imposed a 10-year sentence on each defendant. Mainland newspapers featured the case, and almost all of them were intensely critical of the jury's verdict. Senators and representatives received an extraordinary volume of mail on the issue. Many called for the four to be pardoned. The U.S. secretary of the interior, responsible for many aspects of territorial affairs, sent a cable to Governor Lawrence M. Judd urging a pardon. The next day, after consulting with the heads of the Big Five corporations about a plan of action, Governor Judd commuted each sentence to one hour. Darrow would later comment that "it all came down to the unwritten law," a matter that some mainland newspapers labeled as "honorable lynching."

The reaction of some segments of the American public to the Massie case might have been expected given the barely thawed racial attitudes of the 1930s, but the response by the commanding admirals of the U.S. Navy in Honolulu was notable in two respects: their willingness to influence public opinion and incite violence in both cases, and their recommendations for changes in Hawai'i's criminal justice policies and its form of government. Prior to the first case, the commander of naval forces in Honolulu, Admiral Yates Stirling, Jr., intervened with the governor to demand that the defendants' bail be revoked, ending with the threat "that as long as the defendants were allowed to roam free 'there may be trouble . . . and there may be incidents.' "[33] A gang of sailors subsequently assaulted one of the defendants. Admiral Stirling and another leading naval official in Honolulu, Admiral Pettengill, severely exaggerated statistics on assault, rape, and other crime in Honolulu to Washington, D.C. Their reports led Admiral William Pratt, the chief of naval operations, to threaten to cancel a visit of the Pacific Fleet to Honolulu "unless justice is done at the coming retrial and the police and hoodlum conditions are thoroughly cleaned up by local authorities." Stirling and Pettengill's lurid portrayal of Honolulu as a city in which white women were targets of predatory gangs of young Hawaiian men became the source of headlines for weeks in the widely read Hearst-owned chain of U.S. newspapers.

In January 1932, the U.S. attorney general initiated an investigation into crime conditions in Hawai'i, and congressional hearings were held on a joint resolution to investigate the Hawaiian government.[34] The report of the attorney general's investigation, the Richardson report, was issued on April 4, 1932, and it refuted virtually all of the allegations of high crime rates by Honolulu's Navy brass, finding little reason for any change to Hawai'i's form of government.[35] A red flag in the exhibits attached to the report was a letter from Admiral Stirling, in which he pointed to Hawai'i's Asian population as a potential threat to the military if war broke out in the Pacific. To guard against the potential for violence and treason in the territory during wartime, the admiral recommended that Hawai'i's form of government be changed: that voting be limited to "men primarily of the Caucasian race," and that the appointed governor of the territory be replaced by a commission of officers from the army and navy, who would wield executive authority. If his recommendations had been accepted, Hawai'i would have had a government of, by, and for the U.S. military.

The Massie case is important for understanding how the territorial government actually worked, as it clearly demonstrates that military officers considered themselves to be important "players" in the coalition governing Hawai'i.[36] They had no respect for the autonomy of the territorial government, as they perceived it to be just another agency of the federal government in which departments competed for power and resources. The constitutional rights of U.S. citizens living in the territory were subordinate to the need for the U.S. Navy to create an "orderly" environment for its personnel.

Stirling's arguments stirred vigorous resistance from Governor Judd, the native Hawaiian community, and several prominent members of the business and political establishment. After the second trial's verdict and the commutation of the sentences, Judd insisted to Washington that Stirling be replaced with a new commander. A year later, the admiral was transferred.

Given the attitudes expressed in the Massie case, the U.S. military's overreaching conduct in Hawai'i during World War II was not surprising. The Massie case showed that the U.S. military viewed democratic institutions in U.S. territories as an impediment to military operations rather than as the foundation of an open-access society. Many in the military viewed the islands' Asian-American population as a potential threat during wartime. The Organic Act contained a provision (§67. Enforcement of law) allowing the governor to "call upon the commanders of the military and naval forces of the United States in the Territory of Hawaii . . . to prevent or suppress lawless violence, invasion, insurrection, or rebellion in said Territory" and "in case of rebellion or invasion . . . place the Territory, or any part thereof, under martial law until communication can be had with the President and his decision thereon made known."

The governor of Hawai'i, Joseph Poindexter, declared martial law on the day of Japan's attack on Pearl Harbor—December 7, 1941. President Roosevelt affirmed this action and Congress gave its consent. The military responded to the declaration of martial law by eliminating each and every provision of constitutional government. The territorial constitution was suspended. The legislature, the Hawai'i Supreme Court, and all lower state courts were dissolved indefinitely. The judge of the U.S. District Court in Hawai'i, Ingram Stainback, closed the court's offices and became a little-used advisor to the military governor, General Thomas H. Green. Governor Poindexter nominally remained in office but without any substantive duties or authority. All legal cases through October 1944 were tried in military tribunals, whether they were assaults, violations of price control regulations, or traffic tickets.

The appointment of Ingram Stainback as governor in July 1942 came after negotiations between the Department of the Interior and the Department of War to end military government in Hawai'i. Officially, there was a partial restoration of civilian authority in March 1943.[37] In fact, the restored civilian authorities were ignored by the military authorities, who continued their rule over every aspect of island life. When officers of the U.S. District Court tried to serve General Green with a subpoena, he ordered his men to keep the server away from him.

The March 1944 conviction of a worker ("Duncan") at the Pearl Harbor shipyard by a military ("provost") court led to the end of military rule. The worker petitioned in U.S. District Court for a writ of habeas corpus on the grounds that his trial and conviction in a military court were unlawful when civilian courts were operating. Judge Delbert Metzger granted his petition for habeas corpus[38] and concluded that martial law had been ended by the earlier executive orders restoring the civilian government. Metzger's decision was appealed, and with an appeals court decision imminent, President Roosevelt issued a proclamation on October 24, 1944, ending martial law and suspension of habeas corpus in Hawai'i. The Ninth Circuit ruled against Duncan, and he appealed to the U.S. Supreme Court. The Supreme Court would not rule in his case until long after the war ended. But in a 7–2 decision, the court ruled that the military's imposition of a military government far exceeded the federal government's authority and was inconsistent with the martial law provision in the Organic Act.[39]

A New Competitor for Coalition Rents: The ILWU

As it became more apparent that the United States was winning the war in the Pacific, the military began to face legal challenges to its control over labor markets from Hawai'i unions.[40] The initial labor lawsuit was quickly rebuffed by the U.S. federal court in Hawai'i, but it marked the first of a series of challenges by Hawai'i's labor unions to the three other interests composing Hawai'i's dominant coalition (the U.S. military, the Big Five, and native Hawaiians). The rise and exercise of union power in Hawai'i was part of a nationwide reaction by U.S. workers to the end of the federal government's wartime regulation of wages and employment. Hawai'i's wartime labor regulations differed somewhat from those on the U.S. mainland, as wages in Hawai'i were not capped but workers were restricted from quitting their jobs to take new ones.[41] In 1944, the military government in Hawai'i imposed a wage freeze, which remained in place until the end of the war in August 1945.

As controls on wages, employment, and union activity were gradually lifted in 1945, one union—the International Longshore and Warehouse Union (ILWU)—emerged as a competitor to the Big Five for rents generated by Hawai'i's sugar and pineapple industries. The ILWU organized three industry-wide strikes in the sugar industry (79 days in 1946), in the pineapple industry (5 days in 1947), and on the docks (177 days in 1949).[42] Previous industry-wide strikes in the sugar and pineapple industries had been crushed by the Big Five in 1909, 1921, and 1937. The ILWU's record in extracting concessions varied among the three postwar strikes, with big gains achieved in the sugar strike and almost nothing in the pineapple strike. More importantly, the well-organized and well-executed strikes showed that the ILWU had the power to impose losses on the Big Five and the federal and territorial governments unless its members were provided with a share of the economic rents distributed to the Big Five and their affiliated firms. Either the ILWU would be accommodated in the dominant coalition or industry rents would be totally consumed by conflict among the players. Both the ILWU's power and the limits of its power were laid bare by the lengthy longshoremen's strike in 1949. By the end of that strike, in November 1949, Hawai'i's unemployment rate had soared to 15 percent, businesses reliant on imports and exports were reeling, and the Hawaiian government had seized the territory's docks and started its own stevedoring operations to contain the damage to the overall economy.[43]

For the ILWU, the victory was a double-edged sword. While plantation workers received higher wages, employment in both pineapple and sugar industries would continue to drop over the next three decades, and the federal government would indict ILWU leaders for lying about their connections with the Communist Party. Perhaps most importantly, the ILWU's forced entry into the dominant coalition came just as the punchbowl was being taken away from the party. Hawai'i's transition to an open-access political order with statehood would happen just a decade later, and its hallmark was the dismantling of much of the political architecture that enabled a dominant coalition to exist and to distribute rents to groups like the ILWU.

Conclusion

One of the temptations when analyzing institutional change in Hawai'i is to view the colonial institutions of the territorial government as a prelude to the sovereign democratic institutions established in 1959 at statehood. In a very literal sense, they did provide a gateway to statehood.

But in concept and deed, they were institutions associated with a mature natural state in which the architecture of government was designed to distribute payoffs to important players in the dominant political coalition.[44] Both the overthrow of the monarchy and the new institutions of colonial government led to changes in the distribution of rents among coalition members, but in some other ways the mechanisms and structure of government changed very little. In the first decade of the monarchy, King Kamehameha put in place centralized institutions to monitor the chiefs, and Hawai'i's government remained very centralized throughout the nineteenth century, with decision making and administration focused on king and cabinet rather than the legislature. The colonial territorial government was also very centralized, with power concentrated in the executive in the persons of the governor and the U.S. president, and with the legislature again playing a somewhat limited role in determining the broad sweep of government policies. Even after 1959, when statehood dispersed power among different branches of the new state government, the elected governor retained more powers than most state governors.[45]

Such a long period of centralized government naturally raises the question of whether such centralization ultimately benefited Hawai'i's people. Were the centralized institutions effective in laying foundations for Hawai'i's future development, or were they simply adjusting and distributing flows of rents to various stakeholders to maintain social order and prevent rule by violence? Recent literature in economic history has a lot to say about this question for other states in the nineteenth and twentieth centuries. Consider first the study conducted by economic historian James Fenske examining African states that gained independence from Great Britain and France in the two decades after World War II.[46] Almost all had been governed by centralized colonial governments for 70–100 years, from their colonization in the mid- to late nineteenth century to their independence in the 1950s and 1960s. Fenske's study examines whether African states with centralized indigenous governments in the pre-colonial era did better or worse during the colonial era than other African states that had decentralized governments in the pre-colonial era. He concluded that "the states that existed in Africa before colonial rule continue to shape its modern development. . . . Pre-colonial state centralization is positively correlated with modern cross-country differences in school attainment, literacy, paved roads and immunizations. . . . It better predicts nighttime lights today than country-level institutional quality. . . . The few modern states in Africa that inherited the legitimacy of a pre-colonial predecessor have done better."[47]

The finding of roots of modern development in centralized government institutions prevalent 100–500 years ago is not confined to studies of
African countries. Economists Albert Banerjee and Lakshmi Iyer found
similar results for India.[48] Economists Louis Putterman and David Weil
extended this analysis to a much broader set of countries by examining
whether the ancestors of ethnic populations in each country migrated
from regions with centralized or decentralized governments. Their remarkable finding is that when the ancestors of a country's ethnic populations originated from places with centralized government institutions, the
country's twenty-first-century annual per capita output (GDP) tended to
be substantially higher.[49] The insight to take away from these studies is
that once an effective, centralized government is established, its institutions have a long-lasting influence, often covering several hundred years.

So does this analysis carry over to Hawai'i? Did the centralized monarchy established by King Kamehameha in the late eighteenth century
lay the foundation for growth in the statehood era by establishing government institutions with sufficient capacity to tax, specify and enforce
property rights, and adjudicate contract disputes? There are several indi-
cations that the answer to this question is a resounding "Yes." On the eve
of statehood, political scientist Norman Meller wrote that "Hawaii presents . . . an extreme of centralized administration probably unequalled in
any state on the mainland."[50] Meller argued that the Republic of Hawai'i
had tightened the already centralized rule under the monarchy, and that
its centralized institutions enabled the Caucasian corporate elite and the
Washington, D.C., government to retain control over the territorial government despite having the direct support of only a minority of Hawai'i
voters. Allowed wide discretion by Congress in determining the geographic scope and powers awarded to county and city governments, "the
Territory chose to continue the concentrated administration which had
characterized government throughout the century of independent rule."[51]

One source of continuity across the three governments of the 1890s—
kingdom, republic, and territory—was the transmission of the almost
complete corpus of statute and common laws across regimes. The 1900
Organic Act establishing the U.S. territorial government was very specific
on this matter, mandating "that the laws of Hawaii not inconsistent with
the Constitution or laws of the United States or the provisions of this Act
shall continue in force, subject to repeal or amendment by the legislature
of Hawaii or the Congress of the United States."[52] A second source of continuity was the centralization of strong executive authority in one office.

The monarch, president of the republic, and governor of the territory all had broad executive powers capable of much further extension during emergencies. Throughout the monarchy, there were few direct checks that voters could exercise to restrain the monarch. During the territorial era, Hawai'i voters also had few options available to restrain the power of the Hawai'i governor; the legislature had no power to impeach. Legislatures with relatively weak powers were a third source of continuity. Elections mattered somewhat in the kingdom because the king formed his cabinet and government from the elected representatives. Elections mattered in the territory because they had the potential to force adjustments in the distribution of rents flowing to the two main partners in the Republican political coalition. Native Hawaiians received their share of rents via patronage appointments, and the Big Five sugar agencies received their rents via regulatory protections that reduced entry by potential competitors and allowed them to collude on numerous matters.

Centralized government institutions were first established by King Kamehameha after his 1795 conquests, and government institutions remained centralized in Hawai'i in each of the kingdom, republic, and territorial governments. This continuity may well be the key to understanding how, for over 225 years, Hawai'i survived the difficult transitions from one leading industry to another and from one type of political order to another.

CHAPTER EIGHT

Homes for Hawaiians

Hawai'i reintegrated with the outside world in 1778, and this change led to 180 years of demographic, political, and social disasters for native Hawaiians. Their population fell by more than 90 percent, foreign missionaries and their churches relentlessly repressed Hawaiian culture,[1] and in 1893 a small group of rebels assisted by U.S. Marines overthrew the monarchy that had governed them with considerable success for nearly a century. Annexation by the United States in 1898 continued this long string of disasters, as the loss of sovereignty left native Hawaiians with deeply diminished influence over government policy and actions, reductions in their well-being after two decades of U.S. rule, and loss of the private lands of the deposed queen to the new foreign government.

Hawaiians had a very diminished role in government after the overthrow and after annexation. The Organic Act concentrated power in the office of the U.S. president, who appointed (and could remove at any time) the territorial governor and justices of the Supreme Court. An elected territorial legislature was granted limited powers, with majority approval by both houses required for new laws as well as spending and tax measures. During the first two decades of colonial rule, Hawaiians retained considerable influence in the legislature because they were a majority of the electorate. The cooperation of Hawaiian legislators and their allies was necessary for legislation to pass, and this forced territorial governors to provide Hawaiians with a share of the pool of economic rents distributed to members of the territory's dominant coalition.

The government provided rents to Hawaiians by making a substantial share of patronage appointments to Hawaiian white-collar professionals. The gains to one group of Hawaiians could not, however, hide the broad-sweeping decline in Hawaiian well-being that occurred during the first two decades of U.S. colonial rule. By 1910, Hawaiians had recognized what was happening to them, and they began to organize more effectively to address the trend during the 1910s. They demanded that the territorial and U.S. federal governments take action to address their situation by returning some of the best government lands to Hawaiian use and ownership. In 1921, the U.S. Congress responded by passing the Hawaiian Homes Commission Act (HHCA). Its official goal was to return Native Hawaiians to the land, thereby facilitating the "rehabilitation" of the Hawaiian race.[2] The HHCA designated 203,500 acres of government land and directed the Hawaiian Homes Commission (HHC) to lease it for $1 per year to Native Hawaiians for use as ranches and farms. In 1923, the HHCA was quickly amended to expand the scope of the Hawaiian Homes program, changing its focus from returning people to the land as farmers and ranchers to providing improved residential lots with a 99-year lease.

Persistent and deep administrative scandals and failures have periodically eroded Hawaiians' confidence in the program's ability to fulfill its goals and to treat beneficiaries fairly. In 1930, the federal government took desirable homestead lands at Lualualei, O'ahu, for military use and continues to use them.[3] Long waiting lists for residential leases appeared in the 1940s and have persisted into the twenty-first century. During the 1950s, the HHC lost the list of Native Hawaiians waiting for homesteads, and then did it again in the 1980s. Numerous federal and state government reports and audits, as well as a series of investigative articles published by the *Honolulu Star Advertiser* since 2012, have exhaustively documented a litany of problems with the program, including poor administration, accounting problems, inadequate maintenance of facilities and infrastructure, vacant and run-down properties, unresolved lawsuits over the lost waiting lists, favoritism to political insiders, and delinquent loans to homesteaders. By 2012, the HHC had awarded just 32,713 of its 203,500 acres to just 5,778 Native Hawaiians. Perhaps most troubling were the well-documented findings that both federal and state governments had repeatedly and egregiously violated trust obligations to the Native Hawaiian people established by the HHCA. If the program were to be evaluated by the act's sweeping goal of rehabilitating the Hawaiian race, or even by the less lofty goal of allotting and managing its lands wisely, it would clearly be judged a resounding failure.

This chapter's discussion of the history of the Hawaiian Homes program focuses on two central questions: Why were Hawaiians burdened with such a poorly designed program? And why has the program performed so poorly for so long without major reforms in its basic design and administration? In 1920, native Hawaiians were almost 50 percent of the voting population in Hawai'i. One might expect that Hawaiians would have been able to strike a deal during the 1910s and 1920s because of Hawai'i's history of rewarding vital players in the ruling coalition. One of the essential elements of the monarchy in the early to mid-nineteenth century was its willingness to reorganize property rights in land to cement a ruling coalition. In fact, the ruling chiefs of Hawai'i's archaic states, the first three Mō'ī of the Hawaiian Kingdom, and the president of the Republic of Hawai'i (1893–1898) had all redistributed rights to land. The land redistribution carried out by the Hawaiian Homes program was, however, structured differently from previous ones, as it happened within a colonial institutional environment. I find that the poor design of the program was an extension of the U.S. government's general policy of treating first peoples as dependent peoples, unable to manage their own affairs.[4] It was also a consequence of political infighting between different Hawaiian groups and between Hawaiians and the Big Five firms, which wanted to continue to lease rich agricultural lands owned by the government for sugar production.[5]

Why has the poor performance of the Hawaiian Homes program persisted for almost a century? One reason is that the act's designation of low-quality agricultural lands for the program ensured that Hawaiian homesteaders engaged in ranching and farming would *always* struggle to prosper and that the asset base provided to the program would *always* be insufficient to provide substantial benefits to eligible native Hawaiians. A second reason is that the attenuated property rights in land assigned to native Hawaiian homesteaders substantially reduced the value of the properties being allocated. Program restrictions on the ability to sell leases, to sublet, to mortgage the leases, and to bequeath them to close relatives all reduced the value of Hawaiian Homes program lands. The lower value of the lands reduced incentives for all parties to manage them efficiently. A third reason is the decline in the voting power of native Hawaiians between 1920 and 1960. As the share of Hawaiians in the electorate declined, appropriations for the Hawaiian Homes program as a share of Hawaiian government expenditures also declined. A fourth reason is the poor design of the administrative structure. My argument is that bureaucrats inside the agency and within the broader territorial and state governments had explicit incentives to limit the distribution of lands to native Hawaiians.[6]

My overall conclusion is that the program was never capable of functioning well. Incorporating the program's essential components into the 1959 state constitution helped to solidify Native Hawaiian claims to these lands, but also cemented in place a dysfunctional system of land rights and program administration. A silver lining and a ray of light for the future is that the dedication of these lands to the program has preserved them for future, and perhaps more efficient, use by Native Hawaiians.

Demographic, Political, and Economic Change before and after Annexation

Drastic population decline was one of two key factors driving the *Māhele*, the massive mid-nineteenth-century reorganization of property rights in land. The first accurate census, in January 1850, revealed a drastically diminished full-Hawaiian population of 82,035 and a part-Hawaiian population of 558 that stood in stark contrast to the 400,000 or more Hawaiians living in 1778. The horrific population decline did not, however, end at mid-century, but continued into the early twentieth century. Over the 51 years from the 1849 census to the 1900 territorial census, the resident Hawaiian population continued to decline precipitously, falling to 29,799 full-Hawaiians and 9,857 part-Hawaiians.

As discussed in chapters 4 and 5, I follow other scholars in concluding that the big decline in the Hawaiian population in the early and mid-nineteenth century had wide-ranging effects, transforming Hawai'i's economy, polity, and society. Many of these changes were triggered by the reduced demand for food from the much smaller population. A fall in overall demand for food meant less demand for agricultural lands controlled by *ali'i* and managed by *konohiki*. After 1820, the effect on chiefs' lands and income was magnified by growing urbanization as commoners migrated to three villages (Honolulu on O'ahu, Lahaina on Maui, and Hilo on Hawai'i). The integration of Hawai'i's economy with the world economy in the early to mid-nineteenth century presented an opportunity for *ali'i* to restore the value of their lands by developing them to produce cane sugar. Chapter 5 recounts how a reorganization of property rights in land facilitated conversion of lands owned by crown, government and *ali'i* to sugar production.

A massive influx of migrants in the last third of the nineteenth century

TABLE 8.1. **Hawai'i's Population by Ethnicity**

Ethnic group	1778	1853	1900	1920
Hawaiian	400,000	70,036	29,799	23,723
Part-Hawaiian	0	983	7,857	18,027
Caucasian	0	1,600	10,547	27,740
Japanese	0	0	61,111	109,274
Chinese	0	364	25,767	23,507
Portuguese	0	87	18,272	27,002
Filipino	0	0	0	21,031
Other	0	67	648	5,608
Total population	400,000	73,137	154,001	255,912

Source: Hawaiian population in 1778 is from chapter 4. See Stannard (1989) for additional estimates of Hawai'i's population in 1778. All other data are from Nordyke (1989).

combined with the decreasing native Hawaiian population to disrupt political and economic conditions for Hawaiians. Beginning in 1865, the Hawaiian government and the sugar industry cooperated to bring Chinese, Japanese, Portuguese, Filipino, Korean, and other workers to Hawai'i to labor on the sugar plantations.[7] Combined with a falling Hawaiian population, these big migration flows rapidly reduced the proportion of full- and part-Hawaiians in the total population from 97.1 percent in 1853 to 24.5 percent in 1900 and to 16.3 percent in 1920. Beginning with annexation, U.S. immigration laws restricted Chinese and Japanese workers from entering Hawai'i, prompting the sugar industry to substitute Filipino immigrants. Table 8.1 provides data on the changing ethnic composition of Hawai'i's population.

The flood of foreign workers also rapidly changed the ethnic composition of the sugar plantation workforce. In 1882, 25 of every 100 plantation employees was Hawaiian. By 1900, only 3 of every 100 plantation workers was Hawaiian.[8] Most Hawaiians were dissatisfied with the coercive and strenuous work environment offered by plantations, and many migrated to Honolulu, Hawai'i's largest city, in search of better work opportunities. Table 8.2 presents data from the U.S. census on the occupations of Hawaiians in 1900. Over 33 percent were employed as "unspecified" laborers in a variety of fields, 14.6 percent had their own farms or were overseers on sugar plantations, 10.5 percent worked in agriculture, 5.4 percent worked as fishermen, 4 percent as carpenters, and another 9.6 percent in other manufacturing activities. The remaining 22.8 percent of the workforce was scattered across a wide variety of professional, government, and trade occupations.

Hawaiians were neither the first nor the last workers to escape grinding plantation labor for a more independent existence in growing towns and cities. Chinese workers started to leave the plantations in the early 1880s and successfully established small businesses and rice farms. After 1900, many Japanese field workers also began to leave the plantations after their contracts were voided at annexation. In 1900, the Japanese constituted just 15.7 percent of Honolulu's population, but by 1910, their share had soared to 30 percent.[9] The increased competition with Japanese and Chinese immigrants for jobs and the continued exodus of Hawaiians to urban areas are both reflected in the 1920 census data on occupations of Hawaiian males (see table 8.2). Hawaiians with their own farms or working as

TABLE 8.2. **Selected Occupations of Hawaiians and Part-Hawaiians in 1900 and 1920**

	1900		1920	
Occupation	Number employed	% of total	Number employed	% of total
Agriculture, forestry, animal husbandry:				
Agricultural laborers	784	7.29	2,105	17.39
Farmers, planters, overseers	1,573	14.62	360	2.97
Fishermen	582	5.41	333	2.75
Other agricultural	340	3.16	353	2.92
Professional service:				
Teachers	132	1.23	431	3.56
Lawyers	85	0.79	46	0.38
Other professional service	141	1.31	312	2.58
Public service:				
Watchmen, policemen, and firemen	268	2.49	299	2.47
Government officials	78	0.73	179	1.48
All other public service			466	3.85
Domestic and personal service:				
Laborers, domestic and personal service	3,574	33.22	19	0.16
Servants	148	1.38	204	1.69
Other domestic and personal service	273	2.54	217	1.79
Clerks and copyists	290	2.70	630	5.21
Trade and transportation:				
Boatmen, sailors	244	2.27	236	1.95
Draymen, teamsters, and longshoremen	398	3.70	885	7.31
Laborers, trade and transportation			1,178	9.73
Other trade and transportation	390	3.63	1,236	10.21
Manufacturing:				
Carpenters and joiners	433	4.02	337	2.78
Laborers, manufacturing			703	5.81
Painters	172	1.60	160	1.32
Machinists	21	0.20	183	1.51
Engineers, cranemen, hoistmen			203	1.68
Other manufacturing	832	7.73	1,004	8.30
Mining	0	0.00	23	0.19
Total	10,758	100.00	12,102	100.00

Source: Data for 1920 are from U.S. Bureau of the Census (1923a, 1923b). Data for 1900 are from Twelfth U.S. Census as reported in U.S. Commissioner of Labor (1903, 84–86).

overseers declined from 14.6 percent of the workforce in 1900 to 3 percent
in 1920. Farm laborers expanded from 7.3 percent of the workforce in
1900 to 15.2 percent in 1920. This indicates that Hawaiian farmers sold
their land, with many continuing to work as farm laborers and others moving to urban areas. In 1890, approximately 7.7 percent of male Hawaiian
workers were fishermen, and 79 percent of all fisherman were Hawaiian.[10]
Increasing competition from Japanese fishermen reduced the percentage
of Hawaiians working as fishermen from 5.4 percent in 1900 to 2.8 percent
in 1920. Only 26 percent of all fisherman were Hawaiian in 1920.[11] In 1880,
nearly all longshoremen were Hawaiian. During the 1880s, they began to
be gradually replaced by Chinese workers whose contracts on the sugar
plantations had expired. By 1920, only 49.9 percent of the dock workforce
was Hawaiian.[12] Hawaiians working as clerks increased from 2.7 percent
of the labor force in 1900 to 5.2 percent in 1920, indicating a movement
from blue-collar jobs to low-status white-collar jobs.

The 1920 census also reveals that secondary school enrollment of Hawaiians lagged behind that of other ethnic groups. Among children aged
16–17 living in Honolulu in 1920, 56.5 percent of Japanese, 57.3 percent
of Chinese, 63.8 percent of Caucasians, and 51 percent of Hawaiians were
enrolled in school.[13] Adult male labor force participation rates also lagged
behind those of other groups. In 1920, 78.8 percent of full-Hawaiian males,
60.5 percent of part-Hawaiian males, 85.6 percent of Japanese males, 82.5
percent of Chinese males, and 80.3 percent of Caucasian males participated in the labor force.[14] Adult female labor participation rates were also
lower for full-Hawaiians (7.7 percent) and part-Hawaiians (13.7 percent)
than the general population (20.1 percent).

After 140 years of Western contact, the economic, political, cultural,
and demographic conditions of Hawaiians had severely deteriorated. The
Hawaiian population was drastically diminished; the independence of the
Hawaiian Kingdom had been lost; public expressions of native Hawaiian
culture, including the teaching of the Hawaiian language in schools and its
use in public life, were repressed; Hawaiians had sold, lost, or abandoned
most of their lands; increasing competition from Chinese and Japanese immigrants was reducing the relative economic position of Hawaiians; and
Hawaiians were lagging behind other groups in educational attainment,
providing a worrisome signal that their situation was unlikely to improve
in the near future. A temporary salvation would emerge, however, due to
Hawaiian participation in the dominant coalition. Their rising demands for
a bigger share of the rents created by the coalition set in motion a search

for new government policies to halt their deteriorating circumstances, a demand for return of valuable lands from the territorial government, and a debate over the right paths to political, cultural, and economic renewal.

Origins of the Hawaiian Home Lands Program

The economic impact of World War I on the native Hawaiian population was the trigger that motivated Hawaiians to become more politically active. The general price inflation of World War I was coupled with particularly high price increases for such Hawaiian staples as poi (made from the taro plant) and fish. Consider that "in 1914 the selling price of a 100-pound bag of taro from the farmer to the poi mill was $1.25 . . . in the early part of 1918, it was $2.05."[15] Disruptions in shipping during the war and meat rationing combined to increase the price of fish "by almost 100 percent. For example, fish that normally had sold for 20 cents a pound sold for 35 to 40 cents a pound."[16] Hawaiians complained about the higher prices and noted that poi was now grown by Chinese farmers, processed in Chinese poi mills, and distributed by Chinese and Japanese trade networks.

Declining economic circumstances were coupled with problematic demographic dynamics. The crude birth rate for full-Hawaiians (29.16 per 1,000) was much lower than the rate for all groups (34.76 per 1,000), and the crude death rate for full-Hawaiians (39.42 per 1,000) was 157 percent higher than the rate for all other groups (15.36 per 1,000).[17] Local Hawaiian civic clubs bemoaned the concentration of the dwindling Hawaiian population in crowded urban tenements, blamed high and rising Hawaiian death rates on this urban crowding, and began to formulate plans for the rehabilitation of the Hawaiian race.[18]

The Hawaiian studies scholar Davianna McGregor identified the November 1914 formation of the Hawaiian Protective Association as the signal event triggering political and social activities by Hawaiians on behalf of the Hawaiian race.[19] The association published a newspaper, engaged in social and educational work in the community, and was active in a 1918 campaign against run-down tenement housing. Public discussion among Hawaiians of their changed economic circumstances intensified. In 1918, Princess Abigail Kawānanakoa, the heir to the Hawaiian throne[20] and a prominent figure in the Hawaiian community, toured farm districts in the midwestern United States to gather information about U.S. wartime programs that moved urban workers to farms that had suddenly lost their labor force to the army. Upon her return to Hawai'i, she urged Hawaiians to return to agricultural occupations and enterprises to avoid the ills of urban crowding.[21] The Hawaiian Protective Association drafted a resolution urging that Hawaiians be allowed to homestead government lands when leases of those lands to sugar companies expired. The association's leaders presented their resolution to John Wise, an influential member of the Hawaiian community and Republican member of the territorial senate, and urged him to spearhead a response.

In December 1918, Wise announced a plan for rehabilitation that focused on reforming Hawai'i's existing homesteading law.[22] That existing law, the Land Act of 1895, was designed to attract white farmers from the U.S. mainland to farm in Hawai'i and establish a white, middle-class electorate. The Land Act provided several mechanisms for potential homesteaders to claim public land for farming, including one that provided for a 999-year lease that could be transferred only to the lessee's descendants. Between 1895 and 1908, nearly 5,000 homestead lots were claimed, with Hawaiians receiving about 30 percent of the 84,484 acres taken up, but only about 17 percent of the value of these lands.[23] The public lands used for the program were, however, ones that had not been leased by the sugar companies, a strong signal of their marginal quality or lack of access to roads or markets.

Wise's plan for a new homesteading program for Hawaiians was centered on a provision of the Organic Act, adopted via amendment in 1910, requiring that upon petition of 25 qualified individuals, agricultural lands be opened to homesteading if they were unoccupied or leased subject to a notice of withdrawal.[24] Some leases of government-owned sugarcane lands had expired during World War I, but the Woodrow Wilson administration ordered that these lands not be taken out of cane production or released for homesteading while the war continued.[25] Other leases were scheduled to expire over the next few years. Wise introduced a resolution in the territorial senate (H.C.R. 2) asking the U.S. Congress to open 80 percent of the government's sugarcane lands for homesteading and to reserve a portion for native Hawaiian homesteaders. The territorial legislature endorsed H.C.R. 2 in April 1919.

The legislature also passed a parallel resolution, H.C.R. 28, that urged Congress to adopt *exactly the opposite policy*, to amend federal law to keep leased lands in the hands of Hawai'i's sugar interests. In February 1920, Congress held extensive hearings on the lease of federal lands in Hawai'i.[26] After the hearings, the two contradictory resolutions—H.C.R. 2

and H.C.R. 28—were merged into a single bill, H.R. 12683. Prince Jonah Kūhiō Kalanianaʻole, Hawaiʻiʻs nonvoting delegate to the U.S. House of Representatives, was its sponsor.

The new bill was massively tilted toward the Big Fiveʻs interests. It specified that Congress would retain the power to decide whether to release the sugarcane lands for homesteading or to continue to lease them at auction. Given the network of contributions by the sugar industry to Congress, the new law ensured that they would be allowed to renew their leases on government-owned sugarcane lands. Only second-class agricultural lands would be opened for Hawaiian homesteading. To put this more bluntly, only federal lands that sugar and pineapple corporations had previously judged to be unprofitable to farm would be opened to Hawaiian homesteaders to farm. To make this dismal deal more attractive to the Hawaiian community, the bill provided for a $1 million fund to finance development of these unproductive lands.[27] Rental payments to the territory on government-owned sugarcane lands and territorial receipts from annual water licenses would be dedicated to the new Hawaiian Homes Loan Fund. All individuals with any Hawaiian ancestry would be eligible to be homesteaders, and leases on the lands assigned to Hawaiian homesteaders would last 999 years.

The territorial legislature formed a group of legislators (the Territorial Legislative Commission) to lobby for the new bill in Washington, D.C., but after the commission returned to Hawaiʻi in March 1920, Hawaiian groups, island newspapers, and the Hawaiʻi Chamber of Commerce all voiced opposition to some provisions of H.R. 12683. After discussions among the various parties and deliberations by the U.S. House Committee on Territories, a new, substantially changed bill (H.R. 13500) was introduced. Important changes included restricting access to land to individuals who were at least 1/32 Hawaiian; shortening the duration of leases from 999 to 99 years; specifying the particular tracts of lands to be placed under control of the program; and transferring from Congress to the territorial administration the right to decide whether to continue to lease government sugarcane lands or to open them to homesteading. The revamped bill passed the House in May 1920, but the Senate failed to act on it during either the 1920 or 1921 sessions of the sixty-sixth Congress.

After the failure of H.R. 13500, Delegate Kūhiō returned to Hawaiʻi to try to fashion a bill capable of congressional passage. After extensive discussions, the territorial legislature passed new resolutions endorsing amendments to H.R. 13500. The U.S. House and Senate passed the new bill (S. 1881) in June 1921, and President Harding signed it into law on July 9, 1921.

The Hawaiian Homes Commission Act

Hawaiian leaders had originally proposed a government program that would rehabilitate Hawaiians by returning them to agricultural work on their own small sugarcane farms. The final Hawaiian Homes Commission Act retained some of the original proposal's form, but little of its substance. None of the high-quality lands leased to sugar plantations were opened to homesteading. Instead, the act designated about 203,500 acres of very marginal public lands (approximately 5 percent of the islands' total acreage) as "Hawaiian home lands" and transferred their control to the newly created Hawaiian Homes Commission (HHC). The commission consisted of the governor and four of his appointees. The HHC could lease lands as homesteads to Native Hawaiians for a term of 99 years; HHC lands that were not leased as homesteads had to be returned to the territorial land commissioner. Homesteaders could obtain 20–80 acres of agricultural land, 100–500 acres of first-class pastoral land, or 250–1,000 acres of second-class pastoral land. The annual rent on leases, regardless of acreage, was one dollar, and there was a moratorium on county property tax payments for five years. Lessees were required to occupy and to use or cultivate the site within one year after the lease was made and to continue to cultivate or use it. The HHC could terminate the lease if this provision was violated. Within any five-year period, the HHC could open no more than 20,000 acres for settlement.

Only Native Hawaiians—that is, persons with at least 50 percent "blood quantum"—were eligible for a homestead lease. Upon the death of a lessee, the lease passed to statutorily specified relatives only if they, too, satisfied the blood quantum requirement. A lessee was allowed to transfer or mortgage the lease only with the permission of the HHC and only to Native Hawaiians who satisfied the blood quantum requirement. Subletting of any kind was strictly prohibited.

The HHCA prohibited lessees from applying for loans under the 1919 Farm Loan Act of Hawaii, which provided loans to other small Hawai'i farmers. Combined with the prohibition on mortgaging leased land to a non-Hawaiian, the HHCA's provisions effectively cut off homesteaders from most private and governmental sources of capital. This meant that the only source of capital for homesteaders, beyond personal savings and unsecured personal loans, was the Hawaiian Homes Loan Fund, which was authorized to loan up to $3,000 per homesteader. For all intents and purposes, the Hawaiian Homes Commission was set up as a monopoly supplier of capital to homesteaders.

The Hawaiian Homes Loan Fund was initially used to pay the commission's operating and capital costs as well as to make loans to homesteaders. All revenues from the leasing of public lands "made available" as Hawaiian home lands and 30 percent of the revenues from the leasing of territorial sugarcane lands and receipts from water licenses were to be accumulated in the fund until it reached $1,000,000. The legislature periodically increased the funding cap until it finally abolished the cap in 1959.[28]

From Agricultural Homesteads to Public Housing

The HHC moved quickly to prepare the first settlement, on Moloka'i. By February 1923, 13 settlers had assumed leases at the Kalanianaole Settlement, and by August 1924, the settlement had 278 residents.[29] While the settlement's experiment with diversified farming was initially successful, the lack of irrigation water induced many settlers to abandon their farm lands. A second settlement, on the Ho'olehua Plain on Moloka'i, was leased in October 1924, and the settlers there continued to experiment with diversified farming. In 1926, the HHC allowed homesteaders to sublet their lands to the pineapple grower Libby, McNeil and Libby, despite the HHCA's ban on such arrangements. The contracts with pineapple companies paid land rents to the Native Hawaiian settlers, but did not use their labor. The HHCA's goal of rehabilitating Native Hawaiians by encouraging their labor on homestead lands had been quickly abandoned. The acreage in pineapple cultivation expanded over the next few years and stabilized in the 1930s. Moloka'i's pineapple operations continued for four decades but begin to close in the 1970s. The last company left in 1988.

Given the mixed results of the initial agricultural settlements on Moloka'i, HHC officials quickly petitioned Congress to allow the program to provide applicants with improved house lots and mortgage loans in Hawaiian Home Lands (HHL) residential subdivisions. In 1923, Congress passed legislation amending the HHCA to enable Native Hawaiians to lease half-acre house lots. The limited success of diversified agriculture, the realization that other assigned lands were also likely to be marginal agricultural investments, and the demand by the highly urbanized Hawaiian population on O'ahu for house lots induced the HHC to expand its goals to developing Hawaiian residential areas.[30] While the program still relocated Hawaiians from crowded urban tenements, the rehabilitative work component of the program was discarded. The HHL program had been deftly transformed from a program emphasizing the value of labor on small family farms into a housing program that provided free house lots and neighborhood infrastructure to Hawaiian families willing to build a home and wanting to live in an exclusively Hawaiian community.

The goal of the new housing program was to provide improved residential lots of less than a half acre along with loans to build homes on the lots at below-market rates. The first house lot development was on the island of Hawai'i in the South Hilo area (Pana'ewa and Keaukaha in Waiākea). By 1927, it contained 158 improved lots. In 1928, Congress extended the HHCA from the islands of Moloka'i and Hawai'i to the islands of O'ahu, Maui, and Kaua'i. The popularity of the South Hilo development prompted the HHC to open a second residential settlement at Nānākuli, O'ahu, in 1930. Settlements followed at Kawaihae, Hawai'i (1936); Kewalo and Papakōlea, O'ahu (1937); Waimānalo, O'ahu (1938); Anahola, Kaua'i (1957); Kekaha, Kaua'i (1958); Paukukalo, Maui (1959); Kapa'akea, Moloka'i; Wai'anae, O'ahu (1971); Kuhio Village, Hawai'i (1971); Lualualei, O'ahu (1985); Kula and Waiehui, Maui (1986); and Waiākea, Hawai'i (1989). Settlement locations are shown in figure 8.1. After the disastrous experience with diversified farming on Moloka'i, only the HHC settlement at Waimea, Hawai'i, was developed with farming and grazing lots.[31]

The Hawaii Admission Act, passed by the U.S. Congress to admit Hawai'i as a U.S. state in 1959, contained specific provisions regarding the Hawaiian Homes program. It required that the 1921 Hawaiian Homes Commission Act be made a part of the Hawai'i state constitution, and it mandated the inclusion of a provision in the state constitution establishing a trust relationship between the federal government and the state for the program.[32] The Admission Act granted administrative control of the program to the state, but Congress retained the power to approve all amendments to the HHCA. Hawai'i's 1978 constitutional convention amended the act (as embodied in the constitution) to make changes in the program's administration and in some substantive requirements. Congress approved the changes eight years later, in 1986. The most important amendment allowed homesteaders to leave their homesteads to Hawaiians with at least one-fourth Hawaiian "blood quantum" and required the HHC to give preference to Native Hawaiians when leasing unassigned lands.[33]

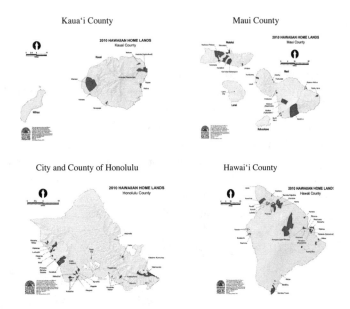

Kaua'i County   Maui County

City and County of Honolulu   Hawai'i County

FIGURE 8.1. Location of Hawaiian Home Lands settlements. Source: Office of Planning, City & County of Honolulu.

The HHL housing program has been characterized by excess demand for house lots since it was started in the 1920s. The HHC compiled long waiting lists for various projects, and many applicants were never awarded a lease. Several times in the postwar period, the HHC lost its waiting list, and Hawaiians frequently charged the HHC with irregularities concerning the allocation of lands. In 1991, the legislature established the Individual Claims Review Panel to receive and review applications from persons who were harmed by mismanagement of the program from 1959 to 1988. The state disbanded the claims panel in 1999. Hawaiian beneficiaries filed suit against the state in the same year, and the case was resolved in their favor in 2009.[34] The state and the beneficiaries were unable to resolve claims regarding damages. A trial to determine damages was finally held in October 2014. Final judgment for a subclass of plaintiffs was entered on January 9, 2018; the state of Hawai'i then appealed the final judgment, contending that it did not breach trust obligations. Thus, more than 27 years after the Individual Claims Review Panel was established, none of the beneficiaries on the lost waiting list had received either land or money compensation from the state of Hawai'i.

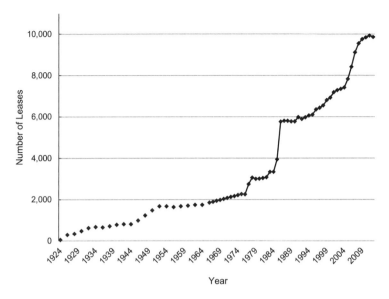

FIGURE 8.2. Number of Department of Hawaiian Home Lands leases, 1924–2012. Source: DHHL Annual Reports.

Beginning in the 1970s, Hawaiians lobbied and litigated to have the federal government act in its capacity as trustee for the Hawaiian Homes program, and federal court decisions agreed that the federal government had a trust responsibility for the program.[35] In 1982, a joint federal-state task force was established to investigate allegations of mismanagement and trust violations. The task force's 1983 report substantiated many of the allegations, made recommendations for reform, and suggested that the HHC end its policy of distributing land only after it had been improved sufficiently to meet county zoning and building codes.[36] The HHC responded by increasing the number of leases from 3,332 in 1984 to 5,803 in 1987 (fig. 8.2). Many of the new leases in the mid-1980s were granted in areas without any infrastructure to support housing.

During the 1990s, Hawai'i's economy went through a deep recession. Over the course of the decade—known as the "lost decade"—the inflation-adjusted value of Hawai'i's output (real GDP) decreased by 0.2 percent annually.[37] While the 1990s were a lost decade for the state's economy, they saw several steps forward for the Hawaiian Homes program. Total leases grew substantially, from 5,778 in 1990 to 7,292 in 2002; the HHC recovered part of its land base; and it reached a settlement regarding past breaches of the trust by the territory and state. The process of land recovery started in the 1980s when the Department of Hawaiian Home Lands (DHHL) began to reclaim certain trust lands that had been illegally set aside by executive orders and proclamations for purposes not benefiting the trust. In October 1994, the state corrected many of these past wrongs by signing over 16,518 acres of land to the Hawaiian Home Lands Trust. Enactment of the Hawaiian Home Lands Recovery Act in 1995 established procedures for the federal government to return lands of equivalent value to replace ones that it had taken earlier. These state and federal actions brought the HHL trust up to 203,500 acres, the amount specified by the HHCA. In 1995, the state of Hawai'i agreed to pay $30 million per year for 20 years to the Hawaiian Home Lands Trust to settle past breaches of the trust. All payments to the trust were completed in 2016.

By the early twenty-first century, the Hawai'i economy was entering a boom period. Real GDP growth averaged 3.0 percent annually from 2000 to 2007, and state tax revenues surged. In 2002, Linda Lingle was elected as the first Republican governor in 40 years, and her first term saw a renewed commitment to the HHL program, as DHHL expenditures and leases awarded both increased. The Lingle administration's policies were shaken by the Great Recession (2007–2009), which dragged Hawai'i real GDP growth down to 0.5 percent in 2008 and −3.6 percent in 2009. State tax revenues fell, and legislative support for DHHL programs evaporated. The legislative appropriation for DHHL operating and administrative expenses was $900,000 for the 2008 fiscal year and $0 for the 2009–2012 fiscal years. The Hawaiian Homes Commission responded by filing suit against the state of Hawai'i, arguing that the Hawai'i state constitution required a minimum appropriation. In 2012, the Hawai'i Supreme Court ruled that the minimum legislative appropriation for DHHL operating and administrative expenses is a judiciable question.[38] The legislature responded to this ruling in May 2013 by appropriating $9.1 million to DHHL for the 2014 fiscal year. A November 2015 district court ruling ordered the legislature to appropriate at least $28 million to DHHL for operating and administrative expenses for the 2017 fiscal year.[39] In May 2016, following the recommendation of Governor David Ige, the legislature appropriated $23.9 million to DHHL for the 2017 fiscal year. In February 2018, the Hawai'i Supreme Court overturned the district court's finding regarding the minimum appropriation for DHHL operating and administrative expenses, ruling that it was limited to $1.6 million (an amount discussed at the 1978 constitutional convention), adjusted for inflation; using the

Honolulu Consumer Price Index, the inflation-adjusted minimum appropriation for 2017 would be $3.94 million.[40]

How did the reduced support by the state during and after the Great Recession affect awards of new leases by DHHL? The number of new leases awarded increased slowly, with the total (residential, farm, and pastoral) increasing from 9,539 leases in June 2008 to 9,838 leases in June 2014.[41] The next section tries to makes sense of DHHL decisions regarding lease allocation by identifying how important political and economic factors could affect these decisions.

Understanding the Bureaucratic and Political Underpinnings of the HHL Program

Politicians and bureaucrats make decisions regarding DHHL funding and new HHL leases. So what factors guide the decisions of politicians and bureaucrats? In earlier research on the HHL program, I developed a simple model of Hawaiian Homes Commission decision making that abstracts from layers of complex relationships in the DHHL and the HHC by assuming that the commissioners for the HHC, who are appointed by the governor, act as the governor's agents.[42] In the model, the HHC commissioners make decisions designed to maximize the sum of votes for the governor from Hawaiians and non-Hawaiians.[43] Both Hawaiian and non-Hawaiian voters are more likely to vote for the governor when they face lower tax rates and are provided with more government services. In the model, I assume that non-Hawaiian voters do not value expenditures on the HHL program, while Hawaiians value the allotment of more Hawaiian Homes program lands to Hawaiian lessees and higher HHL program expenditures.[44]

I use the model to examine how decision making by the governor and his agents on the commission changes when the program's political support and the cost of providing program services change. One important question is how the government's choice of land leases and HHL program expenditures changes as the share of Hawaiian voters in the electorate increases. The model shows that the government issues more land leases and increases HHL program expenditures, essentially because a vote-maximizing government is willing to devote more resources to programs benefiting Hawaiians exclusively as they become a larger share of the electorate.

A second important question is how government choice of land leases and HHL program expenditures changes when the market rent on undispersed HHL lands increases. For both of these choices, the answer depends on two factors that have offsetting effects on votes: rent control on HHL residential leases and lost commercial lease revenues. Rent control on HHL residential parcels—leases are capped at $1 per year—increases Hawaiian demand for HHL parcels when market rents increase because the surplus to a lessee from obtaining a land parcel increases. This higher demand provides incentives for vote-maximizing HHC commissioners to release more parcels to Hawaiians on the waiting list and to support additional expenditures to provide complementary infrastructure. When DHHL releases lands for use by new lessees, it also loses revenue from commercial leases on those lands, pushing down DHHL expenditures on programs. This loses votes from Hawaiian voters who receive program benefits unless revenues from the state's general fund are transferred to the program to offset the revenue loss. However, transfers from the general fund reduce spending on programs benefiting non-Hawaiians, leading them to offer fewer voters to the vote-maximizing governor. The bottom line is that an increase in the market value of DHHL lands could lead a vote-maximizing governor to release more land or less land depending on how much increased benefits are valued by native Hawaiian voters and decreased expenditures on other programs are evaluated by the general public.

Are the model's predictions supported over the life of the program by two measures of program performance, the number of program leases and program expenditures? The number of leases issued by DHHL to Native Hawaiians (*DHHL.Leases*) has increased in fits and starts from the beginning of the program, from 45 in 1924, to a total of 9,849 in 2012 (see fig. 8.2). Periods in which DHHL issued new leases at a relatively rapid pace are 1946–1952, 1976–1978, 1983–1986, and 2003–2008. Estimated program expenditures (*DHHL.Expenditures*) include all funds expended for administration, operation, and capital improvement projects. The expenditure series and all of the series expressed in dollars have been annualized and deflated to constant 1982–1984 dollars (fig. 8.3). Although HHL expenditures have fluctuated significantly over the years, expenditures have generally trended upward since 1969. The ratio of HHL expenditures to Hawai'i state expenditures follows a quite different pattern. HHL expenditures began as a relatively high percentage of state expenditures in the 1920s (10–19 percent), declined rapidly in the 1930s, and have since stayed in the 1–2 percent range.

Consider now measures of the two variables that affected decision making by the governor, DHHL, and the commission: the real value of Hawai'i

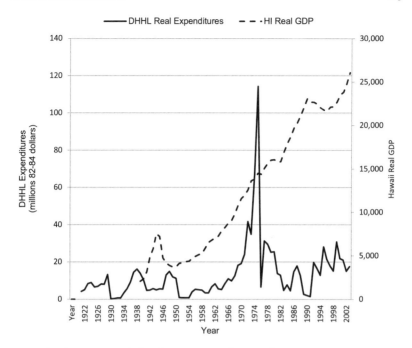

FIGURE 8.3. Department of Hawaiian Home Lands expenditures and Hawai'i real GDP, 1922–2003. DHHL expenditures includes all funds for administration, operation, and capital improvement projects. Sources include the Hawaiian Homes Commission's biennial reports to the territorial legislature, the DHHL's annual reports, the session laws, revised statutes of the territory and the state, and interviews during 1992–1993 with personnel at DHHL and HHC. Hawai'i GDP is from Schmitt (1977) and various issues of the *State Data Book*. All dollar values deflated by spliced Honolulu Consumer Price Index and U.S. Consumer Price Index with 1982–1984 base.

land (*Real.Land.Value*) and the share of Hawaiian voters (*Hawaiian.Voters*). As a (rough) measure of the value of an HHL parcel, I use Hawai'i's aggregate assessed value of land deflated to 1982–1984 dollars (fig. 8.4).[45] This series has trended up from 1921, albeit with some relatively long periods (1981–1984, 1991–1998, 2008–2010) during which assessed values fell. My measure of the proportion of registered Hawaiian voters splices several different series together and mixes together two similar but slightly different series, actual voters and registered voters (fig. 8.5).[46] Despite these inconsistencies, the data display two unambiguous trends. First, there was a long decline in the share of Hawaiians in the electorate, falling from 69 percent in 1902 to 56 percent in 1921 (when Congress passed the HHCA), to 40 percent in 1930, 26 percent in 1940, 21 percent in 1950, and 13 percent in

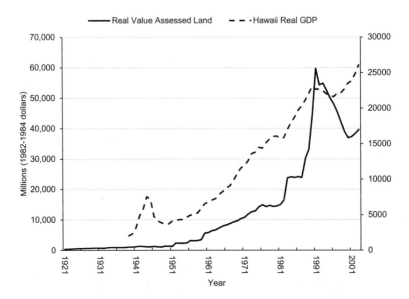

FIGURE 8.4. Real assessed value of Hawai'i land and Hawai'i real GDP, 1921–2003.

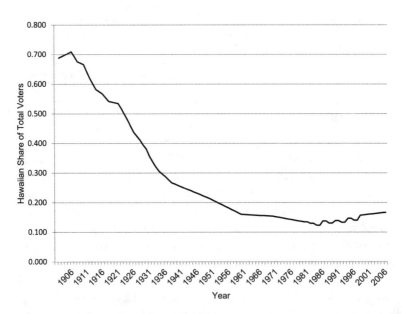

FIGURE 8.5. Native Hawaiian share of total voters, 1902–2006.

TABLE 8.3. **Error Correction Regressions: Number of Leases and DHHL Expenditures, 1924–2002**

Dependent variable	Log of HHL leases	Log of HHL expenditures
Log *Real.Land.Value*	−2.63***	2.38***
	(0.32)	(0.32)
Log *Hawaiian.Voters*	2.74***	−0.47
	(1.03)	(0.95)
Dem.Governor	−0.50	−0.09
	(0.40)	(0.40)
Dem.Legislature	5.64***	−6.16***
	(0.70)	(0.70)
Constant	17.65	−34.63
N	40	40
$\chi2$	185.4	93.4
$P > \chi2$	0.0	0.0

Note: Data set incorporates information for even years to allow for missing values in odd years.
Numbers in parentheses are standard errors. *** denotes statistical significance at the 1 percent level.

1980. Second, over the next 26 years, the Hawaiian share of the electorate gradually rebounded, with the national exit poll revealing a 16.7 percent share of Hawaiians among actual voters in the 2006 midterm elections in Hawai'i.[47]

To investigate whether changes in assessed land value and Hawaiian vote share are actually associated with changes in DHHL leases and program expenditures, I estimate a standard econometric model ("the error correction model") designed to identify long-run relationships between variables.[48] The findings from the econometric analysis are straightforward (table 8.3). Increases in the share of Hawaiian voters are associated with a positive and statistically significant effect on the number of DHHL leases outstanding, but do not yield a statistically significant effect on DHHL expenditures. Increases in the real value of land are associated with fewer DHHL leases outstanding and higher DHHL expenditures. Both of the estimated coefficients on *Real.Land.Value* are statistically significant at the 1 percent level.

Conclusion

My econometric analysis of two performance measures for the Hawaiian Home Lands Program, number of leases and program expenditures, yields

two important findings. First, the share of native Hawaiian voters is positively related to the number of leases issued by the program. Over the HHL
program's first 50 years, the share of native Hawaiian voters declined from
54 percent in 1920 to around 12–13 percent in 1970, and this decline coincided with a period of slow growth in the number of leases. The program's
revival from the mid-1970s also coincides with a small but significant increase in the share of voters (16.7 percent) who identify as Hawaiian or part-
Hawaiian. Second, the number of program leases and program expenditures are affected differently by the real assessed value of Hawai'i land, with
the number of leases outstanding falling and program expenditures rising as
the real value of land increased. From the perspective of a state bureaucracy
focused on maintaining future employment and elected officials focused on
maximizing votes, it is understandable that DHHL became more reluctant
to give away lands as they become more valuable and yielded more income
for the program.[49] Increases in real land value also led to increased DHHL
expenditures, and this was at least in part due to increases in revenue from
leasing its increasing valuable lands on the open market.

Reform of the HHL program was made deliberately difficult when
Hawai'i became a state: the 1959 Admission Act mandated that Hawai'i
embed the Hawai'i Home Lands program in its constitution. Thus, any
substantial reform of the program requires both state and federal legislation to pass. Reforms would probably have occurred if the U.S. Congress had passed legislation ("the Akaka bill") proposed several times by
former U.S. Senator Daniel Akaka to establish a process that would allow Hawaiians to be recognized as a first people by the U.S. government,
thereby enabling them to form a sovereign government.[50] Akaka's legislation contained provisions encouraging negotiations between the U.S.
government, the state government, and the new Hawaiian government
over a variety of grievances, including resources and lands taken by the
U.S. government at annexation. DHHL lands and programs would surely
have been part of these negotiations, but they never happened. Despite
widespread support for the bill as well as concentrated opposition to it
within Hawai'i and the Hawaiian community, the bill has never become
law due to its failure to find sixty votes in the U.S. Senate. Reform of the
Hawaiian Home Lands Program seems a distant mirage.

CHAPTER NINE

Statehood and the Transition to an Open-Access Order

The 1940s were the perfect storm for Hawai'i. Despite the U.S. victory in the Pacific war, Hawai'i suffered through a string of events that tested the fabric of its society and dimmed its prospects of becoming a state.[1] The Pearl Harbor attacks of December 7, 1941 (fig. 9.1), were followed later the same day by Governor Poindexter's declaration of martial law. In the hands of the new military governor, General Thomas H. Green (the army's chief executive officer), martial law quickly expanded into the suspension of all civilian government and military control of every aspect of government. Military courts tried all criminal and civil cases, the territorial legislature was suspended, and General Green ruled with absolute authority. Thousands of Japanese-Americans living in Hawai'i were interned. Curfews and blackouts were rigorously enforced through the very end of the war, long after Japan's military was no longer a threat to Hawai'i.

The restoration of civilian government in October 1944 and the elimination of most wage, employment, and price controls in the six months following the end of the war were bright lights, but they rapidly dimmed after a series of self-inflicted wounds extended the pain endured by residents during the war. A surge of well-organized industrial actions carried out by a single labor union, the ILWU, in key industries—sugar (1946), pineapple (1947), and stevedoring (1949)—disrupted a Hawai'i economy already shaken by the demobilization and departure of sailors and

FIGURE 9.1. Japanese attack on Pearl Harbor, December 7, 1941. Photo: Naval photographer.
Source: National Archives and Records Administration, 295993.

soldiers. The ILWU's success with strikes varied across industries (negotiating big wage gains in sugar and stevedoring and negligible wage gains in
pineapple), but more importantly, the strikes established the union as the
fourth powerful player in Hawai'i politics. Its blue-collar workers would
have to be accommodated with a share of the dominant coalition's rents;
otherwise, much of the economic rent created for the coalition would be
dissipated by labor-management conflicts.[2]

The ILWU's inclusion as a member of the dominant coalition that ruled
Hawai'i would be fleeting. In the late 1940s and early 1950s, the territory
became embroiled in the anticommunist fever that swept the mainland
United States, with the national and Hawai'i press publicizing allegations that Hawai'i's ILWU leaders had been members of the Communist
Party. In April 1950, the U.S. House Un-American Activities Committee held hearings in Honolulu, during which the committee members
gained testimony from ILWU leaders that would be used to indict them
in 1951. Seven journalists, union leaders and Communist Party activists
("the Smith Seven"), among them Jack Hall, the leader of the ILWU in
Hawai'i, were charged with violations of the Smith Act, a federal statute

that criminalized advocacy of the overthrow of the federal government. After a two-year trial, all seven defendants were convicted, with six sentenced to five years in prison and $5,000 fines. The U.S. Ninth Circuit Court of Appeals took five years to review the case and finally overturned all seven guilty verdicts in 1958.[3]

In the decade leading up to the Ninth Circuit's ruling, Hawai'i's prospects for statehood were diminished by the combination of ILWU industrial actions and the tainting of the ILWU's reputation by the initial Smith Seven verdicts and allegations of ILWU misconduct by Hawai'i's daily newspapers. Many in Congress viewed Hawai'i as potentially unstable, far from fit for self-government. The downsizing of two of its three biggest economic sectors—sugar and the military—and the uncertainty generated by the ILWU's strikes left a haze of uncertainty lingering over Hawai'i's politics and economy. This uncertainty was compounded by the United Nations decision in 1946 to place Hawai'i on its list of "Non-Self-Governing Territories"; this listing raised the question of whether Hawai'i would someday regain its status as an independent country, continue as a U.S. colony, or be admitted to the U.S. economic and political union as a U.S. state.[4]

Despite continued opposition to statehood from some U.S. senators and representatives, particularly those from the U.S. South, mainland opinion in the 1940s and 1950s shifted toward support for statehood. One reason was the combat record of Japanese-American soldiers serving in Hawai'i's 442nd Battalion and 100th Regiment. Their well-publicized heroism during major battles in Italy, France, and Belgium had tempered U.S. attitudes toward Hawai'i's Asian-American population, and various branches of the federal government began to consider Hawai'i for statehood more seriously.

In 1947, the U.S. House of Representatives passed a bill approving statehood by a large margin, but it died in the U.S. Senate. President Harry Truman called for statehood in his 1948 State of the Union address, and the Democratic Party's national platform contained a statehood plank in 1948.[5] A vote on Hawai'i statehood would not, however, be taken again until 1953, when the House passed a Hawai'i Statehood bill, with 274 for and 138 against. The Senate again postponed consideration until the next session.

Congressional fear of communist influence in Hawai'i and concerns over how Hawai'i's new congressional representatives would vote on civil rights legislation reduced support in Washington, D.C., for statehood. In Hawai'i, the difficult economic times encountered in the postwar period only reinforced long-standing support for statehood among the majority

of Hawai'i residents. A 1940 plebiscite asking voters whether they supported statehood for Hawai'i had passed by more than a 2–1 margin. Testimony from Hawai'i residents at 1946 congressional hearings on statehood was overwhelmingly favorable.[6] This strong support for statehood
was partly due to still-fresh memories of absolute rule by the U.S. military
in Hawai'i during the war and to longer memories of the dismal performance of the territorial government in providing desired public goods and
services to Hawai'i's emerging middle class.

Congressional reluctance to support statehood in the late 1940s fundamentally changed the course of the statehood debate because it forced
backers of statehood to affirmatively demonstrate that Hawai'i people
were ready and able to assume the responsibilities of governing. Thus,
the decision was made by Hawai'i's leading politicians to elect a constitutional convention that would, via its deliberations and outcome, demonstrate that Hawai'i was capable and worthy of becoming a state.[7] During its 1949 session, the territorial legislature passed a bill authorizing a
constitutional convention.[8] Its elected members would write a constitution for the new state government. If approved by a two-thirds vote in
a public referendum, the constitution would take effect when the U.S.
Congress and president approved statehood.[9] The convention marked the
second time in Hawai'i's history that a group of representatives from a
broadly representative electorate explicitly devised institutions to govern
Hawai'i.[10] The convention, which met in June and July 1950 in Honolulu
(fig. 9.2), was widely applauded for the manner in which the proceedings
were carried out and for the final document's provisions.[11] Statehood proponents then won an overwhelming endorsement for the new constitution
from an electorate eager to establish a government more in tune with
their interests and to bring the sovereign democratic institutions of U.S.
states to Hawai'i.[12] The vote was 82,788 in favor of ratification and 27,109
against, about a 3–1 margin of victory.[13] The bipartisan undertaking was a
huge accomplishment for Hawai'i's electorate and political leadership, yet
it did little to change the decisions of U.S. senators still worried about pig-
tailed Chinese senators representing Hawai'i in Washington, communist
influences in Hawai'i labor unions, and how Hawai'i elections for the U.S.
Senate might affect party control of the Senate and the body's looming
votes on civil rights legislation. But as the nation and Hawai'i moved away
from the McCarthyite Red scares, blacklists, and Smith Act prosecutions,
the prospects for Hawai'i statehood began to improve as political winds
shifted in Washington, D.C.

FIGURE 9.2. Delegates at the Hawai'i state constitutional convention, held at the National Guard Armory in Honolulu, Hawai'i, in 1950. Photo: City Photo Studio. Source: Bishop Museum.

In 1953, statehood for Hawai'i and Alaska was proposed in a single bill, which was approved by the U.S. Senate but then bottled up in the U.S. House of Representatives. Its approval stalled partly because Alaska's and Hawai'i's situations were very different. Alaska had a much more restrictive territorial government and faced different problems with incorporating first peoples into its system of government. In 1957, the Hawai'i delegate to the U.S. House of Representatives, John Burns, pushed for an unpopular (in Hawai'i) change in strategy that would decouple the two statehood bills and allow Alaska to become a state first. The strategy worked. Alaska became a state in 1958 and Hawai'i followed in 1959.[14]

Gains to Hawai'i from Statehood

For a U.S. territory to become a state, its voters must approve the change in status, both houses of Congress must pass an admission act, and the

U.S. president must approve. In other words, both a territory's people
and representatives of the other states' peoples must expect to gain from
federal recognition of the territory as both a democratic sovereign state
and a peer of the other states. Consider now the gains that might accrue to
one of the big players in Hawai'i's dominant coalition, the Big Five firms.

For the first three decades of Hawai'i's territorial government, the Big
Five firms did not support statehood petitions because their firms' economic rents did not depend on whether Hawai'i was organized as an incorporated U.S. territory or as a U.S. state. Industry revenues depended
on the U.S. Congress setting a sufficiently high tariff on imports of raw and
refined sugar, while industry costs depended on whether U.S. immigration law allowed Hawai'i sugar producers to recruit low-cost temporary
labor from another U.S. possession, the Philippines. On both counts, Congress treated Hawai'i's sugar producers just like other sugar producers
located in any of the U.S. states. Most importantly, there were no quotas
or other regulatory restrictions on Hawai'i's sales of raw or refined sugar
to the U.S. market. From the Big Five's perspective, there were no expected gains from statehood, so why upset the status quo?

Everything changed in 1934. Hawai'i's status as an incorporated territory without voting representation in the U.S. Congress forced Hawai'i
sugar planters to watch from the sidelines when Congress passed the
Tydings-McDuffie Act,[15] which restricted immigration from the Philippines
to the United States and its possessions to just 50 people per year. Filipino
migrants had become an important source of low-cost labor for Hawai'i
sugar and pineapple plantations after annexation had cut off access to Chinese migrant workers in 1898 and Japanese migrant workers in 1907.[16] The
plantations had responded to these bans by recruiting temporary Filipino
workers, whose status as U.S. nationals allowed them to freely enter Hawai'i
and to work there. Between 1906 and 1934, the industry recruited more
than 130,000 workers from the Philippines to work in Hawai'i. Most workers stayed only temporarily, returning to the Philippines after accumulating some wealth. Some workers, however—about 18,000 by 1934—settled
down in Hawai'i. The sudden halt to new Filipino migration in 1934 was a
huge blow to the Hawai'i sugar industry, as sugar production had expanded
during the U.S. economy's downward spiral (1929–1933) of the Great Depression, and cheap immigrant labor had helped to fuel this expansion.[17]

Congressional passage of another bill in 1934, the Jones-Costigan Act,
shocked Hawai'i's establishment at least as much as passage of the Tydings-
McDuffie Act, because its provisions opened their eyes to Hawai'i's

second-class status within the U.S. federal system. The act created a new federal regulatory structure for the U.S. sugar industry that substantially reduced the Big Five's economic rents and, even more importantly, treated Hawai'i sugar producers differently from producers in the mainland 48 states. To understand how the act affected Hawai'i producers, we first need to consider how U.S. tariffs on imports of raw and refined sugar evolved between 1900 and 1933 and how their evolution affected the magnitude of economic rents created for Hawai'i's sugar industry.

U.S. tariffs on imported refined and raw sugar more than doubled between 1900 and 1933. Part of the reason for this increase was the dominance of the Republican Party in national American politics for 25 of those 34 years, as it supported trade protection policies more strongly than the Democratic Party did. Consider these major changes in U.S. tariff policy: In 1897, a Republican Congress passed and a Republican president, William McKinley, signed the Dingley tariff bill, which raised the tariff on raw sugar from roughly 1.2 cents to 1.685 cents per pound and on refined sugar from roughly 1.81 cents to 1.95 cents per pound.[18] In October 1913, a Democratic Congress passed and a Democratic president, Woodrow Wilson, signed the Underwood tariff bill. Potentially catastrophic for the Hawai'i sugar industry, the measure reduced the tariffs on both refined and raw sugar by 25 percent on March 1, 1914, and set May 1, 1916, as the sunset date for those tariffs. The world's descent into war in August 1914 disrupted this plan. Sugar production declined in Europe, Asia, and South America, and global sugar prices soared. In April 1916, after negotiations with Great Britain, the United States decided to keep its existing sugar tariffs and to put in place a system of price controls on raw and refined sugar that lasted through the war. Warren Harding, a pro-tariff Republican, was elected president in 1920, and Republicans swept to big majorities in both the Senate and the House. The new Congress passed the Emergency Sugar Tariff Act of 1921, which raised the tariff on raw sugar from 1.685 cents to 2 cents per pound and the tariff on refined sugar from 1.95 cents to 2.16 cents per pound. Two further increases in the sugar tariff were enacted during the Republican-dominated period that followed: the 1922 Fordney-McCumber tariff, which raised rates on raw and refined sugar to 2.206 cents and 2.39 cents per pound, respectively, and the 1930 Hawley-Smoot tariff, which raised rates on raw and refined sugar to 2.5 cents and 2.65 cents per pound, respectively. For a summary of these rate changes, see table 9.1.

The surge in U.S. sugar tariffs during the 1920s allowed the Big Five sugar producers to reap much bigger gains. Under various scenarios, I

TABLE 9.1. **U.S. Tariff Rates on Raw and Refined Sugar per Pound, 1883–1934**

	Raw		Refined	
	Full	Cuba	Full	Cuba
Morrill Act (1883)	2.24	2.24	3.50	3.50
McKinley Tariff (1891)	0.0	0.0	0.50	0.50
Wilson-Gorman Tariff (1894)	40%	40%	40%	40%
Dingley Tariff (1897)	1.69	1.69	1.95	1.95
1903 Cuban Tariff Cut	1.69	1.35	1.95	1.56
Payne-Aldrich Tariff (1909)	1.69	1.35	1.95	1.52
Underwood Tariff (1913)	1.26	1.005	1.36	1.09
Emergency Tariff Act (1921)	2.00	1.60	2.16	1.73
Fordney-McCumber Tariff (1922)	2.21	1.76	2.39	1.91
Hawley-Smoot Act (1930)	2.50	2.00	2.65	2.12
Roosevelt May 1934 Proclamation	1.88	1.50	1.99	1.59

Notes: All rates are given in U.S. cents unless otherwise noted. Domestic producers were paid a 1.75–2-cent bounty per pound under the McKinley Tariff. From May 1, 1900, Puerto Rican sugar was admitted at 85 percent of the full duty and was exempted from the full duty from 1901. Philippine raw sugar was admitted at 75 percent of the full duty from 1902 and Cuban raw sugar at 85 percent of the full duty from December 1903 (under the Cuban Reciprocity Act). As of August 1909, the first 300,000 tons of Philippine raw sugar became exempt from the tariff, and from mid-October 1913, all Philippine sugar became exempt.

estimate that the gains to the Big Five firms from selling at the 1930 sugar tariff rate were massive, ranging between 500 percent and 1,200 percent more than the gains that would have been realized under the 1897 rate. The first third of the twentieth century was truly the golden age for the Hawai'i sugar industry, and it happened because Hawai'i became more embedded in the U.S. market after annexation and because the U.S. market became much more protective of domestic sugar production.

The Great Depression changed everything for Hawai'i sugar producers. The precipitous drop in U.S. incomes and massive rise in unemployment during the four-year slide into the Great Depression (1929–1933) depressed U.S. sugar consumption from a peak of 7.59 million short tons in 1929 to 6.33 short tons in 1933. Despite the decline in U.S. consumption, sales of Hawai'i sugar in the U.S. mainland market actually increased between 1929 and 1933, by 12 percent! In fact, sales of sugar by mainland cane and beet producers and the two other sugar-producing U.S. insular possessions, Puerto Rico and the Philippines, also increased. All of the decline in U.S. sugar consumption was absorbed by Cuba, which saw exports to the United States fall by 53 percent.

The massive decline in U.S. real income between 1929 and 1932 and a deepening banking crisis in 1932 led to a landslide victory in the November 1932 presidential election for Democrat Franklin Roosevelt and huge majorities for Democrats in both houses of the U.S. Congress. The first 100 days of the Roosevelt administration saw the passage of New Deal programs to provide relief to unemployed workers and new regulations for U.S. firms and industries. Prominent among these regulations was the 1933 Agricultural Adjustment Act (AAA), which imposed a new array of quotas, production regulations, and price controls on agricultural commodity outputs. The AAA's ostensible goal was to raise and stabilize commodity prices. Although the AAA did not regulate sugar, that omission was cured by the passage of the 1934 Jones-Costigan Act, which added sugar to the list of highly regulated agricultural commodities. The act's main effect was to embed mainland producers, Hawai'i, Puerto Rico, the Philippines, Cuba, and other foreign producers in a system of output quotas designed to achieve a targeted market price that would be higher than those observed from 1929 to 1933.

The transition to a regulated U.S. sugar market had surprising and unexpected consequences for Hawai'i. To the dismay of the Big Five, their access to the mainland U.S. sugar market was limited by restrictive quotas based on their average sales over 1930–1932. Perhaps most shocking to the Big Five firms were the new U.S. Department of Agriculture regulations that treated Hawai'i cane producers differently from cane and beet sugar producers in the 48 states. The planters' first reaction was to challenge the constitutionality of the legislation. A decision from the Washington, D.C., circuit court came quickly and was unambiguous in its ruling that Congress had the authority to regulate trade between the continent and Hawai'i:

> But Congress is also given the power "to dispose of and make all needful rules and regulations respecting the Territory or other property belonging to the United States." . . . it has all the power that a state government would have over its own citizens. It would seem then that apart from the Commerce clause it has full power to regulate the commerce of a territory whether organized or not and if necessary or expedient to lay embargoes against exports.
>
> The great distance of Hawaii from the continent, separated by the ocean, the difference in race of many of its inhabitants, the difference in manner of living, in the raising of its agricultural products, all might give rise for many grounds for legislation as to its commerce which would not apply to the Continent.[19]

The federal court decision affirming the constitutionality of the Hawai'i sugar quota added to a series of federal court decisions (known as the "insular cases") that had been unfolding since 1898, when the United States had acquired new possessions after the Spanish-American War that were not perceived by Congress to be on trajectories to become U.S. states. The cases clearly affirmed the ability of Congress to treat a territory's government and residents differently from those of a state.[20] After the decision, the Big Five refocused their political strategy, concentrating on lobbying Congress to amend the Jones-Costigan Act rather than contesting in court whether Congress had the authority to pass such restrictive legislation. In 1936 and 1937, Congress responded to the new lobbying initiatives by first amending the Jones-Costigan Act to raise Hawai'i's sugar quotas and then superseding it with new legislation, the 1937 Sugar Act.[21]

Despite the rollback of some of the more onerous features of the Jones-Costigan Act, the shock of the court's decision forced Hawai'i's establishment to recognize that a long-held expectation—that corporations and individuals in the incorporated and organized territory of Hawai'i would be treated as if they were residents of a U.S. state—had been shattered. In the depression-wracked political environment of the 1930s, Congress had bloodlessly sacrificed the Big Five's interests in order to benefit mainland cane and beet sugar producers. As long as Hawai'i lacked voting representation in the U.S. Senate and House, the economic rents provided to the territory from the sale of sugar under the U.S. tariff umbrella would never be secure.[22]

The restrictive provisions of the Jones-Costigan Act came into effect in 1935, when employment at Hawai'i sugar plantations was still far below its 1926 peak. The 1937 Sugar Act restored some of Hawai'i's privileges to sell in the U.S. market, but did little to revive employment prospects for workers on sugar plantations. From its peak in 1926, sugar employment plummeted over the next three decades, falling from about 52,000 in 1926 to about 14,000 in 1965. The opportunities to earn big money in Hawai'i by coordinating vertical chains of sugar and pineapple production were closing, and new profit opportunities were arising in rapidly growing service industries, many based around tourism, such as banking, insurance, airlines, medium- and large-scale retailing, real estate, and housing and hotel development.

Hawai'i residents also reasonably believed that they would gain increased access to federal spending programs if Hawai'i became a state. Residents had always paid the same federal income taxes that citizens in the 48 states paid, but had access to only a limited number of federal programs. The large number of military bases in Hawai'i meant that the territory received more than its per capita share of federal military spending, but the same could not be said for spending on research and development, highway construction, education, training, or welfare funds. After the enactment of a long line of federal spending programs during the Great Depression, the prospect of a federal fiscal windfall from statehood increased. The expectation was that two votes in the U.S. Senate and one or two votes in the U.S. House of Representatives would bring additional federal spending to Hawai'i and would allow Hawai'i to shape federal legislation to more fully incorporate its interests.

Hawai'i citizens might also have expected to gain from being able to monitor the performance of their government better with an elected governor than with an appointed governor. U.S. and Hawai'i firms without ties to the Big Five could also have expected gains from access to more judicially independent state courts. Judges on the territorial Supreme Court were appointed by the U.S. president, served short 4-year terms, and could be removed by the president at any time for any reason. These conditions provided judges with incentives to be oriented toward enforcing contracts and property rights of individuals and groups associated with the federal government and other members of the dominant coalition. Three factors suggest that statehood did indeed bring more judicial independence to Hawai'i. First, under the 1959 state constitution, justices and circuit court judges served seven-year renewable terms and, after the changes made by the 1968 constitutional convention, ten-year renewable terms. Second, the governor appointed, with advice and consent of the state senate, justices and circuit judges from a "merit" list presented by a judicial selection committee. In other states, election of judges had led to more decisions against out-of-state businesses and more decisions favorable to state agencies.[23] Third, in the first 10–15 years after statehood, there was robust competition between the Hawai'i Republican and Democratic parties; this made it more difficult for a majority party to punish judges for decisions inconsistent with that party's interests.[24] Together, these three factors point to a high degree of judicial independence in Hawai'i state courts in the decade after statehood.

Is there, however, any evidence to support expectations by firms and citizens that when state courts are more judicially independent, they actually make better decisions? Economist Daniel Berkowicz and economic historian Karen Clay studied this issue for the 48 mainland states and found strong empirical evidence that more "judicial independence [in U.S. state courts] is strongly associated with court quality."[25] Economist John

Dove studied court systems in all 50 U.S. states and found that greater judicial independence is associated with higher measures of economic freedom, allows for a bigger state government to emerge, and is associated with higher state economic growth.[26] Numerous cross-country studies investigating the relationship between judicial independence and outcomes of judicial systems have also found that countries with higher degrees of judicial independence have higher-quality courts and better outcomes than countries with less judicial independence.[27]

To sum up, Hawai'i citizens and organizations unaffiliated with the Big Five could have reasonably expected that their liberty and property would be more secure in a state government with independent courts and a citizen-elected governor than in a territorial government with courts and a governor tilted toward protection of the interests of the federal government and other members of the dominant coalition.

Why Did Congress Approve Statehood?

It would have been hard to argue in the late 1940s that citizens of the 48 U.S. states would gain much from approving Hawai'i statehood. After the struggles over the sugar quotas were resolved in Hawai'i's favor by the 1937 Sugar Act, there were no restrictions on trade in either direction. Although Hawai'i had a per capita personal income ($1,585) slightly higher than Colorado's ($1,569) in 1950, it had fewer people (491,000) than New Hampshire (533,000), and in general, large economies tend to gain little from trading slightly more with very small economies. Nor would statehood change the legal framework for migration between Hawai'i and the United States for most residents of the 48 states, as there were no restrictions on migration to and from Hawai'i for U.S. citizens during the territorial era.[28] Likewise, there were no federal or territorial restrictions on passive capital flows or direct investment between the United States and Hawai'i. There would be no benefits to be gained from a currency union, as the U.S. dollar had been Hawai'i's official currency since 1900. Nor would statehood allow the U.S. military to gain increased access to Hawai'i lands and ports. In fact, the military had already worked with previous governors (who were presidential appointees) to gain access to over 15,000 acres of federal lands on O'ahu. They were already one of the four big players in the territory's dominant coalition and had received substantial economic rents stemming from the governor's authority to trigger eminent domain proceedings and to reserve government lands for their use. They had already taken what they wanted. Nor did statehood raise opportunities for new revenue flows from Hawai'i to the federal treasury. Hawai'i residents were already paying the same personal and corporate federal income taxes as residents of mainland states.

Why, then, did Congress admit Hawai'i as a state? One reason is that the dominant coalition to which the territorial and federal governments had distributed economic rents was in tatters. The Republican Party, which had controlled the territorial legislature through 1954, was supported by a coalition of native Hawaiians and Caucasians associated with the Big Five companies and their many affiliates. The party's ability to win elections was shaken in the postwar period because the share of native Hawaiian voters had fallen precipitously, from 69 percent of the electorate in 1902 to just 21 percent in 1950.[29] Without a supportive legislature, it became more difficult to distribute economic rents to Big Five firms or patronage positions to Hawaiian professionals. Adjustment of the dominant coalition to reflect the changing political power of various groups would have been very difficult, as the policies pushed by the new legislative majorities of the Democratic Party—tax reform, land reform, and provision of additional state and local public goods—were diametrically opposed to the interests of the Big Five companies.

In his classic book on statehood, *Last Among Equals*, the historian Roger Bell made a more direct argument for why Congress acted: Hawai'i was ready and could not rationally be denied if it was to be kept within the American political system.[30] It had been a territory with an incorporated government for almost six decades, and Congress had eventually granted statehood to every territory set up with an incorporated government. A constitutional convention had adopted a widely praised state constitution in 1950. The heroism of its soldiers in both World War II and the Korean War was widely recognized and admired. Levels of education were high, and the economy had become more diversified in the 1950s. Bell argued that Hawai'i had demonstrated that it had sufficient resources to organize a well-functioning state government and had developed robust political competition for positions in the territorial legislature. And to cement the deal, a broad coalition spanning Hawai'i's ethnicities had actively campaigned for statehood for more than two decades.[31]

Presidents and congressional leaders had typically worried about how senators from newly admitted states would affect the ability of their parties to organize the Senate and to push legislation favored by their parties.

Democratic senators from Southern states had helped to kill Hawai'i statehood bills in the 1940s and 1950s because of their (correct) concerns that Hawai'i senators and representatives would support civil rights legislation. In the late 1950s, this issue faded somewhat as both President Eisenhower and congressional leaders concluded that the congressional delegations from Alaska and Hawai'i were likely to be a mix of Republicans and Democrats. In fact, Hawai'i elected one senator from each party from 1959 to 1977, while Alaska elected two Democratic senators from 1958 to 1968. After 1977, Hawai'i elected two Democratic senators, and from 1969 to 2008, Alaska elected two Republican senators.

How Did Becoming a Sovereign U.S. State Change Outcomes in Hawai'i?

Territorial government in Hawai'i was designed to create rents and distribute them to a dominant coalition of four powerful interest groups. The distribution of rents had to be consistent with the actual power of the various groups or else one group would have taken action to disrupt collection of rents by the others. This principle was exemplified by the series of strikes initiated by the ILWU in the mid- to late 1940s. As the power of various interests changes, a mature natural state must adjust the share of rents distributed to various groups, and it often does this by redistributing property rights to land. Thus, in a natural state, such as Hawai'i under territorial government, property rights are never secure, as their protection is secondary to maintaining peace among the players in the dominant coalition. The sudden and swift transition to an open-access political order in 1959 raised the expectation that property rights would be better secured, as this is a necessary condition for an open-access political order to function properly.

So, did Hawai'i's shift to an open-access political order actually strengthen property rights? Consider how big mainland firms reacted to statehood. Tom Hitch, the long-serving chief economist at First Hawaiian Bank, found that the number of U.S. and foreign corporations operating in Hawai'i soared between 1955 and 1971, increasing from just 311 to 1,916.[32] National brands, in particular, made their presence known in industries previously dominated by one or two Hawai'i firms and in the new service industries that were more than replacing the thousands of jobs being shed by Hawai'i's sugar industry.

The influx of foreign firms before and after statehood was accompanied by the strongest economic growth ever observed in Hawai'i. Between

1957 and 1970, real GDP grew at more than 5 percent per year and per capita real GDP at more than 3 percent per year.[33] These were the years when new roads, airports, retail stores, hotels, and restaurants were built and opened to serve the new tourism industry and the general public.

Ultimately, it is impossible to separate out the influence on economic growth of the stronger property rights established by statehood and the flocks of Boeing 707s that started to make daily migrations through Hawaiian skies in the late 1950s. The resulting reduction in travel time to and from the mainland fit Hawai'i into the busy life of an upper-middle-class executive, and the reduction in the cost of an airline ticket brought a Hawai'i vacation within the grasp of middle-class U.S. families. In a flash, the potential Hawai'i tourism market expanded from the very rich able to afford lavish, expensive cruises to over 25 million U.S. middle-class families.[34] For the new state government, the tourism boom was particularly fortuitous, as tax revenues from the boom fueled the state's new political institutions by providing funding for new programs directed toward Hawai'i's rising middle class.

At the beginning of this chapter, I emphasized that the transition from territory to statehood placed more limits on executive power and enhanced protection of personal and corporate property rights. A sovereign, more democratic state government also implies that the population's preferences regarding taxes, provision of state public goods, and regulations must be respected, or legislators and the governor will be replaced by the electorate. For Hawai'i, transition to the institutions of statehood allowed big changes in five major public policy areas to be legislated and implemented relatively quickly.

First, the government's focus changed from maintaining and adjusting economic rents distributed to members of the ruling coalition to establishing new frameworks for industrial competition that would allow industry rents to be competed away by new entrants. The government moved quickly to dismantle the interlocking relationships among the corporate boards of the Big Five and other major Hawai'i companies after a report by economists Fred Hung and Vernon Mund found that interlocking directorates had allowed the Matson Navigation Company to charge supracompetitive freight rates between Hawai'i and the U.S. mainland and that its actions had contributed to Hawai'i's high cost of living. The Hung-Mund report was a major impetus behind the Hawai'i state legislature's enactment of strong state antitrust legislation in 1963.[35] The intent of this legislation was to avoid the type of situation faced by Sears Roebuck, a major U.S. department store, when it entered the Honolulu market in

1941. To open a retail store, Sears had to clandestinely assemble property for a site in central Honolulu. Once its plan for a store was revealed, Sears received threats that the Big Five–owned Matson would decline to ship its products to Hawai'i from the mainland.

Second, dismantling the institutions supporting the territorial natural state involved reorganization of rights to residential property (see chaps. 10 and 11). In 1967, the state legislature passed the Land Reform Act (LRA) to allow property owned by sugar and ranch interests and native Hawaiian charitable organizations to be involuntarily sold to tens of thousands of homeowners who leased the land on which their homes were built. Such widespread forced sales of land were inconsistent with the promise of an open-access order to secure property rights more fully. The reorganization came about partly because it was desired by the newly enfranchised majority and perhaps partly because of the Madisonian idea that property rights can never really be secure unless a broad middle class owns property and thereby gains incentives to support enforcement of property rights. A more straightforward reason might also have been responsible for the LRA: land leasing was perceived to be an integral part of the old system of creating and distributing economic rents to landowners in the dominant political coalition. Thus, eliminating residential leasehold tenure may also have been perceived to be another step toward dismantling economic institutions associated with the old political order.

Third, the 1959 state constitution provided the state government with extensive powers to regulate land use and development, and politicians moved quickly to use them. The constitution proclaimed that the "State shall conserve and protect agricultural lands" and provided that "the legislature shall vest in one or more executive boards or commissions powers for the management of natural resources owned or controlled by the State."[36] In 1961, passage of the Land Use Law (Act 187) established the state's Land Use Commission, which was charged with implementing a system of statewide land use regulations.[37] The first state law of its type in the United States, it classified land into four broad categories of uses, within which zoning regulations of the City and County of Honolulu provided more detailed rules for land use. The urban core in Honolulu was (and is) surrounded by land zoned for agricultural use; developing these lands for housing required reclassification by the Land Use Commission. The law also allowed a mechanism for the state to designate particular lands for tourism-oriented development and thereby continue to distribute economic rents to political supporters (see chap. 11).

Fourth, the 15 years following statehood saw a massive expansion of state government spending and employment. State employment rose from 13,700 workers in 1958 to 38,700 workers in 1975. State government operating expenditures rose from $110.7 million (10.0 percent of personal income) in 1958 to $216.9 million (12.5 percent) in 1962 to 1,071.5 million in 1975 (15.2 percent). Some of the additional spending was oriented toward providing public goods for the newly politically empowered Asian-American middle class, and some was oriented toward providing infrastructure to facilitate rapid expansion of the tourism industry. Public expenditures on K–12 education increased substantially, and the state engineered a massive transformation of the University of Hawai'i in a bid to establish its credentials as a world-class research university in the 1960s and 1970s. Spending on transportation infrastructure, including highways, ports, and airports, allowed public infrastructure to expand to cope with the exploding flows of tourists.

Finally, statehood involved redistribution of taxation powers and changes in tax rates. The power to levy the property tax was transferred to the four counties, which during the territorial period had only ad hoc sources of funding. The general excise tax (GET) was increased to replace some of the lost property tax revenues. From the 2 percent rate established during the World War II years, the territorial legislature increased the GET to 3.5 percent in 1959, and the state legislature moved it up to 4 percent in 1965.[38] Because the GET taxes receipts of businesses selling services and goods, it was a highly productive tax for the state in the 1960s and 1970s, as it effectively taxed service sectors associated with the rising tourism industry. The GET was controversial from its inception. It was rightly criticized as a highly regressive tax burdening low-income residents and rightly praised as a tax that allowed some of the state's tax burden to be exported to tourists. Statehood also saw expansion of the personal income tax, with the range of incomes subject to tax broadened and tax rates increased. State revenues from the personal income tax soared from $2.1 million in 1957 (0.19 percent of personal income) to $25.7 million in 1959 (1.97 percent), $185 million in 1976 (2.63 percent), and $1,745 million in 2015 (3.04 percent).

The New Relationship with the Federal Government

From 1900 to 1959, the Hawai'i population went totally unrepresented in the U.S. Senate and had only a nonvoting representative in the U.S.

House of Representatives. But in 1959, Hawai'i, with just 0.36 percent of the U.S. population in 1960, suddenly had 2 percent of the voting representatives in the U.S. Senate and one voting representative in the U.S. House (and two after reapportionment in 1962). Hawai'i's new representatives and senators had twin goals: shape legislation to reflect Hawai'i's interests and gain new or enhanced access to numerous federal spending programs from which territories were excluded or limited.

Senator Daniel Inouye was the key figure in the Hawai'i congressional delegation's drive in the 1960s and 1970s to accomplish these goals. Hawai'i's voters elected him to the U.S. Senate in 1962 and would re-elect him to eight more terms. Inouye started his political career in 1953 as a representative in the territorial legislature, where he focused on forcing Hawai'i's appointed Republican governor to recognize the interests of and demands for public services from Hawai'i's newly enfranchised Chinese, Korean, Japanese, and Filipino voters. The skills he developed at the state capitol translated well to Washington, D.C., where his main job was to develop and implement a strategy that allowed the new state of Hawai'i to be treated like other states in the allocation of federal spending. Three factors aided him in facilitating Hawai'i's rapid incorporation into federal spending programs during the 1960s and 1970s.

First, the strong economy of the early to mid-1960s led to strong growth in federal tax revenues. This growth was fortuitous, as Congress typically resisted modification of rules of existing programs by which it allocated resources to the states. The growth in federal revenues in the 1960s set the stage for Hawai'i to be accommodated within the existing structure of rules for allocating program funds. No state would have to receive an absolutely smaller allocation in order to bring Hawai'i to full participation in federal programs. Of course, it also helped that Hawai'i had just 0.36 percent of the U.S. population and that Alaska, admitted as a state in 1958, had just 0.13 percent. The accommodations that needed to be made were ultimately very small.

Second, Hawai'i received voting representation in Congress just as the federal government was beginning a major expansion in the scale and scope of its spending programs. Hawai'i was fully represented when, between 1964 and 1968, Congress passed President Lyndon Johnson's Great Society legislation, which included an array of anti-poverty programs, a joint federal-state program (Medicaid) providing health care benefits to low-income families, a federal program (Medicare) providing health care benefits to people aged 65 and over, and several programs providing support for K–12 and higher education. Hawai'i's liberal congressional delegation strongly supported these programs and was well represented on important Senate and House committees reviewing the enabling legislation. Its members had ample opportunities to ensure that rules for allocating program expenditures took Hawai'i's interests into account.

Finally, Senator Inouye made a critical alliance with Senator Ted Stevens, a Republican from Alaska. Stevens entered the Senate in 1969 and would be elected to six more terms. Like Inouye, Stevens was focused on ensuring that his new state was fully incorporated into federal spending programs and on putting earmarks for specific Alaska-related projects into federal spending bills. The alliance between the Republican Alaska delegation and the mostly Democratic Hawai'i delegation helped to leverage the voting power of these two small states. Whether there was a Democrat or a Republican in the White House and whether the Democratic Party or the Republican Party controlled the Senate became less consequential for each state's delegation. Given the bipartisan nature of this alliance, communication channels to the president's office were always open. As the seniority of the two senators increased (and small states like to re-elect their senators), the ability of Inouye and Stevens to put earmarks into spending bills became widely known. Abuses of this power by Senator Stevens, such as securing federal funding for the well-known "Bridge to Nowhere" in a lightly populated rural area of Alaska, would lead Congress in 2010 to place a (poorly enforced) moratorium on earmarks. Both senators became widely associated with seeking special privileges for their states. It is, however, important to recall the difficult task faced by the two senators when they arrived in Congress in 1958 and 1959: fight their way into federal programs to which their states had little access when they were territories. From the vantage of their constituents, they excelled in their jobs.

A Very Flawed Constitution?

In many respects, statehood transformed Hawai'i from a colonial society dominated by colonial elites to a vibrant, rich democratic society. This transformation came at a great cost, however, as the long-term economic and political foundations of the Admission Act and the 1950 constitution contained a serious flaw: they failed to address the loss of sovereignty for native Hawaiians and the expropriation of private crown lands from

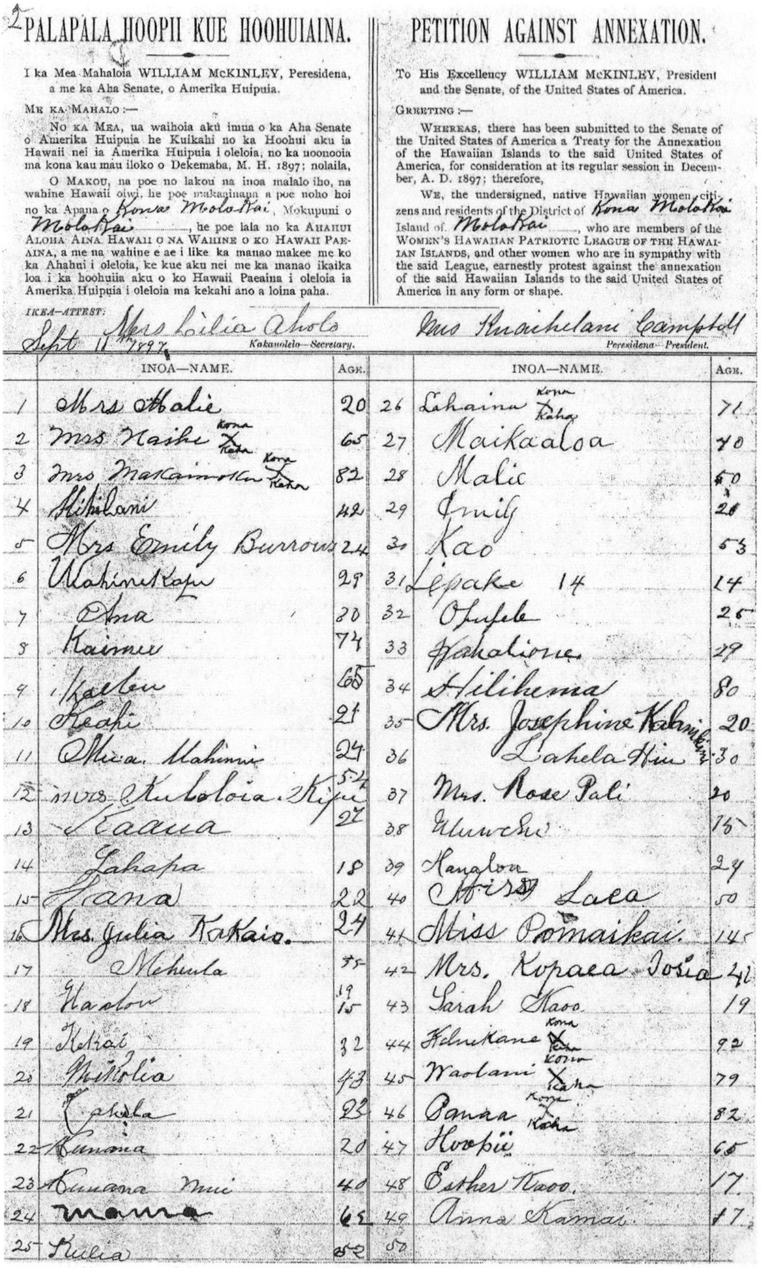

INOA—NAME.	AGE.		INOA—NAME.	AGE.
1 Mrs. Malie	20	26	Lehaina Kona Kahoi	71
2 Mrs. Naike Kona Kaka	65	27	Maikaaloa	70
3 Mrs. Makaimoku Kona Kaka	82	28	Malie	50
4 Hikilani	42	29	Emily	28
5 Mrs. Emily Burrows	24	30	Kao	53
6 Wahine Kapu	29	31	Lepake 14	14
7 Ana	80	32	Opule	25
8 Kainu	74	33	Kahaliou	29
9 Kalu	65	34	Hilihena	80
10 Keahi	21	35	Mrs. Josephine Kahi	20
11 Mrs. Mahinu	24	36	Lahela Kiu	30
12 Mrs. Kuloloia Kiju	54	37	Mrs. Rose Pali	20
13 Kaaua	22	38	Uluwehi	15
14 Kahapa	18	39	Hanalou	24
15 Hana	22	40	Miss Laea	50
16 Mrs. Julia Kakaio	24	41	Miss Poinaikai	14
17 Mehula	55	42	Mrs. Kopaea Iosia	41
18 Haolou	19/15	43	Sarah Kaoo	19
19 Kikiai	32	44	Kelaikane Kona Kaka	92
20 Milolia	43	45	Waolani Kona Kaka	79
21 Lahela	23	46	Oanaa Kona Kaka	82
22 Lunaua	20	47	Hoopii	65
23 Lunaua nui	40	48	Esther Kaoo	17
24 Mawa	65	49	Anna Kamai	17
25 Iulia	52	50		

FIGURE 9.3. Petition against annexation, September 1897. Source: National Archives and Records Administration, Records of the U.S. Senate, Record Group 46.

Queen Lili'uokalani. Virtually all of the adult Hawaiian population had signed petitions protesting the proposed annexation in 1897 (fig. 9.3). When the U.S. flag was raised over 'Iolani Palace in August 1898, there were no Hawaiians present at the ceremony. Many have noted that native Hawaiian voters overwhelmingly approved the state constitution in a November 1950 referendum and three amendments to it required by Congress in a May 1959 referendum. The choice presented to voters was, however, quite stark: to approve the new constitution and statehood or to continue with the existing institutions of territorial government that had brought martial law to Hawai'i in the 1940s and that promised diminished influence to native Hawaiian voters with a declining share of the electorate. Given the limited choices available to voters, it is not surprising that native Hawaiians overwhelmingly choose statehood.

The only concessions provided to native Hawaiian voters in the 1959 constitution were to incorporate the main features of the territorial-era Hawaiian Home Lands program directly into the constitution and to list native Hawaiians as one of several beneficiaries of revenues derived from the public land trust. Two decades later, a state constitutional convention would attempt to remedy the constitution's omissions by creating the Office of Hawaiian Affairs. Few Hawaiians saw the new office as settling fundamental problems of Hawaiian sovereignty or control of the crown lands. In chapter 12, I consider whether Hawai'i can function effectively as an open-access political order when the foundation of that order ignores fundamental issues of Hawaiian sovereignty and government expropriation of crown lands.

CHAPTER TEN

The Rise and Fall of Residential Leasehold Tenure in Hawai'i

A man is not a whole and complete man unless he *owns* a house and the ground it stands on.—Walt Whitman, "New York Dissected" (1856)

In the United States, the owner of a house almost always owns the land on which the house stands. Unless, that is, the homeowner happened to live in Hawai'i during the 1960s.[1] Residential land leasing in the islands grew from just 3.5 percent of all owner-occupied housing in 1940[2] to about 26 percent of the total stock of single-family homes in 1967.[3] Three big private landowners issued 68 percent of these leases, and they worked closely with developers to build and sell leasehold housing in the two decades after World War II, when rural workers and their families were leaving sugar plantations and moving to Honolulu.[4] With the wave of leasehold development came a political backlash, as voters and leasehold homeowners began to view leasehold contracts as a remnant of the territorial economy, which was structured to generate and distribute economic rents to a few powerful corporations, landowners, and the U.S. government.

Statehood in 1959 fundamentally changed the territorial system of government by substantially increasing the voice of Hawai'i's citizens in state decision making and by eliminating the close links between the federal government and Hawai'i's executive and judicial branches. In the early to mid-1960s, the Hawai'i state legislature acted to repeal or reform laws that enabled the territorial system and to dismantle other parts of the system that were enforced by private contract. The large landowners' use of leased land to develop new housing on leasehold was viewed as a contractual method by which large landed estates could maintain their economic power in the land market while also earning profits in the expanded housing market. To remedy this problem, the legislature passed the Land Reform Act (LRA) in 1967. The LRA empowered a state agency to condemn, upon the petition of a majority of owners in a housing tract, residential leased lands and resell them to homeowners. After the U.S. and Hawai'i Supreme Courts both upheld the main provisions of the LRA, Hawai'i homeowners moved quickly to buy the lands under their homes. By 1991, homeowners had purchased the land under about 23,400 of the roughly 28,000 single-family homes built on leased land.

Condominiums in Hawai'i followed a slightly different path of rapid development, political backlash, and land reform. Starting in the early 1960s, new legislation provided a legal basis for condominium sales and associations. By July 1989, 69,969 units had been built, with about 60 percent on leased land.[5] Condo owners tried to convince the state legislature to extend the LRA to include leasehold condos, but when these efforts repeatedly failed, they refocused their attention on the Honolulu City Council. In 1991, the council passed land reform legislation for leasehold condos.[6] The law led to voluntary and involuntary lease conversions. Between 1991 and 2004, the number of leasehold condos in Honolulu fell from 40,916 to 23,193 units.[7] In the early twenty-first century, the political tides shifted again, as opposition to the law among native Hawaiian groups and charitable estates with large landholdings intensified. In January 2005, the council repealed the land reform legislation, thereby ending involuntary condo conversions, even those that had almost been completed before the law's repeal.[8]

This chapter considers the economic and political foundations of the rapid rise and fall of residential land leasing in Hawai'i. Why were so many houses in Hawai'i developed on leased land after World War II, a time when almost all new houses developed in the continental United States were sold as a bundle with the land on which they stood? And why did the economic and political winds shift so suddenly against leasehold tenure, allowing a land reform program to be implemented even as more leasehold housing was being developed and sold? Not surprisingly, the rise of leasehold tenure can be traced to the preferences of landed estates and the federal government's policies on taxation of income and capital gains from land sales. The fall of leasehold tenure can be traced to the transition to more democratic institutions at statehood that allowed the preferences of Hawai'i's electorate to be more directly expressed in state policies.

Structure of Residential Leasehold Contracts in Hawai'i

A prerequisite to an analysis of the rise of residential leasehold tenure in Hawai'i is to understand the terms and mechanics of a typical residential land lease. Here's a brief stylized summary.

Leases on the land under a single-family home were typically set at 55 years.[9] The lease's long length facilitated long-term mortgage financing of the house by the Federal Housing Administration (FHA) and other lenders.[10] Annual land rent was set for 30 years, with a fixed annual rent over the following 25 years determined by a renegotiation process set forth in the lease.[11] Leases typically specified that the rent was to be adjusted to "market levels" at renegotiation. A typical Bishop Estate lease in the early 1970s was based on terms that the estate had negotiated with the FHA in 1967. It specified that the renegotiated lease rent "shall be determined by mutual agreement of Lessor and Lessee, or, if they fail to reach such agreement at least 90 days before the commencement of said period, by appraisal." The new fixed rent "shall be the product of the then prevailing rate of return for similar lands (but not less than the prime rate of interest in Hawaii) multiplied by the then market value of the . . . land exclusive of improvements thereon." Almost all leases stipulated the selection of three appraisers, one each by the lessor and lessee, and the third by those two appraisers. The three appraisers then determined the prevailing rate of return and the market value of the land. A 1975 state law constrained changes in lease rents by placing a ceiling—4 percent of the appraised value of the unencumbered land—on lease rents at renegotiation.[12] The decision of a majority of the three appraisers was final and binding. The cost of the appraisal was divided equally between the two parties. At the expiration of the lease, the lessee had the option to remove his improvements within 30 days; otherwise, both land and improvements reverted to the landowner.[13] Or the two parties could negotiate a new lease, which they would typically do a decade or more before the end of the lease.

Why would owners of land and consumers of land choose to rent land rather than to sell it or buy it? The next two sections examine this choice, the first from the buyer's perspective and the next from the seller's quite different perspective.

Why Leasehold Tenure? The Buyer's Perspective

The financial implications to a home buyer of buying a house bundled with land or buying a house on leased land are very different. To isolate the main differences, I analyze three home purchases in which the same person buys the same house with the same financing but using different types of contracts to obtain the rights to the land on which the house stands.[14] In case 1, the person purchases the house and the land. In case 2, the person purchases the house and leases the land, with the land rent adjusted annually by the Honolulu Consumer Price Index. In case 3, the person purchases the house and leases the land, with the rent fixed for the first 30 years and renegotiated to a fixed market rent for the next 25 years.

Now consider how equity accumulates for homeowners in each of the three cases. In case 1, in which the buyer purchases the house and the land, the owner's real (i.e., inflation-adjusted) equity in the property grows slowly over the first years of the mortgage and then more rapidly at its end (fig. 10.1). When the mortgage is paid off at 30 years, the real value of the homeowner's equity reaches its maximum, which is equal to the market price of the house and land. Equity then declines over the next 25 years due to the 55-year lifespan of the house. Still, after 55 years, the owner retains substantial equity, as the land—an asset with infinite durability—is 50 percent of the asset package and is available for sale or as collateral for rebuilding the house.

Purchase of the land and the house is the typical situation for a 30-year-old home buyer on the U.S. mainland: via the mortgage payment, the owner builds up "life-cycle savings"—that is, savings that could be used to finance consumption during the owner's retirement years. In this case, the owner purchases an asset that has a much longer life (55 years) than the term of the mortgage used to finance its purchase (30 years). At age 60, the owner has the choice of living "rent-free" in the house for 25 years or selling the house, perhaps downsizing, and using the remaining equity for medical care, travel, or other purposes. While there are other ways to accumulate life-cycle savings (e.g., bonds, stocks, commodities,

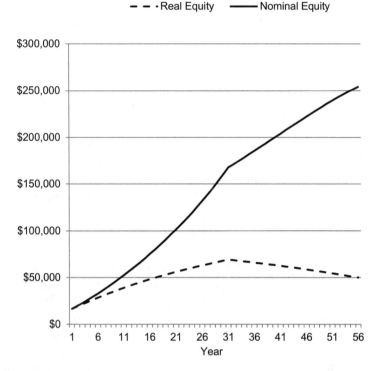

FIGURE 10.1. Buyer equity with house and land purchase.

other real assets), investing in a house-land bundle has some unique tax advantages (e.g., deductibility of interest on home mortgages) and also provides intangible benefits of home ownership.

In case 2, in which the buyer purchases the house and leases the land under a contract in which the lease rent is adjusted annually to reflect increases in the Honolulu Consumer Price Index, the owner's real equity in the property rises for 30 years, reaching a maximum ($7,863) at 30 years when the owner pays off the mortgage (fig. 10.2). The investment in a house on leasehold land is, however, ultimately a *wasting asset*—that is, its value declines to zero at 55 years—because at the end of the 55-year lease, the land must be returned to its owner and the house falls apart. In this case, the owner's real equity in the house continuously falls over the last 25 years of the lease.

In case 3, in which the buyer purchases the house and pays a fixed rent for 30 years on a 55-year land lease and a renegotiated rent for the next

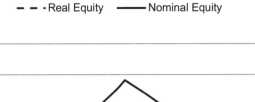

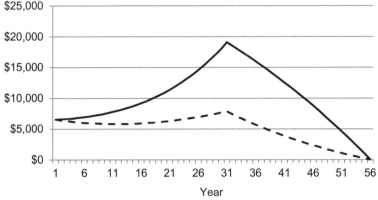

FIGURE 10.2. Buyer equity with house purchase and land lease (lease rents indexed to Honolulu Consumer Price Index).

25 years, the owner's real equity in the property increases for the first 19 years of the lease, reaching a maximum of $9,080 (fig. 10.3). Equity then declines annually for the next 36 years, with the rate of decline accelerating after the mortgage is paid off at 30 years. At 55 years, the house is fully depreciated and the land must be returned to its owner. As in case 2, the owner's equity is zero at the end of the lease.

A central result from cases 2 and 3—that the homeowner has zero equity at the end of a residential lease—raises a big question: Why would any consumer purchase a leasehold residential property if its value is rationally expected to fall to zero at the end of the lease? Economists James Mak and Maxwell Fry provided the answer: to attract a buyer, a house built on leasehold land must sell at a discount, or the lease rent must be set "below market" for the first 30 years of the lease.[15] What types of buyers would be attracted to the combination of a lower purchase price and a lower future price of their home? Younger couples who would have difficulty obtaining a loan are good candidates. Without the discount, some would be unable to buy a home for several more years or would have to buy a home with less space than they need to raise their children. So perhaps leasehold housing exists to provide a mechanism for borrowing-constrained home buyers to gain access to the housing market or to buy better or bigger homes when they are able to access the market.

The buyer-based explanation for leasehold tenure outlined above is logically sound, and it is also a *universal explanation* that should apply to all U.S. metropolitan housing markets, not just the Honolulu market. Leasehold housing, however, is found in only a handful of other U.S. cities. Nor can the high price of housing in Honolulu explain the use of leasehold tenure, as leasehold housing is rarely seen in other U.S. cities with high housing prices. So while a discount on leasehold housing would surely allow greater access for some borrowing-constrained young families in Honolulu, the underlying rationale for the widespread adoption of this form of land tenure in Hawai'i must lie elsewhere, perhaps on the supply side of the housing market. So let's explore that possibility.

Why Leasehold Tenure? The Seller's Perspective

One common element linking most of the U.S. communities with residential land leasing is the presence of large landowning estates. The Irvine Company developed its large "Irvine Ranch" landholdings in Irvine, California, as leasehold housing. Stanford University developed much of the large Palo Alto farm endowed to it by its founder, Leland Stanford,

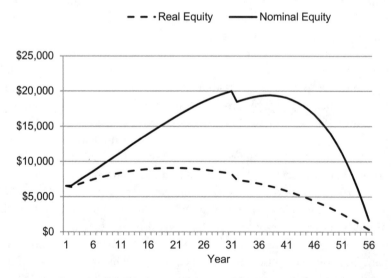

FIGURE 10.3. Buyer equity with house purchase and land lease (lease renegotiation at 30 years).

as leasehold housing. And on O'ahu, the largest private landowner, the Bishop Estate (now known as "Kamehameha Schools"), leased rather than sold most of the lands it developed for housing. The Campbell Estate, the third largest landowner, leased all the land it developed for housing. So why might a large estate prefer to lease rather than sell?

One possible reason is that the will of the estate's founder contains provisions requiring trustees to preserve the estate's landholdings. Consider the case of the Bishop Estate, established in 1884 under the will of Princess Bernice Pauahi Bishop. Her will mandated that all of her lands be held in a charitable trust and that rents from those lands be used to provide for the education of Hawaiians.[16] It further specified that the "trustees shall not sell any real estate, cattle ranches, or any other property, but . . . continue to manage the same, unless in their opinion sales may be necessary for the establishment or maintenance of said schools, or for the best interest of my estate." Throughout the 1950s, the trustees regularly found land sales to be necessary. Between 1912 and 1960, the number of house lots sold (3,356) by the estate actually exceeded the number leased (3,139).[17]

A similar provision limiting land sales appears in the 1900 will of James Campbell, the second largest private landowner on O'ahu. His will specified "that the Trustees and their successors keep intact my estate and administer the same under the name of 'The Estate of James Campbell' . . . and that the realty thereof shall be particularly and especially preserved intact and shall be aliened only in the event, and to the extent, that the obvious interest of my estate shall so demand." Campbell's trustees closely followed the provision "to keep intact my estate" and almost never sold land during the territorial period.[18]

During the 1950s and the 1960s, the Bishop Estate turned away from land sales and began to develop all of its lands—residential, commercial, and industrial—as leasehold properties. One reason to lease rather than sell was that frequent sales of developed lands could have triggered huge federal tax obligations. Whether or not taxes needed to be paid on land sales depended on whether the Internal Revenue Service (IRS) classified the seller as (1) charitable or noncharitable and (2) as a dealer or a nondealer in land.[19]

A charitable classification in the 1950s and 1960s implied very low, or even zero, tax liabilities for income from land sales.[20] Among the largest lessors, the Bishop Estate was classified as charitable and was therefore exempt from the federal capital gains tax. In contrast, the Campbell

Estate was classified as noncharitable, and its land sales were subject to capital gains taxes ranging from 25 to 35 percent from 1945 to 1981. Because the federal capital gains tax is paid only when gains are realized—that is, when the asset is sold—leasing provided these estates with a mechanism for avoiding taxes, as it indefinitely deferred tax payments on the land's capital gains. Incentives to avoid taxes were particularly strong for Hawai'i's estates in the decades after World War II, as most had held their lands since the late nineteenth century and the value of those lands had increased enormously over 75–100 years of ownership. If they had sold land, virtually all of the revenue from the sale would have qualified as taxable capital gains.

Whether estates paid taxes also depended on whether the IRS classified them as dealers or non-dealers in land. A noncharitable landlord, as a dealer, would have had to pay taxes on revenues from land sales at the ordinary income tax rate (which ranged between 70 and 91 percent between 1945 and 1981) instead of at the lower capital gains tax rate (25 to 35 percent). The charitable Bishop Estate, if it had been classified as a dealer, would have lost its exemption from all taxes. If that had happened, rental income would have been taxed at the ordinary income tax rate and capital gains at either the capital gains or ordinary income tax rate. In the early 1950s, the IRS classified all three large estates as non-dealers, thereby allowing each to pay much less in federal taxes.[21]

Estate trustees worried that the IRS might reclassify them as land dealers if they sold land frequently, as the IRS tended to review the tax status of landlords making frequent or large sales and could reclassify the seller as a dealer if the frequency and aggregate value of sales became too large. In a 1973 interview, Bishop Estate trustee Matsuo Takabuki summarized the rationale behind the estate's reluctance to sell land: "Everyone of these [transactions] is subject to the Internal Revenue approval. So we have to be careful that we do not under any circumstances do anything that ruins our status as a tax exempt institution."[22]

In fact, it was a confrontation with the IRS during the 1950s that triggered the estate's shift to residential land leasing. In 1954, the estate had joined with a developer to build homes and sell them with the land.[23] When the IRS learned of the sales, it warned that if such sales continued, the estate would lose its tax-exempt status.[24] In the years following this warning, the estate leased thousands of lots, but made only a few sales of "leased fees"—that is, all remaining interests in the lands leased to homeowners.[25]

Although the tax consequences of dealer classification were less severe for noncharitable estates, they were enough to keep them from making frequent sales. Harold Castle (an individual owner of large tracts of land) seldom sold any land before he died in 1967, and the Campbell Estate made very few voluntary sales in the 1950s and 1960s.[26] When it did sell, the Campbell Estate paid capital gains taxes. Castle & Cooke, the third largest landowner in Honolulu, had a different experience with the IRS. In the mid-1960s, the corporation sold an option to purchase 3,500 acres and paid capital gains taxes on the transaction.[27] The IRS audited the company and required payment of taxes on this transaction at an effective rate somewhere between the capital gains tax rate and the 48 percent corporate income tax rate.

Alongside the economic incentives favoring the estates' choice of leasehold tenure was the clear preference of Bishop Estate trustees to keep their landholdings under native Hawaiian control.[28] In the late 1840s and early 1850s, all traditional landholdings were reorganized into private holdings with fee simple rights. Foreigners quickly gained the right to own land (see chap. 5). Over the next 70 years, many Native Hawaiian recipients of land in the *Māhele* sold, gave away, abandoned, were cheated out of, had mortgages foreclosed, died intestate, or otherwise lost their land. By 1919, individual native Hawaiians owned just 6 percent of Hawai'i's land. The Bishop Estate owned another 9 percent. A number of factors, particularly the post–World War II Hawaiian cultural renaissance, galvanized numerous native Hawaiian groups to oppose further alienation of Hawaiian lands.[29] Native Hawaiian civic organizations pointed to the provisions of Princess Bernice Pauahi Bishop's will, which emphasized the importance of retaining native Hawaiian ownership and control of estate lands. During the 1960s and 1970s, the trustees' commitment to this goal was clearly bolstered by the native Hawaiian community's growing recognition of its historical losses and the trustees' desire for support rather than criticism from these increasingly vocal groups and prominent community leaders.[30]

Another game changer for landowners in the late 1950s was the establishment of the Hawaii Land Development Authority. The bill establishing the authority had bipartisan support. It was passed by a legislature with solid Democratic Party majorities in both chambers and signed by Republican Governor William Quinn, who had energetically lobbied for the bill. The authority was "empowered to declare a development area of not less than twenty-five acres for residential purposes, and to acquire

property for that purpose through negotiations or eminent-domain proceedings."[31] Sociologist Lawrence Fuchs argued that the authority put
pressure on estates and large corporations to develop more lands for residential housing. Given the strong preferences of the Campbell and Bishop
Estates to retain their lands and the high federal capital gains tax on land
sales, the authority's mandate to move the undeveloped lands of large landowners into housing pushed the big landowners onto a clear path: keep
the land and develop it as leasehold housing.[32]

The Fall of Leasehold Tenure: Residential Land Reform

The lawyer George Cooper and the historian Gavan Daws have carefully
documented the political maneuvering that led to the LRA's passage.[33]
They argue that the legislature's enactment of land reform was fueled by
the postwar political revolution in Hawai'i that ended more than 50 years
of dominance by the Republican Party during the territorial era and ush-
ered in more than 60 years of dominance by the Democratic Party in the
statehood era (see chap. 9). Second-generation Asian-Americans, who
were American citizens by right of birth in a U.S. territory, entered the
electorate in the 1940s and 1950s and became strong supporters of Democratic Party candidates. They opposed the dominant Republican coalition in order to force a dismantling of the institutions and policies of the
colonial order and to transfer some of the rents created for the territorial
political coalition to their new ascendant coalition.

Urban land development also moved onto the political agenda, in part
because of the transformation of the sugar industry during the 1930s and
1940s. In 1934, the federal government passed the Jones-Costigan Act
(see chap. 9), setting a sugar production quota for Hawai'i that imposed
more severe cutbacks on its producers than on other U.S. sugar producers. Hawai'i's sugar producers reacted to the market restriction by changing their focus from finding new opportunities for intensification and
expansion of production to developing new technologies to cut the cost
of producing their allocated quota.[34] Sugar planters were already funding
their research and development activities via the Hawaiian Sugar Planters' Association, and many of the industry's most important inventions
during the first third of the twentieth century were developed in Hawai'i.
The industry transformation was reinforced by Hawai'i's passage of the
"Little Wagner" Act, which put in place a state regulatory framework

conducive to the formation of unions in agriculture, and a 1944 National Labor Relations Board ruling that made over 50 percent of plantation workers eligible to join a union. Both developments facilitated unionization of the industry's labor force by the International Longshore and Warehouse Union (ILWU). Mechanization of plantation activities, higher union wages, and U.S. sugar production quotas combined to reduce employment in Hawaiʻi's sugar industry from 52,264 workers in 1933 to just 14,085 workers in 1958.[35]

The 5.24 percent annual decline in employment in the rural sugar industry meant that many plantation workers lost not only their jobs, but also their plantation housing. Taking the interisland ferries to Honolulu and other urban areas, they searched for new employment, new homes, and new lives (fig. 10.4). The post–World War II economic transition was difficult in Hawaiʻi, as the promise of tourism did not manifest itself until the mid- to late 1950s, and other industries were slow to expand. Migrants found not only limited job opportunities but also small, expensive housing units in the crowded, densely populated city that was Honolulu in the 1940s and 1950s. Both veteran and new politicians saw clearly that the demand for homes and home ownership by former plantation workers and young war veterans would be a potent political issue until more homes were built and sold.

After World War II, expansion of the islands' housing stock became intertwined with the idea of reform and perhaps abolition of residential land leasing. The Democratic Party took the lead by advocating for reform of residential land leasing in its party platforms and campaigns. In 1945, Governor Ingram Stainback, a Democrat appointed by Franklin D. Roosevelt, informed the territorial legislature that "there exists on Oahu a grave shortage of lands available on the open market due to the landholding policies of large land-holding monopolies, resulting in an unhealthy increase in the value of small areas which are available—and that this condition is so extreme as to render impracticable any scheme for adequate housing with private capital unless and until sufficient lands at reasonable prices can be made available."[36]

As early as 1949, Democrats introduced bills in the territorial legislature requiring lessors to sell their residential fee interests to their lessees. Beginning in 1952, the Hawaiʻi Democratic Party platform called for land reform to enable homeowners to purchase the fee interests in their residential lots. By the late 1950s, some Republican politicians had also attached themselves to this issue. The liberal wing of the Republican

FIGURE 10.4. Aerial view of a housing subdivision, Pearl City, Oʻahu, Hawaiʻi. Photo: Camera Hawaii. Source: Bishop Museum.

Party began to advocate for land reform, albeit with their proposals more focused on public than private lands. In July 1959, the incumbent Republican governor, William Quinn, would win the first gubernatorial election ever held in Hawaiʻi by promising a "second *Māhele*" that would distribute government land to qualified homesteaders. Although Quinn's plan died in the next legislative session, the adoption of this issue by a Republican governor indicated how significant it had become to voters.

In November 1962, the Democratic Party gained control of both houses of the state legislature and won the first of 10 straight gubernatorial elections. Democrats immediately pushed a bill through the house of representatives that was patterned after the 1884 Maryland Ground Rent Redemption Act.[37] It provided homeowners with the opportunity to purchase fee interests in the land under their homes after living on their property for five years. The bill's provisions applied only to leases initiated after the bill's passage. Opposition came from large landowners and trusts as well as Hawaiian groups who viewed the bill as a threat to the Bishop

Estate. The bill failed by one vote to pass the state senate, an outcome often blamed on the "no" vote of Democratic Senator George Ariyoshi, who cited the bill's dubious constitutionality, exclusion of existing lessees, and potential chilling effects on housing construction as the reasons for his vote.[38]

The death of the Maryland bill prompted Democratic Party strategists to write a new land reform bill that fixed specific aspects of the Maryland bill criticized by a number of different groups. To defuse opposition from small landowners, the new bill exempted them from its leasehold conversion provisions. To bring in Republican legislative support, existing lessees, many of whom lived in Republican legislative districts in East O'ahu, were allowed to convert their leases. To avoid potential adverse tax complications for estates, the Maryland bill's reform mechanism—a requirement that all future leasehold contracts contain a redemption clause—was replaced with a provision for bulk condemnations of entire tracts of leasehold lands. As Cooper and Daws relate, state legislators and representatives from the three big private landowners—the Bishop Estate, Campbell Estate, and the Kaneohe Ranch—visited Washington, D.C., "during or just before the 1967 Legislative session" to meet with an IRS official to discuss how the provisions of the revamped land reform measure would affect their tax obligations and whether conversions would change IRS classifications of estates as non-dealers in land.[39]

In spring 1967, the legislature passed, and Governor John Burns signed, the Land Reform Act (LRA). The law (Hawai'i Revised Statutes 516) enabled single-family homeowners on leasehold land to purchase the lessor's interest. It provided for the Hawaii Housing Authority (HHA), upon the petition of 50 percent of the lessees (or 25 lessees, whichever is less) in a leasehold housing tract, to use its power of eminent domain to purchase lessor land and resell individual parcels to lessees.[40] The LRA's provision for bulk condemnation of whole housing tracts was designed to obtain favorable tax treatment of leasehold sales from the IRS. The strategy worked beautifully. The Bishop Estate kept its tax-exempt status, and the IRS provided noncharitable landowners with the choice of paying the capital gains tax rate on condemnation sales or indefinitely deferring capital gains taxes by rolling over gains from their sales into another investment.[41]

After the LRA's passage, all landowners except the Bishop Estate stopped entering into new leasehold development contracts.[42] There were few conversions from leasehold to fee simple between 1967 and 1975 because Governor Burns objected to the LRA's requirement that the state purchase an entire tract of homes, resell them to lessees willing and able to buy, and become the landlord to the remaining, often quite wealthy lessees. The LRA remained dormant until the death of Governor Burns in 1974 and the assumption of office by Lieutenant Governor George Ariyoshi, who would serve 11 years as governor.

Four acts passed by the legislature in 1975 and 1976 changed the decision calculus of lessees and the state by providing more incentives for lessees to petition for conversions and more incentives for the state to implement the LRA. In 1975, the legislature passed Act 185, which established controls on land rents at lease renegotiation, Act 186, which reaffirmed the LRA's purposes,[43] and Act 184, which required that at the termination of a lease, the lessor pay fair market value to the lessee for unremoved onsite improvements (existing leases provided that the tenant turn over improvements without compensation).[44] In 1976, it passed Act 242, which mandated that appraisers use controlled lease rents to determine the value of condemned lands, thereby reducing compensation to be paid to landowners. This more favorable legal environment for conversion led to the first use of the LRA's leasehold conversion procedures when lessees purchased 182 lots from the Pflueger-Cassiday Trust in a negotiated settlement in 1976. A growing number of petitions to the HHA and conversions followed between 1979 and 1982.

In 1979, the Bishop Estate contested the constitutionality of the LRA in state and federal court cases. A U.S. District Court ruling in favor of the LRA was overturned by the Ninth Circuit Court of Appeals, and the case went to the U.S. Supreme Court. In 1984, the Supreme Court ruled unanimously that the LRA's stated public purpose—to control oligopoly in Hawai'i land markets—was consistent with the public use requirement of the Fifth Amendment.[45] At the state level, the First Circuit Court upheld the act's constitutionality, and the Hawai'i Supreme Court affirmed the First Circuit's decision in 1985.[46]

The U.S. and Hawai'i Supreme Court decisions opened the door to a flood of leasehold conversions in the mid- to late 1980s. In the mid-1970s, about 30 percent of owner-occupied detached homes were on leased land. By 1991, the share of leasehold homes had fallen to 5 percent of the overall housing stock. Four large estates—Bishop Estate (57.3 percent), Castle Estate (16.8 percent), Robinson Estate (9.5 percent), and Campbell Estate (6.7 percent)—accounted for over 90 percent of all conversions.[47]

What were the main economic and political factors leading to the passage of the LRA in 1967 and to its implementation and widespread use starting in the late 1970s? One political factor was the decision by Congress and President Eisenhower to approve statehood for Hawai'i in 1959. The transfer of political power from the federal government to the new state government meant that the state's Democratic voting majority could end policies that transferred economic rents to the Big Five companies and other members of the traditional Republican coalition. One economic factor was the substantial net benefits that the LRA provided to lessees, whether or not they actually used the law. The LRA provided each lessee with an option to buy their land at a legally specified price at any future date. Exercise of this option would allow a lessee to avoid both a diminished ability to borrow against the property toward the end of the lease and the surrender of onsite improvements at the end of the lease.

The LRA's provision of gains to lessees was not fully reflected in the votes of legislators representing lessees. The largest concentrations of lessees were among affluent residents in East and Windward O'ahu, who were represented by Republican legislators, formerly dominant in both chambers but in the minority in the 1960s and 1970s. The four Republican senators representing East and Windward O'ahu supported the bill, while the seven Republican representatives from the same districts voted against the LRA.[48]

The four land reform measures meant to bolster the LRA—Act 186, Act 184, and Act 185 in 1975 and Act 242 in 1976—passed the legislature with big bipartisan majorities and were signed by Governor Ariyoshi. With the passage of these bills, the voting patterns of Republican representatives and senators shifted once again. In the senate, the four Republicans representing East and Windward O'ahu joined the other twenty-one senators in unanimously passing all four bills. All four were re-elected in the 1968 elections. In the house of representatives, where votes in favor of the four bills were almost unanimous, each of the eight Republicans representing East and Windward O'ahu voted for the four bills. Only one representative was defeated in the 1976 election, a year in which the Republican presidential candidate, Gerald Ford, ran a surprisingly close race in Hawai'i against the Democratic presidential candidate, Jimmy Carter.

Why did the close votes on land reform legislation in the 1960s turn into large bipartisan legislative majorities for the 1975 and 1976 land reform bills? Four changes in the intervening eight years stand out. First, the number of single-family leasehold homes had increased from around

14,600 in 1967 to around 22,000 in 1975, thereby increasing the voting power of leasehold homeowners and family members.[49]

Second, the number of lessees with contracts nearing rent renegotiation increased between 1967 and 1975. Voter propensity to participate in the political process depends not only on the costs of gathering and processing information, but also on the wealth at stake for the voter. As the date of rent renegotiation and higher rent payments neared, the wealth at stake also increased, and lessees had increased incentives to vote, lobby, or make political contributions to reduce their lease rent payments.

Third, economic rents from the development of housing increased substantially between 1967 and 1975. A highly regulated land supply, a boom in housing demand due an economy fueled by tourism and the Vietnam War, and unexpectedly high Honolulu inflation all combined to push up Honolulu housing prices.[50] Lease renegotiations were already under way for some properties, and news stories were making lessees aware of the big increases in lease rents that had been negotiated on similar properties and of the difficulties in selling or refinancing their properties as renegotiation neared.[51] Given the big increase in the value of their homes, lessees had incentives to focus their support on state house and senate candidates who would vote for legislation that enabled them to capture a bigger share of the economic rents created by housing price increases.

Fourth, the structure of the fixed-rent leasehold contract implies a substantial rent hike at renegotiation even in the absence of unexpected inflation or real increases in the price of land. In an economic environment with persistent long-term inflation, the leasehold contract has the same payment structure as a long-term mortgage. The fixed lease rent in a long-term contract often exceeds the spot market rent in initial periods and is lower in later periods. At renegotiation, the fixed lease rent must be raised not just to the spot market lease rent, but higher, to compensate for the effects of expected inflation.[52]

Earlier in this chapter, I argued that IRS policy governing taxation of the land sale proceeds of Hawai'i's large estates was one of the main factors behind the rapid rise of residential leasehold tenure in Hawai'i after World War II. Not surprisingly, changes in federal and state income tax rates during the 1970s and 1980s also changed incentives for landowners and homeowners to enter into new leasehold contracts or continue to hold existing contracts. Consider first the homeowner side of the equation. Increases in average marginal tax rates during the 1970s—a result of unexpected inflation pushing homeowners into higher marginal tax brackets—increased homeowners' tax benefits from fee ownership relative to leasing. This is because mortgage interest payments on fee purchases were tax deductible, whereas lease rents were not. Economists Robert Barro and Chaipat Sahasakul used federal income tax data to calculate average marginal federal tax rates from 1960 to 1983 and found that they fluctuated in the 21–26 percent range between 1960 and 1975 and then increased to a range of 29–31 percent between 1978 and 1982.[53] In Hawai'i, the effects of these higher average marginal income tax rates were magnified by big jumps in new and renegotiated lease rents during the 1970s and 1980s due to massive appreciation in housing prices during this period.[54]

Now consider how changes in tax rates and IRS policy affected the seller side of the equation. Prior to 1979, the IRS had conducted after-the-fact, case-by-case audits on all types of estate land sales to determine the estate's tax status and tax liabilities. In 1979, the IRS established a blanket exemption from taxes on lease fee sales of single-family homes by the Bishop Estate.[55] Not only was the estate's uncertainty about taxes eliminated. but all tax issues were resolved completely in its favor! Other large noncharitable estates in Hawai'i also benefited from changes in IRS policies. Between 1981 and 1987, the marginal tax rate on ordinary income applicable to income from lease fee sales fell from 70 percent to 28 percent.[56] The fall in rates reduced the tax liabilities associated with dealer status. This should have reduced the estates' incentives to retain leased fee or fee landholdings given the reduced cost associated with possible IRS reclassification as a dealer.

The rise and fall of leasehold tenure for condominiums and townhouses follows the same basic story as in the case of single-family homes, with two main differences. First, the ownership of land leases for condos was much less concentrated than the ownership of land leases for single-family homes. Whereas one lessor, the Bishop Estate, issued around 20 percent of the leases, the remainder were issued by hundreds of private landowners. Second, land reform for owners of condominiums on leased land was not enacted until 1991, and then only in Honolulu. Reasons for its late arrival include the smaller presence of large landowners in this market and opposition from hundreds of small lessors, many of whom owned only one condo building. Honolulu finally enacted a land reform law after five years of spectacular increases in median condominium prices, which more than doubled between 1985 ($89,800) and 1990 ($187,000). This rapid increase in condo prices motivated owners of leasehold condos to lobby the mayor and city council to enact a land reform law that closely followed the state law.

Condo land reform did not last long, however, as within a few years of its enactment, native Hawaiian trusts and civic groups mobilized to push for repeal of the city law. This change in the political environment took place for several interconnected reasons. First, deep-rooted scandals afflicted the trustees of the Bishop Estate in the mid- to late 1990s.[57] Violations ranged from interference by estate trustees in the management of Kamehameha Schools to payment of outrageous fees to trustees for sales of estate lands that were mandated by the LRA. Hawaiians were shocked to discover how poorly the assets of the Bishop Estate had been shepherded for future generations, and they organized to push for reforms. Once the trustee scandals ebbed in the late 1990s, the Hawaiian groups were strengthened, ready to fight another battle against forced sales of leased land to condominium owners that many Hawaiians found almost as compelling. Second, the law's first decade had been a great success, with many condo owners converting or accepting voluntary offers made by landowners. As the number of leasehold condos and the wealth at stake both fell, resistance to its repeal also weakened. Finally, stories told by leasehold condo owners of abuse by powerful economic players were never as compelling as the ones told by owners of single-family homes on leased land because the lessors were, with the exception of Kamehameha Schools, not "villainous" large landed estates, but rather families with small land holdings.

Conclusion

Hawai'i's big landowners assembled their lands in the nineteenth century, when Hawai'i was a kingdom, and developed them in the twentieth century, when Hawai'i was part of the United States. Their development of those lands as leasehold housing was to a large extent due to cold calculations that their U.S. income tax burden would be much lower if they developed them in leasehold rather than fee simple. In the 1950s, 1960s, and 1970s, minimizing tax burdens really mattered because federal income tax rates were so high. Similarly, the decline of leasehold tenure was partly fueled by the decline in federal income tax rates during the 1980s. In this chapter, I also considered a variety of explanations suggesting that landowners developed leasehold housing because consumers would gain from leasing land rather than purchasing it. I discarded those explanations because they are universal explanations that predict that other U.S. cities with high housing prices should also have been developed with leasehold housing. To the contrary, leasehold housing is rarely seen in major U.S. cities, with the notable exception of Baltimore. In the 1960s, Hawai'i chose to make its housing markets more like those in other U.S. cities and states by dismantling leasehold tenure. In the next chapter, I consider whether this change benefited Hawai'i consumers by reducing the power of large landowners to set housing and land prices and thereby lowering real housing prices in Hawai'i.

CHAPTER ELEVEN

Land Reform and Housing Prices

The 1967 Land Reform Act (LRA) was one of several blockbuster policy initiatives enacted by the state government in the decade after statehood, and its implementation involuntarily transferred large tracts of land from large landed estates to homeowners leasing the land under their homes. The act's preamble sets forth a clear public purpose for the LRA's property rights reorganization: to reduce the market power of the large landed estates and thereby reduce the prices of land and housing.

This chapter takes a close look at the public purpose of the LRA and asks whether its use of coerced sales of leased lands could have been an effective policy for reducing housing prices in Hawai'i. I consider this question from two perspectives. First, I look at the two major federal and state court cases in which the constitutionality of the LRA was challenged. In 1984, the U.S. Supreme Court upheld the constitutionality of the law in a landmark 8–0 decision, *Hawaii Housing Authority v. Midkiff*,[1] and the Hawai'i Supreme Court followed in 1985 with a 5–0 ruling affirming the LRA in *Hawaii Housing Authority v. Lyman*.[2] My examination of the historical and economic arguments put forth by the U.S. Supreme Court finds them to be misleading in some instances and just wrong in others. Second, I use new research on housing prices in U.S. markets to provide a framework for understanding why Honolulu housing prices have been high relative to U.S. mainland prices since at least World War II. I conclude that severe natural restrictions on the supply of land in Hawai'i, state and local

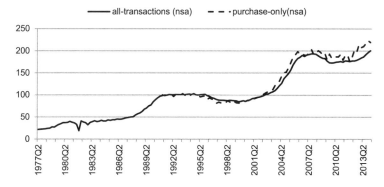

FIGURE II.I. Federal Housing Finance Agency House Price Index (HPI) for single-family houses in Honolulu, 1977–2013 (1990 = 100). As Calhoun (1996) explains, "The HPI for each geographic area is estimated using repeated observations of housing values for individual single-family residential properties on which at least two mortgages were originated and subsequently purchased by either Freddie Mac or Fannie Mae since January 1975." The graph reports the non-seasonally-adjusted (nsa) all-transaction index, which includes sales data and home appraisal data, and the non-seasonally-adjusted purchase-only index, which uses only sales data.

regulations restricting land development, and an economic boom following statehood were the main factors pumping up Hawai'i's land and housing prices.[3] The role of concentrated land ownership in pushing up land prices was small or nonexistent. Nor is there any evidence that the forced sale of land leased by large estates to homeowners ever led to a reduction of land prices in Hawai'i. In fact, Honolulu housing prices have continued to soar since the LRA was implemented in the late 1970s (fig. 11.1).

Given that the LRA was ineffective in reducing housing prices in Hawai'i, is it possible that it could have accomplished a different public purpose? In Hawai'i's earlier natural states, land redistributions had a public purpose, as rulers traditionally used them to rebalance the dominant coalition when there was a transition in rulers or a change in the power of groups in the coalition. Thus, earlier redistributions may have enhanced the stability of new and reorganized governments. Reasoning in the same vein, economic historian Naomi Lamoreaux has suggested that the public purpose of the LRA might not be to control the market power of large landowners, but rather to strengthen the stakes of Hawai'i residents in the open-access political order suddenly established by the transition to statehood just eight years earlier.[4] While confiscation of property rights seems antithetical to the central idea of an open-access order, the LRA did provide (rough) compensation to landowners whose lands were taken, unlike earlier land confiscations. If the compensated redistributions paradoxically had the effect of strengthening the nascent open-access political order emerging in Hawai'i, then perhaps they had a legitimate public purpose.

Prices and Concentrated Land Ownership

This chapter's analysis focuses on the island of O'ahu, which has just one local government, the City and County of Honolulu. This focus is appropriate because when the LRA was enacted, 98 percent of the leasehold owner-occupied dwellings were in Honolulu, and housing and land markets on the islands of Kaua'i, Maui, and Hawai'i were distinctly separate from Honolulu's markets.[5] Home prices were high in Honolulu in 1960 compared with the mainland United States, and the difference more than doubled over the next seven years (table 11.1). According to the Federal Housing Administration (FHA), the average price of a single-family home in Hawai'i in 1960 was $18,570, more than $5,000 higher than the average mainland price. By 1967, the Hawai'i price had risen to $28,447. Home site prices were also high and rising. In 1960, the average price of an existing home site in Hawai'i was approximately $7,000, compared with only $2,000 on the mainland. By 1968, both Honolulu and mainland average site prices had jumped, to $13,000 in Hawai'i and to $4,000 on the mainland.[6]

Many in Hawai'i thought that the main reason for high site and home prices was concentration of land ownership, which allowed large landowners with market power to raise prices. Land ownership had become increasingly concentrated over the previous century due to acquisitions

TABLE 11.1. **Housing and Site Prices in Hawai'i and Mainland United States, 1960 and 1967**

	Average price of existing single-family home		Average price of single-family home site	
	1960	1967	1960	1967
Hawai'i	$18,570	$28,447	$7,000[a]	$13,000[a]
U.S. mainland	13,300[a]	$15,940	$2,000[a]	$4,000[a]

Source: State of Hawaii, Office of Lt. Governor (1969, 22, 24(b), 59, 82).
[a]Approximate values.

TABLE 11.2. **Concentration of Land Ownership on Oʻahu in 1964**

	Acres owned in fee simple	Percentage of land owned
Privately owned land:		
Bishop Estate	59,007	15.49
Campbell Estate	50,260	13.20
Castle & Cooke	42,399	11.13
Harold Castle	9,366	2.46
Zion Securities	6,374	1.67
Combined smaller owners[a]	91,719	24.08
Total	259,125	68.03
Publicly owned land:		
State of Hawaiʻi	56,676	14.88
United States	55,109	14.47
City and County of Honolulu[b]	9,923	2.61
Total	121,708	31.96

Source: Horowitz and Finn (1967).
[a]"Combined smaller owners" is the residual obtained by subtracting acres of publicly owned lands and acres held by the five largest private landowners from Hawaiʻiʻs total.
[b]Acreage for City and County of Honolulu is for the year 1965.

of land by large ranches, sugar plantations, and pineapple plantations as well as large gifts of land from prominent native Hawaiians to charitable estates. Sugar industry consolidation during the Great Depression further concentrated land ownership. Not only did the number of sugar plantations fall from 47 in 1930 to 25 in 1965, but the Big Five companies acquired majority holdings in most sugar plantations during the 1930s, when the plantations were unable to repay loans owed to the Big Five.

Table 11.2 provides information on land ownership on Oʻahu in 1964. Roughly 68 percent of the island was privately owned and 32 percent publicly owned. The three largest private owners—the Bishop Estate, the Campbell Estate, and Castle & Cooke—held almost 65 percent of the privately owned land.[7] Of the publicly owned land, the state of Hawaiʻi owned 47 percent, the United States 45 percent, and the City and County of Honolulu 8 percent. No other urban land market in the United States had more highly concentrated ownership.

The Land Reform Act and the U.S. Supreme Court

In the 15 years after World War II, most of the newly built single-family homes in Honolulu were developed on leased land. Concern grew among the public that large landowners controlled the Honolulu housing market and that home prices were unduly high as a result. Starting in 1952, the Democratic Party platform called for land reform to enable homeowners to purchase the land on which their homes stood. In 1963, a leasehold condemnation bill narrowly failed to pass the Hawai'i state legislature, but in 1967, when some of the earliest ground leases were being renegotiated, the Land Reform Act (LRA) passed both the senate and the house of representatives with substantial majorities and was signed into law by Governor Burns.[8]

The provisions of the LRA (described in more detail in chap. 10) were triggered upon the petition of 50 percent of the owners (or 25 owners, whichever is less) in a leasehold housing tract. The Hawaii Housing Authority (HHA) then condemned the housing tract and resold individual parcels to lessees. The primary stated purpose of the LRA was to increase "the ability of the people to acquire fee simple ownership of residential lots at a fair and reasonable price."[9] This would presumably bring about two of the law's other stated purposes: "the dispersion of ownership of fee simple residential lots to as large a number of people as possible," and to make it possible for "lessees of residential leases to derive full enjoyment from their leaseholds."[10] As section 1 of the law stated:

> (f) The population growth and the increase in demand for residential lots, and the concentration of ownership of private lands in the hands of a few and their practice of leasing, rather than selling in fee simple, the residential lots developed on their lands, have led to a serious shortage of residential fee simple property at reasonable prices in the State's urban areas and have deprived the people of the State of a choice to own or to take leases to the land on which their homes are situated.

> (g) The shortage of single-family, residential, fee simple property, and the restriction on the people of a real choice between fee simple and leasehold residential property have in turn caused land prices for both fee simple and leasehold residential lots to become artificially inflated and have enabled lessors to include in residential leases terms and conditions that are financially disadvantageous to the lessees, restrict unduly their freedom to enjoy their leasehold estates and are weighted heavily in favor of the landlord as against the lessees.[11]

The legislature then concluded that state intervention to force leasehold conversions would create a bigger supply of fee simple lots, a more competitive land market, and lower housing prices.

After the law's passage, Governor John Burns was reluctant to implement it, and condemnation proceedings were delayed until George Ariyoshi became governor upon Burns's death in 1974 and until the legislature passed several amendments to the LRA in 1975 and in 1976. The first condemnation proceedings began in1976, nine years after the LRA's passage. The Bishop Estate filed state and federal lawsuits in February 1979 against the Hawaii Housing Authority, arguing that the LRA violated both the state and federal constitutions.

In 1979, the U.S. District Court found the LRA's compulsory arbitration and compensation formulas to be unconstitutional, but upheld all of its other provisions.[12] In 1983, a three-judge panel from the U.S. Ninth Circuit Court of Appeals reversed that finding in a 2–1 decision. The majority provided a succinct summary of the issue and their decision: "We must decide whether the Federal Constitution permits a state to take the private property of A and transfer its ownership to B for his private use and benefit. It is our view that it was the intention of the framers of the Constitution and the fifth amendment that this form of *majoritarian tyranny* should not occur" (emphasis added).[13] The panel further found the 1967 state legislature's statement of public purpose to be mere "trappings of public use" and that "the statute itself is so structured that it can only aggravate this [land] shortage and resultant inflation of land values."[14]

In 1984, the U.S. Supreme Court upheld the constitutionality of the LRA in an 8–0 decision, *Hawaii Housing Authority v. Midkiff.* Justice Sandra Day O'Connor's forceful opinion responded to each of the Ninth Circuit's arguments, declaring that "the mere fact that property taken outright by eminent domain is transferred in the first instance to private beneficiaries does not condemn that taking as having only a private purpose."[15] Justice O'Connor then asserted that because "the unique way titles were held in Hawaii skewed the land market, exercise of the power of eminent domain was justified."[16]

Justice O'Connor deferred to the basic arguments made by the U.S. Supreme Court in 1954 in its landmark ruling on eminent domain and public use, *Berman v. Parker.*[17] She concluded that

> the "public use" requirement is thus coterminous with the scope of a sovereign's police powers.
>
> There is, of course, a role for courts to play in reviewing a legislature's judgment of what constitutes a public use, even when the eminent domain power is equated with the police power. But the Court in *Berman* made clear that it is "an extremely narrow" one.

She approvingly cited the Berman opinion's reference to an earlier U.S.
Supreme Court decision on eminent domain holding that "deference to
the legislature's 'public use' determination is required 'until it is shown to
involve an impossibility.' "[18] Justice O'Connor then turned to the Hawai'i
state legislature's stated public purpose for the LRA, put forth in the
LRA's "Findings and declaration of necessity." The "Findings" declared
that the cause of high land prices and residential land leasing in Honolulu was the high concentration of ownership in the land market.[19] Justice
O'Connor then found that the Hawai'i state legislature passed the LRA
to rid Hawai'i's land markets of "social and economic evils" traceable to
the nineteenth-century Hawai'i monarchy: "The people of Hawaii have
attempted, much as the settlers of the original 13 Colonies did, to reduce
the perceived social and economic evils of a land oligopoly traceable to
their monarchs. The land oligopoly has, according to the Hawaii Legislature, created artificial deterrents to the normal functioning of the State's
residential land market and forced thousands of individual homeowners
to lease, rather than buy, the land underneath their homes. Regulating
oligopoly and the evils associated with it is a classic exercise of a State's
police powers." She elaborated further in a footnote: "After the American Revolution, the colonists in several States took steps to eradicate the
feudal incidents with which large proprietors had encumbered land in the
Colonies. . . . Courts have never doubted that such statutes served a public
purpose."

Justice O'Connor also declared that the court could not "condemn as
irrational the act's approach to correcting the land oligopoly problem."[20]
The LRA was further praised for providing "a comprehensive and rational approach to identifying and correcting market failure."[21] Given these
multiple sources of support for the LRA, it is not surprising that the court
dismissed the lawsuit. The Hawai'i Supreme Court issued a similar ruling
in 1985, thereby clearing all legal challenges to implementing the LRA.[22]

Justice O'Connor's Use of U.S. and Hawaiian History

Is the comparison between the legislatures of the original thirteen colonies and the Hawai'i state legislature enacting laws "to reduce the perceived social and economic evils of a land oligopoly traceable to their
monarchs" a valid one?[23] Were the circumstances actually similar? Consider first the historical background to the legislation enacted during and

after the American Revolution. In 1777, the Continental Congress passed a law that urged the colonies to confiscate lands and real property of Loyalists and British subjects. Between 1776 and 1787, each of the rebellious colonies passed legislation enabling the confiscation and sale of Loyalist and British property. The historian Forrest McDonald estimated that at least 10 percent of the value of real estate was confiscated by bills of attainder issued by colonies during the war.[24] The states confiscated and sold these traitors' property to raise revenues to finance the war and to reduce the ability of Loyalists to contribute to the British war effort.[25] McDonald found that state after state specifically directed that the larger confiscated estates be sold in small parcels so as to break up "dangerous monopolies of land."[26]

In some ways, the American confiscations were neither unexpected nor unusual, as opposing sides in European civil wars in the early modern period typically confiscated opponents' property during and after the war.[27] They were, however, very unusual in one respect: they were accompanied by reorganizations of *all* property rights to *all* lands in the colony. Consider Virginia's bold proclamation in its 1779 legislation enabling confiscation of Loyalist lands. It declared that the owners

> of lands within this commonwealth may no longer be subject to any servile, feudal, or precarious tenure, and to prevent the danger to a free state from perpetual revenue; *Be it enacted*, That the royal mines, quit-rents, and all other reservations and conditions in the patents or grants of land from the crown of England or of Great Britain, under the former government, shall be, and are hereby declared null and void; and that all lands thereby respectively granted shall be held in absolute and unconditional property to intents and purposes whatsoever, in the same manner with the lands hereafter to be granted by the commonwealth by virtue of this act.[28]

The enabling acts in Maryland, Virginia, and Pennsylvania also allowed for a sweeping reorganization of all rights to all land in each colony, and the *Midkiff* decision cites three state and federal court decisions that provide ringing endorsements of each enabling act's intent and administrative machinery.

Now consider the historical background to the Hawai'i state legislature's 1967 decision to reorganize property rights in residential land markets to "remedy the social and economic evils of land oligopoly." Nine years earlier, in 1958, the measure would probably have failed to pass all of the hurdles required to enact legislation in Hawai'i's territorial system of government. A major reorganization of property rights to land and the resulting redistribution of economic rents would have been unlikely unless it benefited the Big Five companies and the federal government. Statehood changed this calculus, as it established a sovereign, democratic state government that sharply reduced the power of the Big Five and the federal government in Hawai'i's politics and policies and greatly increased the power of Hawai'i's electorate in influencing government policies.

By 1962, the Democratic Party had consolidated power by attracting votes of Asian-Americans, particularly those of Japanese ancestry. Many had moved to urban areas after World War II in the wake of the decline of the sugar industry, were eligible to vote by right of their birth in a U.S. territory, were well educated, and wanted relief from O'ahu's high-priced urban housing. Or to put it another way, it made sense for some political party to pay attention to the demands of urbanized, educated Japanese-Americans who wanted to own a home, find a job beyond Hawai'i's fields of pineapple and sugar, and raise a family away from the confines of barracks-like plantation housing. In the tight housing market of the 1950s and 1960s, the Democratic Party platform called for the government to use its powers of eminent domain to force large landowners who had developed their lands in leasehold to sell those lots to the homeowner. The popular theory behind the proposed reform was that the LRA would not only reduce housing prices but also align incentives for landowners toward future development of fee simple housing.

So how similar were the situations faced by the colonial governments and the Hawai'i state government when they moved to reorganize land rights? A very generous comparison shows the two situations to be completely different. First, the treasonous behavior of Loyalists was the main reason behind confiscation of their lands during and after the Revolutionary War. By contrast, none of the large landowners in Hawai'i had engaged in treasonous conduct against the U.S. government. To the contrary, it was the U.S. government that had collaborated with a small, disaffected Caucasian minority to overthrow the native Hawaiian government in 1893. When it annexed Hawai'i in 1898, the U.S. government confiscated 971,463 acres of crown lands—roughly 24 percent of the land on the eight major islands—without paying any compensation to the deposed queen, and it used eminent domain to take lands from native Hawaiian estates and other large landowners to establish and expand new military bases. In spite of these confiscations and a long record of poor treatment of native Hawaiians, there was no record of native Hawaiians engaging in violent attempts to overthrow either the U.S. territorial government or the new state government when the LRA was passed in 1967.

Second, the colonists passed land reform legislation to eliminate a variety of feudal obligations.[29] In Hawai'i, the land reforms of the 1840s and 1850s (the *Māhele*) had already eliminated vestiges of the prehistoric land system, such as labor dues on crown lands, and established fee simple rights. Most importantly, the concentration of private land ownership in 1967 had little to do with the land institutions of the Hawaiian monarchy. The division of lands undertaken in the *Māhele* created many large and small landowners, but on the four largest islands (O'ahu, Hawai'i, Maui, and Kaua'i), concentration of land ownership was not sufficiently high to raise *any* concerns about market power in the land market. Many of the lands assigned to the government were sold after the *Māhele*, placing more in private ownership and allowing more access to land by the native Hawaiian population and the ascendant sugar plantations.

Finally, in the century between the end of the *Māhele* and the transition to statehood in the 1950s, concentration of private land ownership increased substantially. One reason was that sugar plantations, pineapple plantations, and large ranches all purchased tracts of land on the private market to assemble plantations and ranches that allowed them to achieve economies of scale and lower their average costs of production. A second was the decisions by prominent *ali'i* in the late nineteenth century to consolidate their private lands into larger estates structured to provide services to native Hawaiian beneficiaries. And a third was the consolidation of land in U.S. military bases after Hawai'i became a territory and during World War II.[30] In all of these cases, the consolidation of land ownership served private and public aims related to economic growth or U.S. national security. A comparison with the situation in the American colonies during the 1770s and 1780s has little merit. Land concentration in some colonies, such as Pennsylvania and Delaware, did not grow over time, but was initially quite high due to the British government's practice of making large grants of lands to colonial proprietors.

To sum up, the foundations of the land reforms in the American colonies and of the 1967 Hawaii Land Reform Act were completely different. The large landowners in Hawai'i were not traitors to the United States; feudal aspects of land ownership had already been eliminated in the 1846 *Māhele*; and the increase in concentration of land ownership during the late nineteenth century was primarily due to the sugar industry's need for large consolidated parcels of land and the voluntary assembling of land in charitable estates by Hawaiian chiefs. A rationale for the Land Reform Act would have to be found elsewhere.

The Price of Land and Oligopoly

The stated purpose of the LRA assumes that land prices in Hawai'i contained a premium for market power—that is, that large landowners were coordinating their actions to raise residential land prices. This assumption raises two important questions: If land oligopolists were forced by the LRA to sell land they had already developed as leased residential housing, would they have new incentives to sell rather than lease new residential land in the future, and would they choose to develop more land? The answer to the first question is straightforward. Because the LRA provided homeowners who lease land with an option to buy when circumstances favor them, large landowners gained more incentives to sell rather than lease land. But would this necessarily result in a larger supply of residential land and lower housing prices?

The presumption behind the idea that the LRA would produce a larger supply of residential land is that large landholders were explicitly coordinating their land development activities to restrict the supply of residential land.[31] An effective landowner cartel would have to withhold some of its members' lands from housing use and allocate them to lower-valued uses. If the cartel withheld some lands that would otherwise be released to residential use under competition, the remaining residential lands would then be leased or sold at a price above the competitive price. In 1975, Ronald Coase, a Nobel laureate in economics, threw cold water on the idea of a cartel among producers of durable goods, such as land, which is an infinitely durable good.[32] Coase conjectured that consumers would be reluctant to pay the higher price set by the cartel if they expected the cartel to have a shorter life than the durable good and if they expected firms to produce more of the durable good after the cartel broke up. Under those circumstances, consumers would incur a capital loss on their original purchases. The challenge to cartels is particularly acute in the case of land because the additional product that firms would use to expand market supply—the land withheld from the market—has already been produced. So cartel members would be sorely tempted to cheat by putting more land on the market. To deal with this cheating problem, a cartel in land would need to be very well organized and coordinated or would need to have enlisted state or local governments to enforce the agreement. This could be accomplished by the government enacting land use regulations that increased the cost of developing land initially withheld from the market.

It is much easier for a cartel to operate effectively when its members are relatively homogeneous. Large landowners in Honolulu were very different from one another because some had developed their land more extensively than others. In 1967, for example, the Bishop Estate had already developed and leased a major portion of its residentially suitable land, whereas the Campbell Trust was still leasing almost all of its residentially suitable land for agriculture. Thus, the latter trust would probably prefer more development than the former. If the two had been coordinating their conduct, either side payments or a more balanced plan of residential development would have been necessary. There is no evidence of any side payments between large landowners.

In the early 1980s, several homeowners on leased land brought antitrust lawsuits under the Sherman and Clayton Acts against the Bishop Estate, alleging that the estate had coordinated with other large landowners to raise the price of residential land in Honolulu. In *Souza v. Estate of Bishop*,[33] the district court provided summary judgment to the Bishop Estate. The court ruled that the Bishop Estate had accumulated its lands legally and that it had not taken actions that would prevent other landowners from disposing of their lands as they desired. The Ninth Circuit Court of Appeals upheld the ruling on appeal, finding that "plaintiffs have not offered any evidence of a conscious commitment to a common scheme designed to achieve an unlawful objective."[34]

The Ninth Circuit's finding is backed up by simple measures of competition in the land market. Concentration of land ownership in the Honolulu land market can be conveniently summarized by the Herfindahl-Hirschman index (HHI), a widely used measure of market competition. HHI is defined as the sum of the square of each firm's market share.[35] HHI's value varies from near zero in a market with tens of thousands of small firms to 10,000 in a market with just one firm. Horizontal merger guidelines issued in 2010 by the U.S. Justice Department and the Federal Trade Commission[36] label a market with an HHI below 1,500 as "unconcentrated," between 1,500 and 2,500 as "moderately concentrated," and above 2,500 as "highly concentrated."[37] My calculation of the Honolulu HHI, derived from shares of all privately owned land, equals 1,213.

Restricting the market to house lots subdivided between 1946 and April 1963 reduces the HHI value to 408. The bottom line is clear: one of the most widely used measures of market competition provides little support for the idea that concentration in the Honolulu land market was likely to have led to supra-competitive prices.[38]

Why Have Land Prices Been So High in Honolulu?

In the preamble to the LRA, the 1967 state legislature identified population and land ownership concentration as two forces that were pushing up land and housing prices in Honolulu. The legislators overlooked three other important factors that had generated high prices: natural and cultural amenities, state and county regulations on land use, and natural restrictions on the supply of developable land.[39] In 1960 and in 2016, Honolulu had high housing prices and highly valued natural and cultural amenities. Surveys conducted by media and consulting firms have regularly placed Honolulu among the top cities for quality of life.[40] Consider these four attributes that positively affect the quality of life in Honolulu:

- *The warm water of the subtropical Pacific Ocean.* For people interested in ocean recreation activities, warm water gives Honolulu a huge advantage over such cold-water West Coast cities as San Diego, Los Angeles, San Francisco, and Seattle.
- *The high number of sunny days with moderate temperatures and seasonal trade winds.* Honolulu has, arguably, the best climate in the world. With trade winds acting as a natural air conditioner most days, the high temperature in August averages just 89°F and the low temperature in January averages only 66°F.[41]
- *The multicultural and multiethnic social environment, highlighted by the rich Native Hawaiian culture.* Racial and ethnic tensions are low in Honolulu compared with many other U.S. urban areas, and the culture of the first people—native Hawaiians—is an important part of the lives of many non-native residents.
- *Honolulu's low crime rate.* Murder, rape, and assault rates in Honolulu are lower than comparable rates for other U.S. metropolitan areas.[42]

While increased congestion has reduced the value of this array of amenities, they are often the main reason why people choose to live in Hawai'i and to pay its high price of housing.

Consider next the restrictions imposed by nature, as Honolulu is located on a small island of little more than 380,000 acres. In 1989, University of Hawai'i economist Louis Rose published a pioneering article in which he computed an index of urban land supply that adjusted land availability in U.S. metropolitan areas for the presence of large bodies of water.[43] Honolulu had the lowest land supply index value of any major U.S. urban area, with just 47 percent of the land that would be available to an urban area located on a plain without water boundaries (such as St. Louis or Denver). Louis Rose and I then employed that urban land supply index in a 1989 econometric study of land prices covering the 39 largest U.S. cities for the year 1980.[44] Controlling for a number of other factors, such as population, population growth, income per capita, foreign investment, zoning power, and city amenities, we found that higher land availability was associated with a lower price for land. We then estimated that natural restrictions on land availability should yield a premium of 35 percent for Honolulu's land prices in 1980.

Rose and I also considered how state and local land use regulations affected land prices. We concluded that landowners in Honolulu were subject to the most severe land use restrictions in the United States. The extreme regulatory environment was due to *two* distinct, overlapping zoning monopolies—one at the state level and one at the local level, each of which provided separate regulations on land use throughout the entire island of O'ahu. Developers often had to obtain approval for a housing project from authorities at *both* levels. This double veto power increased the likelihood that any given project to develop land for housing would ultimately not be approved, or even proposed. Because a smaller flow of new housing projects leads to smaller increases in the stock of housing over time, housing prices in future years would need to increase.

By 2017, many states regulated land development, but before the mid-1980s such regulation was extremely rare. In fact, the passage of the Land Use Law in 1961 (described in chap. 9) made the state of Hawai'i a pioneer in imposing regulations on urban development. Once these state-level restrictions on land use had been determined, the City and County of Honolulu implemented several additional layers of zoning regulations. Honolulu's zoning framework was set forth in the Comprehensive Zoning Code, administered by the city's Department of Land Utilization (DLU), and in the Shoreline Management Act, under which the city council approved or denied most development proposals. There were also permitting requirements specified in subdivision and grading ordinances

administered by the DLU and a building code administered by the Honolulu Building Department.

Over the last 50 years, regulation of development in Honolulu has provided county officials and bureaucrats with far more power to affect the
supply of housing than officials have in other U.S. metropolitan areas.
This is not because zoning regulations in Honolulu have explicitly provided officials with more discretion to apply the regulations or because
zoning is much tougher than in other cities. The extra power in the hands
of Honolulu officials is due to the concentration of zoning power in just
one local government: the City and County of Honolulu.[45] Consumers and
developers who do not like zoning decisions made by the Honolulu authorities must move either to the rural neighbor islands or thousands of
miles to the U.S. West Coast. The situation is very different when there are
a large number of local governments operating within a particular metropolitan area. Competition between those governments provides consumers and developers with alternatives to living on or developing land
in any particular suburb or county that chooses to adopt strict zoning
rules because they have the option to migrate to another suburb, city,
or county within the same metropolitan area that has adopted less strict
zoning rules.[46]

So how does the existence of just one government for the Honolulu
metropolitan area make it different from other large U.S. metropolitan
areas? In 1980, the average number of local governments with zoning powers in the 40 most populous U.S. metropolitan areas was 72. At one end
of the distribution, Houston had one, Charlotte two, and Tampa three.
At the other end, New York had 360 and Chicago had 347. The Rose-La
Croix statistical analysis of U.S. urban land prices found that high zoning
power in Honolulu could account for a 34 percent premium in the price of
land in 1980.[47] Now recall that the same statistical analysis found that the
effect of natural restrictions on land availability in Honolulu accounted
for a 35 percent premium on land prices. Together, both restrictions accounted for a 69 percent premium in the price of land in Honolulu in 1980.
In the 1989 study, we noted, however, that the actual premium on land in
"the extraordinary case of Honolulu, Hawaii" above the average price
was 350 percent. A lot of the puzzle of high Honolulu housing prices was
still unexplained.

Now fast-forward 28 years to 2017. Are there new developments in our
understanding of U.S. land and housing prices that might contribute to
our understanding of Honolulu's markets? One important development

TABLE 11.3. **Land's Share of Home Value in Selected U.S. Cities, 1984 and 2004**

U.S. city	1984	2004
Detroit	5	33
Memphis	14	31
New York	32	67
Boston	50	76
Oakland	61	78
Los Angeles	61	79
San Diego	66	81
San Francisco	75	89

Source: Davis and Palumbo (2008, 383–384).

involved efforts by several economists to figure out how much of the appreciation in U.S. housing prices was due to increases in the value of the structure and how much was due to increases in the value of the land. In 2007, economists Morris Davis and Jon Heathcote estimated that the share of the total market value of housing represented by the value of land (the land share) doubled between 1950 and 1970, from 10.4 percent to 19.9 percent.[48] The big increases continued between 1975 and 2006, with U.S. land prices almost quadrupling and the real price of structures increasing only by a third. The higher growth rates of residential land values had the effect of increasing the land share in national housing prices from about 35 percent in 1975 to about 46 percent in 2006. In 2008, Morris Davis and Michael Palumbo were able to extend Davis and Heathcote's analysis to 46 large U.S. metropolitan areas over the period from 1984 to 2004.[49] They found that 43 of 46 metropolitan areas experienced a much faster appreciation of land prices than structure prices. Growth rates for land prices were substantially higher in cities along the coasts, where the supply of residential land tends to be smaller. Even cities with relatively low land shares in 1984 exhibited strong growth in land shares over the period (e.g., Detroit, from 5 percent to 33 percent, and Memphis, from 14 percent to 31 percent), while cities with relatively high land shares also continued to show substantial growth in land shares (e.g., Boston, from 50 percent to 76 percent, and San Francisco, from 75 percent to 89 percent) (table 11.3).[50]

What happened to land shares in Honolulu over the period from 1960 to 2014? It is notable that Honolulu's land share in 1960, 38 percent, was already an outlier compared with the national mean of 18 percent. Within a decade, it had become an even bigger outlier—46 percent, more than twice the national average (19.9 percent) in 1970. My rough calculation of the share of land in Honolulu housing prices in 2004 ranges from 66 to 70 percent.[51] The Honolulu land share was far above the national land share average (51 percent) for major cities in 2004, slightly below the land share for cities in the western region (74 percent), and below the 2004 land shares for other high-priced West Coast metropolitan areas, including San Diego (81 percent), San Jose (82 percent), Oakland (78 percent), and Los Angeles (79 percent).

The high land share in Honolulu housing prices in 1960 (38 percent) and its fast track upward to 66–70 percent in 2004 is critical to understanding the evolution of Honolulu housing prices over the last five decades. The dynamics of housing prices in metropolitan areas where the value of housing is largely accounted for by the value of land (e.g., San Francisco, Boston, and Honolulu) are very different from those in metropolitan areas where the land share is relatively small (e.g., Detroit and St. Louis).[52] The price of housing should be largely pinned down by construction costs in areas where the land share of housing prices is small and the share of the structure in the overall home price looms large. In these metropolitan areas, if demand increases and pushes up housing prices, developers should have incentives to build more housing, and the extra supply should push down the price of housing to the cost of constructing more housing plus the small amount for land. However, in metropolitan areas where the land share of housing is large, such as Honolulu, changes in the demand for housing could translate into big changes in housing prices. Factors affecting housing demand include the tax treatment of housing, nominal and real interest rates, and the metropolitan area's population and income growth rates.

Davis, Heathcote, and Palumbo's work on U.S. housing prices is critical to our understanding of Honolulu's high and increasing housing prices between 1950 and 1990. The high land share in Honolulu housing prices since the early 1960s points to changes in housing demand as the major driver pushing up housing prices in Honolulu. And behind the increase in demand stand increases in population and income.[53] There was a huge increase in Honolulu's population between 1950 and 1990, with the number of nonmilitary residents soaring from 353,000 in 1950 to 631,000 in 1970 and to 836,000 in 1990. Average real per capita personal income in Honolulu also surged, rising from $6,520 in 1950 to $16,210 in 1990 (1984 dollars). The spectacular rise of Honolulu's tourism industry was behind both population and income gains; the population gains were also fueled by migration from the islands of Maui, Kaua'i, and Hawai'i due to declining employment from the 1930s on sugar and pineapple plantations on those islands.

Our understanding of housing prices in U.S. metropolitan areas has also been advanced by new studies examining how a metropolitan area's natural supply of land affects its land prices. Urban economist Albert Saiz refined the earlier Rose-La Croix index of the natural supply of land by applying GIS techniques that allow incorporation of much more detailed information about the landscape into the measure of natural supply. His index calculates the developable area within a 50 km radius from the central city. Oceans, wetlands, lakes, rivers, other internal water, and areas with a slope above 15 percent are defined as undevelopable areas. Saiz finds that "for all MSAs [metropolitan statistical areas] with population over 500,000 in the 2000 Census . . . Ventura (CA) is the most constrained, with 80% of the area within a 50-km radius rendered undevelopable by the Pacific Ocean and mountains. Miami, Fort Lauderdale, New Orleans, San Francisco, Sarasota, Salt Lake City, West Palm Beach, San Diego, and San Jose complete the list of the top 10 most physically constrained major metropolitan areas in the United States. Many large cities in the South and Midwest (such as Atlanta, San Antonio, and Columbus) are largely unconstrained." Honolulu is not included in Saiz's data set, so I have calculated Honolulu's natural land supply using his methodology. Figure 11.2 is a map of Honolulu overlaid with concentric circles centered on the downtown business district with radii in 5 km increments out to a 50 km boundary. Roughly 92 percent of the 50-km-radius circle is not developable. This figure is much higher than the 80 percent measure of undevelopable land for the next most constrained U.S. metropolitan area, Ventura, California. To provide some perspective on how much of an outlier Honolulu is among U.S. metropolitan areas, table 11.4 reports the natural supply of land for 39 selected U.S. metropolitan areas.

In his empirical work on housing prices, Saiz also makes use of a new index measuring the extent of regulations in metropolitan area housing markets, the Wharton Residential Land Use Regulatory Index.[54] Developed by economists Joseph Gyourko, Albert Saiz, and Anita Summers, the Wharton Index aggregates 11 sub-indexes: a local political pressure index, a state political involvement index, a state court involvement index, a local zoning approval index, a local project approval index, a local assembly index (measuring whether a community meeting and vote is required for project approval), a supply restrictions index (measuring

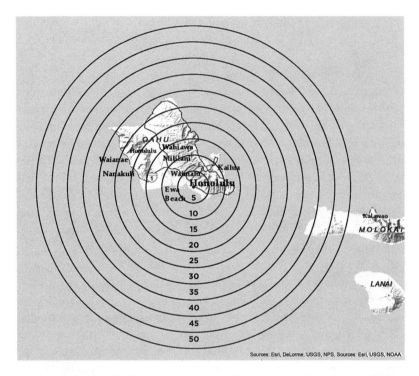

FIGURE 11.2. Land availability within a 50-mile radius of downtown Honolulu. Credit: Map composed by Adele Balderston.

"explicit constraints or caps on supplying new [housing] units to the market"), a density restrictions index, an open space index, an exactions index, and an approval delay index.[55] How does Honolulu compare with other U.S. cities in its score on the Wharton Index? Its score shows that Honolulu has far more regulation of residential development than any other U.S. metropolitan area. In fact, Honolulu's score of 2.32 is an outlier in the sample of U.S. metropolitan areas, far exceeding the next highest score of 1.79 for the metropolitan area encompassing Providence, Rhode Island, Warwick, Rhode Island, and Fall River, Massachusetts.

Honolulu's high score stems from the multiple layers of rigorous, lengthy review required by both state and county governments for all new development projects. Here's a quick summary of the obstacle course. A land development project requires the state Land Use Commission's approval if the land needs to be reclassified from conservation, rural, or agricultural status to urban status, and the commission must determine the

TABLE 11.4. **Physical and Regulatory Constraints on Land Development in Selected U.S. Metropolitan Areas with Populations Greater than 500,000**

Rank[a]	Metropolitan area	Percentage of area undevelopable[b]	WRI[c]
1	Ventura, CA	79.64	1.21
2	Miami, FL	76.63	0.94
3	Fort Lauderdale, FL	75.71	0.72
4	New Orleans, LA	74.89	−1.24
5	San Francisco, CA	73.14	0.72
10	San Diego, CA	63.41	0.46
11	Oakland, CA	61.67	0.62
12	Charleston-North Charleston, SC	60.45	−0.81
13	Norfolk-VA Beach-Newport News, VA-NC	59.77	0.12
14	Los Angeles-Long Beach, CA	52.47	0.49
15	Vallejo-Fairfield-Napa, CA	49.16	0.96
20	Tampa-St. Petersburg-Clearwater, FL	41.64	−0.22
21	Cleveland-Lorain-Elyria, OH	40.50	−0.16
22	New York, NY	40.42	0.65
23	Chicago, IL	40.01	0.02
24	Knoxville, TN	38.53	−0.37
25	Riverside-San Bernardino, CA	37.90	0.53
45	Tucson, AZ	23.07	1.52
46	Colorado Springs, CO	22.27	0.87
47	Baltimore, MD	21.87	1.60
48	Allentown-Bethlehem-Easton, PA	20.86	0.02
49	Minneapolis-St. Paul, MN-WI	19.23	0.38
50	Buffalo-Niagara Falls, NY	19.05	−0.23
60	Little Rock-North Little Rock, AR	13.71	−0.85
61	Fresno, CA	12.88	0.91
62	Greenville-Spartanburg-Anderson, SC	12.87	−0.94
63	Nashville, TN	12.83	−0.41
64	Louisville, KY-IN	12.69	−0.47
65	Memphis, TN-AR-MS	12.18	1.18
76	Houston, TX	8.40	−0.40
77	Raleigh-Durham-Chapel Hill, NC	8.11	0.64
78	Akron, OH	6.45	0.07
79	Tulsa, OK	6.29	−0.78
80	Kansas City, MO-KS	5.82	−0.79
90	Columbus, OH	2.50	0.26
91	Oklahoma City, OK	2.46	−0.37
93	Indianapolis, IN	1.44	−0.74
94	Dayton-Springfield, OH	1.04	−0.50
95	McAllen-Edinburg-Mission, TX	0.93	−0.45

Source: Saiz (2010, 1258–1259).
[a]Rank among the 100 largest U.S. metropolitan areas for the natural supply of land.
[b]Percentage of area undevelopable is Saiz's measure of the natural supply of land.
[c]WRI refers to the Wharton Residential Land Use Regulatory Index.

project's compliance with state planning statutes. It also requires county approval for zoning compliance, and counties' zoning decisions are required to conform to those counties' general plans. If the development is residential, the developer must file a subdivision plat, receive comments on the plat, and obtain final approval for the plat. Development projects near the coast need to be in compliance with the county's implementation of the federal government's Coastal Zone Management Act.[56] All development projects need to be in compliance with the federal government's Endangered Species Act. Finally, the developer must be in compliance with state rules requiring all development projects to obtain a review from the Hawai'i State Department of Land and Natural Resources (DLNR) to determine whether the proposed site might be historic property or a burial site or contain aviation artifacts. If DLNR finds this to be the case, then the developer must commission an archaeological inventory survey and seek review and comment from DLNR's Historic Preservation Division. If human remains or cultural artifacts or aviation artifacts are located, then a plan to make appropriate arrangements for their preservation, reburial, or relocation must be developed and approved.

For a parsimonious model emphasizing just a few factors, the Saiz model of U.S. metropolitan area housing prices does a good job of explaining Honolulu's high ranking among U.S. cities, even if it fails to explain the full magnitude of the city's housing price premium.[57] Honolulu had the most stringent regulatory environment for new housing development in 2004 (when the survey for the Wharton Index was conducted) and the smallest natural supply of land of all U.S. metropolitan areas. Its natural and cultural attributes are among the best in the United States. All this considered, it is not a big surprise that in September 2017, Honolulu had the fourth highest median home price ($760,200) among U.S. metropolitan areas.[58]

Conclusion

High land prices in Honolulu during the 1960s and 1970s were attributable to the natural and cultural amenities of Honolulu, a small natural supply of land, and regulatory restrictions on the supply of land for housing. In the LRA's preamble, legislators contended that high housing prices were also due to concentration of ownership in the land market and leasing of land for housing. During the 1980s, 1990s, and early in the first decade of the twenty-first century, the LRA and Honolulu's land reform law for leasehold condominiums allowed more than 75 percent of leased lands under homes and condos to be purchased by their owners. There is, however, no evidence that these purchases led to lower housing prices or to increased incentives for landowners to develop more land in housing. The 13 years that Castle & Cooke required to obtain regulatory approval for the Koa Ridge housing development (3,500 homes near Pearl City and Waikele) and the 7 years that D. R. Horton required for the Hoʻopili housing development (11,750 homes near Kapolei) provide clear evidence that regulatory constraints remain the biggest barriers to housing development.

If the LRA's implementation did not yield lower housing prices, then was the act's use of eminent domain justified by some alternative public purpose? Economic historian Naomi Lamoreaux and economists Robert Fleck and Andrew Hanssen have argued that governments regularly encounter situations in which they need to reorganize property rights to accommodate technological and economic change.[59] They catalog numerous examples in the United States in which property has been involuntarily reallocated from one private owner to another private owner (sometimes with little or no compensation) to facilitate development of a booming industry. Nineteenth-century examples include uses of eminent domain to take property to facilitate development of grist mills; to provide rights-of-way to bring water to mining sites and fields; and to allow a railroad to lay tracks. Twentieth-century examples include taking property to clear and redevelop city slums and to facilitate entry of new firms deemed vital to an area's economic development.[60] Lamoreaux argues that while voters are willing to give government the benefit of the doubt to facilitate the process of transitioning to new industries, these cases do not give governments a blank check to use the power of eminent domain. Rather, the widespread ownership of land in the United States provides a self-enforcing mechanism that "prompts voters to mobilize whenever they think redistribution in favor of the top is getting out of hand."[61]

The use of eminent domain in Hawaiʻi to redistribute land differs from the cases mentioned above, as it was clearly not used to accommodate technological change, but rather to accommodate a big change in Hawaiʻi's political institutions: the swift, sudden transition to an open-access political order—statehood—in 1959. The use of eminent domain might seem to be totally at variance with an open-access political order, as enforcement of property rights is one of the hallmarks of an open-access order. Support for the use of eminent domain in Hawai'i after statehood can be explained by appealing to James Madison's argument in the *Federalist Papers* that property rights in a democratic society can never be secure if the majority does not own property. The LRA's (mostly) compensated redistribution of property to achieve a more egalitarian distribution could well be understood as a means to make the new open-access political order work better. With the majority owning more property, there would be more support for laws and expenditures designed to enforce property rights.

A simpler explanation, also tied to institutional change, could be behind the passage of the LRA. In the early 1960s, many in Hawai'i perceived land leasing by large estates to be part of the former limited-access economic and political order, in which economic rents were funneled to members of the dominant governing coalition. For the new open-access institutions of statehood to work effectively, it was understood that old colonial institutions had to be dismantled. Thus, the passage and implementation of the LRA could also be viewed as just one more measure designed to sweep away the vestiges of the old order.

CHAPTER TWELVE

The Long Reach of History

"The further backward you look, the further forward you can see."—Queen Elizabeth II, quoting a remark attributed to Winston Churchill in her 1999 Christmas Message

Hawai'i's transition from a U.S. colony to a U.S. state came abruptly and yet was implemented quickly. Territorial leaders had been pushing for statehood since the first statehood bill was introduced in Congress by Prince Jonah Kūhiō Kalaniana'ole, Hawai'i's nonvoting representative to Congress. The road to statehood was seemingly coming to a successful end in 1950 with overwhelming voter approval of a state constitution, but eight years later statehood was stalled in Congress, particularly in the Senate. It came as a bit of a surprise when John Burns, Hawai'i's congressional representative, was successful in brokering a deal in which Alaska would be admitted first, in January 1959, and Hawai'i second, in August 1959. In the decade following President Eisenhower's signature on the Hawaii Admission Act, a new constitution was implemented, laws supporting the old territorial political order were replaced, the new state government was expanded to provide services demanded by the growing middle class, and the Hawai'i economy boomed. Some of Hawai'i's success in overcoming its colonial legacy was clearly due to the fortuitous growth of the tourism industry over the first three decades of statehood. There were, however, several other reasons why Hawai'i escaped many of the colonial hangovers that have beset other countries attempting to make the transition to an open-access political order. They include Hawai'i's avoidance of slave labor on sugar and pineapple plantations, the persistence of indentured labor for less than 50 years, the ability of competing economic and political groups to form organizations to compete away some economic rents, and long experience (over 450 years) with relatively centralized government institutions. I discuss each of these factors more fully below.

The effects of colonialism in Hawai'i are far from gone, as the welfare of Native Hawaiians is still affected by lost sovereignty, lost lands, and lost opportunities. In 2013, the per capita income of native Hawaiians was about 30 percent lower than those of other ethnic groups.[1] Confiscation of crown lands at annexation, loss of patronage jobs over the course of the twentieth century, loss of the monarchy and sovereign control of their country, and suppression of the use of the Hawaiian language in schools and government during the territorial era have all reduced the overall welfare of native Hawaiians. Over the 60 years since statehood, native Hawaiians have had considerable success in rebounding from these losses. Hawaiian culture has thrived, and use of the Hawaiian language has massively expanded since the 1960s. Despite this, native Hawaiians have been only partly successful in finding redress for the uncompensated transfer of the crown lands and their loss of sovereignty. In this chapter, I review the progress that has been made toward restoring a sovereign Hawaiian government and recent decisions by the U.S. government that have slowed progress toward that goal.

Labor Markets and Hawai'i's Colonial Legacy

From 1876 to 1960, the Hawai'i sugar industry boomed. That boom was driven by protection provided by high U.S. sugar tariffs, cheap contract labor from Asia and Europe, and rapid technological change.[2] A slow but persistent decline in industry employment started in the 1930s due to mechanization and unionization, and a slow but persistent decline in industry output began after 1960 due to changes in the U.S. sugar program, increases in the value of Hawai'i land, changes in international prices, and new aviation technologies and planes that reduced Hawai'i's ability to compete in growing and processing sugar and pineapple but increased its ability to compete for domestic and international tourists. In 2016, the last Hawai'i sugar plantation closed. It is remarkable that during the long decline of Hawai'i's sugar and pineapple industries, Hawai'i's overall economy continued to grow, albeit at a much slower pace after 1990 than previously. What is notable about Hawai'i's successful transition from the sugar industry is how starkly its post-transition success contrasts with the poor outcomes that followed similar transitions in other islands and countries where there once was extensive sugar cultivation.

Hawai'i's outcomes differ from those of island groups in the Caribbean Sea that were colonized between 1492 and 1900 and had much of their land developed as sugar plantations because Hawai'i's sugar plantations never used slave labor. During the first 300 years of the colonial period in North America, the Caribbean, and South America, slave labor was the choice of plantation owners. Planters in those colonies could expect to attract a sufficient supply of slaves from slave traders at a price that would enable them to earn normal or above-normal profits. In the places where cane sugar was grown—Brazil, Cuba, Jamaica, the Dominican Republic, Haiti, St. Croix, Barbados, and the U.S. Southern states, slavery crushed the spirit and welfare of workers for centuries, and its burden has persisted long after it was eliminated. Hawai'i escaped this burden by never having slavery.

One reason why Hawai'i did not have slavery was that its sugar plantations were established much later than those in the Caribbean and the Americas. Most owners and managers on Hawaiian and other Pacific island plantations saw the institution of slavery flashing by in the rearview mirror, as other countries were eliminating it during the mid- to late nineteenth century. The exception was "blackbirding," a uniquely Pacific form of slavery that was common in the mid- to late nineteenth century. Slaving ships kidnapped Australian Aboriginals, Polynesians, Melanesians, and Micronesians and sold them to work in servitude on sugar plantations, in guano mines, in pearl harvests, and other forms of hard labor. Blackbirding never came to Hawai'i and never became the primary source of labor for colonial enterprises in the Pacific Ocean, in part because it was strongly opposed by the colonial powers and in part because it failed to provide a sufficient supply of reliable labor to plantations.

As the slave trade wound down in the early nineteenth century, countries began to emancipate slaves, and plantation owners and managers had to find ways to attract migrant and indigenous workers to come and work in the fields voluntarily.[3] Some sugar planters in Cuba and Peru replaced African slave labor with contract labor from China, but contract labor was also gradually phased out in the late nineteenth and early twentieth centuries in both countries.[4] In Hawai'i, as in Fiji and in Queensland, Australia, bound immigrants working on three-year contracts became the main source of plantation labor from the early 1870s until 1900. Most workers in Hawai'i spent relatively few years working as bound labor because either they decided not to renew their fixed-term indenture contracts or their contracts were terminated in August 1900 by a provision of the Organic Act, the federal law that established Hawai'i's territorial government.[5] The termination of all indentured labor contracts in 1900 meant that even the first big wave of Japanese workers who arrived in 1885 never spent more than 15 years working under an indenture contract. In fact, most of the Japanese field workers in Hawai'i arrived after the overthrow of Queen Lili'uokalani in 1893, and the majority of these workers spent less than three years working under an indenture contract. The short time spent by most migrants working as coerced labor was particularly important, as the social, physical, and personal costs of working day after day as gang labor in tropical fields were real and have been well documented for Hawai'i and other parts of the world by social and economic historians.[6] Migrants' fast escape from the crushing burdens of coerced labor meant that those who worked in field and factory suffered less personally and had more capacity to pass on cultural and social capital to future generations.

Did the end of bound labor actually lead to better working conditions on the plantations? With the transition from bound-labor to free-labor market institutions, Hawai'i planters were faced with a more complex labor supply problem: they sought a long-term labor force, but also had to offer an attractive enough package to convince people to work in their fields voluntarily. One sure way to attract workers, particularly after they have been worked excessively hard for long hours, is to reduce hours of work and raise wages. The economist Wayne Liou has shown that after the termination of indenture contracts in 1900, wages for field workers rose and hours of work decreased.[7] And one way to attract migrant workers is to pay them more than they would earn in their home countries. The economic historian Price Fishback and I have shown that between 1900 and 1915, sugar plantations paid higher wages to workers from high-wage countries than to workers from low-wage countries.[8] In both cases, the wages paid far exceeded average earnings in the migrants' home countries.

All that said, the history of labor relations in Hawai'i in the first half of the twentieth century was marked by company collusion, violent strikes, and personal suffering by sugar and pineapple plantation workers.[9] Dissatisfaction with pay, field supervisors, and prospects for advancement led Japanese workers to organize a large-scale strike in 1909. Management ruthlessly crushed the strike, yet responded to it over the next few years by making numerous improvements in working conditions. These improvements included increasing the pay of Asian workers, improving living conditions on the plantations, and employing a much larger percentage of workers under tenancy contracts that required less supervision and allowed more worker initiative. In 1920, a second major strike on six sugar plantations by Japanese and Filipino workers lasted five months, but was again crushed by management.[10] Unionization of Hawai'i sugar and pineapple workers in the mid-1940s led to strikes in both industries in the mid- to late 1940s and ultimately to payment of premium wages and benefits over the next seven decades in the two industries.

The Short Duration and Changing Circumstances of U.S. Colonial Rule

The American-imposed colonial government did not last long in Hawai'i—just 61 years, a short time compared with, say, the 375 years of Spanish and American rule in the Philippines. Could the short duration of explicit colonial rule have been one of the factors underpinning Hawai'i's strong economic performance in the first three decades of statehood? Or could American colonization have facilitated the transfer and establishment of higher-quality government institutions associated with an open-access political order? This is unlikely to be the case for Hawai'i, as its government had already adopted many Western governance institutions in the mid-nineteenth century, 50–60 years prior to explicit colonization. Adoption of British common law is also associated with somewhat better postcolonial outcomes, but, again, Hawai'i's government had already adopted it as part of its mid-nineteenth century reforms.[11] Others have argued that shorter colonization periods might be associated with higher post-independence economic growth. With a shorter period of colonization, "extractive" colonial institutions would have had less time to become deeply ingrained in the population, and the people's knowledge of a sovereign political order would have had less time to decay and would thus be easier to restore when colonization ended.

Two empirical studies have looked at the relationship between length of colonization and postcolonial economic growth. A 1999 study by the economist Robin Grier statistically analyzed this relationship for 61 former European colonies and found that countries held longer as colonies tended to have higher rates of output growth after independence.[12] A 2009 study by the economists James Feyrer and Bruce Sacerdote examined 81 island groups in the Pacific and Atlantic Oceans that had been or were still colonized.[13] They contend that their sample provides the best data to test the relationship between length of colonization and economic performance because islands are more similar to one another than countries and because colonization of islands happened more randomly than colonization of countries.[14] Feyrer and Sacerdote's results reveal that islands held longer as colonies had higher per capita GDP in the year 2000. Hawai'i's experience is an outlier in their study (i.e., an observation that doesn't follow the statistical patterns found in the overall sample), as it was colonized for less than a century and in 2000 had one of the highest per capita outputs (GDP) of any island in their sample. More consistent with Hawai'i's colonial experience is Feyrer and Sacerdote's finding that islands colonized after 1700 had higher GDP in the year 2000 than countries colonized before 1700.[15]

Are there any other variables related to colonization that might affect postcolonial economic performance? Two studies suggest that the extent of education among the general population during the colonial years is important. Grier's study finds that the differences in educational attainment at independence between British and French colonies help to explain superior GDP growth after independence in British colonies.[16] Economists William Easterly and Ross Levine's cross-country statistical study of 130 colonies finds that the share of the European-American population at colonization is positively related to per capita GDP in 1995–2005.[17] They hypothesize that the mechanism connecting the European-American population with current economic performance is that its presence facilitated investment in human capital (i.e., skills, knowledge, experience) by the remainder of the population as well as technology transfers.

So, how high was the European-American share of the population in Hawai'i at colonization? In 1900, it was 18.7 percent, and it would grow to 32 percent in 1960.[18] For Hawai'i, the presence of fewer than 200 American missionaries starting in 1820 was particularly important for investment in native Hawaiian human capital, as their sponsor, the American Board of Commissioners for Foreign Missions, heavily subsidized an island-wide system of mission schools that by the 1850s had educated tens of thousands of Hawai'i's elite and non-elite population. In 1900, the first

U.S. census of Hawai'i identified almost two-thirds (64.8) of the overall population of Hawai'i over age 15 as literate (i.e., able to read and write in some language), a remarkable status for a population of which 61.7 percent were foreign born.[19] By 1960, the literacy rate had growth to 95 percent of the population over age 14, and the median number of years of school completed in Hawai'i was 11.0 years, higher than the U.S. median of 10.6 years.[20]

Perhaps the most important part of the Hawaiian experience of colonization was that the U.S. Congress did not design its colonial political institutions to persist for long periods—say, 50 to 100 years. The Organic Act's incorporation of the full Bill of Rights of the U.S. Constitution meant that the central feature of a limited-access political order—limitation of access by non-elite groups to legal mechanisms used to form important types of organizations—could not be enforced in many important situations.[21] It is unsurprising to see that political groups organized in Hawai'i to protest political institutions designed to generate and distribute economic rents to members of the dominant political coalition. Their pressure on the federal government would ultimately bring an end to those territorial colonial institutions.

In this context, consider the territorial government's decision in the mid-1920s to regulate the curriculum of 147 Japanese-language schools in the territory.[22] Around 20,000 students attended these "after-school" language schools, which employed about 300 instructors. Japanese and Japanese-American parents had formed these schools during the first two decades of the twentieth century to ensure that their children learned the Japanese language and important elements of Japanese culture. Concerned that the language schools were promoting allegiance to the Japanese emperor, the Hawai'i territorial legislature passed the "Act relating to foreign language schools and teachers thereof" in 1920. It authorized the Territorial Department of Public Instruction to promulgate regulations affecting virtually every aspect of the schools' operations.[23] Operating permits were required; lists of pupils and instructors had to be submitted to the department; instructors needed to be licensed by the department; hours of operation were limited; pupils below a certain age and pupils who had not completed the fourth grade were not allowed to enroll; textbooks would be chosen by the department; subjects taught required the department's approval; and instructors were required "to the best of [their] ability, so direct the minds and studies of pupils in such schools as will tend to make them good and loyal American citizens." In sum, the territorial government acted to severely restrict the ability of Japanese and Japanese-American residents to form and operate cultural organizations because the government perceived that those organizations might weaken Hawaiʻi's colonial political order.

Outraged at the government's interference in their privately organized and privately financed language schools, school sponsors brought suit in 1925, charging that the "Act relating to foreign language schools" and the regulations issued to implement it violated their constitutional rights. In 1927, the U.S. Supreme Court resoundingly struck down the act in *Farrington v. Tokushige*.[24] The court concluded that "enforcement of the Act probably would destroy most if not all of [the language schools], and certainly it would deprive parents of fair opportunity to procure for their children instruction which they think important, and we cannot say is harmful. The Japanese parent has the right to direct the education of his own child without unreasonable restrictions; the Constitution protects him as well as those who speak another tongue." The court's definitive ruling, that the territory's act and regulations would violate parents' Fifth Amendment rights not to be "deprived of life, liberty, or property, without due process of law," was possible only because the Organic Act had provided that the territory's residents be able to enjoy the full protection of the U.S. Constitution.[25]

Hawaiʻi newspapers and political organizations were also protected by various provisions in the Bill of Rights, and this protection allowed them to influence public opinion and compete effectively for political power without fears of government restraints. The rise of competing organizations between 1900 and 1958 in the realms of politics, economics, and civil society set the stage for Hawaiʻi to be admitted as a U.S. state in 1959, as the broader society was no longer reliant on organizations sponsored by members of the dominant coalition.

Racially inclusive legislative elections were also a key to the transition to an open-access political order. During the first five decades of territorial government, the Hawaiʻi Republican Party dominated territorial elections with its uneasy coalition of colonial Caucasian voters, native Hawaiian voters, and plantation workers coerced by their employers to vote for Republican candidates. The Organic Act's provisions for a racially inclusive electorate would ultimately break apart that coalition, as the percentage of the electorate that was native Hawaiian declined sharply through the territorial years (see fig. 8.5). The large second generation of Hawaiʻi-born Asian-Americans who became part of the electorate after World War II allowed the Democratic Party to compete effectively in elections starting in 1946 and to elect Democratic Party majorities in both the territorial house and senate in 1954. Initial efforts of the new legislative majorities to repeal the policies underpinning the distribution of rents to some of the interest groups associated with the Republican Party's voting coalition were rebuffed by the federally appointed governor and courts. Despite these setbacks, it was obvious to all parties and politicians that the ability of people outside the dominant coalition to form a strong political party had severely eroded the coalition's ability to create and distribute economic rents. As the economic rents available to distribute dwindled, the old limited-access order lost support, thereby allowing statehood to emerge.

Have Open-Access Institutions Worked in Hawai'i?

Ideally, institutions in an open-access order facilitate cooperation between some groups to generate economic rents and cooperation between other groups to compete away economic rents when they are generated. Did Hawai'i's new open-access institutions work this way? One way to answer this question is to take a critical look at the development of the tourism industry in the three decades after statehood. For Hawai'i, it was fortuitous that the sudden introduction of new political institutions and policies was accompanied by an improvement in Hawai'i's terms of trade with the outside world, as economic growth lubricated a smoother transition to the new institutional arrangements. Although Hawai'i was one of the most geographically isolated places on the globe in the early nineteenth century, a century-long decline in shipping costs allowed its markets in sugar, pineapple, and consumer goods to become closely integrated with global markets by the end of the century. A more abrupt decline in transportation costs came in 1958 with the introduction of jet plane passenger service. Regular passenger service from the U.S. mainland and Japan provided big reductions in both the money and time costs of traveling to Hawai'i and ignited a three-decade boom in the tourism industry that completely transformed the Hawaiian economy.

Behind the growth in tourism also stood the open-access political order of statehood. Hawai'i's new sovereign state government no longer had incentives to create economic rents and distribute them to the Big Five companies that had dominated the state's economy. Instead, the establishment of more independent judicial institutions and the ability of citizens to choose their own governor meant that the state had incentives to provide more secure property rights to new firms and their investors rather than just funneling new opportunities to the Big Five. Another way in which the new sovereign state government facilitated the growth of new industries and the transformation of old ones was by dismantling the entry restrictions and interlocking directorates that fed rents to Big Five firms and limited the formation of independent local businesses. Initiatives to reduce the cost of entry into many industries prompted out-of-state domestic and foreign firms to enter markets and compete away economic rents previously assigned to the Big Five corporations and their affiliates.

The state's more open policies facilitated the entry of new local, mainland, and foreign corporations into the Hawai'i market and the fast growth of a mass tourism industry. Visitor arrivals soared from 296,000 in 1960 to 6,724,000 in 1990—an annual growth rate of 10.4 percent. New competition spurred by elimination of entry restrictions triggered growth across a spectrum of enterprises associated with the tourism industry. But for the one sector that was crucial to the new tourism industry—land development—government tightened rather than loosened its control. The 1961 Land Use Law established a comprehensive state regulatory framework for all lands and allowed rents from development to be redistributed to particular landowners who were important players in the new political coalition assembled by the Democratic Party. If they could obtain timely state reclassification of land from a rural or agricultural designation to the urban designation needed for tourism development, they, rather than other players with fewer connections, would receive a stream of economic rents. Hawai'i's economy would also benefit, with the 15 years following statehood marked by a burst of economic growth that propelled Hawai'i into the middle third of U.S. states in terms of per capita output. Hawai'i's transition to a sovereign state government and the concurrent growth of a booming new industry led to a massive improvement in its citizens' welfare, yet did not mean a complete abandonment of the mechanisms used by the territorial government to create and redistribute rents for political supporters. In fact, open-access political orders limit such rent seeking, but are never successful in eliminating it.

Several scholars have argued that Hawai'i's transition to an open-access political order has been incomplete. Their line of argument is that adoption of the formal institutions of an open-access political order will not be enough to establish an open-access order if informal or even formal rules and organizations left over from the limited-access order continue to operate. In their classic 1985 book on post-territorial Hawai'i politics, *Land and Power*, the lawyer George Cooper and the historian Gavan Daws documented how Hawai'i politicians used state and county zoning regulations to selectively zone for development those lands with access to unpriced resources such as beautiful beaches, scenic views, and mountain trails. In most cases, those lands selected for development were owned by supporters of the new dominant political coalition, anchored since 1954 in the big-tent Democratic Party.

The swift, sudden transition to an open-access order clearly led to huge transitions in some policy areas, increases in wealth, and a government more subject to checks and balances. But what if people are slower to change than government policies? Many politicians and political organizations had skills and connections that were more suited to the network-based politics of patronage associated with limited-access political orders. Cooper and Daws describe in great detail how local networks of businessmen and landowners gained access to opportunities in the 1960s and 1970s because of their networks of political and social connections. Or perhaps that was just what happens in U.S. states with small populations, where people often refer to governors by their first names—Linda, Ben, and Neil—and have just two or three degrees of separation from them and one another.

More than two decades after Cooper and Daws floated their story of state and local governments distributing rents to favored supporters, three economists—Majah-Leah Ravago, James Roumasset, and Kimberly Burnett—offered a modern version of this story.[26] They argued that even after 50 years of statehood, Hawai'i still retained some political institutions that allowed a dominant political coalition to redistribute property and rents to its supporters. Their existence was due, in part, to what the three economists neatly labeled the "Curse of Paradise." An eightfold increase in the number of tourists coming to Hawai'i between 1958 and 1990 was accompanied not just by huge expansions in the hotel, restaurant, and transportation industries serving tourists, but also by a crowding out of more dynamic industries. Without the good jobs generated by those industries, many people with high levels of human capital migrated to the U.S. mainland or never came to Hawai'i. On top of this, expansion of the tourism industry led to congestion of roads, surf breaks, island beaches, and public schools. The quality of life deteriorated, primarily because Hawai'i's policymakers struggled to find and implement policies to prevent, or at least limit, the dissipation of economic rents from unpriced natural resources, environmental attributes, and public infrastructure. In this take on life in Hawai'i, corruption of the state's politics grew more pervasive over time because the changes in zoning required at both the state and county levels to develop coastal land for tourism businesses funneled economic rents to political insiders.

Democratic and Republican politicians in Hawai'i have often espoused variants of the Curse of Paradise thesis. The politicians' reformulations usually incorporate a role for government policies designed to subsidize emergence and growth of the dynamic industries that were crowded out by the rise of the state's tourism industry. These politicians have made "diversification of the economy" a mantra and have used the rationale of diversification to justify experimentation with a long trail of subsidies, taxes, and special programs designed to foster alternative dynamic industries that would eventually surpass tourism as future sources of economic growth. The emphasis on designing policies to foster new industries arose primarily because the rapid economic growth achieved over the first 30 years of statehood was followed by slow and volatile growth over the next 25–30 years, partly due to a big slowdown in the tourism industry. Consider that visitor arrivals grew at an annual rate of 10.4 percent from 1959 to 1990, but only 0.8 percent from 1990 to 2013. More importantly, total inflation-adjusted visitor expenditures fell by 11.1 percent from 1990 to 2013, decreasing at an average annual rate of 0.5 percent.

The search for new industries to complement Hawai'i's tourism industry began well before the industry's decline in the mid-1990s. By the mid-1970s, after almost two decades of rapid property development, Hawai'i's residents had already become somewhat uncomfortable with the ever-expanding supply of resorts located on beautiful beachfront lands and offering an array of jobs (think janitors, maids, parking attendants, and front desk clerks) with limited opportunities for future wage gains and promotions within the organization. Parents began to worry: Where would their children work when they graduated from the University of Hawai'i with that esteemed degree in engineering or chemistry? Would their future depend on relocation to the distant U.S. mainland and result in the splintering of close Hawai'i families?

During the late 1970s and 1980s, the state of Hawai'i responded to the public's demand to create jobs for its newly educated baby boomers by creating a gaggle of quasi-public entities to foster start-up high-technology firms, such as the High Technology Development Corporation, the Hawaii Information Network Corporation, the Office of Space Industries, the Hawaii Innovation Development Program, the Hawaii Strategic Development Corporation, and the Research and Development Industry Promotion Program.[27] Despite these efforts, economists George Darby and Meheroo Jussawalla complained in the early 1990s that "the state has yet to attract one sizeable company. In fact, Hawai'i is losing, not gaining, high tech jobs." Technology consultant Peter Kay concluded that new companies start up in Hawai'i, and when they become successful, they relocate to the U.S. mainland.[28] Examples include companies affiliated with these state-subsidized incubator programs in the 1990s—such as AdTech, Verifone, Pihana Pacific, and Digital Island—that grew into bigger ventures and, showing a shocking lack of gratitude to the state that subsidized their birth and growing pains, relocated to the U.S. mainland.

The sharp decline of Hawai'i's economy during the 1990s and the mediocre performance of its quasi-public high-technology incubators set the stage for state government to improvise a new set of diversification policies.[29] Rather than providing more direct services to firms in the few industries it had targeted, the state of Hawai'i initiated a major policy change by offering investment tax credits to local firms in selected high-technology industries with roots in Hawai'i's environment and natural resource endowments. Act 221, a state law enacted in 2001, provided a 100 percent tax credit to people who invested in the few vital industries targeted by the law. Act 221 found many supporters among owners of and investors in firms in the targeted industries, as they realized that the act would allow them to expand the scale of their enterprises and would provide them with a stream of economic rents even if their businesses were not particularly successful. Act 221 was notable for the huge size of its tax credits relative to those provided by other states, the lack of transparency regarding the sizes of benefits claimed by particular firms, and the elimination of strict enforcement provisions used by the U.S. government to monitor similar programs.[30]

Over 15 years (2001–2015), Act 221 provided investors with more than $1.2 billion in subsidies. The legislature repealed the law in 2010, but the state continued to pay out subsidies promised to investors through 2015. So, was the act successful in promoting the establishment of new industries? There is no evidence for a surge in jobs associated with high-technology industries, or for a surge in investment in high-technology industries, in the periods after the subsidies were paid. Evaluation of the impact of the law has been hampered by its lax reporting requirements and by the Department of Taxation's refusal to release critical information required to evaluate it, even to the state's Tax Review Commission. Regardless, it is hard to conclude that the high-technology subsidies achieved anything meaningful beyond distributing $1.2 billion in economic rents to private investors.

How could such an extreme form of rent seeking have arisen in a sovereign U.S. state with political institutions designed to limit the blunt exercise of such power? One general and obvious answer is that all U.S. state governments regularly engage in rent-seeking ventures. The separation of powers built into state governments limits rather than prohibits such behavior. In fact, provision of tax credits to favored firms and industries is observed in just about every state. Support for such tax credits has spanned the partisan political spectrum, as both Republican Party–dominated Texas and Democratic Party–dominated Massachusetts have made widespread use of tax credits and complicated tax subsidies in the first two decades of the twenty-first century. Hawai'i enacted its high-technology credits after a decade (1990–2000) without economic growth, and it is not hard to understand how a legislature and governor desperate to find ways to jump-start growth might favor experimenting with high-tech investment tax credits.[31] There is also some support in the economics literature for providing *limited* government support to start-up firms in some types of new industries.

Economists Daron Acemoglu, Simon Johnson, Douglass North, Steven Webb, and John Wallis and political scientists James Robinson and Barry Weingast have carried out numerous studies analyzing transitions by newly independent countries from colonial to sovereign political institutions. Their studies are relevant to understanding modern Hawai'i political history, as the same type of transition occurred when the U.S. Congress finally agreed to change Hawai'i's status from colonial territory to sovereign state. Their main finding was that the establishment of new, more democratic governance institutions with limitations on executive power was ineffective in curbing rent seeking and corrupt practices in many of these developing countries. This was partly because the new institutions failed to obliterate politicians' memories of the rents available to them in the previous era, or to destroy the human capital of politicians skilled in operating within the rules and culture of the ancien régime, or to change the underlying circumstances that originally brought forth and sustained limited-access political orders.[32] Politicians used their skills to subvert the new government institutions and to re-establish governance by imposing de facto limited-access institutions over the new de jure open-access institutions.

Hawai'i's transition to an open-access order was much more successful than such transitions in many other countries. When August 1959 arrived, the formal institutions of the territorial era were dissolved by the new state constitution. The legislature moved quickly to dismantle the entry barriers and tax policies that created economic rents and distributed them to the Big Five corporations, and to provide the expanded set of public goods demanded by Hawai'i's voters. One exception to this flood of changes was the set of new laws regulating land development, such as the state Land Use Law of 1961, which concentrated zoning functions in the state of Hawai'i. These laws allowed creation and distribution of economic rents to favored players in the emerging tourism industry who were members of the dominant political coalition. I have set forth a number of reasons why such development regulations might persist: a lack of competition from neighboring jurisdictions (Los Angeles, a mere 2,558 miles to the east, is a little too far to commute); lobbying of county governments by homeowners to keep growth-impeding regulations in place to preserve their elevated home values (the "home voter hypothesis"); provision of valuable environmental amenities; and a lack of competition among political parties within the state to force changes to undesirable policies.

Most state residents have rightly concluded that Hawai'i has too little political competition, as most of the competitive elections happen in the Democratic Party primary rather than the general election.[33] This situation could allow inefficient policies, such as regulations on land development, to persist if their benefits are concentrated among the majority group within the Democratic Party. Of course, the flip side to the "lack of political competition" argument is that the state legislature greatly weakened Act 221 in 2005 and then repealed it in 2010 as legislators and the public gradually became more aware of the law's harmful impacts and its egregious transfers of wealth. Of course, reform is easiest when simple repeal is a good option, and simple repeal is surely not an option for the entire set of land development regulations in a fragile island environment. Reform might become more attractive if the public had a better idea of what an "efficient" set of land development regulations looks like and how better regulation would affect land development, the Hawai'i economy, and the welfare of a typical voter.

The Legacy of Colonialism in Hawai'i

The effects of the colonial political order are seen today in the lower incomes of native Hawaiians, while remnants of colonial institutions are found in the loss to native Hawaiians of their crown lands and sovereign government. Both the crown lands and Hawaiian sovereignty were considered by the 1950 constitutional convention and the 1978 constitutional convention. The compromises struck over these issues were approved by native Hawaiians participating in both constitutional conventions and were embodied in both of the resulting constitutions. But 40 years after the 1978 "Con Con," native Hawaiians have a much less favorable view of current constitutional arrangements. Some favor the end of the U.S. occupation and restoration of the Hawaiian Kingdom (fig. 12.1). Others favor establishment of a new government for a country independent of the United States. More favor establishment of a sovereign Hawaiian state within the larger framework of a U.S. state and return of the crown lands to that new Hawaiian state. A wide spectrum of views exists regarding proper institutions for a Hawaiian government, its relationship to federal, state, and county governments, and its capacity to generate revenue and provide services. I intentionally bypass issues of how a sovereign Hawaiian government should be structured and instead focus on the recent Hawaiian constitutional convention and the constitutional compromises, court decisions, and congressional inaction that have shaped the environment for future policy decisions affecting crown lands and Hawaiian sovereignty.

Consider first the issue of the lost crown lands. On the one hand, their redistribution with the change in government follows a familiar pattern, as Hawaiian governments have for centuries redistributed land to bolster the strength of ruling coalitions. Ruling chiefs redistributed land in the sixteenth, seventeenth, and eighteenth centuries when they came to power or conquered new lands (see chap. 3). King Kamehameha redistributed land when he conquered Maui, Moloka'i, and O'ahu in 1795 (see chap. 4). King Kamehameha III (Kauikeaouli) redistributed land in the mid-nineteenth century *Māhele* (see chap. 5). And President Sanford Dole redistributed land when the Republic of Hawai'i confiscated the monarch's private lands after the 1893 coup d'état (see chap. 7).

On the other hand, previous land redistributions took place before private property rights in land had been established in Hawai'i via the *Māhele*. With the recognition of private property in land, the government stopped using land redistribution to solidify the governing coalition when a new king took power. In fact, the confiscation of the crown lands by an autocratic government that had taken power in a coup d'état is the type of property confiscation that is often reversed when a government that respects property rights finally comes to power.

FIGURE 12.1. Royal seal on entrance gates of ʻIolani Palace. Photo: Sumner La Croix.

The crown lands were explicitly considered by the Hawaiʻi constitutional conventions in 1950 and 1978 and by the U.S. Congress in 1959, and provisions in both Hawaiʻi constitutions and in the Hawaii Admission Act address them. Consider how Congress constrained the state of Hawaiʻi's use of revenues from these lands. Section 5(b) of the Hawaii Admission Act turned over 1.4 million acres of public lands, including crown lands, to the new state government.[34] The act established a new "public land trust" and dedicated revenues from that trust to five different uses. Four were very general uses, specifically "support of the public schools and other public educational institutions . . . for the development of farm and home ownership on as widespread a basis as possible, for the making of public improvements, and for the provisions of land for public use." But in an acknowledgement of the origins of these lands, their revenues were also dedicated to "the betterment of the conditions of native Hawaiians, as defined in the Hawaiian Homes Commission Act, 1920, as amended."

The dedication of revenues from the crown lands became much more specific after the 1978 constitutional convention created the Office of Hawaiian Affairs (OHA). An ensuing 1980 state law provided OHA with

"20 percent of all funds derived from the public land trust."[35] The "20 percent of all funds" requirement led to disputes between the state of Hawai'i and OHA over the meaning of the clause; a 1990 state law (Act 304) to refine the meaning of the phrase "20 percent of all funds"; a 1993 payment by the state to OHA to settle claims on this issue; and another round of litigation on the same issue initiated by OHA that was dismissed by the Hawai'i Supreme Court in 2001.[36] In April 2012, Governor Abercrombie signed Hawai'i Senate Bill 2783, which settled all claims (through 2012) over the "20 percent" stipulation by providing OHA with several valuable parcels of land near Kaka'ako Waterfront Park. Political fights between OHA, the state, and environmental groups followed regarding the extent of development that would be allowed on these properties.

The question of the status of the crown lands came to the forefront again in 1993, the 100th anniversary of the overthrow of the Hawaiian Kingdom. At the urging of Hawai'i's congressional delegation, the U.S. Congress passed, and President Bill Clinton signed, a joint resolution of "apology to Native Hawaiians on behalf of the United States for the overthrow of the Kingdom of Hawaii."[37] The heart of the apology was its acknowledgement that "without the active support and intervention by the United States diplomatic and military representatives, the insurrection against the Government of Queen Lili'uokalani would have failed for lack of popular support and insufficient arms" and that "the indigenous Hawaiian people never directly relinquished their claims to their inherent sovereignty as a people or over their national lands to the United States, either through their monarchy or through a plebiscite or referendum." The apology also specifically referred to the crown lands ceded to the United States by the Republic of Hawai'i: "*Whereas*, the Republic of Hawaii also ceded 1,800,000 acres of crown, government and public lands of the Kingdom of Hawaii, without the consent of or compensation to the Native Hawaiian people of Hawaii or their sovereign government."

Whether the apology resolution committed the federal government to any changes in its current or future policies toward native Hawaiians was tested in 1995 when the state of Hawai'i decided to transfer a parcel from the public land trust for development as low-income housing. OHA was to receive monetary compensation for the loss of revenues from this crown lands parcel, but it saw broader issues behind the state's actions. OHA filed suit, noting that the federal government had acknowledged in the apology resolution that native Hawaiians had never relinquished claims in these lands. It asked that no lands be removed from the public land trust until claims to them by the native Hawaiian people had been resolved. The Hawai'i Supreme Court agreed and ruled that the apology resolution required Hawaiian claims to be resolved. Its decision stopped the land transfer.[38] The state of Hawai'i appealed the case to the U.S. Supreme Court, and in a 2009 unanimous ruling, the court overturned the part of the Hawai'i Supreme Court's decision that relied on the apology, sending the case back to the Hawai'i Supreme Court for further review.[39] Justice Alito wrote that the apology resolution did not restructure Hawai'i's "rights and obligations" and that it "did not strip Hawaii of its sovereign authority to alienate the lands the United States held in absolute fee and granted to the State upon its admission to the Union."

The legislative pronouncements and court rulings pertaining to Hawai'i's crown lands force consideration of a more fundamental question: Can a large, uncompensated confiscation of land from a political opponent—Queen Lili'uokalani—continue to be recognized as legitimate when an open-access political order is established? As discussed above, when the overthrow occurred, Hawai'i had over 40 years of experience with private property rights in land, and its government had put in place public and private mechanisms for their enforcement. The decision by the U.S. government when it annexed Hawai'i to consider the confiscated crown lands as lands legitimately owned by the government was not surprising, as the United States was not establishing the open-access political order of a U.S. state in Hawai'i. Rather, it was establishing a limited-access colonial political order, in which the government traditionally uses land transfers to enhance its stability and ability to generate and distribute economic rents.

Hawai'i's transition to an open-access political order in the 1950s provided an opportunity for resolving the seizure of the crown lands. Such a transition often involves a restitution of property unjustly seized by previous governments or compensation for the property's loss. Governments take these steps because they reinforce the government's commitment to future enforcement of property rights. The reunification of East and West Germany in 1990 provides a well-known example. Claims for restitution of properties seized without compensation by the Third Reich and the East German government were settled by a legal process overseen by a government agency, in which property rights were returned or compensation paid to the original owners of more than 2.5 million parcels. Other open-access political orders have realized that property rights in land cannot be secure when previous uncompensated confiscations have not been addressed. Since the 1970s, federal court decisions in Canada and Australia have led to dialogue and negotiations between those governments and first peoples that have resulted in the return of some seized lands and the transfer of resource rights to first peoples. In New Zealand, the Waitangi Tribunal was established in 1975 to hear grievances related to government taking of land from Maori *iwi* (tribes), which may have violated the 1840 Treaty of Waitangi between Maori tribes and the British government. Since 1990, the Office of Treaty Settlements has negotiated 66 settlements that were subsequently approved by Parliament, and it was in the process of negotiating 49 more settlements as of September 2017.[40] The New Zealand, Australian, and Canadian reconciliation processes have all been criticized in some respects, but have also served to resolve many of the grievances held by first peoples regarding confiscated lands.

By contrast, since the decisions by the 1978 constitutional convention and the 1980 state legislature to create OHA and to dedicate 20 percent of revenues from crown lands to fund its programs, OHA and private native Hawaiian groups have made little tangible progress in gaining more control over the crown lands or receiving a larger share of revenue from them. In addition, proposals to give more control over the crown lands to OHA seem less promising in light of two federal court decisions regarding eligibility to participate in OHA elections and qualifications to be an OHA trustee.

In 2000, the U.S. Supreme Court, in *Rice v. Cayetano*, overturned provisions in the Hawai'i state constitution that restricted participation in elections for OHA trustees to Hawaiian voters.[41] One of the hallmarks of Hawai'i's 1978 constitutional convention was its establishment of OHA. The new constitution (article XII, section 5) specified that "there shall be a [nine-member] board of trustees for the Office of Hawaiian Affairs elected by qualified voters who are Hawaiians, as provided by law. The board members shall be Hawaiians." Article XII, section 6, provided the OHA Board of Trustees with the power "to manage and administer the proceeds from the sale or other disposition of the lands, natural resources, minerals and income derived from whatever sources for native Hawaiians and Hawaiians," including a pro rata share of all income and proceeds from a public land trust set aside to benefit native Hawaiians and the general public; "to formulate policy relating to affairs of native Hawaiians and Hawaiians; and to exercise control over real and personal property set aside by state, federal or private sources and transferred to the board for native Hawaiians and Hawaiians."

In 1996, Freddie Rice, a non-native Hawaiian rancher and a registered voter on the island of Hawai'i, brought suit against the state's restriction of the 1996 election of OHA trustees to Hawaiian voters. Rice claimed that this restriction violated the Fifteenth Amendment of the U.S. Constitution, which prohibits a state government from denying a citizen's right to vote based on race. In a 7–2 opinion, Justice Anthony Kennedy wrote that such restrictions did indeed violate the Fifteenth Amendment. He rejected arguments that Hawaiians had the de facto status of an Indian tribe. Kennedy emphasized that the federal government did not recognize native Hawaiians as an Indian tribe, and said that even if it did, the state of Hawai'i could not restrict participation in a state-sponsored election to members of a tribe.

A group of Hawai'i voters saw potential for the *Rice* decision to serve as the basis for a legal challenge to the Hawai'i state constitution's requirement that OHA "board members shall be Hawaiians."[42] Thirteen plaintiffs challenged this requirement, claiming that it violated the Fourteenth and Fifteenth Amendments to the U.S. Constitution. After the U.S. District Court issued a summary judgement for the plaintiffs, the state of Hawai'i brought the case to the Ninth Circuit Court of Appeals. In its unanimous 2002 decision, *Arakaki v. State of Hawaii*,[43] the court ruled that race could not be used as a qualification to be a candidate for the OHA Board of Trustees in this state-sponsored election.

Together, the *Rice* and *Arakaki* decisions raised fears in the Hawaiian community that other federal government programs restricted to native Hawaiian beneficiaries, including the Hawaiian Home Lands program, could be struck down by the federal courts.[44] In addition, the two decisions left OHA in a tenuous position as a vehicle for formulating policy and managing resources relating to the affairs of native Hawaiians. Hawaiians feared that the expansion of the electorate for and eligibility to serve on the board of trustees would provide incentives for the trustees to pay more attention to interests of the broader Hawai'i community than to those of the native Hawaiian community when making OHA policies and allocating OHA resources.

After the *Rice* and *Arakaki* decisions, politicians and community activists in Hawai'i expanded their efforts to gain federal recognition of native Hawaiians and to establish a federally recognized process by which a Hawaiian governing entity could be formed. Multiple organizations promoting the establishment or restoration of a sovereign Hawaiian government have flourished since the 1970s, and over the last 50 years their efforts have found increasing support among the native Hawaiian population for some form of sovereign Hawaiian government.[45] By the beginning of the twenty-first century, efforts to establish a sovereign Hawaiian government within the overall state-federal framework had gained widespread support from Hawai'i's politicians and the general public.

The *Rice* and *Arakaki* decisions increased the resolve of Hawai'i Senator Daniel Akaka to push for federal legislation that would grant native Hawaiians a status similar to that of an Indian tribe and create a process for native Hawaiians to form a government. During the George W. Bush administration, there was little prospect for passage of the Native Hawaiian Government Reorganization Act (popularly known as the "Akaka bill") due to that administration's strong opposition to federal recognition of native Hawaiians. Various versions of the bill were repeatedly introduced in Congress between 2001 and 2007. The House passed different versions of the bill in 2000 and 2007; another version came to the Senate floor for debate in 2006, but was four votes short of winning a cloture vote (56 ayes–41 nays).[46]

Three factors changed the calculus for passage of the Akaka bill between 2006 and 2009. First, the Democratic Party took control of the U.S. Senate and House in 2007—an important development, as most Republican senators and representatives opposed federal recognition of native Hawaiians, contending that it would lead to an unconstitutional race-based government. Second, the incoming Obama administration indicated its support for recognition. Third, and most importantly, the Akaka bill gained a broad spectrum of bipartisan support within Hawai'i, with strong supporters including Hawai'i's two Democratic senators (Inouye and Akaka) and two Democratic representatives (Abercrombie and Hirono), Republican Governor Linda Lingle, Hawai'i Attorney General Mark Bennett, all but a few members of the Hawai'i state legislature, and many prominent people and groups in the Hawaiian community.[47]

On February 23, 2010, the Akaka bill (H.R. 2314) passed the U.S. House of Representatives by a vote of 245–164, but it had insufficient support to be brought up for a vote in the U.S. Senate. With the loss of the Democratic Party majority in the U.S. House in the November 2010 midterm elections, sovereignty activists were forced to consider other strategies for achieving recognition of native Hawaiians by the federal government. One such alternative was to form a native Hawaiian governing entity and then ask the federal government to recognize it. This strategy would involve identifying eligible native Hawaiian voters, electing delegates to a constitutional convention, writing and approving a constitution at the convention, holding a vote to ratify the constitution, electing government officials, and forming a government.

The new strategy was facilitated by a process initiated by the U.S. Department of the Interior. In 2014, the department held a series of hearings in Hawai'i designed to gather input on a new administrative rule that would establish procedures governing establishment of a relationship between a governing entity formed by native Hawaiians and the federal government. The Department of the Interior issued the administrative rule on September 23, 2016, thereby providing a path to federal recognition that bypassed approval by the U.S. Congress.[48] The department's summary of the final rule states that it "does not attempt to reorganize a Native Hawaiian government or draft its constitution, nor does it dictate the form or structure of that government. Rather, the rule establishes an administrative procedure and criteria that the Secretary would use if the Native Hawaiian community forms a unified government that then seeks a formal government-to-government relationship with the United States. Consistent with the Federal policy of self-determination and self-governance for indigenous communities, the Native Hawaiian community itself would determine whether and how to reorganize its government."[49]

The first step taken by the native Hawaiian community to (re)organize a government was to work with the Hawai'i state legislature to gain passage of a bill authorizing collection of a "roll" of Hawaiians who could meet ancestry requirements to vote on a new government entity. In 2011, the legislature passed, and Governor Neil Abercrombie signed, Senate Bill 1520 into law (Act 195). Next, the governor appointed a five-member Native Hawaiian Roll Commission (*Kana'iolowalu*) to begin collection of the roll. By April 2014, over 120,000 native Hawaiians had joined the roll, and in November 2015, a volunteer community organization, Na'i Aupuni, conducted a mail-in ballot election in which voters on the roll could choose delegates to a constitutional convention (*Na'i Aupuni 'Aha*). But the election was placed in peril by a federal lawsuit charging that it was unconstitutional because its requirement that voters be native Hawaiians violated the *Rice* decision. The plaintiffs argued that OHA's indirect funding of a grant made to Na'i Aupuni to pay for the delegate election meant that the election was state-sponsored and thus voter eligibility could not be restricted on the basis of race. On November 26, 2015, the U.S. Supreme Court issued an order prohibiting Na'i Aupuni from counting the votes in the election and certifying the results.[50] Rather than continuing to fight the case in court, Naʻi Aupuni responded on December 15, 2015, by cancelling the election and inviting the 196 candidates running for election as delegates to attend the constitutional convention (ʻaha). One hundred thirty delegates convened on Oʻahu on February 1, 2016, for a closed-door convention with a scheduled closing of February 26.

On February 26, the delegates approved a 15-page "Constitution of the Native Hawaiian Nation" and a "Declaration of the Sovereignty of the Hawaiian Nation" by a vote of 88–30 and one abstention. The constitution describes a government consisting of the usual three branches, with a unicameral 43-member "Legislative Authority."[51] The rights enumerated include rights of the nation, rights of the individual, customary rights, and collective rights.[52] The constitution states that "the Nation has the right to self-determination," but the document is silent regarding whether the new government would pursue independence or federal recognition.[53] Regarding the issue of return of crown lands, the document provides that "the Government shall pursue the repatriation and return of the national lands" or receive "just compensation for lands lost."[54]

After the convention, Naʻi Aupuni bowed out of any future involvement in the process in order to avoid more lawsuits based on the *Rice* decision and urged that future elections and educational forums regarding the proposed constitution be privately funded. The Council for Native Hawaiian Advancement, an umbrella organization with over 100 native Hawaiian community organizations as members, announced plans in 2016 to raise funds to conduct ratification elections and, if the constitution is approved, conduct elections to select officials of the new government. Two years later, organizers were still working to raise sufficient funds to hold a privately funded ratification vote.

Opposition to the Akaka bill and to the new efforts to form a Hawaiian governing entity has come from both sides of the political spectrum. Numerous Hawaiian groups favor the restoration of the Hawaiian Kingdom or the establishment of a new, independent Hawaiian nation. These groups are opposed to any efforts to gain recognition from the federal government or to establish a Hawaiian government that would coexist with the state and federal governments. Roughly 40 native Hawaiian groups have banded together under an umbrella organization—ʻAha Aloha ʻĀina—to oppose ratification of the proposed constitution and to persuade native Hawaiians to withdraw their names from the roll of people meeting ancestry requirements. Conservative and libertarian groups in Hawaiʻi and the mainland United States have also opposed federal recognition and formation of a

Hawaiian government. Their main objection is that the new government would be race-based and that it would serve to balkanize Hawai'i. Some opponents question whether the new government is needed and whether the welfare of native Hawaiians could be better enhanced by focusing political action on the federal and state governments.

Whether any of these groups will be successful in stopping formation or federal recognition of a Hawaiian government remains an open question. The U.S. Department of the Interior's new administrative rule governing federal recognition of a Hawaiian government means that congressional approval is no longer required and thus closes one pathway for stopping recognition. This will undoubtedly force opposition groups to refocus on using federal and state courts to stop the ratification process; raising doubts about the viability of the proposed constitution during the ratification process; or pushing the U.S. Department of the Interior to repeal its administrative process for recognizing a Hawaiian government. Whether a Hawaiian governing entity is formed and recognized by the federal government will also depend on how fast its supporters are able to move and whether they will be able to raise sufficient private resources to galvanize support among the broader native Hawaiian population.

Conclusion

The immigrants who voyaged from East Polynesia to Hawai'i in the thirteenth and fourteenth centuries established independent settlements that were neither controlled by nor dependent on their home governments. Hawai'i's early political institutions were most likely microcosms of the institutions they brought with them from their home islands. Centuries of isolation in a resource-rich archipelago allowed new political institutions and economically and culturally rich Hawaiian societies to emerge. Competition among fluid archaic states for territory and influence within Hawai'i spanned several centuries and coincided with expansion of production and population. Reintegration with the rest of the world in the late eighteenth and nineteenth centuries allowed a unified Hawaiian nation to emerge that would be recognized as an independent country by Japan, the United States, and major European countries and that would successfully modernize its economic and political institutions in order to preserve both its independence and its culture. The imposition of colonial rule by the United States interrupted more than 600 years of Hawaiian independence, but paradoxically, the colonial political order contained the seeds of its own destruction, as it allowed both the Hawaiian people and the new Asian and European immigrants and their children to establish social and political organizations that would ultimately undermine that order. The constitutions that emerged in 1950, 1968, and 1978 from these efforts allowed a more open political order—statehood—to be established, yet failed ultimately to adequately address the confiscations of private property from Hawaiians and the loss of sovereignty by the Hawaiian people. The growing recognition during the 1960s and 1970s of the rich cultural, economic, and political inheritances from both ancient and modern Hawaiian societies provided the inspiration for Hawaiian sovereignty groups to take action to redress the issues of confiscated property and lost sovereignty. Progress toward these goals has stalled in the twenty-first century, but prospects for future progress remain bright as long as recognition of the long tradition of independent and successful governments in pre-colonial Hawai'i continues to grow.

A Model of Political Orders

Throughout this book, I use a framework for analyzing political orders that enables me to tie together more than 800 years of Hawai'i's
economic and political history. The use of models in historical analysis
can be both frustrating and illuminating. Their use often annoys informed
observers who are aware of the intricate networks and details of time,
circumstances, and place that affect political and economic behavior and
outcomes. Criticism is often particularly fierce regarding the use of simplifying assumptions that reduce the determinants of human behavior to
a just a few factors, as this comes at the cost of obscuring complexities associated with social networks and particular circumstances. However, the
use of models also forces us to identify those factors that loom particularly large in human decision making across different times and societies
and to consider carefully how those important factors work together to
generate outcomes.

The explicit and implicit models used in this book's narratives embody
two very strong assumptions that allow for consistent analysis over time
and a narrowing of the frame of analysis. First, the models are applied
under the strong assumption that decision makers were rational—that
is, that they based their decisions on information they gathered on their
environment, their own capabilities, and the capabilities of others in the
society. Second, the models assume that people in Hawai'i maximized
their own well-being and that they made the best of their opportunities as

mediated by the ideology, conventions, and rituals of the overall society surrounding them, regardless of whether they were chiefs, prayer specialists, warriors, or workers in the fields.

My analysis of Hawai'i's political institutions is guided primarily, but far from solely, by a theory of the state recently developed by an interdisciplinary team of social scientists: economic historian and Nobel laureate Douglass North, economic historian John Joseph Wallis, and political scientist Barry Weingast. In their 2009 book *Violence and Social Orders*,[1] the North-Wallis-Weingast research team identifies the control of violence as the critical challenge faced by every society. Their basic insight is that it is impossible for people in a society to achieve a high level of welfare if they live in an atmosphere charged with frequent outbreaks of violence. If violence reigns, then in the immortal words of Thomas Hobbes, "life is nasty, brutish, and short." Whereas no society can ever eliminate violence, a society can prosper only if violence is "controlled and managed."[2] Societies living in the shadow of violence try to solve this fundamental problem by devising social arrangements to "deter the use of violence by creating incentives for powerful individuals [and their supporters] to coordinate rather than fight." This approach involves specifying formal and informal rules to limit competition between individuals and groups, a task that is partly accomplished by placing limits on the use of violence. In the conceptual framework developed by North-Wallis-Weingast, there are two general ways in which societies can be ordered to control violence. In a *limited-access order*, violence is controlled primarily by devising institutions that limit people's rights to form new organizations that could compete with established organizations. In an *open-access order*, violence is largely restricted to the military and police, which are controlled by well-established lines of authority in the government. Political institutions support open entry of new organizations into economic and political markets to compete with organizations run for and by established interests.[3]

What is the mechanism used in a limited-access order to control the use of violence?[4] Leaders of powerful groups and powerful individuals first agree to form a *dominant coalition*, whose members divide up resources and opportunities among themselves and agree to maintain one another's privileged access to those resources. Such privileges generate streams of *economic rent* (defined as a premium above and beyond the normal returns to an activity) and, if incentives are properly structured, ensure that all leaders and their groups keep the peace rather than fight. Because self-enforcing agreements between the members of the dominant coalition often break down, the dominant coalition acts to provide an "organization of organizations"—often called "the state"—that provides third-party enforcement of privileges.[5] If individuals or groups inside or outside the dominant coalition fail to respect member privileges, then individual members of the coalition, as well as the state, have incentives to take action to enforce member rights. In fact, to maintain their exclusive access to economic rents, the key action that members of the dominant coalition must take is "to *limit* the possibility for others to start rival organizations."[6]

How are the economic rents created by the dominant coalition distributed to its members? Distribution is heavily influenced both by the violence potential of powerful individuals and organizations and by established networks of unique personal, family, and group relationships. Networks are important for rent distribution because most of the relationships between individual members of elites in the dominant coalition are personal, not impersonal. Because important relationships among elites are personal in nature, enforcement of agreements between members of the elite depends on the identity and status of the particular members rather than impersonal rules of law. In Hawai'i, the identity of chiefs mattered when agreements were made and enforced, as a chief's status was determined by genealogical background and the chief's network of relationships with other chiefs. Intermarriage across leading families in different states was common, a practice also simultaneously observed in European states.[7] Use of impersonal rules to enforce agreements between chiefs of different ranks was impossible, and this meant that agreements requiring high levels of trust could be concluded only by chiefs of similar genealogical rank.

As these networks of personal relationships change over time and particular groups gain more power, maintaining the stability of the dominant coalition requires that those groups and individuals who have gained more power also gain access to more economic rents. In agricultural societies, rulers would typically redistribute productive lands to accomplish this objective. It has, for example, long been the historical norm that winners of international and civil wars redistribute lands to their supporters in order to build a governing coalition that reflects the new distribution of power in the society at the end of the war.

In Hawai'i, the transition to a new ruling chief or king meant that the new ruler's network of supporters and warriors, genealogically close, high-ranking relatives, and important opponents would be provided with economic rents. To accomplish this objective, the new ruling chief or king typically redistributed productive lands to members of the network. Examples abound: Māʻilikūkahi redistributed lands when he assumed power on Oʻahu in the late 1400s or early 1500s and specified boundaries for *ahupuaʻa*. ʻUmi-a-Līloha redistributed lands when he took power on the island of Hawaiʻi in the early 1500s. Kamehameha redistributed lands in 1795 when he took control of the islands of Hawaiʻi, Lānaʻi, Maui, Molokaʻi, and Oʻahu. Liholiho and the regent Kaʻahumanu redistributed rights to the sandalwood trade when they took power in 1819. Kauikeaouli redistributed lands in the 1840s via the *Māhele*. The U.S. government redistributed lands when it confiscated crown lands on assumption of power in 1898, and then redistributed some lands back to Native Hawaiians in 1921 when the territorial government needed to bolster its ruling coalition. In the 1960s, a newly ascendant democratic legislature and Governor John Burns authorized redistribution of lands to middle- and upper-income supporters by enacting the Land Reform Act of 1967.

Historian Lilikalā Kameʻeleihiwa sees the same functional purpose in land redistribution—to reward close supporters and cement the ruling coalition—but also argues that it was a critical ritual through which every new ruling chief gained *mana*, what Patrick Kirch has called the "manifestation of that power [of their ancestors and their gods] in the human world."[8] The ritualistic nature of redistribution was important in Hawaiʻi, Aztec Mexico, Wankan Peru, Second Dynasty Egypt, and other very similar limited-access political orders, primarily because it imbued the activity and the ruler with a legitimacy that a "naked" redistribution always lacks in any time or place.

North, Wallis, and Weingast distinguish between three types of limited-access orders, which they label fragile, basic, and mature natural states. A *fragile natural state* "can barely sustain itself in the presence of internal and external violence. . . . In a fragile natural state, commitments within the dominant coalition are fluid and unstable, often shifting rapidly, and depending on the individual identity and personality of the coalition members. The coalition is fragile and sensitive to small changes in the situation of the coalition members—changes in relative prices, any number of shocks from climate, neighboring peoples, disease, and so on—can upset the coalition."[9] Fragile natural states are characterized by simple institutional structures. The dominant coalition "successfully provides order when the political interests of coalition members are balanced by their economic stakes in the existing order—the double balance."[10] Violence is always just below the surface of politics, and mistaken political decisions can result in death or war among the parties. Military conquest and successful political action within the coalition are both routes to augment a group's resources.[11] Chiefdoms are usually fragile natural states, and Hawai'i chiefdoms from settlement to sometime in the late fifteenth or sixteenth century had many features consistent with the fragile natural state.

A *basic natural state* "sustains a durable and stable organizational structure for the state." New public institutions are established to structure relationships within the state and between the state and members of the elite. These public institutions "provide standard solutions to recurring problems: succession of the leader, succession of elites, determination of tax and tribute rates and division of the spoils of conquest."[12] These problems are difficult to resolve when they occur and can lead to the breakup of the state. Specifying rules for how to proceed in these situations reduces the danger of a breakup and solidifies participants' expectations that they can rely on agreements made within the framework of the basic natural state. The dominant coalition in a basic natural state is bolstered by the new public institutions but still fears competition and disruption of existing arrangements from new organizations. To constrain this kind of unwanted competition, "only organizations with direct connections to the state possess durability." The archaic states that developed in Hawai'i in the late fifteenth and sixteenth centuries had many features consistent with the basic natural state, including the collection of taxes during the *makahiki* festival, the importance of genealogical background in determining elite status, conventions whereby a ruling chief passes certain offices to designated individuals, and the presence of a large class of prayer specialists to ensure that rituals are conducted to legitimize actions of ruling chiefs and to provide alternatives to violence for enforcing rules.

A *mature natural state* "is characterized by durable institutional structures for the state and the ability to support elite organizations outside the immediate framework of the state."[13] A private law emerges that informs individuals regarding the types of relationships between individuals that will be enforced under that law, and a public law emerges that "specifies the offices and functions of the state and the relationship between the offices and functions, and provides for methods of resolving conflicts within the state and, by extension, within the dominant coalition."[14] Most importantly, mature natural states are capable of supporting elite organizations without close ties to the state. Recognition of organizations as persons under the law allows contracting among and within organizations to be governed by courts, and this allows for more, and more specialized, organizations to operate effectively, generating more opportunities and income for the society. From the 1840s to 1893, the Hawaiian Kingdom had many features of a mature natural state, including a functioning court system that resolved private disputes, a public law that specified offices of the government and their relationship with one another, and numerous perpetually lived organizations (i.e., those that "live beyond the life of individual members") that were somewhat independent of the state, such as the Bishop Estate, other large charitable and landed trusts, and the Big Five companies that provided a variety of agency services to the sugar industry.

The transition from a limited-access order to an *open-access order* occurs when "the society transforms from one based on personal relations and personal exchange to one based on impersonal relations and impersonal exchange." Open-access orders "rely on competition in the political and economic systems to sustain order." Their hallmark is the establishment of a "perpetual state in which the rules and institutions of government do not depend on the identity of political officials." Only some military and police organizations can legitimately use violence, and their use of violence is overseen by well-specified lines of authority in the government. Groups compete for control of the government, with the competition "subject to clear and well-understood rules."[15] Because governments in open-access orders must be responsive to the demands of a broad electorate, they tend to grow larger than when they are creating and distributing rents only to groups in the dominant coalition.[16]

Shared beliefs among citizens are necessary features of open-access orders, and such belief systems typically emphasize "equality, sharing and universal inclusion."[17] Elites no longer have special status under the law, but are subject to the same laws applicable to the rest of the population. This is because elites are no longer parties to agreements that divide up resources and generate rents for specific people and groups.

The takeover of Hawai'i by the United States, a country that in 1900 had many aspects of an open-access order, did not result in an open-access order being established in Hawai'i. Instead, a colonial version of a limited-access order was put in place wherein the state did not emerge as an organization created by players in the dominant coalition to facilitate and enforce agreements, but rather was forced on players in the dominant coalition by the colonial power. In Hawai'i, only the legislative branch of government was contestable by a broad electorate while the executive and judiciary branches were imposed and controlled by the U.S. government.

A colonial power that annexes a country is likely to be particularly interested in redistributing rents and property within the country shortly after its takeover, as the new colonial government usually faces the immediate task of establishing its authority. It undertakes redistribution not just to bolster the strength of the government's coalition, but also to reduce the strength of supporters of the just overthrown government who may be waiting on the sidelines to violently overthrow or to disrupt the new regime if given the chance.

Hawai'i's territorial government was actually quite similar to governments established for other mainland territories that were expected to become U.S. states. Like those territories, it coupled institutions typical of a limited-access order with a few features of an open-access order. Most importantly, the Organic Act brought the Bill of Rights of the U.S. Constitution to all Hawai'i citizens and a smaller but still considerable package of rights to noncitizen residents. In addition, it placed no explicit limits on the formation of private organizations. The organizations of civil society and the political parties that developed in Hawai'i during the territorial era would be essential to the drive to gain statehood and to a functioning open-access order after statehood.

North-Wallis-Weingast emphasize that transitions from a limited-access order to an open-access order tend to occur as three "doorstep conditions" are satisfied: rule of law for elites; perpetually lived organizations in the public and private spheres; and consolidated control of the military.[18] These doorstep conditions were, however, not very relevant for Hawai'i's transition from a colony to a U.S. state. Consolidated control of the military was not an issue for Hawai'i, as neither territories nor states have any substantial control over U.S. military forces or decisions. Rule of law for elites was in place during the territorial era, but perpetually lived private and public organizations were not in place due to the power of the U.S. Congress to alter the territory's "constitution," the Organic Act, at any time.[19] For Hawai'i, the relevant doorstep conditions were those that increased the likelihood of the members of the U.S. Senate and House voting for statehood. As described in chapter 9, these conditions included the reduced presence of Communist Party members in leadership positions in Hawai'i unions, the demonstration of patriotism and bravery by Japanese-Americans and other Asian-Americans during World War II, and the adoption of a "typical" state constitution in 1950.

Notes

Chapter One

1. See Voigtländer and Voth (2013) for an analysis of the relationship between a country's per capita income 300–500 years ago and its per capita income today. See Putterman and Weil (2010) for an analysis of the relationship between your ancestors' income centuries ago and your income today. For an excellent survey of the deep historical roots of economic development, see Spolaore and Wacziarg (2013).

2. See Nunn (2008) for an empirical analysis of the legacy of more than three centuries of slave capture and sales in West Africa.

3. Voigtländer and Voth (2012, 1139) use pogroms during the plague era of the mid-fourteenth century "as an indicator for medieval anti-Semitism. They reliably predict violence against Jews in the 1920s, votes for the Nazi Party, deportations after 1933, attacks on synagogues, and letters to Der Stürmer."

4. See Kirch (2010) and Earle (1997) for similar but different stories of the rise of archaic states in Hawai'i. See D'Arcy (2014) for a remarkable overview of conditions in the Central and Eastern Pacific Ocean and how they compared with regions spanned by the Atlantic Ocean. See Allen (2014) for a discussion of whether new evidence on the later settlement of Polynesia still allows for the Marquesas Islands to be a source of early migration to Hawai'i.

5. See Mann (2011) for an excellent analysis of how the Columbian exchange (i.e., the transfer of plants and animals across continents after the voyages of Christopher Columbus) triggered transformation of societies and landscapes throughout the world.

6. See Kirch (2014, chap. 7) for a description of a Maui *heiau* that is exactly oriented around the constellation of the Southern Cross, the astronomical guide used by voyagers to return to Tahiti. Kirch also concludes that the discovery of a stone adz mined on Kaho'olawe, Hawai'i, on the atoll of Napuka in the Tuamotu Archipelago, more than 2,500 miles south of Hawai'i, "is the 'smoking gun' that archaeologists had long searched for, the incontrovertible evidence of two-way voyaging between Hawai'i and Kahiki [Tahiti]." See Kirch (2012, chap. 7).

7. For the origins of this argument, see Earle (1997, 45).

8. Samuel Kamakau (1991), a nineteenth-century Hawaiian historian, and Abraham Fornander ([1878–1885] 1969), a nineteenth-century historian living in Hawai'i, provide accounts of foreign ships that stumbled upon Hawai'i during this period of isolation and people from the ships who stayed in Hawai'i.

9. Rapa Nui, a remote Polynesian island in the Southern Pacific, also known as Easter Island, might be another example. See Hunt and Lipo (2011) for a brilliant new history of Rapa Nui based on recent archaeological discoveries.

Rulers of some societies, such as Japan for more than 250 years during the feudal military rule of the Tokugawa (1603–1867), have made decisions to voluntarily isolate themselves from other countries. From the seventeenth to the mid-nineteenth century, Japan virtually eliminated contacts with European countries, keeping just a small window open to the European world via an island at the port of Nagasaki. Less noticed is that Japan remained integrated with Asia, retaining its extensive trade contacts with Korea and China.

10. Kirch (2010, 237) noted that "elites can isolate themselves by various means. And with isolation comes mystery. 'Perhaps those people with the feathered cloaks are gods on earth,' the common people may wonder to themselves, occasionally glimpsing the exalted ones from afar."

11. See Earle (1997) and Allen (1997).

12. Some European societies had sumptuary laws that restricted consumption of certain goods to the nobility. See Sheilagh Ogilvie's (2010) study of sumptuary laws in Württemberg, Germany.

13. See Hommon (2013) for a comprehensive analysis of life in ancient Hawai'i.

14. See Kirch (2010) for extended reflections on the history of Hawai'i's competing states.

15. The suppression of Hawaiian culture lasted until the 1870s, when King Kalākaua and Queen Lili'uokalani revived long-suppressed chants and hulas and wrote new ones. With the overthrow of Queen Lili'uokalani in 1893, U.S. territorial government restrictions on the use of the Hawaiian language in schools and government led to a dramatic fall in the use of the language and a shrinkage in Hawaiian cultural activity. A Hawaiian cultural renaissance began after World War II and flourished particularly in the 1960s and 1970s.

16. See La Croix and Fishback (1989 and 2000) for a more detailed discussion of indentured servitude and its aftermath in Hawai'i.

17. Glick (1980, 19).

18. Moriyama (1985, tables 8 and 10).

19. Hawaiian Homes Commission Act, 42 Stat. 108 (1921). I follow convention in using "Native Hawaiian" to refer to any person who is at least 50 percent Hawaiian and use "Hawaiian" and "native Hawaiian" (with a small n) to refer more inclusively to any person with any Hawaiian lineage.

20. The federal government initially retained 0.375 million acres of public lands.

21. See Saiz (2010). In a recent paper (La Croix 2016), I provide a more complete accounting of the factors underpinning residential housing prices in Hawai'i.

Chapter Two

1. See Beaglehole (1968a, 154). As quoted in Howe (2006, 77–79).

2. See Beaglehole (1968b, 87, Thursday, April 3, 1777). Cook concluded that "this circumstance very well accounts for the manner the Inhabited islands in this Sea have been at first peopled; especially those which lay remote from any continent and any other." For his formulation of the accidental drift hypothesis, see Sharp (1957). For a convincing refutation, see Finney (1994).

3. See Levison, Ward, and Webb (1973) and Irwin, Bickler, and Quirke (1990).

4. For a fascinating and lively review of the influence of new advances in radiocarbon dating on archaeology in Hawai'i, see Kirch (2012, 73–109).

5. See Wilmshurst et al. (2008, 2011), and Rieth et al. (2011).

6. A recent study using seafaring simulations of potential voyages from the Central to the Eastern Pacific Ocean concludes that "seasonal and semiseasonal climatic changes were highly influential in structuring ancient Pacific voyaging." See Montenegro, Callaghan, and Fitzpatrick (2014).

7. Allen (2014, 1) concludes that radiocarbon dates "unambiguously place Polynesians in the archipelago in the 13th century, while numerous dates on other materials point to the likelihood of colonization from the 11th to 12th centuries." She also finds (2014, 1) that "other evidence (ceramics and stone tool geochemistry) indicates multiple and unusually far-ranging regional contacts between roughly the 12th to 15th centuries, a situation which suggests superior and sustained voyaging."

8. Rieth et al. (2011, 2747).

9. See Athens et al. (2014).

10. See Hunt and Lipo (2006).

11. For example, I formerly endorsed Kirch's (1985) estimate of Hawai'i settlement between AD 400 and 500 (La Croix 2004).

12. See Terrell (2011) for an analysis of the importance of the later dates of colonization for our understanding of the history of East Polynesian societies.

13. See Baines (1995) for an application of push-pull migration theory to nineteenth- and twentieth-century European migration to the Americas, Australia, and New Zealand.

14. See Terrell (1988, 11–16). For example, a Marquesan oral history relates that a voyage from the Marquesas to Tahiti took several months and was so long that "from Eiao [an island in the Marquesas chain] they travelled to the middle of the ocean. Their food ran out, the water ran out, and the men died." There were 140 rowers on the double-hulled canoe, and 100 died during the voyage (14).

15. See Bell et al. (2015, 406).

16. See Finney (1985 and 2003). Contributions by archaeologists to this discussion include Anderson et al. (2006) and Irwin (1992).

17. More recent analysis of voyaging windows has focused on a 450-year period (AD 900–1350) known as the "Medieval Climate Anomaly" and how the end of that anomaly might have closed those windows in the fourteenth century. See Goodwin, Browning, and Anderson (2014).

18. See Anderson (2003).

19. See Anderson (2003, 175). "A productive strategy would have been to keep moving toward the southeast while also searching regularly at right angles to intercept each new archipelago across its long axis, where the target angle was broadest . . . Unlike the laborious search pattern in the orthodox model, this alternative strategy is effectively reduced to a simple axis of sailing directions—southeast, with offsets to southwest and northeast—and it required sailing across the prevailing wind direction from the beginning, using suitable tail winds as these occurred. Relatively few voyages would have found all the islands in the main band quite quickly. Once exploration had reached well to the southeast, the discovery of the marginal archipelagos, though more difficult, may have been simply in continuation of that strategy, with Hawai'i and, later, New Zealand being found by interception voyages that travelled further than usual in easterlies."

20. Kirch (2012, 55–56).

21. Handy, Handy, and Pukui (1991, 321, 324–325) argue that the Polynesians found an aboriginal people, the *kauwa*, who were subsequently enslaved and marginalized,. One Hawaiian observer estimated that there were roughly 1,000 *kauwa* at the time of Western contact. While the historical record of Western visitors to Hawai'i acknowledges a small enslaved class of undetermined size, the modern archaeological record provides no evidence that Polynesian settlers encountered an aboriginal people.

22. Curtin (1989, 1998) shows that European soldiers, sailors, bishops, and bureaucrats living in colonies in the tropics had extremely high morbidity and mortality rates. The absence of first peoples also meant that the disease environment introduced to the islands by the waves of colonists from Central Polynesia did not decimate populations of first peoples, as did the post-1492 waves of European colonists to the non-European world.

23. Resource distribution varies considerably across islands in archipelagos, with some being very dry (Kaho'olawe in Hawai'i) and others being so close to sea level that their resources could have been prone to destruction during natural disasters. Many of the "resource-rich" archipelagos, like Hawai'i, lacked critical foods, such as staple starches—wheat, rice, taro—needed for a large population to be established.

24. Hunt and Lipo (2017), who discuss push-and-pull migration theories in the context of the Polynesian migration into the Eastern Pacific between 1000 and

1300, are skeptical that population pressure could provide a rationale for additional voyaging. Instead, they hypothesize that "some kind of voyaging technology or navigational innovation" coupled with changing climate conditions, could have been the main factor behind the continued pulse of voyaging (2017, 210–211).

25. Bell et al. (2015, 398). See also Irwin and Flay (2015) for additional discussion.

26. See Page (1995) and Jóhannesson ([1974] 2006). There is some, not totally reliable, archaeological evidence and references in written Irish sources suggesting that the first Norse settlers encountered a few very small settlements of hermit Irish monks and priests.

27. Page (1995, 59).

28. Page (1995, 58–59).

29. See Alston, Libecap, and Mueller (1998).

30. See Umbeck (1977) for the seminal analysis of how groups of miners established de facto property rights to unclaimed land during the 1848–1855 California gold rush and how rights to mine gold in the California/Nevada Sierra adjusted to changes in the number of new claimants. In an earlier paper (La Croix 1992), I extended Umbeck's discussion by considering the role of government in the establishment of property rights during the 1851–1854 gold rush in Victoria, Australia. Libecap (1978, 1994) analyzes how property rights in natural resources in the United States were established. Lueck (1995) considers why rules of first possession to claim property rights in land and natural resources are likely to be efficient in a wide range of circumstances.

The economist Harold Demsetz (1967) was the first to suggest that a property rights structure cannot be taken as an institutional datum, but rather changes as more fundamental demographic, economic, and social factors change. As constraints on individuals' behavior change, property rights and institutions change in response, sometimes in a punctuated fashion. Umbeck (1981) adds to this analysis by arguing that property rights structures are based "on the abilities of individuals, or groups of individuals to forcefully maintain exclusivity" (1981, 39). Unless the property rights structure endows each individual with the same amount of wealth that he could achieve through violence, it will pay for this individual to contract with other individuals to obtain a new distribution using or threatening violence (Umbeck, 1981, 40).

Umbeck argues that the important factor determining property rights, at least in a closed-access political order, is the relative violence potential of various individuals and groups of individuals.

31. See Alston, Harris, and Mueller (2012) and Dye and La Croix (2013).

32. Dye and La Croix (in press) find similar behavior by Dutch sheep and cattle farmers in the Cape Colony during the eighteenth century.

33. Many Pacific islands and atolls have only small amounts of arable land, and these lands could have been fully claimed and occupied just a few decades after

initial settlement began. Since Polynesians reached the Society Islands just 80–150 years before voyages to Hawai'i began, would this have been sufficient time for an initial group of voyagers—say, 150 to 500 people—to grow to a population large enough to restrict land access for larger younger generations? While this is highly implausible, the Society Islands were close enough to the discoverers' home that return trips, facilitated by downwind sailing, could have led to new waves of migrants. See Kirch (2012) and Carolyn K. Cachola-Abad (1993) for evidence of such return trips to home islands in Central Polynesia. Clark et al. (2014) discusses the trade between the centralized state of Tonga, which emerged in the twelfth and early thirteenth centuries, and Samoa, Fiji, and the Society Islands.

34. The classic analysis of the different challenges, constraints, and opportunities that present themselves on windward and leeward coasts of Pacific islands is Patrick Kirch's 1994 book *The Wet and the Dry*.

35. Patrick Kirch (2012, 66) has argued that the first settlers probably arrived at beaches where their *vaca moana*s could safely land, such as O'ahu's Waimanolo-Bellows Beach, Waikiki Beach, or the Waihee coast on Maui.

36. The earliest volcanic formations in the Hawai'i archipelago—the islands in the northeastern part of the archipelago, namely, Necker Island, Nihoa Island, and French Frigate Shoals—have been subject to erosion and have slowly subsided into the earth's crust. Most are now barely above sea level. Necker's highest elevation is 156 feet, and Nihoa's highest point is 910 feet. French Frigate Shoals has a small 121-foot pinnacle, but otherwise its highest point is just 9.8 feet above sea level.

37. This section closely follows Kirch's (2012, 101–109) lively descriptions of the analyses of pollen in sedimented marsh and pond cores set forth in Athens (1997); of Polynesian rat fossils set forth in Athens et al. (2002); of flightless bird fossils set forth in Ziegler (2002, chap. 22); and of fossilized land snails set forth in Christensen and Kirch (1986).

38. Kirch (2012, 103).

39. We know this because the number of shells from a non-native snail often found in the roots of taro plants increased. See Kirch (2012, 108).

40. See Hunt and Lipo (2011, 27–35).

41. Engerman and Sokoloff (2002).

42. Engerman and Sokoloff (2002, 4).

43. Engerman and Sokoloff (2002, 3).

44. Engerman and Sokoloff (2002, 4).

45. With taro production, there were few spillovers of costs or benefits across valleys, although the experience of the late nineteenth and early twentieth century with sugar, pineapple, and livestock grazing clearly shows the potential for such spillovers. Kaiser (2014) shows how close O'ahu came to ecological disaster in the late nineteenth century before cooperation among plantation owners reversed deteriorating conditions in the watershed forest. See Kaiser and Roumasset (2014)

for an analysis of Hawaiian history that emphasizes the relationship between resources and institutional development.

46. In the nineteenth century, rapidly declining shipping costs integrated Hawai'i markets more closely with global sugar and labor markets. As Hawai'i's comparative advantage in sugar emerged, plantations and the government cooperated to bring bound labor to Hawai'i to work in the sugar fields. The shift to bound labor as the choice of crop shifted is consistent with Engerman and Sokoloff's analysis of changes over time in property rights to labor.

47. North, Summerhill, and Weingast (2000).

48. For example, government grants or sales of small contiguous farm lands with well-defined property rights were often made to replicate the system of land rights found in European farm communities at the time. The decisions of some colonists to ignore the official system of land rights and move beyond the official settlement boundaries of the colony to clear and claim new lands opened a number of paths by which the transplanted property rights and governance institutions could eventually adapt to the new environment.

49. See Kirch (2011) and the discussion in chapter 4 of the 1778 population.

50. Dye and Komori (1992) found that population peaked in 1440 and then declined until the end of the eighteenth century. Kirch (2007b, chap. 4) provides an excellent review of population trends until 1778. He concludes (66) that "between around AD 1500 and contact at 1778, the rate of population growth dropped off significantly" and that "population dynamics in the critical two to three centuries prior to European contact (AD 1500–1778) remain hazy." Archaeologists have emphasized that the rate of population growth varied across and within islands between initial settlement and contact.

51. Hommon (2013, 229) concludes that the minimum viable size for an initial settlement was 200 people.

52. The net total fertility rate is net of infants who die at birth or before age 5.

53. See Livi-Bacci (2012, 57–61).

54. One of the highest population growth rates in the Pacific islands was for the English-Tahitian population that lived on Pitcairn Island. Its 3 percent growth rate lasted 66 years, from 1790 to 1856.

55. Another possibility is that immigration to Hawai'i started at an earlier date. Suppose, for example, that the first migrants arrived in 1160, 100 years earlier than assumed in the main text. Starting again from an initial population of 100 people, this scenario would require only a 2.29 percent annual growth rate for the full 340-year period to produce the same AD 1500 population.

56. Cachola-Abad (1993) organizes stories from numerous *mo'oelo* that support the hypothesis that several waves of migrants came to Hawai'i during the thirteenth and fourteenth centuries. Clark et al. (2014) provide evidence that there was extensive inter-archipelago voyaging around this same time in the Polynesian core if not necessarily the periphery. Walpole (2014) furnishes a reconciliation

of the new archaeological findings on thirteenth-century East Polynesian settlement with the linguistic theories and evidence of East Polynesian language development. Given the extensive voyaging that took place within Polynesia over the twelfth through the fifteenth centuries, she argues that regular contact among island groups led to interlinked development of such regional languages as Hawaiian, Marquesan, Tahitian, Mangarevan, Tuamotuan, and Māori.

Suppose that there was one return voyage to Polynesia and that news rapidly spread that Hawai'i had been discovered and settlement started. What would have then happened? Christopher Columbus's return to Spain and Portugal from his first voyage in March 1493 shows how widely news of new lands can spread and how rapidly new voyages can be organized. Columbus's letter reporting on his discovery of resource-rich islands was reprinted and circulated through Spain and Portugal within a few weeks of his return to Spain and through Europe within a few months. Adventurers throughout Europe flocked to Spain to join new voyages of discovery, and it took only about six months (September 1493) for the Spanish government to launch a 17-ship expedition to the Americas.

57. See Hommon (2013, 229–231). Hommon (231) cites "a mo'oelo genealogically dated to around the year 1420 that tells of Lakona, who served as chief of the island of O'ahu but exercised direct rule only over 'Ewa and Wai'anae districts, while another chief controlled Kona and a third held Ko'olauloa and Ko'olaupoku." Hommon (231) suggests "that the estimated population of 29,535 would have been sufficient for interacting districts . . . to have formed by the time of Lakona."

58. Consider, for example, one alternative assumption, changing the assumed population in 1350 from 30,000 people to 50,000 people. This assumption would lower the growth rate for the 1350–1500 period to 0.92 percent, but would not affect the qualitative analysis presented in the text (i.e., that population growth declines after 1350 and again after 1500).

59. Livi-Bacci (2012, table 1.3). See also Biraben (1979, 16).

60. On the origins of the sweet potato in Polynesia and Hawai'i, see Ballard et al. (2005), Ladefoged, Graves, and Coil (2005), and Horrocks and Rechtman (2009). Compare with Miller (1927) on nutritional value of taro and poi.

61. See Spriggs and Kirch (1992, 157–164).

62. See Ladefoged et al. (2009, 2381).

Chapter Three

1. Ladefoged et al. (2009) estimate that the five largest islands had 189.79 km^2 in land that could be used in irrigated agriculture ("good land") and that it would take 28,701 people to farm this land annually. Now suppose that each farmer initially produced enough food for three dependents. This implies that all of the good

land would be farmed when the overall population reached 114, 804. Using the alternative population scenario developed in chapter 2, in which the population grew at 5.57 percent from 1260 to 1350 and then by 1.26 percent from 1350 to 1500, this would have happened in 1452.

2. Earle (1997, 44).

3. Earle (1997, 43).

4. See North, Wallis, and Weingast (2009). North, Wallis, Webb, and Weingast (2012) apply their model to the modern history of 10 developed and developing countries.

5. North, Wallis, and Weingast (2009, 18).

6. North, Wallis, and Weingast (2009, 42, 52–58).

7. North, Wallis, and Weingast (2009, 43).

8. See Earle (1997). Later extensions include Earle and Doyel (2008) and Earle (2012).

9. See Kirch (1992, vol. 2).

10. For Pharaonic Egypt, see Trigger (1993). For the United States and United Kingdom in 1850, see Broadberry and Irwin (2006). For France circa 1800, see Hoffman (2000).

11. My discussion of the rise of competing states in Hawai'i, including the unification of O'ahu's chiefdoms, draws heavily from Patrick Kirch's many magisterial books on Hawai'i's prehistory. In particular, see *The Wet and the Dry* (1994); *How Chiefs Became Kings: Divine Kingship and the Rise of Archaic States in Ancient Hawai'i* (2010); *A Shark Going Inland Is My Chief: The Island Civilization of Ancient Hawai'i* (2012); and *Kua'āina Kahiko: Life and Land in Ancient Kahikinui, Maui* (2014).

12. See Caldeira et al. (2015) for a spectacular documentation of the complexity and spiritual power of royal Hawaiian featherwork. See Linnekin (1988) and Cordy (2003) for discussions of who made the feather cloaks. Both commoners and specialists would collect feathers and make feathered helmets.

13. See Malo (2006, Hawaiian text p. 50, English translation p. 62).

14. For original sources, see Malo (2006, Hawaiian text pp. 119–129, English translation pp. 164–177). For a discussion of the cultural significance of the games, see Valeri (1985, chap. 7).

15. See Kolb (1994).

16. Kolb (2006, 657) argued that "temple development follows a cycle of construction and use characteristic of incipient state development, coinciding with distinct periods of political tension when it was important to encourage and control social allegiances." See also McCoy et al. (2011).

17. Hommon (2013, 12) estimated 525,000 people in 1778. On the basis of his detailed studies of Kihikinui, Maui, Kirch (2014, 146–157) speculates that the population of Maui in 1778 could have been as large as 280,000 people, which would certainly imply an overall population for the islands far exceeding 500,000.

18. See Cachola-Abad (1993, 13–32) for analysis of additional *mo'oelo* that provide support for inter-archipelago voyaging during the initial years of Hawaiian settlement.

19. The analysis changes if the initial migrants coming to Hawai'i were mostly in their early twenties and did not bring children with them. Suppose that the migrants were all 20-year-old male-female couples. In this case, the workforce would decline slightly for the next 16–17 years and then start to grow as the first 16-year-old children entered the workforce. The number of people in the workforce would then grow rapidly as large numbers of young people entered.

The analysis changes if waves of new 20-year-old migrants came to Hawai'i during, say, the first 40 years of settlement. In this case, the labor force would have rapidly increased over the first two to three decades of settlement, in part because the initial population and labor force were small and the flows of migrants were large relative to the initial population.

20. There was only limited barter trade across *ahupua'a*. On the island of Hawai'i, the missionary William Ellis observed "trade fairs" at which goods were bartered, including hogs, tobacco, tapas, condensed *poi*, and dried salt fish. See Ellis ([1827] 1963, 229–230) and discussion in Hommon (2013, 107–109).

21. See Ladefoged, Graves, and McCoy (2003), Ladefoged and Graves (2007), Ladefoged, Lee, and Graves (2008), and McCoy and Graves (2010).

22. See Williamson and Bloom (1998) and Mason and Lee (2007).

23. In the Solow neoclassical growth model, a decline in the rate of population growth will also produce a one-time increase in output per person; its realization can take a few years or a few decades, depending on how fast the economy is able to adjust to the change in population growth.

24. North, Wallis, and Weingast (2009, 43).

25. North, Wallis, and Weingast (2009, 43).

26. See Jorgenson (1967) for a simple general equilibrium model of food surpluses. The idea traces back to V. Gordon Childe's highly influential 1936 book *Man Makes Himself.*

27. See Olson (1993).

28. Carneiro (1970). See also Barzel (2012) for discussions of the role of monitoring costs in state formation.

29. Small groups working large tracts of thinly utilized rich lands would generally have had incentives to cede some land rather than fight, at least through a few rounds of newcomers.

30. See Stigler (1966, chap. 13).

31. Wittfogel (1957, 238–246).

32. See Earle (1997, 68–69, 75–76).

33. See Allen (1997, 136) for an application of Carneiro's theory of the state to the formation of the Egyptian state during the fourth millennium BC.

34. See Hommon (2013, 139–199, 218). There is some evidence for voyaging between Hawai'i and the Tuamotu Archipelago, where adzes with basalt heads

mined on Kahoʻolawe have been discovered. Similarities between varieties of rats in Hawaiʻi and the Cook Islands provide evidence for at least an indirect linkage between the two island groups. See also Matisso-Smith et al. (1998).

35. See Hommon (2013, 187–199) and Kirch (1990). For a stimulating discussion of trade in adzes between Tonga and other Polynesian chiefdoms and states in the Central and Eastern Pacific Ocean, see Clark et al. (2014).

36. Malo (2006, Hawaiian text p. 5, English translation p. 6).

37. Fornander ([1878–1885] 1969, vol. 2, 33–38). See also the discussion in Kirch (2012, 69). Jim Bayman and Tom Dye warn social scientists and historians that research combining *mo ʻoelo* and archaeological findings needs to be tempered by the thought that "we don't really know whether any of these people actually lived." See Bayman and Dye (2013).

38. The discussion in the text draws from the seminal discussion in Kirch (2010, 88–92) regarding how a state first formed on Oʻahu.

Economists and political scientists have closely studied how U.S. states imitate and adapt successful institutions in neighboring U.S. states. It helps to have a good neighbor. See Besley and Case (2003). Stewart (1830, 97) tells the story of King Kamehameha who, after boarding a ship returning from Canton, found "a bill of charges amounting to 3000 dollars! In the items of the bill were *pilotage and anchorage* and custom-house fees to a large sum; and when told that maritime states in other countries derived large revenues in this manner, he immediately said, 'Well then, I will have fees for my harbour too'; and from that time the harbor at Oahu has been taxed in the amount mentioned."

In the post–World War II era, states have often coalesced more quickly when they face external threats. Modern examples include Western European states facing the large armies of the Soviet Union at their borders; South Korea facing the North Korean army and its thousands of short-range weapons and missiles within striking range of Seoul; Taiwan facing Chinese armies and missiles just across the Taiwan Strait; and Singapore facing nearby Indonesian and Malaysian forces in the 1960s and 1970s. (Thanks to Yoram Barzel for the Singapore example.)

39. Hommon (2013, 241–242). See Higgs (1987) for the argument that a series of crises allowed power to be gradually consolidated in the executive branch of the U.S. government during the first half of the twentieth century.

40. Hoffman (2015, 135–136).

41. Fornander ([1878–1885] 1969, vol. 2, 67–68). An army of Kauaʻi chiefs led by the *Mō ʻī*, Kukona, defeated the invading forces, captured Kalanuiohua, and then sent Huapouleilei back to Oʻahu.

42. Fornander ([1878–1885] 1969, vol. 2, 88).

43. Kamakau (1991, 54).

44. See Kamakau (1991, 54–55). See also the careful discussion in Kirch (2010, 88–92).

45. See Kamakau (1991, 152). Throughout this book, I argue that Hawaiian chiefs, kings, and territorial and state governors have repeatedly redistributed lands to bolster the strength of their coalition of supporters.

46. Kirch (2010, 88–92); Fornander ([1878–1885] 1969, vol. 2, 93).

47. Some *ahupua'a* did not stretch from the mountains to the ocean and some were not geographically contiguous.

48. See Kirch et al. (2012). Hommon (2013, 107–109) provides a summary of institutions providing for exchange of goods across communities via gift and barter.

49. For the classic statement of this proposition, see Taylor (2010).

50. Walther (1997) provides a history of the Pearl Harbor oyster fishery. King Kamehameha regularly placed a *kapu* on selling goods to foreign ships in order to restrict supply and force up the price.

51. Hommon (2013, 32).

52. Hommon (2013, 33).

53. Kamakau ([1969] 1992, 35, 45–46, 55, 66–67, 230).

54. See Kolb and Dixon (2002).

55. Walled fortifications played only a minor role in Hawaiian wars. Vulnerable non-fighting populations sometimes moved to designated areas of refuge that were declared to be *kapu* and thus off-limits to invading warriors. These areas of refugee may have served important purposes, but their overall extent seems small.

56. Hommon (2013, 32).

57. Malo (1951, 53). In this instance, the 1898 Emerson translation of Malo's book more accurately reflects the text than the 2006 Chun translation, as it explicitly refers to the "art of war."

58. Hoffman (2012, 605).

59. Hoffman (2012, 605).

60. Kirch (2010, 37–40).

61. Religious ceremonies and festivals on the islands of Hawai'i and Maui, both of which had primarily rain-fed fields, were more focused on worship of Lono, while those on the islands of Kaua'i and O'ahu, both of which had primarily irrigated fields, were more focused on Kāne, "the god of fresh-water springs and thus of irrigated agriculture, as well as fishponds and forests." See Hommon (2013, 87–88).

62. Voigtländer and Voth (2013, 165–186).

63. These would include such battlefield diseases as typhoid, cholera, and dysentery. The situation changed radically after visits by Captain Cook's ships in 1778, during which crew members transmitted venereal diseases to Hawaiians, and by other American, British, and French ships over the next two decades, which introduced numerous new bacterial and viral diseases. Kamehameha's war of conquest, in which he brought an invading and occupying army to O'ahu in 1795, provides one of the first examples in which a victory in Hawai'i was followed not just by starvation, but also by disease.

64. McCoy and Graves (2010, 90–107).

65. McCoy and Graves (2010, 95). The statistic on ponded acreage for the island of Hawai'i is from Ladefoged et al. (2009).

66. McCoy and Graves (2010, 95).

67. Agricultural innovations in Hawai'i tended to be shared, and it is possible, though not yet established, that the same innovations were used on East Maui volcanic slopes.

68. I bypass the classic question posed by the economist Ester Boserup: Did increases in population drive expansion of cultivated area and agricultural innovation, or did expansion and innovation drive population increases? Boserup (1965, 1981) argued that population increases drove expansion of cultivated land area and innovation. McCoy and Graves (2010, 103) venture an answer: they find that in Hawai'i, "the motivation for widespread expansion into more and more marginal areas, was an increase in the need for surplus to support chiefly competition that ultimately helped push the entire economy from subsistence to surplus."

69. See Ladefoged et al. (2009).

70. For a discussion of the workings of China's central granaries, see Shiue (2004).

71. Malo (2006, Hawaiian text p. 100, English translation pp. 151–152).

72. Kamakau ([1961] 1992, 105). See also Fornander ([1878–1885] 1969, vol. 2, 200), who tells of discontent among ali'i and maka'āinana in Kohala where Kalaniopu'u had moved his court after leaving Kona. Fornander attributes the discontent to "the same eat and be merry policy" that had caused discontent in Kona.

73. The Pleiades constellation is also known as the "Seven Sisters." It was significant in many ancient civilizations and is mentioned several times in the Bible. For the Hawai'i context, see Kyselka (1993).

74. Malo (2006, Hawaiian text pp. 84–85, English translation pp. 112–113).

75. Kamakau ([1961] 1992, 181).

76. Ellis (1831, 416).

77. This is some disagreement regarding whether the polities in the seventeenth and eighteenth centuries were chiefdoms or states. My analysis bypasses this controversy, as I have concluded that essential ingredients of a state were already present in O'ahu from the late 1400s or early 1500s.

78. McCoy et al. (2013, 1537).

79. The same question has not been adequately investigated for Maui.

80. Kirch (2010, 153).

81. Ladefoged and Graves (2008).

82. See Bayman and Dye (2013, chap. 4) and Dye (2011).

83. See, for example, Kirch (1994).

84. Ladefoged and Graves (2008, 783–786).

85. Cheung (1969).

86. See Ladefoged and Graves (2008), Ladefoged et al. (2009), and Ladefoged et al. (2011).

87. The analysis does not rely on the existence of explicit markets in land or in food products, although explicit markets in factors and goods would provide additional channels for competition to be fully manifested. All that is needed for the analysis to work is for labor not to be completely tied to the land, as serfs were in early medieval Europe. For an example of how Northern Europeans during the late seventeenth and eighteenth centuries worked more hours to grasp more opportunities, see de Vries (2008).

88. See McCoy (2005), Ladefoged and Graves (2008), Ladefoged et al. (2009), McCoy and Graves (2010), and Ladefoged et al. (2011).

89. See Kolb and Dixon (2002); Kirch (2010); and Hommon (2013, chap. 15).

90. Most of the islands are separated by manageable distances for outrigger canoes to transport warriors. Kaua'i and Ni'ihau are much farther from their closest neighbor island, O'ahu, than the other major islands are from their close neighbors. This did not stop ruling chiefs from controlling both O'ahu and Kaua'i.

91. Hommon (2013, chap. 15).

Chapter Four

1. The *mele* (chant) celebrating Kamehameha's birth is from Morrison (2003, 71–72), who tells us (72) that "the Hawaiian version appeared in the *Ka Nupepa Kuokoa*, June 9, 1911, p. 7. The translation is by Mary Kawena Pukui (1895–1986) and can be found in the Bishop Museum Archives MS SC Pukui Box 17.4. Pukui chose to delete punctuation from her translation, and neither version was written with diacritical marks."

2. See Diamond (1999), *Guns, Germs and Steel: The Fates of Human Societies*, for a sweeping analysis of how environment and geography have shaped human history.

3. See Davenport (1969) for another analysis of the events detailed in this chapter.

4. See Sahlins (1992, chaps. 3–4). A large part of the army returned to the island of Hawai'i to put down a rebellion in 1796 and returned to O'ahu in 1804.

5. To further avoid the possibility of a revolt by one of the important chiefs, Kamehameha kept the chiefs in his immediate entourage. See Kuykendall (1938, vol. 1, 51–54). The comparison with Louis XIV is intriguing. His reign (1666–1712) was marked by frequent wars and a consolidation of power toward the center and away from a decentralized nobility. To prevent revolts, Louis XIV brought much of the nobility together at Versailles, a veritable theme park for nobility, featuring a vast complex of luxurious apartments, massive parks, and infamous indoor tennis courts.

6. "Most of these men carried muskets. He had eight cannon, forty swivel guns, and six mortars, together with a substantial amount of ammunition. In addition to

a great fleet of double-hulled canoes, his navy comprised twenty-one armed schoo-
ners, a more potent fleet than his first armada." See Joesting (1984, 62).

7. See Schmitt (1970b), Stannard (1989), and Shanks (2016) for more discussion
of the causes of the *oku'u* and estimates of the population decline from this episode.

8. The political scientist Robert Bates has proposed a Ricardian view of the
rise of central states that emphasizes the role of trade in state formation when ac-
tors encounter new trade opportunities that would be enhanced by cooperation:
"One of the basic arguments linking political centralization with economic reward
rests upon the desire of people to benefit from the gains in welfare which can be
reaped from markets. In essence, the argument is Ricardian . . . the contribution
of the state is to provide order and peace and thereby to render production and
exchange possible for members of society. The origins of the state, then, lie in the
welfare gains that can be reaped through the promotion of markets." Bates (1983),
as quoted in Fenske (2014, 613).

9. During the conquest of the island of Hawai'i in 1794, Kamehameha's men
had killed the ruling chief of a rival island state who had traveled to Kamehameha's
headquarters in Kohala to negotiate with him.

10. See Kuykendall (1938, vol. 1, 49–51), and Joesting (1984, 57–69).

11. Two different takes on the Hawai'i-Russia interactions are Pierce (1965)
and Mills (2002).

12. In the 1980s, three historians and social scientists put forth estimates of
population for 1778 and arrived at vastly different conclusions: Robert Schmitt
(1968) proposed between 200,000 and 250,000 people; Eleanor Nordyke (1989)
310,000 people; and David Stannard (1989) 795,000 people. Stannard's book revolutionized the study of population in Hawai'i, as it forced a full examination of assumptions made to estimate historical populations. Andrew Bushnell (1993, 127)
carefully reviewed these estimates and sharply criticized Stannard's estimate: "The
historical record does not support the 'die-off,' the disappearance of 50 percent
of the pre-contact population (400,000 people), that Stannard's model requires
during the first twenty-five years of contact (1778–1803). People aboard dozens
of ships passed through Hawai'i after 1786 and before 1804, but not one of them
made mention of a major epidemic (except that venereal disease was noted by a
number of visitors)." Bushnell suggested a 1778 population of between 300,000 and
400,000 people. Tom Dye, in a 1994 study, estimated just 110,000–150,00 people,
with population peaking in the early sixteenth century. Jean-Louis Rallu's 2008
study shows the sensitivity of population estimates for various islands in Polynesia
to small changes in assumptions regarding the number of initial voyagers, voyages,
natural disasters, extent of contact with Westerners, and incidence of infanticide
and human sacrifice. Patrick Kirch (2011) provides the most recent reviews of dis-
parate estimates from the 1970s and 1980s.

13. Ladefoged et al. (2009, table 2) present evidence from the archaeological
record regarding the maximum amount of rain-fed and irrigated land cultivated in

pre-contact Hawai'i and the total annual labor input required to obtain estimated yields.

14. See Kirch (2011). It is much debated how the population declined by 270,000 or more in the five decades after contact. Battlefield deaths during Kamehameha's wars of unification were substantial, reported by some sources at over 30,000 for O'ahu alone, yet are unlikely to be responsible for more than 20 percent of the decline. Venereal diseases were extensively spread by ships' crews from the first and second Cook voyages, and most people visiting Hawai'i in the 1780s and 1790s commented on the numerous Hawaiians with venereal diseases. Their effect on population probably was less through higher death rates than through lower birth rates. Andrew Bushnell's (1993, 127) extensive review of visitor reports from 1778 through the 1820s found that except for the 1804 *oku'u* (a dysenteric disease), there are no reports of introduced illnesses until 1818, and no reports of epidemics until 1825 and 1826, when thousands "died of an epidemic of 'cough, congested lungs and sore throats.'" See Shanks (2016) for the case that the *oku'u* was due to bacillary dysentery caused by shigella carried by crew from a visiting Western ship.

15. Gibson (1992).

16. Imposition of the *kapu* did not provide Kamehameha with a complete monopoly, as captains of visiting ships recorded numerous clandestine sales.

17. Thrum (1905, 59).

18. Merlin and Van Ravenswaay (1990, 49–50).

19. Thrum (1905, 59–61).

20. See Shineberg (1967, chap. 1) for an overview of the expansion of the sandalwood trade in the Southern Pacific during the first half of the nineteenth century. The book documents the rapid exhaustion of sandalwood wherever it was discovered in the Southern Pacific.

21. Morgan (1948, 61–62).

22. A picul is a Chinese unit of measure equal to 133⅓ pounds.

23. Morgan (1948, 62). Sandalwood deliveries reported in table 1 reflect total American shipments from all Pacific islands that were officially logged in Canton. Historians have identified exports from Hawai'i that were larger than the official Chinese import statistics for the period and have speculated that the difference was due to smuggling.

24. An exclusive contract would have reduced the cost to Kamehameha of monitoring chiefs' behavior and would have extracted more of the gains from trade for him.

25. Kuykendall (1938, vol. 1, 86–87).

26. Boston and New York trading firms, including such major players as John Jacob Astor, J. and T. H. Perkins, and Bryant and Sturgis, entered the Hawai'i sandalwood trade. Initially, they combined a voyage to the Pacific Northwest to obtain furs with stop(s) in Hawai'i for provisions. As furs became increasingly scarce, sandalwood from Hawai'i became a larger part of the ships' trade with Canton merchants.

27. See Corden (1984).

28. The analysis above is not fully complete because less labor in the nontraded good sector reduces the supply of the nontraded good and leads to excess demand in the nontraded good market. Restoring equilibrium requires an increase in the price of the nontraded good. This price increase draws more labor into the traded good sector from the agriculture sector, an effect known as *indirect deagriculturalisation*. See Corden (1984, 362–363).

29. See Broadberry et al. (2015, table 1.06) for English population totals between 1086 and 1541, and Clark (2010, table 1) for data on English wage rates.

30. See Bailey (2014, chap. 2).

31. The spending effect generated by increases in wealth from the sandalwood boom would also have drawn resources from agriculture into the nontraded goods sector.

32. Kamakau ([1961] 1992, 204).

33. The accounts provided by officers from visiting Russian ships closely follow Kamakau's account. See Tumarkin (1983, 22).

34. Tyerman et al. (1832, 43).

35. La Croix and Roumasset (1984, 161–164) and Sahlins (1992, 49–54).

36. Acemoglu and Wolitzky (2011) present a formal model of labor coercion in which the increased power of elites to coerce workers both reduces wages and increases hours of work.

37. La Croix and Roumasset (1984, 157–163) and Sahlins (1992, 82–83).

38. Roumasset and La Croix (1988, 322–328).

39. Mathison (1825, 451), as quoted in Sahlins (1992, 87).

40. Kamakau ([1961] 1992, 204).

41. de Freycinet ([1821] 1978, 20–21).

42. In Hawai'i, there were two necessary conditions for this proposition to hold: (1) the supply of sandalwood from the Hawai'i market must not have been sufficiently large to substantially affect the price offered by sandalwood buyers in Canton; and (2) consolidated control over harvesting must not have allowed Kamehameha to exercise additional monopsony power in the Hawai'i labor market.

43. Kamakau ([1961] 1992, 209–210).

44. Dibble ([1843] 1909, 60).

45. See also accounts in Fornander ([1961] 1969).

46. See Kame'eleihiwa (1992), Kirch (2010, 2012), and Hommon (2013).

47. See Fornander ([1961] 1969, vol. 1, 300).

48. Fifty-seven years old, that is, if one believes that the *mele* celebrating his birth refers to Halley's comet, which passed the island of Hawai'i in 1758.

49. If Ka'ahumanu did not redistribute lands, rivals would have had incentives to overthrow her and redistribute lands to form their own dominant coalition. In either case, the expectation was likely that land would be redistributed at the transition to a new ruling chief.

50. See my earlier paper (La Croix 2015) for discussion of how the rulers of other natural states redistributed land to support the ruling coalition.

51. La Croix and Roumasset (1984).

52. Lieutenant R. P. Boyle from the 1819 Russian expedition to Hawai'i related in his notes on the expedition that the sale of 800 rifles from the brig *Arab* to Liholiho's forces just prior to the battle was critical to his victory, as his opponents had few firearms. See Tumarkin (1983, 18, 29).

53. Kuykendall (1938, vol. 1, 65–66).

54. Two political scientists, Sergei Guriev and Konstantin Sonin (2009), devised a game-theoretic model to analyze how a group of chiefs will choose between weak and strong candidates to be the ruling chief. A strong ruler has the virtue of being able to set rules that increase economic growth, but the ruler's strength also increases the probability that the ruler will expropriate the chiefs' wealth. A weaker ruler cannot enforce rules that increase economic growth, but is also less likely to expropriate chiefs' wealth.

55. After this boom, sandalwood exports declined in the mid-1820s. In 1827 and 1828, there was a brief revival of the sandalwood trade due to a tax levied on the common people to be paid in sandalwood. But after 1830–1831, harvests never exceeded 5,600 piculs, and after 1837, they fell to less than 1,000 piculs annually. After 1856, it was impossible to locate any significant stock of sandalwood in Hawai'i's forests.

56. Sahlins (1992, chap. 3).

57. Sahlins (1992, 76–81).

58. Joesting (1984, 99–112).

59. See Bradley (1942) and Kuykendall (1938, vol. 1, appendix D, 434–436) for details of the loans.

60. Kamakau ([1961] 1992, 276).

Chapter Five

1. For a transaction cost–oriented analysis of how and why rights evolve as property becomes more valuable, see Barzel (2012).

2. North and Thomas (1973), North (1981), and Chambers (1953).

3. Feeny (1988).

4. Alston, Harris, and Mueller (2012).

5. A simple closed-economy general equilibrium model with just land and labor as factors of production generates this implication.

6. Bogart and Richardson (2011b). See also Bogart and Richardson (2009, 2011a) for elaborations of these theories and statistical tests using seventeenth- and eighteenth-century data from Britain.

7. James Roumasset and I (1990) developed this argument. North's view, that property rights reorganizations tend to originate with the state, has not gone un-

challenged, as more recent research on changes in property rights in Ghana and Côte d'Ivoire (Bubb, 2013, 557) has emphasized that "nonstate sources of norms shape the de facto rules governing property in land." See Williamson and Kerekes (2011) for a cross-country study of the effect of formal and informal rules for securing property rights. See also Libecap (1994) and Anderson and Hill (2009) for classic analyses of the role of private contracting in establishing property rights to land and natural resources in the United States.

8. Feeny (1982, 273–282). Williamson (2011) highlights how wages and land rents in periphery countries were linked to factor endowments when they were more closed economies, but became more closely linked to international product prices as their economies became more open to trade and investment flows.

9. 'I'i (1959).

10. Nogelmeier (2010).

11. Dittmar and Meisenzahl (2016).

12. Dittmar and Meisenzahl (2016, 2).

13. Dittmar and Meisenzahl (2016, 4).

14. The 1831–1832 census counted 13,344 people in Honolulu and 8,415 people in the district of Lahaina, which included some rural areas. The 1835–1836 census counted 7,087 people in the districts of North Hilo and South Hilo, which included some rural areas. See Schmitt (1977, table 1.6, 12). Missionaries stationed on the island of Hawai'i estimated 4,181 people for Hilo in 1833–1834. See Sandwich Islands Missions (1834). A report from missionaries to their American sponsors estimates the population of Lahaina at 4,000 people in 1833–1834. See American Board of Commissioners for Foreign Missions (1835, 78–79).

15. Some Hawaiians lost rights to lands after the transition because they did not understand the mechanics of the system: how to make claims, how the new system of courts worked, and the importance of having a will when they owned land. Stauffer (2004) makes a case that many *kuleana* lands were lost because of onerous provisions in Act 33 ("An Act to Provide for the Sale of Mortgaged Property without Suit and Decree of Sale"), enacted in 1874. Stauffer (2004, 97) finds that "the law permitted a lender to unilaterally and privately auction off a borrower's deed without due process or judicial oversight." In a detailed case study of Kahana Valley on windward O'ahu, Stauffer documents numerous cases in which insiders opportunistically used the law to acquire *kuleana*s mortgaged by native Hawaiian owners. Van Dyke (2008, 223) notes that many *kuleana*s were leased by their owners to sugar plantations and were ultimately lost because the markers of their lot boundaries, determined under metes-and-bounds surveying, had been obliterated when the sugar plantations transformed the leased lands for planting sugarcane.

16. North, Wallis, and Weingast (2009, 47).

17. North, Wallis, and Weingast (2009, 47).

18. Kuykendall (1938, vol. 1, 278). Dr. Gerrit P. Judd was a medical missionary from Scotland who immigrated to Hawai'i from the United States in 1827. After the Declaration of Rights of 1839 and the constitution of 1840 transformed

Hawai'i's government, several missionaries entered the king's government, including Judd, Lorrin Andrews, Richard Armstrong, and Edwin Hall. Gavan Daws (1968, 108) observed that each man, "as a condition of his employment, had signed an oath of allegiance to the king. Among the noisy expatriates of the foreign community this was enough to ruin any man's reputation." See Daws (1968, 106–112) and Osorio (2002, chaps. 2–4) for detailed discussions of the role of missionaries and other foreigners in Kamehameha III's government.

R. C. Wyllie, the minister of foreign affairs, also argued that land reform would have salutary effects on Hawaiians (Hawai'i, Department of Foreign Affairs, 1847, report dated Dec. 1, 1847, 67):

> Thus even the poorest of Your Majesty's subjects would stand on a footing of independent right—he would know that the land which he cultivated was his own, and could not be taken from him; and he would have the powerful stimulus of self interest to improve it, and to put a good dwelling on it; every child would be of value to him as he grew up, to help him in cultivating the ground; laborers would be induced to marry, in order to have children to help them; those children would be better taken care of, and would become more moral by being removed from the haunts of vice in the seaports.

19. Chinen (1958, 15–16). Other important renditions of the *Māhele* are Kuykendall (1938, vol. 1, chap. 15), Morgan (1948, chap. 8), Daws (1968, 124–131), Sahlins (1992), and Linnekin (1990).

20. Kuykendall (1938, vol. 1, 288).

21. Kuykendall (1938, vol. 1, 289).

22. Kuykendall (1938, vol. 1, 291).

23. See Libecap and Lueck (2011) for a comparison of metes-and-bounds and rectangular survey methods of demarcation of land boundaries. A metes-and-bounds demarcation is "decentralized with plot shapes, alignment, and sizes defined individually," while a rectangular survey demarcation is a "centralized grid of uniform square plots that does not vary with topography (Libecap and Lueck, 2011, 426). The division of land according to its traditional name is a much more vague demarcation of land boundaries even if parties have an informal understanding as to unspecified metes-and-bounds measures that define the boundaries. A century after the *Māhele*, some of the awards to *ali'i* had not been surveyed.

24. Moffat and Fitzpatrick (1995, 63).

25. Lyons (1889/1890), as quoted in Moffat and Fitzpatrick (1995, 58, 60).

26. Moffat and Fitzpatrick (1995, 62).

27. Moffat and Fitzpatrick (1995, 58).

28. Corvée labor, in which a tenant is required to provide labor services to a private landlord, the king, or the state, was observed in other states during periods

when most transactions were barter and tenants were unlikely to have money to pay taxes and other levies.

29. For a discussion, see Ladefoged et al. (2011).

30. Letter of March 12, 1851. Hawaiian Mission Children's Society Library.

31. Journal of the Legislature, July 9, 1850.

32. *Penal Code and Laws of 1850*, 146–147. For discussions of the process by which foreigners were allowed to own land, see Kuykendall (1938, vol. 1, 294–298) and Kame'eleihiwa (1992, 298–306).

33. Kuykendall (1938, vol. 1, 153–169); Daws (1968, 106–112, 124–131).

34. See the discussion in Kuykendall (1938, vol. 1, 153–159).

35. Earlier disputes between the Hawaiian government and foreign governments had resulted in foreign warships visiting the islands to "influence" the course of negotiations. Two American warships arrived in 1826 to press for the repayment of debts incurred by the chiefs in the course of sandalwood trading. Ships returned later that year and in 1829 to remind the *ali'i* of their unpaid debts and to threaten attacks if they were not repaid. Questions about the treatment of native Catholics, French priests, and foreign consuls also prompted a succession of visits by American, French, and British ships during the 1830s.

36. Wyllie (1848, 7–13).

37. See Feeny (1982, chap. 3, appendix 2) for a more complete discussion concerning the inference of prices of land and labor from sparse data.

38. Schmitt (1970b, 363) found that thousands "died of an epidemic of 'cough, congested lungs and sore throats'" in 1825 and 1826.

39. *The Friend*, vol. 7, no. 10 (Nov. 15, 1849): 79, as quoted in Schmitt (1970b, 363).

40. Schmitt (1971, 238–239).

41. The number of missionaries and their families, merchants, deserters from visiting ships, and other foreigners grew with arrival of missionaries in 1820 and the expansion of the whaling industry in the 1830s and 1840s; 1.9 percent of the total population was foreign-born in 1850.

42. As quoted in Schmitt (1968, 39).

43. Demand by visiting ships for food supplies offset some of this decline in demand.

44. See Lind (1938, 61–62). There is more qualitative than quantitative evidence concerning land rents and wages during this period.

45. Galloway (1989, 135).

46. See Kuykendall (1938, vol. 1, 315–316).

47. Morgan (1948, 154–158) presents data on exports of important agricultural products which indicate that the increased "demand was bunched into a three-year interval, from the fall of 1848 through part of 1851, though it continued at a higher level after 1851 than it had before 1849." An additional effect of the gold rush was to stimulate migration of Hawaiians to California and Southern Oregon. See Blue (1924, 20).

48. See the letters sent to and from Joel Turrill and his friends in Hawai'i (Hawaiian Historical Society, 1958). Consider a few excerpts regarding Turrill's investment in several lots laid out on the Waikiki plain. On 12/28/1850, Judge Lee wrote to Turrill that "real Estate has advanced to a high figure, and has not yet reached its height. All of Waikiki Plain has been laid out into lots 100ft × 150ft and sold at auction, at an average price of over $100. per lot. The 5 lots owned by us, I have been offered $500. for, but have thought best not to sell." On 4/13/1855, Charles Bishop wrote to Turrill that "those lots that you and Judge Lee own situated at the east of the town are not in demand, and would not now bring much if anything over fifty dollars each. Lots are plenty, and money is scarce." On 5/31/1958, Charles Bishop wrote to Turrill that "those 'lots on the plain,' which were in such demand at one time, are now almost worthless, only two or three of all that were sold having been improved. I had two which cost me over $100. each, and about two years ago I sold them by auction at $25 each. Yours would probably bring $20 to $25 each, and I think not more than that, and there is no prospect at present of their rising in value." On 2/27/1860, Charles Bishop wrote to Mrs. Turrill that "the lots on the plains are not desirable for investments, and are not in demand for use, and I see no prospect of improvement in their value; and would advise you to have them sold even at a considerable loss. The lots on the plain would not bring one third their cost."

49. MacLennan (2014, 86).

50. MacLennan (2014, 86).

51. MacLennan (2014, 87).

52. See North and Thomas (1971), North and Thomas (1973, 39–40), and North (1981, 129–131).

53. *Constitution and Laws*, 1842, chap. 3, sec. 3.

54. *Constitution and Laws*, 1842, chap. 3, sec. 1.

55. *Constitution and Laws*, 1842, chap. 3, secs. 5 and 6.

56. In response to the large population losses from the Black Death, England's Parliament enacted a series of laws intended to restrict the mobility and wages of workers and to force labor services from some workers. The initial law, the 1349 Statute of Laborers, was ineffective, and subsequent measures to tighten enforcement proved equally ill fated. See Postan (1972, 152).

57. *Constitution and Laws*, 1842, chap. 3, sec. 4.

58. Alexander (1890, 119).

59. Kuykendall (1938, vol. 1, 298).

60. See Surveyor General (1887). The two sets of data correspond almost exactly. The only discrepancies are in the 1849 Maui acreage and the 1857 Moloka'i acreage. Review of these entries indicates that the private report probably double-counts acreage for those two observations.

61. A small amount of acreage was sold prior to the institutional reforms in 1847, but I have been unable to discover how such sales were executed.

62. For additional detail, see North (1981), chap. 3.

63. North (1981, 28).

64. North (1981, 139).

65. North (1981, 138–142).

66. For a comparison of how the British colonial government in Fiji and the Hawaiian government reacted to their new opportunities to sell sugar in global markets, see La Croix (2004).

Chapter Six

1. John Tyler (1842), Special Message to the Senate and House of Representatives of the United States, December 30.

2. A sixth large sugar firm, Irwin & Co., was also operating during this period. It was later absorbed by one of the Big Five firms, C. Brewer.

3. See, for example, the comments in the U.S. press quoted in Pratt (1932, 274–275), and Beard and Beard (1927, 359–360). Raburn Williams (1993, 13–25) emphasized the importance of the McKinley Tariff in precipitating the overthrow.

4. Pratt (1932); Russ ([1959] 1992, [1961] 1992).

5. Tate (1965, 1968). Merze Tate (1965, 308) wrote that her work could bear the subtitle "An Economic Interpretation of the Hawaiian Revolution," but political and diplomatic considerations dominated her analysis. Noel Kent ([1983] 2016) discussed nineteenth-century Hawai'i in a broader work that put forward a dependency hypothesis. For other perspectives on annexation, see Budnick (1992) and Dougherty (1994).

6. Kuykendall (1967); Silva (2004).

7. Coffman (1998).

8. William Morgan (2011) rehashes ideas originally set forth in La Croix and Grandy (1997).

9. I measure a country's size by the value of its annual output of goods and services (i.e., gross domestic product [GDP]). Suppose that two countries of different size, A, with $500 billion GDP, and B, with $5 billion GDP, enter into a trade treaty in which each country reduces tariffs on imports from the other country by, say, 20 percent. Suppose that the result is that each country exports additional goods and services worth $200 million to the other country. For large country A, the additional exports amount to just 0.04 percent of GDP, an amount that would not substantially change the consumption and output of various industries or be likely to affect domestic politics. But for small country B, the additional exports amount to 4.0 percent of GDP, an amount sufficiently large to substantially change the consumption and output of various industries and to affect domestic politics.

10. Other examples of reciprocity treaties between large and small countries that resulted in similar strategic problems are the 1876 Treaty of Kanghwa

between Japan and Korea, which increased Japan's influence in Korea and led to Korea's annexation in 1910, and Nazi Germany's preferential trading agreements with Central European countries in the 1930s, which paved the way for their absorption at the start of World War II.

11. See Kuykendall (1938, vol. 1, 175–176).

12. See Lind (1938, 67) and Schmitt (1977, 539). The value of exports is unavailable for this time period.

13. See Kuykendall (1938, vol. 1, 309–310) and Morgan (1948, chaps. 5 and 9).

14. Lind (1938, 70).

15. Kuykendall (1938, vol. 1, 199–226, 388–407) provides an overview of these events. A documentary history from the American perspective appears in U.S. Senate (1893b).

16. See Carter et al. (2006, vol. 1, Aa2540–2602, Aa6249–6311, Aa5342–5404). Compare these figures with Hawai'i's 1870 population of about 60,000; see Schmitt (1977, 223).

17. Per pound tariffs are converted into ad valorem tariffs.

18. The 1855 treaty, reproduced in U.S. Senate (1901, at 407–409), referred to "unrefined sugar." The 1867 treaty, transmitted by President Andrew Johnson in a confidential message, allowed duty-free access for sugar "not above number twelve (12) Dutch standard." See U.S. Senate (1867). The Dutch standard classifies sugar by using sugar color as a measure of purity, which increases with the classification number. Grades below no. 7 are typically crude sugars purged of molasses. Grade no. 12 generally represents the dividing line between manufactured sugars and sugars that have been subject to an independent process of refining. See Wells (1878, 24–29).

19. Robinson (1904, 115–116).

20. Tate (1968, 70).

21. Annexation and reciprocity issues had been tangled together since the 1840s. On the heels of the dispute with the French in the 1840s, the Hawaiian and American governments negotiated a formal annexation treaty in 1854. The treaty provided for Hawai'i's admission as a state, U.S. citizenship for all subjects, and an annuity to the royal family. A secret article provided that if prior to ratification, another power threatened Hawai'i, the king could declare the islands annexed to the United States, and the U.S. commissioner to Hawai'i (a position similar to an ambassador) would protect the islands until the U.S. Senate voted on ratification. A copy of the treaty is in U.S. Senate (1893b, at 123–124). Kamehameha III died before the treaty was signed, and his successor, Kamehameha IV, opposed annexation. Indeed, one of the new king's first acts was to break off annexation negotiations and begin reciprocity discussions. See Kuykendall (1938, vol. 1, 426) and Kuykendall (1967, vol. 3, 38).

22. Kuykendall (1953, vol. 2, 220–230) discussed the relationship between reciprocity and annexation at the end of the Civil War. See also Tate (1968, 71, 76).

23. Secretary of State John Clayton to William C. Rives, U.S. Minister to France, July 5, 1850, reproduced in U.S. Senate (1893b, at 83–84).

24. See Kuykendall (1967, vol. 3, 247–250).

25. Kuykendall (1967, vol. 3, 249, 255) and Tate (1968, 95–100).

26. Emma Naʻea Rooke married King Kamehameha IV (William Lunaliho) in 1856 and was known thereafter as Queen Emma.

27. King Kalākaua opposed the proposed cession of Pearl Bay in 1873. See Kuykendall (1967, vol. 3, 19). Pearl Bay could serve as a major harbor only if substantial improvements were made to widen the channel providing access from the bay to the Pacific Ocean.

28. See Kuykendall (1967, vol. 3, 30, 34, 39).

29. U.S. House of Representatives (1876, 11).

30. U.S. House of Representatives (1876, 16).

31. U.S. House of Representatives (1876, 5).

32. One of the first American economics professors, Frank Taussig, anticipated some of these arguments over one hundred years ago. See Taussig (1892).

33. See Panagariya (2000) and Freund and Ornelas (2010) for excellent surveys of the economics literature on preferential tariff reductions. Michaely (1998) carefully analyzes how asymmetric country size affects the distribution of gains from a preferential trade agreement. The "trade diversion effect" may be compared with the "trade creation effect," in which a tariff reduction lowers the price paid by consumers, raises domestic consumption, decreases higher-cost domestic production, and increases lower-cost imports. Trade creation is missing in this case of the U.S.-Hawaiʻi reciprocity treaty because the preferential access of Hawaiʻi sugar to the U.S. market neither affected the price of sugar received by U.S. producers nor the price paid by U.S. consumers. Prices did not change because the reciprocity treaty affected neither U.S. sugar output nor the profitability of U.S. sugar producers.

34. The reciprocity agreement also generated some transfers across sugar refiners. Hawaiʻi sugar exports displaced other foreign sugar exports that had been shipped to the U.S. East Coast and refined by East Coast refiners. The new Hawaiʻi sugar exports were shipped to the U.S. West Coast and were refined by West Coast refiners. Since the trade diversion left East Coast refiners with excess capacity, they were generally opposed to the reciprocity treaty with Hawaiʻi.

35. Economists call this waste of resources a "deadweight loss." Some of the transfer of tariff revenue to Hawaiʻi sugar producers could have been passed on to sugar workers if increased production led to increases in wage rates in the Hawaiʻi sugar industry.

36. Thus, additional profits earned by U.S. manufacturing firms from additional sales in Hawaiʻi would be close to zero.

37. The tariff revenues on manufactures lost by Hawaiʻiʻs government were transferred to Hawaiʻi consumers and Hawaiʻi sugar plantations purchasing machines and parts.

38. The export elasticity is a measure of how responsive sugar exports are to a higher export price. A higher export elasticity means that suppliers are more responsive to a change in the price they receive for their product in a foreign market. More formally, it is the ratio of the percentage change in sugar exports over the percentage change in the export price.

39. The economist Murray Kemp (1969) demonstrated that in certain cases the formation of a free-trade area between two countries could reduce the welfare of one country if it was not compensated with a side payment.

40. See Mayer (1981) and Kennan and Riezman (1988).

41. McLaren (1997).

42. The 1876 treaty provision represented a compromise between the U.S. government's demand for exclusive access to Pearl Bay in 1873 and the Hawaiian government's rejection of any side payment.

43. The real value of Hawai'i's net sugar output more than doubled between 1870 and 1880 and then almost tripled between 1880 and 1890. See Mollett (1961, 35). In line with the partial equilibrium theoretical analysis of the tariff's effects, Louisiana sugar production expanded throughout this period. See "The Tariff Bill," 21, Pt. 5 *Cong. Rec.* 4991–5002 (May 20, 1890), at 4995.

44. Acreage is estimated by multiplying the number of plantations by the average plantation size in Mollett (1961, 28).

45. By 1893, sugar plantations rented 14,126 acres of crown lands, representing approximately 14 percent of cultivated cane lands. See Iaukea (1894). The king received income from crown lands, which were his private property. In 1864 and 1865, the legislature imposed restrictions on property rights to crown lands by restricting inheritance to the heir to the throne, restricting the term for which crown lands could be leased, and prohibiting mortgage or sale of the lands. See Van Dyke (2008, chaps. 8 and 9) for a comprehensive treatment of important issues relating to crown lands. King Kalākaua's income from sugar leases on crown lands surely contributed to his support for the reciprocity treaty in the face of strong opposition from many Native Hawaiians.

46. Mollett (1961, 21). See also Wilcox (1998) and Kaiser (2014).

47. Shoemaker (1940, 34).

48. Shoemaker (1940, 34).

49. See La Croix and Fishback (1989 and 2000) for a more complete analysis of the inflow of contract workers and wages paid to them. We compared purchasing power wages across countries, with purchasing power wages calculated for Hawai'i in 1910 using methods from Williamson (1995).

50. Morgan (1948, 190).

51. See Kuykendall (1967, vol. 3, chaps. 5 and 6, especially 172–185). In 1892, "An Act Restricting Chinese Immigration" (Hawaii Session Laws, 1892, chap. 80) prohibited new immigrants from engaging in any but agricultural, sugar or rice mill, and domestic occupations. See Kuykendall (1967, vol. 3, 546).

52. U.S. House of Representatives (1883, 1).

53. U.S. House of Representatives (1883, 1).

54. U.S. Senate (1883, 5).

55. Our results parallel those of Davis and Huttenback (1988), who found that Britain probably suffered net losses from its empire despite gains by particular British manufacturing interests. Coelho (1973) calculated that Britain experienced significant losses in its commercial relations with its West Indies colonies in the eighteenth century. We have not included gains to U.S. manufacturing interests in our calculations, as our theoretical analysis indicates that they are very small. See Accominotti, Flandreau, and Rezzik (2011) for a critique of the literature measuring empire effects.

56. Searle (1886, 9).

57. The estimated economic losses do not include costs and benefits accruing to the United States from the strategic and political impacts of the treaty.

58. The treaty extension appeared in U.S. Senate (1893b, at 166–168).

59. McLaren (1997) applies these arguments to the 1988 Canada-United States Free Trade Agreement, a precursor to the North American Free Trade Agreement. Canadian opponents of the agreement emphasized that its termination clause—requiring a mere six months' notice—would leave Canada vulnerable to future U.S. demands after Canadian industries had made big new investments to service the U.S. market.

60. Claus Spreckels, Hawai'i's famed "Sugar King," owned about 25–35 percent of the sugar industry's capital. This was surely a large enough share for him to consider the effects of his investment on Hawai'i's future negotiating position.

61. By contrast, in a trade war, each government acts unilaterally and does not consider how their actions affect interest groups in the other country. If politicians in both countries switch from noncooperative choices of trade policy to a cooperative agreement (negotiated in trade talks), the welfare of both countries can be improved (with appropriate lump sum transfers). See Grossman and Helpman (1995).

62. De Varigny (1981, 205).

63. De Varigny (1981, 205).

64. Galloway (1989, 220) and Laughlin and Willis (1903, 559).

65. Canadian tariffs are from Brown (1879, 41). Tariffs in Victoria and New South Wales are from Patterson (1968, 67) and converted at the prevailing exchange rate of $5.42/£ for 1876. The Canadian population for 1881 is from Government of Canada (2017). The Australian population is from Government of Australia (2014, table 1.1). The U.S. population for 1880 is from Carter et al. (2006, vol. 1, table Aa1–5).

66. See King Kalākaua's comment to Commissioner J. H. Wodehouse, quoted in Kuykendall (1967, vol. 3, 395). The king's cabinet urged him to initiate reciprocity negotiations with Canada in late February 1887. See Kuykendall (1967, vol. 3, 393).

67. This temporary decline in the property tax share may have motivated the increase in real and personal property tax rates from 0.75 percent to 1.0 percent in October 1886. Hawaii Session Laws, 1886, chap. 32, October 8, 1886.

68. Kuykendall (1967, vol. 3, 355).

69. Dukas (2004) documents the small size of the military resources available to the Hawai'i government in 1887 and 1893 to defend against a coup d'état.

70. Article 41. A copy of the 1887 constitution appeared in U.S. Senate (1898a, at 50–59). Under the previous constitution of 1864, the king enjoyed an absolute veto.

71. Compare Article 62 of the 1864 constitution with Article 59 of the 1887 constitution. See U.S. Senate (1898). Rowland (1943) examined the limited extension of the franchise to Asians and the complications for annexation raised by the disenfranchisement of Japanese residents in 1887. See also Russ ([1961] 1992, chap. 4).

72. Kuykendall (1967, vol. 3, 397).

73. The economist Noel Mauer has carefully analyzed how U.S. corporations investing overseas have regularly called on the U.S. government to intervene to support their interests and the dilemmas that such intervention has created for both parties. See Mauer (2011).

74. Taussig (1914, 275–277). In this case, raw sugar was defined as that below no. 16 Dutch standard.

75. For producers exporting from non-reciprocity countries, the elimination of the tariff either would have no effect on the net-of-tariff price (if world supply was infinitely elastic) or would increase it by up to the amount of the rescinded tariff (if the world supply of sugar to the United States had a positive elasticity).

76. Debates featuring the effect of the McKinley Tariff on Hawai'i took place on May 9 and 20, 1890. See "The Tariff Bill," 21, pt. 5 *Cong. Rec.* 4385–4397 (May 9, 1890), at 4390–4392, and "The Tariff Bill," 21, pt. 5 *Cong. Rec.* 4993–5002 (May 20, 1890).

77. See "The Revenue Bill," 21, pt. 10 *Cong. Rec.* 9535–9540 (September 2, 1890).

78. Opportunism is defined, following Oliver Williamson, as maximizing with guile.

79. Hawai'i special envoy John Mott-Smith broached the possibility of extending the sugar bounty to Hawai'i, but U.S. Secretary of State James Blaine rejected this as politically impossible. See Kuykendall (1967, vol. 3, 492). Later in the session, McKinley introduced a bill to ensure that the new tariff law would not impair treaty obligations with Hawai'i. See U.S. House of Representatives (1891). Passed and signed just before the McKinley Tariff went into effect, the law's provisions neither restored the tariff umbrella to Hawai'i sugar producers nor extended the bounty paid to domestic sugar producers to them.

80. The quoted weekly price for 96 degree sugar (raw sugar containing 96 percent sucrose) fell from 5.68 to 3.53 cents per pound in late March 1891. The price had not fallen below 5 cents per pound in the previous year and did not rise above 3.5 cents per pound in the following year. See *Willett & Gray's Weekly Statistical Sugar Trade Journal* 16, December 29, 1892, 3.

81. See Schmitt (1977, 540). To put this change in context, the value of Cuban sugar exports to the U.S. rose over this period from $35 million in 1890 to $45 million in 1891 and to $61 million in 1892. Furthermore, world production of cane sugar expanded over this period. See Laughlin and Willis (1903, 556, 570–573).

82. The value of real physical capital invested in Hawai'i sugar production rose by 228 percent between 1880 and 1890. See Mollett (1961, 23).

83. The earliest gross state product estimate for Hawai'i is $38 million in 1901 (Schmitt, 1977, 164). Merchandise exports reached $28 million in that year, of which $27.9 million went to the United States (Schmitt, 1977, 543). Between 1885 and 1900, the share of Hawai'i merchandise exports that went to the U.S. never fell below 98 percent (Schmitt, 1977, 542). Pineapple remained a minor commercial crop until after 1898, when annexation eliminated the 35 percent U.S. tariff on canned fruit. See Hitch (1992, 99–100).

84. Queen Lili'uokalani ([1898] 1990) suggested that King Kalākaua signed the 1887 constitution under threat of assassination. Helena G. Allen (1982) quoted Lili'uokalani's diary entry opposing the cession of Pearl Harbor.

85. Kuykendall (1967, vol. 3, 548–559).

86. Lili'uokalani ([1898] 1990, 230–231).

87. A draft of the proposed constitution appeared in U.S. Senate (1898).

88. Article 62. Usual age, residence, and tax payment requirements also applied. The copy found in U.S. Senate (1898) specified a property qualification for voting, but the signatories to the validity of the document questioned this feature.

89. Article 31 required the queen to sign all laws to make them valid. Article 49 provided for an override of a royal veto by a two-thirds vote of the legislature, but the queen also had to sign the act to make it law.

90. Queen Lili'uokalani certainly had precedent for promulgating a new constitution, as previous monarchs had already done so in 1840 and 1864. See Lili'uokalani ([1898] 1990, 238–239) and Kuykendall (1967, vol. 3, 547).

91. A number of works cover the events sketched in this paragraph in much more detail, including Russ ([1961] 1992), Kuykendall (1967, vol. 3), Coffman (1998), and Silva (2004).

92. Pratt (1932, 289–290, 294).

93. Seven of the 13 members owned stock in the sugar industry. The economic fortunes of other firms and most professionals were, however, closely tied to prosperity in the sugar industry.

94. Russ ([1959] 1992, 87–88).

Chapter Seven

1. See Osorio (2002, chap. 6).

2. Joint Resolution to Provide for Annexing the Hawaiian Islands to the United States, 30 Stat. 750 (1898).

3. U.S. Government, Hawaiian Commission (1899).

4. S. 222, with extensive amendments, became the basis for the Organic Act. See State of Hawaii, Legislative Reference Bureau (1946).

5. The Organic Act: An Act to Provide a Government for the Territory of Hawaii, Pub. L. 56-331, 31 Stat. 141 (1900).

6. See Van Dyke (1992).

7. Organic Act, § 66. The executive power.

8. Organic Act, § 82. Supreme Court.

9. The Organic Act, § 86, specified a term of six years for a district judge and seven years for a Supreme Court justice "unless sooner removed by the President."

10. The Hawai'i courts were not created under Article III, Section 1 of the U.S. Constitution and thus were not subject to its provisions mandating life terms and no diminishment of compensation. Rather, they were created under Article IV, Section 3, which allows the government to "make all needful Rules and Regulations respecting the Territory or other Property belonging to the United States."

11. Lee (2011, 6). These restrictions on the authority of the territorial legislature were not unique to Hawai'i, but were applied by Congress to all governments of U.S. territories.

12. See Meller (1958, 99).

13. See Meller (1958, 100).

14. See Organic Act, § 85. Delegate to Congress.

15. Van Dyke (2008, 172).

16. Joint Resolution to Provide for Annexing the Hawaiian Islands to the United States (1898).

17. Joint Resolution to Provide for Annexing the Hawaiian Islands to the United States (1898).

18. See State of Hawaii, Legislative Reference Bureau (1946, 2438–2449). Senator Clark of Wyoming offered an amendment that would pay $250,000 in compensation to the queen. Several senators spoke in support of the amendment, but it was rejected by the Senate.

19. See Van Dyke (2008, 229–234) for an excellent discussion of Liliuokalani v. United States, 45 Ct. Cl. 418, 1909 WL 905 (Ct. Cl. 1910).

20. Fuchs (1961, chap. 2).

21. There were four smaller sugar agencies (C. Afong, G. W. McFarlane & Co., W. G. Irwin & Co., and J. T. Waterhouse) that competed with the Big Five in 1879. They were either absorbed by the Big Five or exited the market by the first decade of the twentieth century.

22. See also Shoemaker (1940, 12).

23. If the U.S. government decided to protect sugar via a subsidy rather than a tariff, then Hawai'i producers would be eligible for that subsidy if Hawai'i were to be annexed.

24. MacLennan (2014, 96).

25. MacLennan notes that the British-owned Big Five firm, Theo H. Davies, was excluded from purchasing any of Hackfeld's Hawai'i assets. See MacLennan (2014, 97).

26. See MacLennan (2014, chaps. 5 and 10) and Kaiser (2014).

27. Since the mid-1890s, some Big Five companies had used, with limited success, a variety of other strategies designed to evade the American Sugar Refining Company's market power.

28. This discussion of industry organizations largely follows MacLennan (2014, chap. 10).

29. MacLennan (2014, 230).

30. See U.S. Department of Justice (1932).

31. North, Wallis, and Weingast (2009, 169–180).

32. This account draws heavily on David Stannard's riveting and beautifully written account of the Massie cases. See Stannard (2005), *Honor Killing: Race, Rape, and Clarence Darrow's Spectacular Last Case*. A more recent account emphasizes the role of the case in shaping social and ethnic identities in Hawai'i. See John P. Rosa (2014), *Local Story: The Massie-Kahahawai Case and the Culture of History*.

33. Stannard (2005, 159). The quote from Governor Judd is taken from his autobiography (Judd, 1971, 171–172). After indictments of the three sailors and Grace Fortescue for the kidnapping and murder of Joseph Kahahawai, Admiral Stirling demanded that the four prisoners be housed on a Navy ship in Pearl Harbor.

34. U.S. Senate (1932).

35. U.S. Department of Justice (1932).

36. Later in the 1930s, Stirling again made the case for a change of government in Hawai'i when he published his memoirs (Stirling, 1938): "Self government in Hawaii is a menace to the nation's naval security in the Pacific Ocean and the sooner curtailed the better for the nation."

37. See Anthony (1955) for a more complete account.

38. Ex parte Duncan, 66 F. Supp. 976 (D. Haw. 1944).

39. Duncan v. Kahanamoku, 327 U.S. 304, 66 S. Ct. 606, 90 L. Ed. 688 (1946).

40. See Anthony (1955).

41. Military judges often compelled convicted defendants to purchase U.S. war bonds as part of their penalty for violating the law. The military courts altered the terms of U.S. bonds by placing a stamp on them restricting redemption until after the end of the war or six months after its end. See Anthony (1955, 57–58).

42. For an account of the strikes from the perspective of the ILWU leaders, see Zalburg (1979).

43. See Schmitt (1976). For the year 1949, the unemployment rate was 11 percent.

44. "Mature limited access orders have durable institutional structures for the government and can support a wide range of elite organizations that exist apart from the government. A mature limited access order, therefore, has a body of public law that specifies the offices and functions of the government, the relationship between the offices and functions, and provides for methods of resolving conflicts within the government, and by extension, within the dominant coalition." North, Wallis, and Weingast (2012, chap. 1).

45. For an insightful study of Hawai'i's government in the nineteenth century, see Osorio (2002).

46. Fenske (2014).

47. Fenske (2014, 612). Some references in footnotes in the Fenske quote were omitted: Gennaioli and Rainer (2007); Michalopoulos and Papaioannou (2010); and Englebert (2000). See also Michalopoulos and Papaioannou (2013, 2015).

48. Banerjee and Iyer (2005).

49. The hypothesis that institutions from antiquity provide the foundations for modern economic growth has many parents; some modern fathers and mothers include Bockstette, Chanda, and Putterman (2002); and Putterman and Weil (2010). See Comin, Easterly, and Gong (2010), who show that a country's state of technological development 500–1,000 years ago helps to predict its twenty-first-century GDP.

50. See Meller (1958, 98).

51. Meller (1958, 98).

52. Organic Act, Article 1 § 6.

Chapter Eight

1. See Silva (2000) for an extended discussion of the repression of Hawaiian culture after annexation.

2. Hawaiian Homes Commission Act, 42 Stat. 108 (1921).

3. Department of Hawaiian Home Lands claims against the federal government for the uncompensated taking of Lualualei were recognized in 1998 with the federal government's exchange of other federal government lands for continued use of Lualualei. The exchange was facilitated by the U.S. Congress's enactment in 1995 of The Hawaiian Home Lands Recovery Act, Pub. L. 104-42.

4. See Parker (1989) and the classic papers by Carlson (1981a, 1981b) for analysis of U.S. government policy toward Native Americans. Anderson and Lueck (1992) provide the classic study relating attenuated property rights on Indian reservations to reduced agricultural productivity.

5. A number of scholars, including Anderson (1995), have long considered that the flawed governance mechanisms and attenuated property rights in land

imposed by the U.S. Congress on Native American populations were key reasons for their persistent and deep poverty. For a contrary view, see recent work by economic historian Leonard Carlson (2011, 13), who argues that despite serious flaws, the U.S. reservation system evolved to allow "Indians to maintain a degree of autonomy within the federal U.S. structure that Indians value highly."

6. For additional analysis, see La Croix and Rose (1993, 1998).

7. See Eleanor Nordyke (1989, 22–57) and La Croix and Fishback (1989, 2000).

8. Fuchs (1961, 70).

9. Fuchs (1961, 122).

10. Bureau of Public Instruction (1891, 26). The report also observed that "there is quite a common impression abroad in the community that the Chinese have superseded the Natives in this business to a much greater extent than these figures would indicate. It is quite possible that some of the Natives returned as fisherman may be working for Chinese bosses."

11. U.S. Bureau of the Census (1923b, 1277).

12. U.S. Bureau of the Census (1923b, 1277).

13. U.S. Bureau of Census (1923a, table 14, 1183).

14. U.S. Bureau of Census (1923a, table 16, 1271).

15. See McGregor (1990, 11).

16. McGregor (1990, 10).

17. U.S. Department of the Interior (1919, 65–67).

18. "Back to Land Move," *Honolulu Advertiser*, July 16, 1918, sec. 2, 1.

19. See McGregor (1990, 1–4). The following section draws extensively from McGregor's (1990) excellent article and Vause's (1962) superb thesis detailing the history of the HHCA.

20. Her husband, Prince David La'amea Kahalepouli Kawānanakoa Pi'ikoi, had been the previous designated heir to the Hawaiian throne. With his death in 1908, Princess Kawānanakoa assumed this role.

21. "Princess Will Urge Hawaiians to Go Back to the Land," *Honolulu Advertiser*, October 2, 1918, 1.

22. "May Ask U.S. to Give Land to Hawaiians," *Honolulu Advertiser*, February 15, 1919, 2.

23. U.S. Department of the Interior (1908, 35).

24. The May 27, 1910, amendments to Section 73 of the Organic Act provided that land leases contain a provision that the territorial government could withdraw the land from lease "for homestead or public purposes."

25. U.S. President (1918, 1804), Proclamation of June 24, 1918.

26. U.S. House of Representatives (1920).

27. The Big Five firms would surely have improved the land if they had judged such investments to be profitable. Their choice not to improve it provides a strong inference as to the profitability of improvements made by other farmers leasing the land.

28. Spitz (1963).

29. See Spitz (1964) for an excellent summary of how the HHL program allocated its lands over its first four decades.

30. In addition to the private benefits derived by Native Hawaiian homesteaders, the HHL program also produces public benefits for some individuals in the broader Hawaiian community. Underlying some Hawaiians' desire to retain land ownership for Hawaiians is a deeply held cultural belief that the land (*'āina*) is more than a mere commodity to be traded for other goods. Many Hawaiians respect and revere the land as a form of spiritual and emotional sustenance. Hawaiians with these beliefs benefit from the knowledge that the government's holding of the land in trust retains it for the benefit of Hawaiians and keeps it out of the hands of other Hawai'i residents and foreigners.

Almost all of the residential homesteaders are located in settlements and housing projects reserved exclusively for Native Hawaiians. The exclusivity of these communities of Native Hawaiians living in close proximity to one another should increase benefits from a public good, the Hawaiian culture. If these homogeneous settlements reduce the communication and transportation costs of interacting with other Hawaiians, more Hawaiians will engage in Hawaiian cultural activities. This could lead to higher rates of cultural transmission and innovation.

Language is central to all cultures. If ethnically homogeneous Hawaiian communities contribute to the expanded use of the Hawaiian language, this may be their biggest contribution toward preserving and enhancing Hawaiian culture. Knowledge of the Hawaiian language would facilitate the transmission of cultural traditions in their original state. Community centers, schools and churches, some businesses, and neighborhood associations in a purely Hawaiian community on HHL lands could reduce the cost of transmitting cultural knowledge and practices from one generation to another in an environment partially sheltered from the rest of society.

31. Information obtained from interviews by former University of Hawai'i economics professor Louis Rose with Kenneth Tokoguchi and Stanley Wong at DHHL and annual reports of the HHC.

32. An Act to Provide for the Admission of the State of Hawaii into the Union (Act of March 18, 1959, Pub. L. 86-3, § 1, 73 Stat. 4). The trust responsibilities of the federal and state governments are spelled out in Sections 4, 5(a), and 5(f) of the Admission Act.

33. See Parker (1989).

34. Kalima v. State, 37 P.3d 990—Haw. S. Ct. 2006.

35. The U.S. Court of Appeals for the Ninth Circuit ruled that neither individual Hawaiians nor Hawaiian groups had standing to sue to enforce the application. Keaukaha-Panaewa Cmty. Ass'n v. Hawaiian Homes Comm'n, 588 F.2d 1216 (9th Cir. 1978), cert. denied, 444 U.S. 826 (1979).

36. Federal-State Task Force on the Hawaiian Homes Commission Act (1983).

37. State of Hawaii, Department of Business, Economic Development and Tourism (DBEDT) (2009, table 13.03).

38. Nelson III vs. Hawaiian Homes Commission, 127 Hawai'i 185 (2012). Article XII, § 1 of the Hawai'i state constitution states that "the legislature shall make sufficient sums available for the following purposes: . . . (4) the administrative and operating budget of the department of Hawaiian home lands."

39. Nelson III vs. Hawaiian Homes Commission, 1st Cir., State of Hawaii, Civil No. 07-1-1663-08 (JHC), November 27, 2015. In February 2016, the judge clarified her decision, stating that she was not ordering a specific appropriation but instead was "ordering that the State must comply with its constitutional duty to make sufficient sums available to the Department of Hawaiian Home Lands for its administrative and operating budget."

40. Nelson III vs. Hawaiian Homes Commission, 141 Haw. 411.

41. See State of Hawai'i, Department of Hawaiian Home Lands (2015).

42. See La Croix (2013).

43. A more complex model would include a legislature, as native Hawaiians are not uniformly spread across state house and senate districts.

44. A more complex model would relax this model's simplifying assumption that Hawaiian voters are a homogeneous group, as different groups of Hawaiian voters are likely to place different values on land allotments by the HHL program and program expenditures. Hawaiian voters who do not qualify for land allotments (due to a less than required blood quantum) are likely to be less supportive of allotments than Native Hawaiian voters who do qualify; and some Native Hawaiian voters who have already received land allotments could also be less supportive since they have already received their slice of the pie. Hawaiian voters who are on the waiting list or have close relatives and friends on the waiting list may also be more supportive.

45. The assessed value of Hawai'i land is calculated from land values assessed by counties and legal assessment ratios. Prior to 1935, there are no data on the legal assessment ratio, and I have assumed that it was equal to the ratio prevailing between 1935 and 1950. In addition, assessment data on land values between 1920 and 1934 are unavailable. I use data on the assessed value of real property (which includes the series for assessed land value) to infer the assessed value of land for this period. Hawai'i GDP is from Schmitt (1977) and various issues of the *State Data Book*. All dollar values are deflated by spliced Honolulu Consumer Price Index and U.S. Consumer Price Index with 1982–1984 base.

46. Data from 1902 to 1950 measure the proportion of registered Hawaiian voters among total voters. They are taken from Aguiar (1996, table 2–3). Data from 1980 to 1998 measure the proportion of voters who voted in Office of Hawaiian Affairs (OHA) elections, which were restricted to native Hawaiian voters until a U.S. Supreme Court decision overturned this provision of the Hawai'i state constitution. See Rice v. Cayetano, 528 U.S. 495 (2000). The court ruled that

non-Hawaiians could vote in state elections for the Board of Trustees of the OHA and could serve as trustees. The number of voters in OHA elections is reported in various editions of Office of Elections, State of Hawaii (2013). Data from 2000 to 2006 measure the share of native Hawaiian voters as reported by national exit polls (Cornell University, Roper Center 2004–2012). Data from 1952 to 1978 are more problematic, as they are interpolated from 1950 and 1980 benchmarks and use two additional benchmarks for the share of the Hawaiian electorate in 1960 and 1970. These benchmarks are derived from the share of Hawaiians in the 1960 and 1970 censuses and the share of the Hawaiian population who voted in pre–World War II elections.

47. In my statistical analysis, I also include two binary variables indicating which political parties held the governorship and controlled the legislature: *Dem. Governor*, which equals one for a Democratic governor and zero for a Republican, and *Dem.Legislature*, which equals one for Democratic Party control of both houses and zero otherwise. Because of changing political allegiances during the 1921–2010 period, I do not offer predictions as to the signs of these control variables. Hawaiians were generally aligned with Caucasians in an ethnic voting bloc between 1904 and 1946, when a dominant Republican Party controlled both the territorial senate and house of representatives. In the decade following World War II, the Democratic Party gained strength, seizing control of both houses of the legislature in 1954. Democrats have controlled both the senate and the house through 2018 and the governor's office from 1962 to 2002. During this period, native Hawaiian votes were split between the two parties. In 2002, the Democratic gubernatorial dominance was broken by a two-term Republican governor (2002–2010) who gained sizable support from native Hawaiian voters.

48. Adjusted Dickey-Fuller tests for stationarity reveal that a unit root cannot be rejected for *Hawaiian.Voters*, and the log of *DHHL.Leases*, *DHHL.Expenditures*, and *Real.Land.Value*. Additional tests show that the series are cointegrated. To derive the long-run relationship between the series, I estimate an error correction model with the following two equations:

$$\Delta DHHL.Leases_t$$

$$= \delta_0 + \sum_{i=1}^{2} \delta_i \, \Delta DHHL.Leases_{t-i} + \sum_{i=1}^{2} \delta\mu_i \, \Delta Hawaiian.Voters_{t-i}$$

$$+ \sum_{i=1}^{2} \alpha_i \, \Delta Real.Land.Value_{t-i} + \beta_1 Dem.Governor_t$$

$$+ \beta_2 Dem.Legislature_t + \gamma_0 \left(v_t \right) + \varepsilon_t$$

and

$$\Delta DHHL. Expenditures_t$$

$$= \delta_0 + \sum_{i=1}^{2} \delta_i \Delta DHHL. Expenditures_{t-i}$$

$$+ \sum_{i=1}^{2} \delta\mu_i \Delta Hawaiian. Voters_{t-i} + \sum_{i=1}^{2} \alpha_i \Delta Real. Land. Value_{t-i}$$

$$+ \beta_1 Dem. Governor_t + \beta_2 Dem. Legislature_t + \gamma_0 \left(v_t \right) + \varepsilon_t$$

49. This analysis points to a more important general implication for government programs that administer assets: programs that are funded by income from an asset to be given away to beneficiaries will be characterized by complaints that the agency gives away too little of the asset.

50. See Native Hawaiian Government Reorganization Act of 2009, S. 1011 and H.R. 2314. The Akaka bill was introduced in slightly different forms in 2000, 2001, 2003, 2005, and 2007.

Chapter Nine

1. Numerous historians, lawyers, and political scientists have analyzed the events leading to statehood. See Daws (1968), Fuchs (1961), Coffman (2003), Kinevan (1950), Bell (1984), Hunter (1959), and Spitz (1967).

2. The sugar industry's demand for labor was already falling at about the same time that the ILWU began to exercise its power. Labor-saving mechanization and federal controls on sales of Hawai'i sugar in U.S. mainland markets led to a wave of plantation closings and a 5.2 percent annual decline in industry employment over the 1935–1960 period.

3. See Horne (2011) for a more complete discussion.

4. See Charter of the United Nations, chap. XI (Declaration regarding Non-Self-Governing Territories), Article 73.

5. "We should also consider our obligation to assure the fullest possible measure of civil rights to the people of our territories and possessions. I believe that the time has come for Alaska and Hawaii to be admitted to the Union as States." See Truman (1948).

6. U.S. Congress, House of Representatives, Committee on Territories (1946).

7. An end to the war between Hawai'i daily newspapers over statehood facilitated more collective action. Walter Dillingham, a leading developer and the largest stockholder in the Honolulu morning newspaper, the *Honolulu Advertiser*, was strongly opposed to statehood. The *Advertiser*'s anti-statehood policy led to fierce editorial battles with the pro-statehood Honolulu afternoon newspaper, the *Honolulu Star Bulletin*. In 1947, the newspaper wars over statehood ended when

the *Advertiser's* editor, Lorrin Thurston, unexpectedly switched camps, endorsing statehood and becoming chair of the Hawai'i Statehood Commission. Support from both major dailies as well as the leading Japanese-language newspaper (*Hawaii Hochi*) was a vital element in the 1950s campaigns for statehood.

8. Hawaii Session Laws, 1949, Act 334.

9. Hawai'i's action was the norm, not the exception. Fifteen U.S. territories drafted constitutions before Congress approved their statehood bills. Wyoming and Idaho, in 1890, were the most recent territories to do this.

10. King Lot Kapuāiwa (Kamehameha V) called a constitutional convention in 1864 to reform the constitution of 1852. Unhappy with the qualifications for voters approved by the convention, the king promulgated the new constitution in 1864 without 20 articles that he found objectionable.

11. See Bartholomew and Kamins (1959) for a discussion of the constitution's provisions.

12. The ILWU objected to the broad powers assigned to the state governor. For discussions of the 1950 constitution, see Lee (2011), Lowrie (1951), and Meller (1971).

13. In 1954, Buck Buchwald, an editor with one of Honolulu's two daily newspapers, the *Honolulu Advertiser*, laid down a roll of newsprint stretching one block on Bishop Street, one of the main streets in downtown Honolulu. People were urged to sign the roll in support of statehood. It was submitted to Congress with over 120,000 names. See Bob Siegal, "A Tsunami Tale, and the Man Behind the 1954 Honor Roll," *Honolulu Star Advertiser*, April 10, 2015.

14. Recent critics of the statehood vote have rightly observed that it did not supply an option for Hawai'i voters to choose to be an independent country, as required by international law, or an option for native Hawaiians to form their own governing entity. Objections were also registered to migrants from the United States, the colonizing country, being allowed to vote in an election on the political status of Hawai'i. Most scholars agree that the mechanisms used by the United States to annex Hawai'i violated international law. A smaller group of scholars and activists have argued that the current U.S. presence in Hawai'i should be viewed as an occupation of a sovereign country. For a clear rendition of these arguments and other perspectives on the U.S. presence in Hawai'i, see Sai (2008).

15. The Philippine Independence Act, Pub. L. 73-127, 48 Stat. 456 (March 24, 1934).

16. The U.S. government's law banning Chinese immigration to the United States, the 1882 Chinese Exclusion Act, became applicable to Hawai'i at annexation. Hawai'i's recruitment of plantation workers from Japan ended in 1907 when the U.S.-Japan "Gentlemen's Agreement" banned new migration of male Japanese workers.

17. In July 1946, Congress passed the Luce-Celler Act (Chap. 534, 8 U.S.C.A. § 703, July 2, 1946), which allowed Philippine spouses of U.S. citizens to enter

without any quotas and raised Filipino immigration quotas by a token amount, from 50 to 100 persons per year. Earlier in 1946, Hawai'i plantations had recruited more than 7,000 workers and family members from the Philippines ("the 1946 Boys") to work on plantations during the ILWU sugar industry strike. The action completely backfired, however, as an ILWU recruiter found his way onto the boat bringing the workers to Hawai'i and signed up most of them to become ILWU members during their voyage.

18. More precisely, the 1894 Wilson-Gorman tariff, which the Dingley tariff superseded, had set 40 percent as the rate for raw sugar and 40 percent plus ⅛ of a cent per pound as the rate for refined sugar. The 1909 Payne-Aldrich tariff bill left sugar tariffs unchanged while establishing a lower preferential rate for refined Cuban sugar.

19. See Ewa Plantation Co., et al. v. Wallace, 62 Wash. Law Rep. 830 (1934). Some provisions of the Jones-Costigan Act were overturned by the Supreme Court in the 1936 Hoosac Mills case, United States v. Butler, 297 U.S. 1 (1936). Quota restrictions on Hawai'i sugar sales were, however, not affected by this decision and were reaffirmed by Congress in its passage of the 1937 Sugar Act.

20. For a discussion of 35 important insular court cases, see Sparrow (2006). Hawai'i's status as an incorporated territory provided citizens with more rights than residents in unincorporated territories.

21. Congress amended the Jones-Costigan Act in 1936 (Act of June 19, 1936, c. 612, § 1, 49 Stat. 1539). After a 1936 U.S. Supreme Court decision (*Butler*) overturned the act's processing tax, Congress adopted new legislation regulating sugar sales and production (Act of 1937, c. 898, § 510, 50 Stat. 903, 916).

22. For a discussion of the insecurity of property rights in a limited-access order, see La Croix (2015).

23. See Berkowitz and Clay (2006, 419).

24. See Berkowitz and Clay (2006, 419).

25. See Berkowitz and Clay (2006, 399). Berkowitz and Clay also found that U.S. states initially settled by common-law countries had higher-quality judicial institutions than states initially settled by civil-law countries. The first judges in Hawai'i's judicial system, established in the 1840s, were U.S. lawyers, and Hawai'i's legal system was structured along the lines of U.S. and British common law. The common-law basis of Hawai'i territorial law also provides a basis for firms to expect a high-quality court system under statehood.

26. See Dove (2016).

27. See, for example, Feld and Voight (2003) and Glaeser et al. (2004). A recent line of cross-country studies has examined the relationship between democracy and economic growth; an excellent study that uses a semi-parametric matched difference-in-differences model to control for endogeneity is Persson and Tabellini (2008). The authors find evidence that transitioning to democracy causes growth and that transitioning away from democracy reduces growth. See also Acemoglu

et al. (2008) for an argument that other historical variables drive both income and democracy and that higher income does not cause democracy and democracy does not cause higher income.

28. Chinese residents of Hawai'i who were not U.S. citizens were not allowed to travel to the mainland United States until the Chinese Exclusion Act was repealed by Congress in 1943. Other Asian residents of Hawai'i who were not U.S. citizens could enter the mainland United States only if they showed a birth certificate upon entry.

29. During the 1950s, Imua, an anti-Japanese and anticommunist coalition of Hawaiians, part-Hawaiians, and Caucasians, lobbied heavily in Washington, D.C., against statehood. Bell (1984, 260) writes that Imua believed that an appointed governor was the best defense against reform of a territorial tax system that favored wealthy landowners, such as the Big Five.

30. Bell (1984, chap. 9).

31. Bell found that Chinese, Japanese, and Filipino communities, which were oppressed under the territorial government, overwhelmingly supported statehood, while Hawaiians and Caucasians, many of whom were supporters of the dominant Republican Party, were sharply split over statehood.

32. Hitch (1992, 181–182).

33. Hawai'i's GDP statistics are a composite of three different series (1957–1962, 1963–1997, and 1997–2015), which were compiled using different assumptions and industrial classifications. Neither the U.S. Bureau of Economic Analysis nor the Hawai'i Department of Business, Economic Development and Tourism have calculated a reliable GDP deflator that incorporates prices of investment and consumption goods for any of the three series. I follow the established practice of computing real GDP by deflating nominal GDP by the Honolulu Consumer Price Index.

34. An excellent history of the tourism industry in Hawai'i is James Mak (2008), *Developing a Dream Destination: Tourism and Tourism Policy Planning in Hawai'i.* Andrew Kato and James Mak (2013) attribute the pattern of growth in Hawai'i's tourism industry to the speed of technological progress in air transportation.

35. See Hung and Mund (1961). The 1932 Richardson report (U.S. Department of Justice, 1932) had already identified the spaghetti-like interlocking directorates of major corporations as a problem for Hawai'i's economy. See figure 7.2 for the classic depiction of the network of connections among major corporations.

36. Constitution of the State of Hawai'i, Article XI, Conservation, Control and Development of Resources; Conservation and Development of Resources, Sections 2 and 3.

37. 1961 Hawaii Session Laws, 299–305, codified at Hawaii Revised Statutes 1955, 1963 Supp., chap. 98h.

38. The GET was established in 1933 to tax business revenues from sales of goods and was expanded during the 1930s to tax business revenues from sales of

goods and services. The GET has been criticized for taxing sales associated with the resale of goods and services and thereby allowing the effect of the tax to pyramid when production of a product or service involves numerous vertical transactions. The law was amended in 1969 to set a lower rate for business receipts involving resale of goods and in 1995 for business receipts involving resale of services.

Chapter Ten

1. In Great Britain, Israel, Hong Kong, Singapore, New Delhi, Canberra, Amsterdam, Stockholm, and Vancouver (Canada), residential land leasing is more common. In most cases, a municipal government leases land to residents in a competitive land market. See McDonald (1969). In Great Britain, the Church of England owns large tracts of land that it leases to homeowners. Residential land leasing is also widely practiced in many Pacific island countries where land cannot be sold to non-natives. In the Pacific, only New Zealand, Australia, Guam, and Hawai'i permit land to be sold to non-natives. Ward (1992) argues that the desire to protect indigenous landowners from the loss of their land was a feature of colonial policy in many Pacific island countries. For an analysis of the evolution of land rights and widespread use of land leasing in nineteenth-century Fiji, see my chapter in *Land Rights, Ethno-nationality, and Sovereignty in History* (La Croix 2004). The largest of the U.S. leasehold developments is in Irvine, California where, in the 1960s, the Irvine Company developed several leasehold housing communities. There are also small pockets of leasehold homes on Indian reservations and federal lands.

2. Leasehold tenure already had a presence in Hawai'i in 1900. The *Report of the U.S. Commissioner of Labor on Hawaii,* 1901 (U.S. Commissioner of Labor 1902) surveyed 225 families about their housing tenure. Of the 36 families who owned their homes, 12 families leased the land.

3. See Vargha (1964) for prewar data and Economics Research Associates (1969) for data through 1967.

4. See Vargha (1964, 12). The three big landowners were a charitable trust, the Bishop Estate, with 33 percent; an individual, Harold Castle, with 29 percent; and a noncharitable trust, the Campbell Estate, with 6 percent. Ownership data are for 1963 and include tenant-occupied as well as owner-occupied leasehold units. After Harold Castle's death in 1967, his landholdings were left to the Castle Estate.

5. The Bishop Estate, Honolulu's largest private landowner, owned approximately 20 percent of condo leases, with the remainder widely dispersed among a large number of charitable estates and individual owners with small landholdings.

6. The provisions of this legislation (chap. 38) closely paralleled those of the LRA, empowering an agency of the City and County of Honolulu to use powers of eminent domain to buy leased lands under condos and resell them to participating condo owners.

7. About 13,000 of the remaining 23,193 leasehold condos were located in 358 buildings in which some owners had already purchased their interest in the land. During the period (1991–2004) when the city's condo conversion law was in force, just 452 of 18,624 newly built condo units were sold as leasehold units. Data are from Mitrano (2004).

8. See Ching Young v. City and County of Honolulu, 639 F.3d 907 (9th Cir. 2011). After repeal of the city's land reform law, many landowners continued to offer opportunities to condo owners to buy their land.

9. The Bishop Estate's standard lease ran 55 years. See Economics Research Associates (1969, VI-2–VI-8). Prior to 1940, most leases ran just 30 years. From 1946 to 1952, the typical lease ran 50 years to conform to Federal Housing Administration (FHA) standards. The FHA's change to a 55-year term in 1952 quickly pushed the term of most new Hawai'i leases to 55 years.

10. Some leases established in the 1970s and 1980s specified rents that increased by fixed amounts at set dates, typically at 10-year or longer intervals, during the first 30 years. In some cases, "below-market" lease rents were set for the first 30 years; in exchange, the lessee paid more than the market value of the house. Buyers of homes on leased land often preferred this arrangement because the interest component of payment on a larger home mortgage loan is deductible against both federal and state income tax, whereas lease rent on residential land is not.

11. In 1975, the median (mean) annual lease rent on existing single-family dwellings in Hawai'i was $245 ($512). Data are from Survey and Marketing Services (1976).

12. 1975 Hawaii Session Laws, 419–423 as codified in Hawaii Revised Statutes 1976, chap. 519. In the early 1970s, the Bishop Estate's policy was to set lease rent at 4.5 percent of the land's value. For the Bishop Estate, the rent control law meant an unexpected decline in its future rent collections. See Zalburg, "Bishop Estate Trustees Discuss Job," *Honolulu Advertiser*, August 1, 1973, sec. 2-A-7. The law also specified that lease rents could be renegotiated after the initial fixed-rent period no more than once every 15 years.

13. For leases negotiated after 1975, new provisions governed reversion of improvements at expiration of the lease. See La Croix, Mak, and Sklarz (1989).

14. I make several assumptions to ensure that our cases are comparable and easy to understand. First, I assume that the buyer finances the purchase of the house (or the house and the land in case 1) with a 30-year fixed-rate (5 percent) mortgage covering 80 percent of the purchase price. Second, I assume that at the time of purchase, the buyer expects the rental value of the house and the land to appreciate annually at the same rate as the Honolulu Consumer Price Index. This is equivalent to assuming that the real rental value of the house and land remains constant. Third, I assume a constant 3 percent rate of inflation, an initial annual land rent of $1,000, and house rent of $2,000. The main implications of the analysis stay the same if, instead, I assume that the buyer anticipates increasing rental

values or I change the initial shares of the house rent and the land rent in the bundle's overall value. From the rental values of the house and land, I derive the price that a purchaser would pay for the house (or the house and the land when the buyer purchases both, as in case 1). I do this by assuming that the house lasts for 55 years and then falls apart. This admittedly unrealistic assumption sidesteps problems associated with the turnover of a house to the landowner at the end of the lease. I also assume that all off-site improvements—such as roads, schools, and sewers—and all on-site improvements—such as landscaping and driveways—that affect the value of the land are in place when the house is built and that they last for 55 years. This assumption sidesteps problems at rent renegotiation regarding how the improvements affect the land rent and who paid for them.

15. See Fry and Mak (1984).

16. In compliance with the will, the trustees established the Kamehameha Schools in 1887.

17. Midkiff (1961, 24–25, 32).

18. Similarly, the Stanford family's grant of their Palo Alto farm in 1885 to help establish Stanford University prohibited the university from ever selling those lands. Much of the acreage has since been developed as residential leasehold.

19. The governance structure of the Bishop Estate might also help explain its trustees' reluctance to sell land. The Bishop Estate, like other large landholding estates in Hawai'i, is organized as a dynastic trust. The purpose of a dynastic trust is to preserve the trust principal and, secondarily, to provide a reasonable income for beneficiaries. Prior to 1947, Hawai'i constrained trustees to make investments from specified lists. In 1947, these constraints were relaxed somewhat when the territorial legislature enacted a model "prudent man rule" statute that specified duties of trustees when making investment decisions for the trust. See Hawaii Revised Statutes 1955, 1960 Supp., chap. 179-14, added 1947, subsequently amended 1959, and Hawaii Revised Statutes 1955, chaps. 177-21–177-26. The main provision of chap. 179-14 states:

> Investments. (a) Fiduciary accounts. In acquiring, retaining, exchanging, selling, investing and managing property of another, including investments for account of their trusts by trust companies acting as trustees or guardians, a trust company shall exercise the judgment and care under the circumstances then prevailing, which men of prudence, discretion and intelligence exercise in the management of their own affairs, not in regard to speculation but in regard to the permanent disposition of their funds, considering both probable income as well as the probable safety of their capital.

The law of dynastic estates and the prudent man rule, applicable under the wills establishing the Bishop and Campbell trusts, encouraged conservative investment, including land retention. Had the estate trustees sold the land, they would have had to manage the sales proceeds. Of course, since residential land represented only a small percentage of their landholdings, one could argue that sales would have been beneficial to both estates by diversifying the asset portfolios held by these land-rich but cash-poor estates. While asset diversification is beneficial in reducing variation in income flows over time, investing the proceeds from land sales in a diversified portfolio could have provided other trustees and media critics with even more ammunition to generate attacks under the prudent man rule against any one investment that lost value. This is because the number of investments made would have sizably increased and the chance that one would lose value would also have increased. Given provisions of the wills advising against the sale of real estate and the prudent man rule emphasizing preservation of trust principal, it was surely less risky for individual trustees to favor lease rather than sale of estate land and to bear the wealth reduction from poor returns on reinvested proceeds. See Blair and Heggstad (1978) for a more complete discussion of the prudent man rule, Friedman (1964) for a good discussion of dynastic trusts, and King and Roth (2006) for applications to Kamehameha Schools/Bishop Estate.

Bishop Estate trustees have often publicly criticized and even sued one another over allegedly imprudent financial decisions and investments. See "Richards Sues Fellow Trustees for Higher Lease Rental for Choice Parcel of Kona Beach Property," *Honolulu Advertiser*, September 9, 1961, A-1; "Royal Hawaiian Center Lost $6.4 Million in 1981 Fiscal Year, According to Trustee Takabuki in His Suit Against Hung Wo Ching," *Honolulu Advertiser*, February 10, 1982, D-10. Beneficiaries sued the estate over "imprudent" land sales. See "Sued by Friends of Kam Schools Over Kapua Land Sales," *Honolulu Advertiser*, December 18, 1973, A-1; "Kam School Students Law Suit Against Bishop Estate Over Value of Kapua Lands Dismissed," *Honolulu Advertiser*, March 20, 1974, A-12.

In 1997, Hawai'i adopted the Uniform Prudent Investor Act. Its updated prudent man rule provided trustees with more flexibility to make investments in accord with modern portfolio theory. Schanzenbach and Sitkoff (2007, 681) show that after adoption of the act in other states, non-commercial trusts held about 1.5–4 percentage points more stock at the expensed of "safe" investments.

20. Hawai'i state income taxes have mostly mirrored federal income taxes. This means that the same arguments set forth in the text regarding the effects of federal income taxes also apply to the effects of state income taxes.

21. Many small noncharitable landowners in Honolulu leased rather than sold land developed with single-family homes. Like the large owners, they could avoid capital gains taxes by leasing. Why, then, did small landowners on the U.S. mainland sell rather than lease their lands? One possible but not exactly convincing explanation is that home buyers and landowners in Honolulu were more familiar with and accepting of the leasehold contract due to its widespread use by Hawai'i's large estates. This could have made it easier for smaller landowners in Honolulu to lease in emulation of the larger estates.

22. Zalburg, "Bishop Estate Trustees Discuss Job," *Honolulu Advertiser*, July 31, 1973, sec. 1-A-13.

23. The estate's original intent was to sell these homes in leasehold, but the FHA would not insure them, thereby cutting off mortgage financing to buyers. Because the estate could not sell the new homes in leasehold, it sold them in fee simple. Subsequently, major Hawai'i landowners worked out standard lease forms with the FHA and Veterans Administration (VA), which enabled those agencies to insure mortgages on leasehold homes. In an interview, former Bishop Estate trustee Oswald Stender emphasized the importance of the standard forms and FHA and VA mortgage insurance in accelerating the rise of leasehold tenure. Almost all residential leases initiated since the 1960s have used these standard forms or a minor variant of them.

24. Information from an interview by University of Hawai'i economics professor Louis Rose with Bishop Estate trustee Oswald Stender on August 30, 1994.

25. Cooper and Daws (1985, 406) indicated that in the mid-1960s, the estate sold leased fees in Halawa Hills after the failure of a land reform bill in the legislature. In 1972, the estate also sold 791 leased fees in a single bulk transaction organized to avoid dealer classification. Information on the 1972 transaction is from a personal conversation between Wesley Hillendahl, former chief economist at Bank of Hawaii, and University of Hawai'i economics professor James Mak.

26. In an interview with Louis Rose, a Campbell Estate trustee recalled only two sales through the early 1990s: 200 acres to an oil company and 65 acres to a residential developer.

27. Castle & Cooke did not develop any residential leasehold property.

28. Not all the economic incentives were tilted toward leasehold contracts. The choice of a leasehold contract typically involves higher transaction costs than a fee simple contact. Most of the additional transaction costs are incurred at renegotiation, as determining the new lease rent is a costly process. If a leasehold property is part of a large leasehold housing tract without fee simple house lots, transaction prices on comparable fee simple land do not exist. The presence of homeowner-financed site-specific assets and lessor-financed off-site assets increases the cost of determining the price of the unimproved land. Once the price of the land is determined, the two parties must still agree on the rate of return on the asset. If the two parties are unable to agree on a new lease rent, a board of three appraisers determines the rent. Such costs do not exist when a land-house package is purchased in fee simple. Given that the lessee must also incur upfront costs to understand the "non-standard" leasehold contract, the transaction cost differential is clear.

29. See, for example, Kanahele (1986).

30. See, for instance, Amalu, "Critical of Estate's Decision to Sell Land; Says Land Is Better Than Worthless Money," *Sunday Star Bulletin & Advertiser*, August 27, 1978, A-25; "Akaka Says Land Sales Create Crisis," *Honolulu Star Bulletin*, July 20, 1973, A-12; "Sales Criticized by Hawaiians," *Honolulu Star Bulletin*, July 21, 1973, A-12.

31. Fuchs (1961, 430–433).

32. Fuchs (1961, 431–432) provides several examples of estates and corporations that moved land into leasehold residential development, ostensibly in response to the new eminent domain threat hanging over their lands.

33. Cooper and Daws (1985).

34. The change would have occurred in any case, as by the mid-1930s there was little acreage available for expansion of production.

35. Schmitt (1977, 360–361).

36. See Ingram M. Stainback, "Special Message Recommending the Hawaii Home Development Authority by Ingram M. Stainback, Governor of Hawaii, to Twenty-Third Session of the Territorial Legislature," *Honolulu Star-Bulletin*, March 20, 1945.

37. Maryland's land reform laws provide a precedent for Hawai'i's reform laws. In Maryland, long-term residential leases paying ground rent date back to the colonial period. In 1884, the state of Maryland passed legislation enabling tenants with leases taken out after 1884 and lasting longer than 15 years to redeem ground rents at any time more than 15 years into the lease. A clear method for calculating the redemption value was specified (Md. Laws 1884, chap. 485). Maryland courts quickly upheld the redemption law (Stewart v. Gorter, 70 Md. 242, 16 A. 644, 1889). While many lessees took advantage of the legislation (and subsequent updates) to redeem their ground rents, there are still homes in the Baltimore metropolitan area subject to ground rents. Since 2007, Maryland has required lease owners to register ground rents in a central registry. Other attempts to reform the ground rent system or to enforce registration have been overturned by the Maryland Supreme Court; see, for example, State of Maryland v. Stanley Goldberg et al., in the Court of Appeals of Maryland, No. 8, September Term 2013, opinion issued February 26, 2014.

38. See Horowitz and Meller (1966, 52–54) and Cooper and Daws (1985, 403–409). In an interview with the author (December 12, 2017), Governor Ariyoshi stressed that his main reason for voting against the bill was the different situations that existing and new lessees would have faced if the Maryland bill passed.

39. Cooper and Daws (1985, 416–417).

40. For a chronology of the land reform measures affecting single-family residences, see State of Hawaii, Hawaii Housing Authority (1982).

41. The IRS rules were modeled along the lines of 1031 exchange rules. IRS policies toward sales by charitable and noncharitable landowners were implemented sale by sale, through post-sale audits, until 1978, when the IRS provided a blanket ruling for the Bishop Estate. See Kato, "Bishop Estate Allowed to Sell 15,000 Lots, Stay Tax-Exempt," *Honolulu Advertiser*, July 18, 1978, A-1, A-5.

42. The Bishop Estate did not stop entering into new leases until the mid-1980s, and fulfillment of those contracts brought new leasehold homes onto the market as late as 1991. Strong pressure from the native Hawaiian community for the estate to

keep its lands intact was probably the main reason why the trustees did not adjust faster to the LRA.

43. See Cooper and Daws (1985, chap. 13).

44. This provision applied to both existing and future leases. A Hawai'i court overturned the retroactive provisions of the law in Anthony v. Kualoa Ranch, Inc., 69 Haw. 112, 736 P.2d 55 (1987). For an analysis of *Kualoa*, see La Croix, Mak, and Sklarz (1989).

45. Hawaii Housing Authority v. Midkiff, 467 U.S. 229 (1984).

46. 704 P.2d 888 (Hawaii 1985).

47. Locations, Inc. (1992, 19).

48. Only one of the four Republican senators was defeated in the 1968 election.

49. The conventional wisdom is that larger groups are not always more politically influential than smaller groups, as they tend to have higher costs of organizing for political action due to free-riding problems and smaller per capita gains when more individuals are added to the majority group. As a group becomes larger, the incentive of individual members to vote or contribute to lobbying efforts falls, diluting its political effectiveness. The politics of land reform in Hawai'i represents an important exception to the standard analysis because, as in the case discussed in the text, each additional lessee brought additional economic rents to the political process for redistribution.

50. U.S. census data on the median price of single-family homes in Hawai'i show strong annual growth in prices during the 1950s (5.32 percent) and the 1960s (5.18 percent) and accelerating annual growth in the 1970s (12.13 percent). Deflating by the U.S. Consumer Price Index (CPI-U) leaves a similar pattern of annual growth rates for the 1950s (3.25 percent), the 1960s (2.69 percent), and the 1970s (5.51 percent). John Child and Co., a Honolulu appraisal firm, analyzed resale prices of single-family homes in 20 Honolulu subdivisions between 1967 and 1980 and found that the appreciation of a carefully selected sample of homes during this period averaged 10.75 percent. See John Child and Co., Inc. (1980–1981). The range of annual appreciation across subdivisions ranged from 9.0 to 13.7 percent, a large increase even if the annual increase of 6.6 percent in the Honolulu CPI during this period is considered.

51. Mortgage lenders would typically not make mortgage loans when the lease was due for either renegotiation or expiration within 10 years.

52. One of the earliest rent renegotiations came in 1964 for homes in the posh Portlock Road area located on Bishop Estate land near Hawai'i Kai. Rents jumped by 300–600 percent for the first 15 years and another 20–25 percent for the final 15 years. See "Portlock Road Residents Fight Bishop Estate Lease Rent Hikes," *Honolulu Advertiser*, February 5, 1964, A-1, A-2. In 1971, rent renegotiation for a small subdivision on Bishop Estate land in Kailua resulted in a 624 percent increase for the final 26 years of a 48-year lease. See "Bishop Rent Hike Draws a Complaint," *Honolulu Advertiser*, September 23, 1971, A-13. In 1976–1977, the Waialae-Kahala Tract A lease rents jumped from $250 to nearly $3,000 per year, an increase of over 1,000 percent (Cooper and Daws, 1985, 424). In the early

1990s, condominium lease rents typically increased by 1,000 to 1,200 percent at renegotiation. See "Alshire, Lease Rent Up 8,742% for Townhouse," *Sunday Star Bulletin and Advertiser*, March 24, 1991, A-1, A-11.

53. Barro and Sahasakul (1986).

54. Hawai'i is not the only U.S. experiment with residential leasehold tenure that floundered as the time of rent renegotiation neared. Consider the Irvine Company's leasehold housing development in Orange County, California. Terms of leasehold contracts were set in the late 1950s and early 1960s, with annual rents fixed for 25 to 30 years and then set at 5–7 percent of the "fair market value" of the land. At renegotiation in the late 1970s and early 1980s, rents increased by as much as 3,233 percent. Stunned, angry homeowners organized the Committee of 4000 to seek restructuring of their leases. They filed a class action suit alleging price gouging in rent renegotiations and, more importantly, organized politically to block the company's plans for new commercial developments on its undeveloped lands. In 1983, the Irvine Company, stymied in its efforts to have new developments approved by regulatory authorities, essentially conceded the fight and agreed to sell fee interests to those lessees electing to purchase at market value. To those unwilling to purchase, it offered new 55-year amended leases with annual rents indexed to the U.S. Consumer Price Index. See Gary Hector, "The Land Coup in Orange County," *Fortune Magazine*, November 14, 1983, 90–102. Lease rents are also tied to the Consumer Price Index on many residential leasehold properties located on privately held Aqua Caliente tribal lands in Palm Springs, California. See Akee (2009) for an analysis of residential leasing in Palm Springs.

55. In July 1993, the IRS provided the Bishop Estate with a similar blanket ruling for sales of lease fee interests in condominiums and townhouses. After the ruling, the Bishop Estate offered to sell the fee to virtually all condo and townhouse lessees. See Greg Wiles and Vickie Ong, "Bishop Given Go-Ahead for All of Condos," *Honolulu Advertiser*, July 31, 1993, A1–A2.

56. From 1946 until 1963, the highest federal marginal tax rate on ordinary income was an extraordinary 91 percent. Congress reduced it to 70 percent in 1964, 50 percent in 1982, and 28 percent in 1988. Between 1991 and 2018, it fluctuated over a narrower range, between 31 and 39.6 percent.

57. See the iconic book detailing the massive corruption at the Bishop Estate by King and Roth (2006).

Chapter Eleven

1. *Midkiff*, 467 U.S. 229 (1984).

2. Hawaii Housing Authority v. Lyman, 704 P.2d 888 (1985).

3. A prominent legal scholar, Richard Epstein, anticipated some of this chapter's findings. In a brief analysis of *Midkiff*, Epstein (1985, 181) wrote, "No

antitrust expert thinks 'oligopoly' because there are 'only' seventy or twenty-two or eighteen landowners in a given market. Why then allow the legislature to so find? ... The better place to look for land shortages and high prices is in the extensive network of state land use regulations that is today beyond constitutional challenge, even though it facilitates the very oligopolistic practices that land reform statutes are said to counteract." See also Merrill (1986).

4. See Lamoreaux (2011).

5. Economics Research Associates (1969). In 1967, less than 20 percent of O'ahu was classified as urban. Data are from State of Hawaii, Office of the Lt. Governor (1969, 24b) and Schmitt (1977, 295).

6. The average Honolulu site price per square foot in 1968 was $1.76, or 3.6 times the average price on the mainland. The Honolulu data include leasehold observations, but do not reveal the extent to which the average prices reflect the presence of lessor interests. See Economics Research Associates (1969, VI-3–6).

7. In 1964, the Bishop Estate was the largest private landowner in the state.

8. Hawaii Revised Statutes 1968, chap. 516, and Hawaii Session Laws, Regular Session, 1967, Act 307. Act 307 applied strictly to single-family homeowners, and not to leasehold condominiums, townhouses, or cooperatives.

9. Hawaii Session Laws, 1967. Act 307, pt. I, sec. 1(j).

10. Hawaii Session Laws, 1967, Act 307, pt. I, sec. 1(j).

11. Hawaii Session Laws, 1967, Act 307, pt. I, secs. 1(f) and 1(g).

12. Midkiff v. Tom, 483 F.Supp. 62 (1979).

13. Midkiff v. Tom, 702 F.2d 788 (1983), at 790.

14. Midkiff v. Tom, 702 F.2d 788 (1983), at 805, 806. The panel also found that the LRA's use of eminent domain could be clearly distinguished from other cases in which the court previously found private-to-private takings to be constitutional.

15. *Midkiff*, 467 U.S. 229 (1984), at 243.

16. *Midkiff*, 467 U.S. 229 (1984), at 244.

17. *Berman v. Parker*, 348 U.S. 26 (1954).

18. *Midkiff*, 467 U.S. 229 (1984), at 240. O'Connor is quoting from the court's decision Old Dominion Co. v. United States, 269 U.S. 55, 66 (1925).

19. *Midkiff*, 467 U.S. 229 (1984), at 241–242.

20. *Midkiff*, 467 U.S. 229 (1984), at 242.

21. *Midkiff*, 467 U.S. 229 (1984).

22. The *Midkiff* decision was both reaffirmed and eclipsed in 2005 as the standard for public use in eminent domain cases by the U.S. Supreme Court's decision Kelo v. City of New London, 545 U.S. 469 (2005). That decision allowed for the use of eminent domain in cases of private redevelopment of land when it could be expected that the general public would benefit from increased economic growth due to the project.

23. Epstein (2009, 164) approvingly cited the oligopoly rationale for the *Midkiff* decision: "Beginning in the early 1800's, Hawaiian leaders and American settlers repeatedly attempted to divide the lands of the kingdom among the crown,

the chiefs, and the common people. These efforts proved largely unsuccessful, however, and the land remained in the hands of a few. In the mid-1960's, after extensive hearings, the Hawaii Legislature discovered that, while the State and Federal Governments owned almost 49% of the State's land, another 47% was in the hands of only 72 private landowners" (*Midkiff*, 467 U.S. at 231). Epstein's data on land concentration are correct, but his representation that "Hawaiian leaders and American settlers repeatedly attempted to divide the lands of the kingdom" and that "these efforts proved largely unsuccessful" is just plain wrong. The 1846 *Māhele* reorganized property rights in land, established fee simple rights, and fully delineated ownership of land by the king, government, chiefs and land managers, and *kānaka maoli* farming the land.

24. McDonald (1985, 92).

25. See Van Tyne ([1902] 1959, 268–285, 331–341) for an account of the colonies' land laws and the land confiscations and sales during and after the revolution. A bill of attainder is a legislative act that pronounces one or more persons to be guilty of violating a law and often prescribes a penalty.

26. McDonald (1985, 91).

27. See La Croix (2015).

28. Act of May 1779, 10 Henning's Statutes At Large 64, chap. 13, § 6 (1822) (Virginia statute).

29. State confiscations of land during and after the Revolutionary War and state laws to reorganize property rights in land both happened prior to the ratification of the Bill of Rights in December 1791. States enacting land reform legislation did not have to satisfy a still-to-be-adopted public use clause of the Fifth Amendment. By contrast, the Hawai'i LRA had to satisfy restrictions on eminent domain staked out in both the Hawai'i and U.S. constitutions.

30. See Melendy (1999).

31. Suppose coordination between estates was tacit. A clear case cannot be made that the LRA's conversion provisions changed estates' incentives to tacitly coordinate.

32. See Coase (1972).

33. Souza v. Estate of Bishop, 594 F. Supp. 1480 (1984).

34. Souza v. Estate of Bishop, 799 F.2d 1327, 1329 (9th Cir. 1986). The court is quoting *Wilson v. Chronicle Broadcasting Co.*,794 F.2d 1359, 1365 (9th Cir. 1986), which is quoting *Edward J. Sweeny & Sons, Inc. v. Texaco, Inc.*, 637 F.2d 105, Ill (3d Cir. 1980).

35. All HHI calculations refer to ownership of the stock of land rather than to an annual flow of land sales or rentals.

36. U.S. Department of Justice and Federal Trade Commission (2010).

37. The 1992 DOJ and FTC merger guidelines are much stricter: a market with an HHI below 1,000 is unconcentrated, between 1,000 and 2,500 moderately concentrated, and above 2,500 highly concentrated. See U.S. Department of Justice and Federal Trade Commission (1992).

38. Because the total lots in our data do not include fee simple lots developed prior to 1946, but include all leasehold lots, the measured HHI is biased upward. The measured HHI would also be lower if we defined the residential market to include condominiums, as ownership of leased land for condominiums and apartment buildings is even less concentrated than ownership of leased land for single-family homes. Data for the HHI calculation for lots subdivided between 1946 and April 1963 are from Vargha (1964, 11–12).

39. Another factor that increased demand for housing in the 1960s was the spectacular rise of Hawaiʻi's tourism industry and expectations for its continued growth over the next 15–20 years. Expectations of higher future incomes would have been capitalized into the current price of housing.

40. Rankings tend to be higher when Honolulu consumers are surveyed as to their satisfaction with living in Hawaiʻi. Rankings tend to be lower when tax rates and congested infrastructure, such as the ever-crowded and slowly moving H1 and H2 highways, are included in the rankings.

41. The record high temperature recorded at the Honolulu International Airport is 95°F and the record low temperature is 52°F.

42. The presence of highly valued amenities in a metropolitan area can induce migration and population growth, which can, in turn, lead to congestion. Costs of congestion would offset to residents and visitors some of the value generated by the area's amenities—think Honolulu traffic. See Ciccone and Hall (1996) for the classic statements of the tradeoffs between amenities, population density and productivity spillovers, and congestion. Roback (1982) shows that people in metropolitan areas with highly valued amenities either are paid lower wages or pay higher housing prices, or face a combination of lower wages and higher housing prices.

43. Rose (1989a, 1989b).

44. Rose and La Croix (1989). Houston was dropped from the sample because it had no zoning laws in 1980.

45. In the mainland United States, villages and towns equivalent to Hawaiʻi Kai, Waipahu, or Nānākuli (all on Oʻahu) often have separate city or county governments.

46. See Hamilton (1978) and Fischel (1980, 1985).

47. In our regressions, we included an index of zoning power developed by urban economist William Fischel to control for government zoning power. The mean index value in the 39-urban-area sample is 0.35; values range from 0.83 in Richmond to 0.04 in Minneapolis. See Fischel (1981).

48. Their estimate is derived using data from the U.S. Decennial Censuses of Housing on metropolitan statistical area housing prices and data from the Bureau of Economic Analysis on the replacement cost of structures. See Davis and Heathcote (2005, 2007).

49. See Davis and Palumbo (2008). Honolulu is not in their sample of the 46 largest U.S. metropolitan areas as it ranked 68th by population in the 2000 U.S. census.

50. Land price appreciation over the last 15 years in coastal U.S. metropolitan areas was also accompanied by considerable volatility due to the crisis in housing finance and the U.S. Great Recession of 2007–2009, the effects of which lingered in many housing markets into the 2010s.

51. The calculation is rough because I use aggregate R. S. Means data on Honolulu construction costs rather than disaggregated R. S. Means data.

52. See Davis and Heathcote (2007, 2610–2612) for an extended analysis of the factors influencing housing prices in metropolitan areas with high land shares.

53. The Hawai'i state legislature mentioned that increases in population were another factor pushing up the demand for land, but failed to mention other important factors affecting land prices, in particular, widely held expectations of strong household income growth.

54. Gyourko, Saiz, and Summers (2008).

55. Gyourko, Saiz, and Summers (2008, 698–702).

56. See Honolulu City Council (2017a, 2017b, and 2017c).

57. These two variables and others in his regression explain about half of the premium in Honolulu's housing price.

58. National Association of Realtors (2017). Monthly rental rates in Hawai'i are also high, with a study based on U.S. Bureau of the Census data showing the monthly median housing rent ($1,448) in 2015 to be 55 percent higher than the national average. See Darian Moriki, "Tight Supply Drives Rental Rates Up," *Pacific Business News*, September 25, 2015, 4.

59. Lamoreaux (2011). Three articles by economic historians Dan Bogart and Gary Richardson (2009, 2011a, 2011b) show how reorganization of property rights in Great Britain facilitated the transition from an agricultural to an industrial society.

60. See also Fleck and Hanssen (2010).

61. Lamoreaux (2011, 301).

Chapter Twelve

1. Per capita incomes of native Hawaiians peaked at 73.4 percent of state per capita incomes in 2007, fell during the Great Recession to 66.2 percent in 2010, and then recovered to 69.2 percent in 2013. The gap in median household incomes is smaller. In 2013, U.S. census surveys show that median household incomes were only 3.4 percent lower for Hawaiian households ($65,688) than for households across the entire state ($68,020). Hawaiian households were, however, larger (3.51 persons) than households across the entire state (3.01 persons). Adjusting for household size, the median income of Hawaiian households was 82.8 percent of the median income for all households. For a summary of the data on native Hawaiian incomes in 2013, see Office of Hawaiian Affairs (2014).

2. Hawai'i's pineapple industry also boomed during this period, in part because of U.S. tariffs on processed pineapple products.

3. For a more complete discussion, see Engerman (1992).

4. For histories of bound labor in Peru and Cuba, see Stewart (1951) and Hu-Dehart (1993).

5. The act prohibited new bound labor contracts and voided all existing contracts. See La Croix and Fishback (2000) for an analysis of compensation paid to migrant labor in early twentieth-century Hawai'i. For a discussion of the rise of the sugar industry and coevolution of property rights in Fiji, see La Croix (2004).

6. See, for example, Takaki (1983).

7. Liou (2015, chap. 3).

8. La Croix and Fishback (2000). See Williamson (2000) for data on wages in Asian countries at the turn of the twentieth century. See Williamson and Hatton (1998) for an analysis of forces driving global migration in the late nineteenth and early twentieth centuries. See Patterson (1988) for discussion of migration from Korea.

9. See Ichioka (1988) and Wakukawa (1938) for extended description and analysis of the life of first-generation Japanese migrants—*Issei*—in Hawai'i.

10. Beechert (1985, chap. 10).

11. Olsson (2009).

12. Grier (1999).

13. Feyrer and Sacerdote (2009).

14. Feyrer and Sacerdote (2009, 246).

15. See also Ertan, Fiszbain, and Putterman (2016).

16. Grier (1999, 325–328). Grier (1999, 319) also finds that "British colonial education policies made a conscious effort to avoid alienating the native culture, by teaching in the vernacular languages and training teachers from the indigenous tribes."

17. Easterly and Levine (2016).

18. Schmitt (1977, table 1.12) and Nordyke (1989, Appendixes).

19. See Schmitt (1977, tables 3.1 and 9.11) for data on 1900 and 1960.

20. See Schmitt (1977, table 3.10) for 1960.

21. North, Wallis, and Weingast (2009, 17–21, 134–142).

22. The laws also regulated 9 private Korean-language schools and 16 private Chinese-language schools.

23. Special Session 1920, Legislature of Hawaii, Act 30, entitled "An act relating to foreign language schools and teachers thereof," as amended by Act 171 of 1923 and Act 152 of 1925, and certain regulations adopted by the Department of Public Instruction on June 1, 1925.

24. Farrington v. Tokushige, 273 U.S. 284 (1927).

25. In the late 1930s, the U.S. government conducted a covert investigation to determine whether Hawai'i's Japanese and Japanese-American population would

remain loyal to the United States if war between Japan and the United States broke out. The investigation concluded that the population would remain loyal (as it actually did) and found no evidence of any groups supporting the Japanese government.

26. Ravago, Roumasset, and Burnett (2008).

27. See Darby and Jussawalla (1993, 45–49). During the administration of Governor John Waihee, there was a formal policy to concentrate state resources on the creation of jobs outside the tourism industry. See also Mak (2008, 62–64).

28. See Peter Kay, "Should Hawaii Pursue a High-Tech Future?" *Honolulu Star Bulletin*, September 1, 2002, D1, D6.

29. Hawai'i's "lost decade" was primarily due to the collapse of tourism and of foreign investment from Japan, the closure of several U.S. military bases, and the shutdown of more sugar and pineapple plantations.

30. For a more complete description and more critical analysis of Act 221, see Kato, La Croix, and Mak (2009).

31. Over the entire "lost decade" of the 1990s, real GDP increased by just 1 percent (1990–2000). See State of Hawaii, Department of Business, Economic Development and Tourism (2002, table 13.02).

32. See, for example, Acemoglu, Johnson, and Robinson (2001) and North, Wallis, and Weingast (2009).

33. Since 1962, Republicans have won just two gubernatorial elections (2002 and 2006) and have not controlled either the house or the senate since 1964.

34. The federal government initially retained 0.375 million acres of public lands.

35. Hawaii Session Laws, 1980, Act 273, at 525.

36. See Office of Hawaiian Affairs v. State of Hawai'i, 96 Haw. 388, for a more complete description of the issues involved in the litigation.

37. Pub. L. 103-150, 107 Stat. 1510.

38. For the Hawai'i Supreme Court ruling, see Office of Hawaiian Affairs v. Housing and Community Development Corp. of Hawaii, 117 Haw. 174.

39. For the U.S. Supreme Court ruling, see Hawaii v. Office of Hawaiian Affairs, 129 S. Ct. 1436 (2009).

40. See Office of Treaty Settlements, New Zealand Department of Justice (2017).

41. Rice v. Cayetano, 528 U.S. 495 (2000).

42. Constitution of the State of Hawai'i, Article XII, Section 5.

43. Arakaki v. State of Hawai'i, 314 F.3d 1091 (9th Cir. 2002).

44. There was also litigation over the Hawaiian-only admission policy of Kamehameha Schools. A narrow 8–7 ruling by the U.S. Ninth Circuit Court of Appeals in favor of Kamehameha Schools left some observers pondering whether the policy would survive future challenges in federal court. See Doe v. Kamehameha Schools/Bernice Pauahi Bishop Estate, 470 F.3d 827 (9th Cir. 2006) (en banc).

45. Some organizations have focused on establishing a Hawaiian governing entity that would have a relationship to the state and federal government similar to that of an Indian tribe. Others have focused on ending the American occupation of Hawai'i and restoring the institutions of the Hawaiian Kingdom as specified in its constitution or on establishing a new, independent Nation of Hawai'i.

46. Senator Akaka repeatedly rewrote major provisions in the bill to try to win over some of the bill's opponents in Congress.

47. Both the Hawai'i state senate and house of representatives passed resolutions supporting the Akaka bill almost unanimously.

48. U.S. National Archives and Records Administration (2016).

49. U.S. National Archives and Records Administration (2016, 71278).

50. Akina v. Hawaii No. SCOTUS injunction 15A551.

51. Constitution of the Native Hawaiian Nation, Articles 27–33.

52. Constitution of the Native Hawaiian Nation, Articles 4–7.

53. Constitution of the Native Hawaiian Nation, Article 4.

54. Constitution of the Native Hawaiian Nation, Article 10, Sec. 9.

Appendix

1. See North, Wallis, and Weingast (2009). North et al. (2012) use their model to provide case studies of institutional change in 10 developed and developing countries.

2. North, Wallis, and Weingast (2009, 13).

3. North et al. (2012, 4).

4. North et al. (2012, 4).

5. Some types of organizations (known as "adherent" organizations) are able to specify a set of incentives that is self-enforcing—that is, all parties within the organization have incentives to follow the incentives and to enforce them. Third-party enforcement of contracts with the organization greatly expands the number of viable organizations, some of which are more complex and some of which are more specialized, and increases opportunities within the society.

6. North et al. (2012, 4)

7. See Linnekin (1990).

8. Quote is from Kirch (2010, 1031). See Kame'eleihiwa (1992).

9. North, Wallis, and Weingast (2009, 42).

10. North, Wallis, and Weingast (2009, 42).

11. North, Wallis, and Weingast (2009, 42).

12. North, Wallis, and Weingast (2009, 43).

13. North, Wallis, and Weingast (2009, 47).

14. North, Wallis, and Weingast (2009, 47).

15. North, Wallis, and Weingast (2009, 47).

16. See Acemoglu and Robinson (2006).

17. North, Wallis, and Weingast (2009, 110–111).

18. North, Wallis, and Weingast (2009, 150–151).

19. North, Wallis, and Weingast (2009, 151–152). Rule of law for elites does not mean that elites are treated the same as other citizens or that laws are fair with respect to elites and other citizens. Rather, it means that each member of an elite group is treated the same under the law as other members of the group.

References

Accominotti, Olivier, Marc Flandreau, and Riad Rezzik. 2 11. "The Spread of Empire: Clio and the Measurement of Colonial Borrowing Costs." *Economic History Review* 64:385–407.

Acemoglu, Daron, Simon Johnson, and James A. Robinson. 2001. "The Colonial Origins of Comparative Development: An Empirical Investigation." *American Economic Review* 91:1369–1401.

———. 2005. "The Rise of Europe: Atlantic Trade, Institutional Change, and Economic Growth." *American Economic Review* 95:546–579.

Acemoglu, Daron, Simon Johnson, James A. Robinson, and Pierre Yared. 2008. "Income and Democracy." *American Economic Review* 98:808–842.

Acemoglu, Daron, and James Robinson. 2006. *Economic Origins of Dictatorship and Democracy*. New York: Cambridge University Press.

Acemoglu, Daron, and Alexander Wolitzky. 2011. "The Economics of Labor Coercion." *Econometrica* 79:555–600.

Aguiar, Gary George. 1996. "Party Mobilization, Class, and Ethnicity: The Case of Hawaii, 1930–1954." PhD diss., Indiana University.

Akee, Randall K. Quinones. 2009. "Checkerboards and Coase: Transactions Costs and Efficiency in Land Markets." *Journal of Law and Economics* 52:395–410.

Alexander, W. D. 1890. "A Brief History of Land Titles in the Hawaiian Kingdom." In *Hawaiian Annual for 1891*, ed. Thomas G. Thrum. Honolulu.

Allen, Helena G. 1982. *The Betrayal of Liliuokalani, Last Queen of Hawaii 1838–1917*. Honolulu: Mutual Publishing.

Allen, Melinda S. 2014. "Marquesan Colonisation Chronologies and Postcolonisation Interaction: Implications for Hawaiian Origins and the 'Marquesan Homeland' Hypothesis." *Journal of Pacific Archaeology* 5:1–17.

Allen, Robert C. 1997. "Agriculture and the Origins of the State in Ancient Egypt." *Explorations in Economic History* 34:135–154.

Alston, Lee J., Edwyna Harris, and Bernardo Mueller. 2012. "The Development of Property Rights on Frontiers: Endowments, Norms, and Politics." *Journal of Economic History* 72:741–770.

Alston, Lee J., Gary Libecap, and Bernardo Mueller. 1998. *Titles, Conflict and Land Use: The Development of Property Rights and Land Reform on the Brazilian Amazon Frontier.* Ann Arbor: University of Michigan Press.

American Board of Commissioners for Foreign Missions. 1835. *Report of the American Board of Commissioners for Foreign Missions, Read at the Twenty-Sixth Annual Meeting held in the City of Baltimore, September 9, 10, & 11, 1835.* Boston: Crocker & Brewster.

Anderson, Atholl. 2003. "Entering Uncharted Waters: Models of Initial Colonization in Polynesia." In *Colonization of Unfamiliar Landscapes: The Archaeology of Adaptation*, ed. Marcy Rockman and James Steele. New York: Routledge.

Anderson, Atholl, John Chappell, Michael Gagan, and Richard Grove. 2006. "Prehistoric Maritime Migration in the Pacific Islands: An Hypothesis of ENSO Forcing." *Holocene* 16:1–6.

Anderson, Terry L. 1995. *Sovereign Nations or Reservations? Indian Economies: An Economic History of American Indians.* San Francisco: Pacific Research Institute.

Anderson, Terry L., and Peter J. Hill. 2009. *The Not So Wild, Wild West: Property Rights on the Frontier.* Stanford, Calif.: Stanford Economics and Finance.

Anderson, Terry L., and Dean Lueck. 1992. "Land Tenure and Agricultural Productivity on Indian Reservations." *Journal of Law and Economics* 35:427–454.

Anthony, Joseph Garner. 1955. *Hawaii under Army Rule.* Stanford, Calif.: Stanford University Press.

Athens, J. Stephen. 1997. "Hawaiian Lowland Vegetation in Prehistory." In *Historical Ecology in the Pacific Islands*, ed. Patrick V. Kirch and T. L. Hunt. Honolulu: University of Hawai'i Press.

Athens, J. Stephen, Timothy M. Rieth, and Thomas S. Dye. 2014. "A Paleoenvironmental and Archaeological Model-Based Age Estimate for the Colonization of Hawai'i." *American Antiquity* 79:144–155.

Athens, J. Stephen, H. D. Tuggle, J. V. Ward, and D. J. Welsh. 2002. "Avifaunal Extinction, Vegetation Change, and Polynesian Impacts in Prehistoric Hawai'i." *Archaeology in Oceania* 37:57–78.

Bailey, Mark. 2014. *The Decline of Serfdom in Late Medieval England: From Bondage to Freedom.* Woodbridge, UK: Boydell Press.

Baines, Dudley. 1995. *Emigration from Europe, 1815–1930.* New York: Cambridge University Press.

Ballard, C., P. Brown, R. M. Rourke, and T. Harwood, eds. 2005. *The Sweet Potato in Oceania: A Reappraisal.* Ethnology Monographs 19/Oceania Monograph 56. Pittsburgh: University of Pittsburgh; Sydney: University of Sydney.

Banerjee, Albert, and Lakshmi Iyer. 2005. "History, Institutions, and Economic Performance: The Legacy of Colonial Land Tenure Systems in India." *American Economic Review* 95:1190–1213.

Barro, R., and C. Sahasakul. 1986. "Average and Marginal Tax Rates from Social Security and the Individual Income Tax." *Journal of Business* 59:555–566.

Bartholomew, Paul C., and Robert M. Kamins. 1959. "The Hawaiian Constitution: A Structure for Good Government." *American Bar Association Journal* 45:1145–1148, 1221–1222.

Barzel, Yoram. 2012. *A Theory of the State: Economic Rights, Legal Rights, and the Scope of the State.* 2nd ed. New York: Cambridge University Press.

Bates, Robert. 1983. *Essays on the Political Economy of Rural Africa.* Berkeley: University of California Press.

Bayman, James M., and Thomas S. Dye. 2013. *Hawaii's Past in a World of Pacific Islands.* Washington, D.C.: Society for American Archaeology.

Beaglehole, John C. 1968a. *The Journals of Captain Cook on his Voyages of Discovery, the Voyage of the Endeavor, 1768–1771.* Cambridge: Hakluyt Society.

———. 1968b. *The Journals of Captain James Cook on His Voyages of Discovery, the Voyage of the Resolution and Discovery, 1776–1780.* 2 vols. Cambridge: Hakluyt Society.

Beard, Charles A., and Mary R. Beard. 1927. *The Rise of American Civilization.* Vol. 2. New York: MacMillan Company.

Beechert, Edward D. 1985. *Working in Hawaii: A Labor History.* Honolulu: University of Hawai'i Press.

Bell, Adrian V., Thomas E. Currie, Geoffrey Irwin, and Christopher Bradbury. 2015. "Driving Factors in the Colonization of Oceania: Developing Island-Level Statistical Models to Test Competing Hypotheses." *American Antiquity* 80:397–407.

Bell, Roger. 1984. *Last among Equals: Hawaiian Statehood and American Politics.* Honolulu: University of Hawai'i Press.

Berkowitz, Daniel, and Karen Clay. 2006. "The Effect of Judicial Independence on Courts: Evidence from the American States." *Journal of Legal Studies* 35: 399–440.

Besley, Timothy, and Anne Case. 2003. "Political Institutions and Policy Choices: Evidence from the United States." *Journal of Economic Literature* 41:7–73.

Biraben, Jean Noël. 1979. "Essai sur l'évolution du nombres des hommes" [Essay on the growth of human population]. *Population* 34:13–25.

Blair, Roger D., and Arnold A. Heggstad. 1978. "The Prudent Man Rule and Preservation of Trust Principal." *University of Illinois Law Forum* 1978:79–101.

Blue, George V. 1924. "Early Relations between Hawaii and the Northwest Coast." In *Thirty-Third Annual Report of the Hawaiian Historical Society for the Year 1925,* 17–23. Honolulu: Paradise of the Pacific Press.

Bockstette, Valerie, Areendam Chanda, and Louis Putterman. 2002. "States and Markets: The Advantage of an Early Start." *Journal of Economic Growth* 7: 347–369.

Bogart, Dan, and Gary Richardson. 2009. "Making Property Productive: Reorganizing Rights to Real and Equitable Estates in Britain." *European Review of Economic History* 13:3–30.

———. 2011a. "Did the Glorious Revolution Contribute to the Transport Revolution? Evidence from Investment in Roads and Rivers." *Economic History Review* 64:1073–1112.

———. 2011b. "Property Rights and Parliament in Industrializing Britain." *Journal of Law and Economics* 54:241–274.

Boserup, Ester. 1965. *The Conditions of Agricultural Growth.* London: George Allen & Unwin.

———. 1981. *Population and Technological Change: A Study of Long-Term Trends.* Chicago: University of Chicago Press.

Bradley, Harold. 1942. *The American Frontier in Hawaii: The Pioneers, 1789–1843.* Palo Alto, Calif.: Stanford University Press.

Broadberry, Stephen N., Bruce M. S. Campbell, Alexander Klein, Mark Overton, and Bas van Leeuwen. 2015. *British Economic Growth, 1270–1870.* Cambridge: Cambridge University Press.

Broadberry, Stephen N., and Douglas A. Irwin. 2006. "Labor Productivity in the United States and the United Kingdom during the Nineteenth Century." *Explorations in Economic History* 43:257–279.

Brown, Henry A. 1879. *Revised Analyses of the Sugar Question.* Saxonville, Mass.

Bubb, Ryan. 2013. "The Evolution of Property Rights: State Law or Informal Norms?" *Journal of Law and Economics* 56:555–594.

Budnick, Rich. 1992. *Stolen Kingdom: An American Conspiracy.* Honolulu: Aloha Press.

Bureau of Public Instruction. 1891. *Report of the General Superintendent of the Census, 1890.* Honolulu: R. Grieve, Steam Book and Job Printer.

Bushnell, Andrew F. 1993. "The 'Horror' Reconsidered: An Evaluation of the Historical Evidence for Population Decline in Hawai'i, 1778–1803." *Pacific Studies* 16:115–161.

Cachola-Abad, Carolyn K. 1993. "Evaluating the Orthodox Dual Settlement Model for the Hawaiian Islands: An Analysis of Artefact Distribution and Hawaiian Oral Traditions." In *The Evolution and Organization of Prehistoric Society in Polynesia,* ed. Michael W. Graves and Roger Green, 13–32. Monograph 19. Auckland: New Zealand Archaeological Association.

Caldeira, Leah, Christina Hellmich, Adrienne L. Kaeppler, Betty Lou Kam, and Roger G. Rose. 2015. *Royal Hawaiian Featherwork: Nā Hulu Ali'i.* Honolulu and San Francisco: Fine Arts Museums of San Francisco in collaboration with the Bernice Pauahi Bishop Museum and University of Hawai'i Press.

Calhoun, Charles A. 1996. OFHEO House Price Indexes. HPI Technical Description. Washington, D.C.: Office of Federal Housing Enterprise Oversight.

Carlson, Leonard A. 1981a. *Indians, Bureaucrats and Land: The Dawes Act and the Decline of American Indian Farming.* Westport, Conn.: Greenwood Press.

———. 1981b. "Land Allotment and the Decline of American Indian Farming." *Explorations in Economic History* 18:128–154.

———. 2011. "Similar Societies, Different Solutions: United States Indian Policy in Light of Australian Policy towards Aboriginal Peoples." In *Economic Evolution and Revolutions in Context: Historical Approaches to Social Science*, ed. Paul W. Rhode, Joshua L. Rosenbloom, and David Weiman. Stanford, Calif.: Stanford University Press.

Carneiro. Robert L. 1970. "A Theory of the Origin of the State." *Science* 169 (3947): 733–738.

Carter, Susan B., Scott Sigmund Gartner, Michael R. Haines, Alan L. Olmstead, Richard Sutch, and Gavin Wright, eds. 2006. *Historical Statistics of the United States: From Earliest Times to the Present.* Millennial Edition. Vol. 1, *Population.* New York: Cambridge University Press.

Chambers, J. D. 1953. "Enclosure and Labour Supply in the Industrial Revolution." *Economic History Review*, 2nd ser., 5:319–343.

Cheung, Steven N. S. 1969. *The Theory of Share Tenancy, With Special Application to Asian Agriculture and the First Phase of Taiwan Land Reform.* Chicago: University of Chicago Press.

Childe, V. Gordon. 1936. *Man Makes Himself.* London: Watts.

Chinen, Jon J. 1958. *The Great Mahele: Hawaii's Land Division of 1848.* Honolulu: University of Hawai'i Press.

Christensen, Carl C., and Patrick V. Kirch. 1986. "Non-Marine Mollusks and Ecological Change at Barbers Point, O'ahu, Hawai'i." *Bishop Museum Occasional Papers* 26:52–80.

Ciccone, Antonio, and Robert Hall. 1996. "Productivity and the Density of Economic Activity." *American Economic Review* 86:54–70.

Clark, Geoffrey R., Christian Reepmeyer, Nivaleti Melekiola, Jon Woodhead, William R. Dickinson, and Helene Martinsson-Wallin. 2014. "Stone Tools from the Ancient Tongan State Reveal Prehistoric Interaction Centers in the Central Pacific." *Proceedings of the National Academy of Sciences* 111:10491–10496.

Clark, Gregory. 2010. "The Macroeconomic Aggregates for England, 1209–1869." *Research in Economic History* 27:51–140.

Coase, Ronald S. 1972. "Monopoly and Durability." *Journal of Law and Economics* 15:143–150.

Coelho, Philip. 1973. "The Profitability of Imperialism: The British Experience in the West Indies 1768–1772." *Explorations in Economic History* 10:253–280.

Coffman, Tom. 1998. *Nation Within: The Story of America's Annexation of the Nation of Hawaii.* Kaneohe, Hawaii: Epicenter.

———. 2003. *The Island Edge of America: A Political History of Hawaii.* Honolulu: University of Hawai'i Press.

Comin, Diego, William Easterly, and Erick Gong. 2010. "Was the Wealth of Nations Determined in 1000 BC?" *American Economic Journal: Macroeconomics* 2:65–97.

Cooper, George, and Gavan Daws. 1985. *Land and Power in Hawaii: The Democratic Years.* Honolulu: Benchmark Books.

Corden, W. M. 1984. "Booming Sector and Dutch Disease Economics: Survey and Consolidation." *Oxford Economic Papers* 36:359–380.

Cordy, Ross. 2003. "Who Made the Feather Cloaks in The Hawaiian Islands?" *Journal of the Polynesian Society* 112:157–162.

Cornell University, Roper Center. 2004–2012. *National Election Day Exit Polls.* Accessed June 15, 2013. https://ropercenter.cornell.edu/polls/us-elections/exit-polls/.

Curtin, Philip D. 1989. *Death by Migration: Europe's Encounter with the Tropical World in the Nineteenth Century.* New York: Cambridge University Press.

———. 1998. *Disease and Empire: The Health of European Troops in the Conquest of Africa.* New York: Cambridge University Press.

Darby, George, and Meheroo Jussawalla. 1993. "Why Hasn't the State Been Able to Attract High-Tech Companies?" In *The Price of Paradise*, vol. 2, ed. Randall W. Roth, 45–49. Honolulu: Mutual Publishing.

D'Arcy, Paul. 2014. "The Atlantic and Pacific Worlds." In *The Atlantic World*, ed. D'Maris Coffman, Adrian Leonard, and William O'Reilly. London: Routledge.

Davenport, W. 1969. "The 'Hawaiian Cultural Revolution': Some Political and Economic Considerations." *American Anthropologist* 71:1–20.

Davis, Lance, and Robert Huttenback. 1988. *Mammon and the Pursuit of Empire: The Political Economy of British Imperialism, 1860–1912.* New York: Cambridge University Press.

Davis, Morris A., and Jonathan Heathcote. 2005. "Housing and the Business Cycle." *International Economic Review* 46:751–784.

———. 2007. "The Price and Quantity of Residential Land in the United States." *Journal of Monetary Economics* 54:2595–2620.

Davis, Morris A., and Michael G. Palumbo. 2008. "The Price of Residential Land in Large US Cities." *Journal of Urban Economics* 63:352–384.

Daws, Gavan. 1968. *Shoal of Time: A History of the Hawaiian Islands.* Honolulu: University of Hawai'i Press.

De Freycinet, Louis Claude de Soulses. (1821) 1978. *Hawaii in 1819: A Narrative Account by Louis Claude de Soulses de Freycinet.* Trans. Ella Wiswell, ed. Marion Kelly. Pacific Anthropological Records, no. 26. Honolulu: Bernice P. Bishop Museum.

Demsetz, Harold. 1967. "Toward a Theory of Property Rights." *American Economic Review* 57:347–359.

De Varigny, Charles. 1981. *Fourteen Years in the Sandwich Islands: 1855–1868.* Trans. Alfons L. Korn. Honolulu: University Press of Hawai'i.

de Vries, Jan. 2008. *The Industrious Revolution.* New York: Cambridge University Press.

Diamond, Jared M. 1999. *Guns, Germs and Steel: The Fates of Human Societies.* New York: W. W. Norton.

Dibble, Sheldon. (1843) 1909. *A History of the Sandwich Islands.* Honolulu: T. G. Thrum.

Dittmar, Jeremiah E., and Ralf R. Meisenzahl. 2016. *State Capacity and Public Goods: Institutional Change, Human Capital, and Growth in Early Modern Germany.* Finance and Economics Discussion Series 2016-028. Washington, D.C.: Board of Governors of the Federal Reserve System.

Dougherty, Michael. 1994. *To Steal A Kingdom: Probing Hawaiian History.* Rev. ed. Waimanalo, Hawaii: Island Style Press.

Dove, John A. 2016. "Judicial Independence and Economic Freedom in the US States." *Applied Economic Letters* 23:78–83.

Dukas, Neil Bernard. 2004. *A Military History of Sovereign Hawai'i.* Honolulu: Mutual Publishing.

Dye, Alan, and Sumner La Croix. 2013. "The Political Economy of Land Privatization in Argentina and Australia, 1810–1850: A Puzzle." *Journal of Economic History* 73:901–936.

———. In press. "Institutions for the Taking: Property Rights and the Settlement of the Cape Colony, 1652–1750." *Economic History Review.*

Dye, Thomas S. 1994. "Population Trends in Hawaii before 1778." *Hawaiian Journal of History* 28:1–20.

———. 2011. "The Tempo of Change in the Leeward Kohala Field System, Hawai'i Island." *Rapa Nui Journal* 25:21–30.

Dye, Thomas S., and E. Komori. 1992. "Computer Programs for Creating Cumulative Probability Curves and Annual Frequency Distribution Diagrams with Radiocarbon Dates." *New Zealand Journal of Archaeology* 14:35–43.

Earle, Timothy. 1977. "A Reappraisal of Redistribution: Complex Hawaiian Chiefdoms." In *Exchange Systems in Pre-history*, ed. T. Earle and J. Ericson. New York: Academic Press, 213–232.

———. 1997. *How Chiefs Came to Power: The Political Economy in Prehistory.* Stanford, Calif.: Stanford University Press.

———. 2012. "Taro Irrigation and Primary State Formation in Hawai'i." In *Irrigated Taro (Colocasia esculenta) in the Indo-Pacific: Biological, Social and Historical Perspectives*, ed. M. Spriggs, D. Addison, and P. J. Matthews, 95–114. Senri Ethnological Studies 78. Osaka: National Museum of Ethnology.

Earle, Timothy, and David E. Doyel. 2008. "The Engineered Landscapes of Irrigation." In *Economies and the Transformation of Landscape*, ed. Lisa Cliggett and Christopher Pool, 19–46. Lanham, Md.: Altamira Press.

Easterly, William, and Ross Levine. 2016. "The European Origins of Economic Growth." *Journal of Economic Growth* 21:225–257.

Economics Research Associates. 1969. *Hawaii Land Study, Study of Land Tenure, Land Cost, and Future Land Use in Hawaii.* Los Angeles: Economics Research Associates.

Ellis, William. (1827) 1963. *Journal of William Ellis.* Honolulu: Advertiser Publishing Co.

———. 1831. *Polynesian Researches.* Vol. 4. London: Fisher, Son, & Jackson.

Engerman, Stanley L. 1992. "Coerced and Free Labor: Property Rights and the Development of the Labor Force." *Explorations in Economic History* 29:1–29.

Engerman, Stanley L., and Kenneth L. Sokoloff. 1997. "Factor Endowments, Institutions, and Differential Paths of Growth among New World Economies: A View from Economic Historians of the United States." In *How Latin America Fell Behind: Essays on the Economic Histories of Brazil and Mexico, 1800–1914*, ed. Stephen Haber, 260–304. Stanford, Calif.: Stanford University Press.

———. 2002. "Factor Endowments, Inequality, and Paths of Development among New World Economies." National Bureau of Economic Research Working Paper no. 9259.

Englebert, Pierre. 2000. *State Legitimacy and Development in Africa.* Boulder, Colo.: Lynne Riener.

Epstein, Richard. 1985. *Takings: Private Property and the Power of Eminent Domain.* Cambridge, Mass.: Harvard University Press.

———. 2009. "Public Use in a Post-Kelo World." *Supreme Court Economic Review* 17:151–171.

Ertan, Arhan, Martin Fiszbain, and Louis Putterman. 2016. "Who Was Colonized and When? A Cross-Country Analysis of Determinants." *European Economic Review* 83:165–184.

Federal-State Task Force on the Hawaiian Homes Commission Act. 1983. *Report to United States Secretary of the Interior and the Governor of the State of Hawaii.* Honolulu: State of Hawaiʻi.

Feeny, David. 1982. *The Political Economy of Productivity: Thai Agricultural Development, 1880–1975.* Vancouver: University of British Columbia Press.

———. 1988. "The Development of Property Rights in Land: A Comparative Study." In *Toward a Political Economy of Development*, ed. Robert H. Bates. Berkeley: University of California Press.

Feld, Lars P., and Stefan Voight. 2003. "Economic Growth and Judicial Independence: Cross-Country Evidence Using a New Set of Indicators." *European Journal of Political Economy* 19:497–527.

Fenske, James. 2014. "Ecology, Trade and States in Pre-colonial Africa." *Journal of the European Economic Association* 12:612–640.

Feyrer, James, and Bruce Sacerdote. 2009. "Colonialism and Modern Income Growth: Islands and Natural Experiments." *Review of Economics & Statistics* 91:245–262.

Finney, Ben R. 1985. "Anomalous Westerlies, El Niño and the Colonization of Polynesia." *American Anthropologist* 87:9–26.

———. 1994. *Voyage of Rediscovery.* Berkeley: University of California Press.

———. 2003. *Sailing in the Wake of the Ancestors: Reviving Polynesian Voyaging.* Honolulu: Bishop Museum Press.

Fischel, William A. 1980. "Zoning and the Exercise of Monopoly Power: A Reevaluation." *Journal of Urban Economics* 8:283–293.

————. 1981. "Is Local Government Structure in Large Urbanized Areas Monopolistic or Competitive?" *National Tax Journal* 34:95–104.

————. 1985. *The Economics of Zoning Law*. Baltimore: Johns Hopkins University Press.

Fleck, Robert K., and F. Andrew Hanssen. 2010. "Repeated Adjustment of Delegated Powers and the History of Eminent Domain." *International Review of Law & Economics* 30:99–112.

Fontenoy, Paul E. 1997. "Ginseng, Otter Skins, and Sandalwood: The Conundrum of the China Trade." *Northern Mariner* 7:1–16.

Fornander, Abraham. (1878–1885) 1969. *An Account of the Polynesian Race: Its Origins, and Migrations, and the Ancient History of the Hawaiian People to the Times of Kamehameha*. 3 vols. Rutland, Vt.: Tuttle.

Freund, Caroline, and Emanuel Ornelas. 2010. "Regional Trade Agreements." *Annual Review of Economics* 2:139–166.

Friedman, Lawrence M. 1964. "The Dynastic Trust." *Yale Law Journal* 73:547–592.

Fry, Maxwell J., and James Mak. 1984. "Is Land Leasing a Solution to Unaffordable Housing? An Answer from Fee Simple versus Leasehold Property Price Differentials in Hawaii." *Economic Inquiry* 22:529–549.

Fuchs, Lawrence H. 1961. *Hawaii Pono: A Social History*. New York: Harcourt, Brace & World, Inc.

Galloway, J. H. 1989. *The Sugar Cane Industry: An Historical Geography from Its Origins to 1914*. Cambridge: Cambridge University Press.

Gennaioli, Nicola, and Ilia Rainer. 2007. "The Modern Impact of Precolonial Centralization in Africa." *Journal of Economic Growth* 12:185–234.

Gibson, James R. 1992. *Otter Skins, Boston Ships, and China Goods: The Maritime Fur Trade of the Northwest Coast, 1785–1841*. Seattle: University of Washington Press.

Glaeser, Edward L., Rafael La Porta, Florencio Lopez-de-Silanes, and Andrei Shleifer. 2004. "Do Institutions Cause Growth?" *Journal of Economic Growth* 9:271–303.

Glick, Clarence E. 1980. *Sojourners and Settlers: Chinese Migrants in Hawaii*. Honolulu: University of Hawai'i Press.

Goodwin, Ian D., Stuart A. Browning, and Atholl J. Anderson. 2014. "Climate Windows for Polynesian Voyaging to New Zealand and Easter Island." *Proceedings of the National Academy of Sciences* 111:14716–14721.

Government of Australia, Australian Bureau of Statistics. 2014. *Australian Historical Population Statistics, 2014*. Accessed December 15, 2017. http://www.abs.gov.au/ausstats/abs.nsf/mf/3105.0.65.001.

Government of Canada. 2017. *Statistics Canada*. Population and Growth Components (1851–2001 Censuses). Accessed December 15, 2017. http://www.statcan.gc.ca.

Grier, Robin M. 1999. "Colonial Legacies and Economic Growth." *Public Choice* 98:317–335.

Grossman, Gene M., and Elhanan Helpman. 1995. "Trade Wars and Trade Talks." *Journal of Political Economy* 103:675–709.

Guriev, Sergei, and Konstantin Sonin. 2009. "Dictators and Oligarchs: A Dynamic Theory of Contested Property Rights." *Journal of Public Economics* 93:1–13.

Gützlaff, Karl. 1834. *A Sketch of Chinese History, Ancient and Modern.* Vol. 2. London: Smith, Elder and Co.

Gyourko, Joseph, Albert Saiz, and Anita Summers. 2008. "A New Measure of the Local Regulatory Environment for Housing Markets: The Wharton Residential Land Use Regulatory Index." *Urban Studies* 45:693–729.

Hamilton, B. W. 1978. "Zoning and the Exercise of Monopoly Power." *Journal of Urban Economics* 5:116–130.

Handy, E. S. Craighill, and Elizabeth Green Handy, with the collaboration of Mary Kawena Pukui. 1991. *Native Planters in Old Hawaii: Their Life, Lore, and Environment.* Rev. ed. Bernice P. Bishop Museum Bulletin 233. Honolulu: Bishop Museum Press.

Hatton, Timothy J., and Jeffrey G. Williamson. 1991. "Integrated and Segmented Labor Markets: Thinking in Two Sectors." *Journal of Economic History* 51:413–425.

Hawai'i, Department of Finance. 1847–1880. *Report of the Minister of Finance.* Honolulu.

Hawai'i, Department of Foreign Affairs. 1845–1900. *Reports of the Minister of Foreign Affairs.* Honolulu.

Hawaii, Department of the Interior. 1847–1870. *Report of the Minister of the Interior.* Honolulu.

Hawaiian Historical Society. 1958. "The Turrill Collection, 1845–1860." In *Sixty-Sixth Annual Report of the Hawaiian Historical Society for the Year 1957,* 27–92. Honolulu: Advertiser Publishing Co., Ltd.

Higgs, Robert. 1987. *Crisis and Leviathan.* New York: Oxford University Press.

Hitch, Thomas Kemper. 1992. *Islands in Transition: The Past, Present, and Future of Hawaii's Economy.* Honolulu: First Hawaiian Bank.

Hoffman, Philip T. 2000. *Growth in a Traditional Society: The French Countryside, 1450–1815.* Princeton, N.J.: Princeton University Press.

———. 2012. "Why Was It Europeans Who Conquered the World." *Journal of Economic History* 72:601–633.

———. 2015. *Why Did Europe Conquer the World?* Princeton, N.J.: Princeton University Press.

Hommon, Robert J. 2013. *The Ancient Hawaiian State: Origins of a Political Society.* New York: Oxford University Press.

Honolulu City Council. 2017a. Revised Ordinances of Honolulu. Chap. 21, Land Use Ordinance. Honolulu: City Clerk.

———. 2017b. Revised Ordinances of Honolulu. Chap. 24, Development Plans. Honolulu: City Clerk.

———. 2017c. Revised Ordinances of Honolulu. Chap. 25, Special Management Area. Honolulu: City Clerk.

Horne, Gerald. 2011. *Fighting in Paradise: Labor Unions, Racism, and Communists in the Making of Modern Hawaii.* Honolulu: University of Hawai'i Press.

Horowitz, Robert H., and Judith B. Finn. 1967. *Public Land Policy in Hawaii: Major Landowners.* Report no. 3. Honolulu: Legislative Reference Bureau.

Horowitz, Robert H., and Norman Meller. 1966. *Land and Politics in Hawaii.* 3rd ed. Honolulu: University of Hawai'i Press.

Horrocks, Mark, and Robert B. Rechtman. 2009. "Sweet Potato (*Ipomoea batatas*) and Banana (*Musa* sp.) Microfossils in Deposits from the Kona Field System, Island of Hawaii." *Journal of Archaeological Science* 36:1115–1126.

Howe, K. R., ed. 2006. *Vaka Moana: Voyages of the Ancestors, The Discovery and Settlement of the Pacific.* Honolulu: University of Hawai'i Press.

Hu-Dehart, Evelyn. 1993. "Chinese Coolie Labour in Cuba in the Nineteenth Century: Free Labour or Neo-Slavery?" *Slavery and Abolition* 14:67–86.

Hung, Fred C., and Vernon A. Mund. 1961. *Interlocking Relationships in Hawaii and Public Regulation of Ocean Transportation.* Honolulu: University of Hawai'i Economic Research Center.

Hunt, Terry L., and Carl P. Lipo. 2006. "Late Colonization of Easter Island." *Science* 311:1603–1606.

———. 2011. *The Statues That Walked: Unraveling the Mystery of Easter Island.* New York: Simon and Schuster.

———. 2017. "The Last Great Migration: Colonization of the Remote Pacific Island." In *Human Dispersal and Species Movement,* ed. Nicole Boivin, Rémy Crassard, and Michael Petraglia. New York: Cambridge University Press.

Hunter, Charles. 1959. "Congress and Statehood for Hawaii." *World Affairs Quarterly* 29:354–378.

'Ī'ī, John Papa. 1959. *Fragments of Hawaiian History.* Honolulu: Bishop Museum Press.

Iaukea, C. P. 1894. *Biennial Report of the Commissioners of Crown Lands 1894.* Honolulu: Hawaiian Gazette Company.

Ichioka, Yuji. 1988. *The Issei: The World of the First Generation Japanese Immigrants, 1885–1924.* New York: Free Press.

Irwin, Geoffrey. 1992. *The Prehistoric Exploration and Colonisation of the Pacific.* Cambridge: Cambridge University Press.

Irwin, Geoffrey, S. Bickler, and P. Quirke. 1990. "Voyaging by Canoe and Computer: Experiments in the Settlement of the Pacific Ocean." *Antiquity* 64:34–50.

Irwin, Geoffrey, and Richard G. J. Flay. 2015. "Pacific Colonisation and Canoe Performance: Experiments in the Science of Sailing." *Journal of the Polynesian Society* 124:419–443.

Joesting, Edward. 1984. *Kauai: The Separate Kingdom.* Honolulu: University of Hawai'i Press and Kauai Museum Association, Limited.

Jóhannesson, Jón. (1974) 2006. *A History of the Old Icelandic Commonwealth: Islendinga Saga.* Trans. Heraldar Bessason. Winnipeg: University of Manitoba Press.

John Child and Co., Inc. 1980–1981. *Appraisal Report Covering Leased Fee Interests of the Single-Family Residential Parcels Designated as the Lunalilo Park Tract.* Vol. 2. Honolulu.

Jorgenson, Dale W. 1967. "Surplus Agricultural Labour and the Development of a Dual Economy." *Oxford Economic Papers* 19:288–312.

Judd, Lawrence M. 1971. *Lawrence M. Judd and Hawaii: An Autobiography.* Rutland, Vt.: Charles E. Tuttle.

Kaiser, Brooks A. 2014. "Watershed Conservation in the Long Run." *Ecosystems* 17:698–719.

Kaiser, Brooks A., and James Roumasset. 2014. "Transitional Forces in a Resource-Based Economy: Phases of Economic and Institutional Development in Hawaii." *Review of Economics and Institutions* 5:1–44.

Kamakau, Samuel Mānaiakalani. 1991. *Tales and Traditions of the People of Old* [Nā Moʻoelo a ka Poʻe Kahiko]. Trans. Mary Kawena Pukui, ed. Dorothy B. Barrère. Honolulu: Bishop Museum Press.

———. (1961) 1992. *Ruling Chiefs of Hawaii.* Rev. ed. Translated by Mary Kawena Pukui, Thomas G. Thrum, Lahilahi Webb, Davidson Taylor, and John Wise. Honolulu: Kamehameha Schools Press.

Kameʻeleihiwa, Lilikalā K. 1992. *Native Land and Foreign Desires: Pehea Lā E Pono Ai?* Honolulu: Bishop Museum Press.

Kanahele, George. 1986. *Ku Kanaka: Stand Tall, A Search for Hawaiian Values.* Honolulu: University of Hawaiʻi Press.

Kato, Andrew, Sumner La Croix, and James Mak. 2009. "Small State, Giant Tax Credits: Hawaii's Leap into High Technology Development." *State Tax Notes,* November 30, 2009, 641–652.

Kato, Andrew, and James Mak. 2013. "Technical Progress in Transport and the Tourism Area Life Cycle." In *Handbook of Tourism Economics, Analysis, New Applications and Case Studies,* ed. Clement A. Tisdell, 225–255. London: World Scientific Publishing Company.

Kemp, Murray C. 1969. *A Contribution to the General Equilibrium Theory of Preferential Trading.* Amsterdam: North Holland.

Kennan, John, and Raymond Riezman. 1988. "Do Big Countries Win Tariff Wars?" *International Economic Review* 29:81–85.

Kent, Noel J. (1983) 2016. *Hawaii: Islands under the Influence.* Honolulu: University of Hawaiʻi Press (New York: Monthly Review Press).

Kinevan, Marcos E. 1950. "Alaska and Hawaii: From Territoriality to Statehood." *California Law Review* 38:273–292.

King, Samuel P., and Randall W. Roth. 2006. *Broken Trust: Greed, Mismanagement & Political Manipulation at America's Largest Charitable Trust.* Honolulu: University of Hawaiʻi Press.

Kirch, Patrick V. 1985. *Feathered Gods and Fishhooks: An Introduction to Hawaiian Archaeology and Prehistory.* Honolulu: University of Hawai'i Press.

———. 1990. "Monumental Architecture and Power in Polynesian Chiefdoms: A Comparison of Tonga and Hawaii." *World Archaeology* 22:206–222.

———. 1992. *The Archaeology of History.* Vol. 2 of Patrick V. Kirch and Marshall Sahlins, *Anahulu: The Anthropology of History in the Kingdom of Hawaii.* Chicago: University of Chicago Press.

———. 1994. *The Wet and the Dry: Irrigation and Agricultural Intensification in Polynesia.* Chicago: University of Chicago Press.

———. 2007a. "Hawai'i as a Model System for Human Ecodynamics." *American Anthropologist* 109:8–26.

———. 2007b. "'Like Shoals of Fish': Archaeology and Population in Pre-Contact Hawai'i." In *The Growth and Collapse of Pacific Island Societies: Archaeological and Demographic Perspectives*, ed. Patrick V. Kirch and Jean-Louis Rallu. Honolulu: University of Hawai'i Press.

———. 2010. *How Chiefs Became Kings: Divine Kingship and the Rise of Archaic States in Ancient Hawai'i.* Berkeley: University of California Press.

———. 2011. "When Did the Polynesians Settle Hawai'i? A Review of 150 Years of Scholarly Inquiry and a Tentative Answer." *Hawaiian Archaeology* 12:3–26.

———. 2012. *A Shark Going Inland Is My Chief: The Island Civilization of Ancient Hawai'i.* Berkeley: University of California Press.

———. 2014. *Kua'āina Kahiko: Life and Land in Ancient Kahikinui, Maui.* Honolulu: University of Hawai'i Press.

Kirch, Patrick V., Peter R. Mills, Steven P. Lundblad, John Sinton, and Jennifer G. Kahn. 2012. "Interpolity Exchange of Basalt Tools Facilitated via Elite Control in Hawaiian Archaic States." *Proceedings of the National Academy of Sciences* 109:1056–1061.

Kolb, Michael. J. 1994. "Monumentality and the Rise of Religious Authority in Precontact Hawai'i." *Current Anthropology* 34:521–547.

———. 2006. "The Origins of Monumental Architecture in Ancient Hawai'i." *Current Anthropology* 47:657–665.

Kolb, Michael, and Boyd Dixon. 2002. "Landscapes of War: Rules and Conventions of Conflict in Ancient Hawai'i (And Elsewhere)." *American Antiquity* 67:514–534.

Kuykendall, Ralph S. 1938. *The Hawaiian Kingdom, 1778–1854.* Vol. 1, *Foundation and Transformation.* Honolulu: University of Hawai'i Press.

———. 1953. *The Hawaiian Kingdom, 1854–1874.* Vol. 2, *Twenty Critical Years.* Honolulu: University of Hawai'i Press.

———. 1967. *The Hawaiian Kingdom, 1874–1893.* Vol. 3, *The Kalakaua Dynasty.* Honolulu: University of Hawai'i Press.

Kyselka, Will. 1993. "On the Rising of the Pleiades." *Hawaiian Journal of History* 27:173–183.

La Croix, Sumner J. 1992. "Property Rights and Institutional Change during Australia's Gold Rush." *Explorations in Economic History* 29:204–227.

———. 2004. "Explaining Divergence in Property Rights: Fiji and Hawai'i in the Nineteenth Century." In *Land Rights, Ethno-nationality, and Sovereignty in History*, ed. Stanley L. Engerman and Jacob Metzger. London: Routledge.

———. 2013. "A Theoretical and Empirical Model of the Hawaiian Homes Commission, 1921–2010." Presented at the 2013 Annual Meetings of the Social Science History Association, December 3, 2013.

———. 2015. "Land Confiscations and Land Reform in Natural Order States." In *Resources, Development and Public Policy: Concepts, Practice and Challenges*, ed. Arsenio Balisacan, Ujjayant Chakravorty, and Majah-Leah Ravago. Amsterdam: Elsevier.

———. 2016. "New Perspectives on Land and Housing Markets in Hawaii." UHERO Working Paper, University of Hawaii, January 2016.

La Croix, Sumner J., and Price Fishback. 1989. "Firm-Specific Evidence on Racial Wage Differentials and Workforce Segregation in Hawaii's Sugar Industry." *Explorations in Economic History* 26:403–423.

———. 2000. "Migration, Labor Market Dynamics, and Wage Differentials in Hawaii's Sugar Industry." *Advances in Agricultural Economic History* 1:31–72.

La Croix, Sumner, and Christopher Grandy. 1997. "The Political Instability of Reciprocal Trade and the Overthrow of the Hawaiian Kingdom." *Journal of Economic History* 57:161–189.

La Croix, Sumner J., James Mak, and Michael Sklarz. 1989. "The Impact of Reversionary Rules on Land Use in Hawaii: A Property Rights Perspective." Working Paper no. 89-5, Department of Economics, University of Hawaii.

La Croix, Sumner J., and Louis A. Rose. 1993. "Inalienability, Rehabilitation, and Interest Group Politics: An Economic Analysis of the Origins of the Hawaiian Homes Program." Working Paper no. 93-29, Department of Economics, University of Hawaii.

———. 1998. "The Political Economy of the Hawaiian Home Lands Program." In *The Other Side of the Frontier: Economic Explorations into Native American History*, ed. Linda Barrington. Boulder, Colo.: Westview.

La Croix, Sumner J., and James Roumasset. 1984. "An Economic Theory of Political Change in Pre-missionary Hawaii." *Explorations in Economic History* 21:151–168.

———. 1990. "The Evolution of Property Rights in Nineteenth-Century Hawaii." *Journal of Economic History* 50:829–852.

Ladefoged, Thegn N., and Michael W. Graves. 2007. "Modeling Agricultural Development and Demography in Kohala, Hawai'i." In *The Growth, Regulation, and Collapse of Island Societies*, ed. Patrick V. Kirch and J. Rallu, 70–89. Honolulu: University of Hawai'i Press.

———. 2008. "Variable Development of Dryland Agriculture in Hawai'i: A Fine-

Grained Chronology from the Kohala Field System, Hawai'i Island." *Current Anthropology* 49:771–802.

Ladefoged, Thegn N., Michael W. Graves, and J. H. Coil. 2005. "The Introduction of Sweet Potato in Polynesia: Early Remains in Hawai'i." *Journal of the Polynesian Society* 114:359–373.

Ladefoged, Thegn N., Michael W. Graves, and Mark D. McCoy. 2003. "Archaeological Evidence for Agricultural Development in Kohala, Island of Hawai'i." *Journal of Archaeological Science* 30:923–940.

Ladefoged, Thegn N., Patrick V. Kirch, S. M. Gon, III, O. A. Chadwick, A. S. Hartshorn, and P. M. Vitousek. 2009. "Opportunities and Constraints for Intensive Agriculture in the Hawaiian Archipelago Prior to European Contact." *Journal of Archaeological Science* 36:2374–2383.

Ladefoged, Thegn N., C. Lee, and Michael W. Graves. 2008. "Modeling Life Expectancy and Surplus Production of Dynamic Pre-contact Territories in Leeward Kohala, Hawai'i." *Journal of Anthropological Archaeology* 27:93–110.

Ladefoged, Thegn N., Mark D. McCoy, Gregory P. Asner, Patrick V. Kirch, Cedric O. Puleston, Oliver A. Chadwick, and Peter M. Vitousek. 2011. "Agricultural Potential and Actualized Development in Hawai'i: An Airborne LiDAR Survey of the Leeward Kohala Field System (Hawai'i Island)." *Journal of Archaeological Science* 38:3605–3619.

Lamoreaux, Naomi R. 2011. "The Mystery of Property Rights: A U.S. Perspective." *Journal of Economic History* 71:275–306.

Laughlin, J. Laurence, and H. Parker Willis. 1903. *Reciprocity.* New York: Baker & Taylor.

Lee, Ann Feder. 2011. *The Hawai'i State Constitution.* Rev. ed. New York: Oxford University Press.

Levison, Michael, R. Gerald Ward, and John W. Webb. 1973. *The Settlement of Polynesia: A Computer Simulation.* Minneapolis: University of Minnesota Press.

Libecap, Gary D. 1978. *The Evolution of Private Mineral Rights: Nevada's Comstock Lode.* New York: Arno Press.

———. 1994. *Contracting for Property Rights.* New York: Cambridge University Press.

Libecap, Gary D., and Dean Lueck. 2011. "Land Demarcation and the Role of Coordinating Property Institutions." *Journal of Political Economy* 119:426–467.

Lili'uokalani, Lydia. (1898) 1990. *Hawaii's Story by Hawaii's Queen.* Reprint. Honolulu: Mutual Publishing.

Lind, Andrew W. 1938. *An Island Community: Ecological Succession in Hawaii.* Chicago: University of Chicago Press.

Linnekin, Jocelyn. 1988. "Who Made the Feather Cloaks? A Problem in Hawaiian Gender Relations." *Journal of the Polynesian Society* 97:265–280.

————. 1990. *Sacred Queens and Women of Consequence: Rank, Gender, and Colonialism in the Hawaiian Islands.* Ann Arbor: University of Michigan Press.

Liou, Wayne. 2015. "Three Essays on Policies Affecting Migrants." PhD diss., University of Hawai'i-Mānoa.

Livi-Bacci, Massimo. 2012. *A Concise History of World Population.* Malden, Mass.: Wiley-Blackwell.

Locations, Inc. 1992. *Study of the Resale of Leasehold Properties Converted to Fee Simple Ownership under the Hawaii Land Reform Act of 1967, A Report to the Governor and the Legislature of the State of Hawaii.* Honolulu: Auditor, State of Hawaii.

Lowrie, S. Gale. 1951. "Hawaii Drafts a Constitution." *University of Cincinnati Law Review* 20:215–238.

Lueck, Dean. 1995. "The Rule of First Possession and the Design of the Law." *Journal of Law and Economics* 38:393–436.

Lyons, Curtis. 1889/1890. "Forty Years Ago." Typescript. Hawaiian Mission Children's Society Library.

MacLennan, Carol A. 2014. *Sovereign Sugar: Industry and Environment in Hawai'i.* Honolulu: University of Hawai'i Press.

Mak, James. 2008. *Developing a Dream Destination: Tourism and Tourism Policy Planning in Hawai'i.* Honolulu: University of Hawai'i Press.

Malo, David. 1951. *Hawaiian Antiquities* (*Moolelo Hawai'i*). Bernice P. Bishop Museum Special Publication 2. 2nd ed. Trans. Nathaniel B. Emerson. Honolulu: Bishop Museum Press.

Malo, Davida. 2006. *Ka Moolelo Hawai'i* [*Hawaiian Traditions*]. Trans. Malcolm Nāea Chun. Honolulu: First People's Productions.

Mann, Charles C. 2011. *1493: Uncovering the New World Columbus Created.* New York: Alfred A. Knopf.

Mason, Andrew, and Ronald Lee. 2007. "Transfers, Capital, and Consumption over the Demographic Transition." In *Population Aging, Intergenerational Transfers and the Macroeconomy*, ed. Robert L. Clark, Andrew Mason, and Naohiro Ogawa, 128–162. Northampton, Mass.: Elgar Press.

Mathison, Gilbert Farquhar. 1825. *Narrative of a Visit to Brazil, Chile, Peru, and the Sandwich Islands during the Years 1821 and 1822.* London: Charles Knight.

Matisso-Smith, E., R. M. Roberts, G. J. Irwin, J. S. Allen, D. Penny, and D. M. Lambert. 1998. "Patterns of Pre-historic Human Mobility in Polynesia Indicated by mtDNA from the Pacific Rat." *Proceedings of the National Academy of Sciences* 95:15145–15150.

Mauer, Noel. 2011. *The Empire Trap: The Rise and Fall of U.S. Intervention to Protect American Property Overseas, 1893–2013.* Princeton, N.J.: Princeton University Press.

Mayer, Wolfgang. 1981. "Theoretical Considerations on Negotiated Tariff Adjustments." *Oxford Economic Papers* 33:135–153.

McCoy, Mark D. 2005. "The Development of the Kalaupapa Field System, Moloka'i Island, Hawai'i." *Journal of the Polynesian Society* 114:339–358.

McCoy, Mark D., Anna T. Browne Ribeiro, Michael W. Graves, Oliver A. Chadwick, and Peter M. Vitousek. 2013. "Irrigated Taro (*Colocasia esculenta*) Farming in North Kohala, Hawai'i: Sedimentology and Soil Nutrient Analyses." *Journal of Archaeological Science* 40:1528–1538.

McCoy, Mark D., and Michael W. Graves. 2010. "The Role of Agricultural Innovation in Pacific Islands: A Case Study from Hawai'i Island." *World Archaeology* 42:90–107.

McCoy, Mark D., P. R. Mills, S. Lundblad, Timothy Rieth, J. G. Kahn, and R. Gard. 2011. "A Cost Surface Model of Volcanic Glass Quarrying and Exchange in Hawai'i." *Journal of Archaeological Science* 38:2547–2560.

McDonald, Forrest. 1985. *Novus Ordo Seclorum: The Intellectual Origins of the Constitution.* Lawrence: University Press of Kansas.

McDonald, Ian J. 1969. "The Leasehold System: Towards a Balanced Land Tenure for Urban Development." *Urban Studies* 6:179–195.

McGregor, Davianna Pōmaika'i. 1990. "'Āina Ho'opulapula: Hawaiian Homesteading." *Hawaiian Journal of History* 24:1–38.

McLaren, John. 1997. "Size, Sunk Costs, and Judge Bowker's Objection to Free Trade." *American Economic Review* 87:400–420.

Melendy, H. Brent, assisted by Rhoda Armstrong Hackler. 1999. *Hawaii, America's Sugar Territory, 1898–1959.* Lewiston, N.Y.: Edwin Mellen Press.

Meller, Norman. 1958. "Centralization in Hawaii: Retrospect and Prospect." *American Political Science Review* 52:98–107.

———. 1971. *With an Understanding Heart: Constitution Making in Hawaii.* State Constitutional Convention Studies no. 5. New York: National Municipal League.

Merlin, Mark, and Dan Van Ravenswaay. 1990. *The History of Human Impact on the Genus* Santalum *in Hawai'i.* USDA Forest Service General Technical Report. PSW-122, 46–60.

Merrill, Thomas W. 1986. "The Economics of Public Use." *Cornell Law Review* 72:61–116.

Michaely, Michael. 1998. "Partners to a Preferential Trade Agreement: Implications of Varying Size." *Journal of International Economics* 46:73–85.

Michalopoulos, Stelios, and Elias Papaioannou. 2010. "Divide and Rule or the Rule of the Divided: Evidence from Africa." National Bureau of Economic Research Working Paper 17184 and Centre for Economic Policy Research Discussion Paper 8088.

———. 2013. "Pre-colonial Ethnic Institutions and Contemporary African Development." *Econometrica* 81:113–152.

———. 2015. "On the Ethnic Origins of African Development: Chiefs and Precolonial Political Centralization." *Academy of Management Perspectives* 29:32–71.

Midkiff, F. 1961. *The Origin, Objectives, and Development of the Bernice Pauahi Bishop Estate.* Honolulu: The Bernice Pauahi Bishop Estate.

Miller, C. D. 1927. "Food Values of Poi, Taro, and Limu." *Bishop Museum Bulletin* 37:1–25.

Mills, Peter R. 2002. *Hawai'i's Russian Adventure: A New Look at Old History.* Honolulu: University of Hawai'i Press.

Mitrano, Thomas J. 2004. *Honolulu City Council Leasehold Conversion Task Group: Facilitator's Report.* Honolulu: City and County of Honolulu, April 2, 2004.

Moffat, Riley M., and Gary L. Fitzpatrick. 1995. *Surveying the Māhele: Mapping the Hawaiian Land Revolution.* Honolulu: Editions Limited.

Mollett, J. A. 1961. "Capital in Hawaiian Sugar, Its Formation and Relation to Labor and Output, 1870–1957." *Agricultural Economics Bulletin* 21:9–61.

Montenegro, Alvaro, Richard T. Callaghan, and Scott M. Fitzpatrick. 2014. "From West to East: Environmental Influences on the Rate and Pathways of Polynesian Colonization." *Holocene* 24:242–256.

Morgan, Theodore. 1948. *Hawaii, a Century of Economic Change: 1778–1876.* Cambridge, Mass.: Harvard University Press.

Morgan, William Michael. 2011. *Pacific Gibraltar: U.S.-Japanese Rivalry Over the Annexation of Hawaii, 1885–1898.* Annapolis, Md.: Naval Institute Press.

Moriyama, Alan T. 1985. *Imingaisha: Japanese Emigration Companies and Hawaii 1894–1908.* Honolulu: University of Hawai'i Press.

Morrison, Susan Keyes. 2003. *Kamehameha: The Warrior King of Hawaii.* Honolulu: University of Hawai'i Press.

National Association of Realtors. 2017. "Metropolitan Median Area Prices and Affordability." Accessed December 17, 2017. https://www.nar.realtor/research-and-statistics/housing-statistics.

Nogelmeier, M. Puakea. 2010. *Mai Pa'a I Ka Leo: Historical Voice in Hawaiian Primary Materials, Looking Forward and Looking Back.* Honolulu: Bishop Museum Press.

Nordyke, Eleanor. 1989. *The Peopling of Hawaii.* 2nd ed. Honolulu: East-West Center.

North, Douglass C. 1981. *Structure and Change in Economic History.* New York: W. W. Norton.

North, Douglass C., William Summerhill, and Barry R. Weingast. 2000. "Order, Disorder and Economic Change: Latin America vs. North America." In *Governing for Prosperity*, ed. Bruce Bueno de Mesquita and Hilton Root. New Haven, Conn.: Yale University Press.

North, Douglass C., and Robert Paul Thomas. 1971. "The Rise and Fall of the Manorial System: A Theoretical Model." *Journal of Economic History* 31:777–803.

———. 1973. *The Rise of the Western World: A New Economic History.* New York: Cambridge University Press.

North, Douglass C., John Joseph Wallis, Steven B. Webb, and Barry R. Weingast, eds. 2012. *In the Shadow of Violence.* New York: Cambridge University Press.

North, Douglass C., John Joseph Wallis, and Barry R. Weingast. 2009. *Violence and Social Orders: A Conceptual Framework for Interpreting Recorded Human History.* New York: Cambridge University Press.

Nunn, Nathan. 2008. "The Long-Term Effects of Africa's Slave Trades." *Quarterly Journal of Economics* 123:139–176.

Office of Elections, State of Hawai'i. 2013. *Fact Sheet: Election Registration and Turnout Statistics.* Honolulu: Office of Elections.

Office of Hawaiian Affairs, Research Division. 2014. "Income Inequality and Native Hawaiian Communities in the Wake of the Great Recession: 2005 to 2013." *Ho'okahua Waiwai* [Economic Self-Sufficiency] *Fact Sheet* 2014(2): 1–12.

Office of Treaty Settlements, New Zealand Department of Justice. 2017. *Year-to-Date Progress Report 1 July 2017–30 September 2017.* Accessed January 3, 2018. http://www.govt.nz/organisations/office-of-treaty-settlements.

Ogilvie, Sheilagh. 2010. "Consumption, Social Capital, and the 'Industrious Revolution' in Early Modern Germany." *Journal of Economic History* 70:287–325.

Olson, Mancur. 1993. "Dictatorship, Democracy, and Development." *American Political Science Review* 87:567–576.

Olsson, Ola. 2009. "On the Democratic Legacy of Colonialism." *Journal of Comparative Economics* 37:534–551.

Osorio, Jonathan Kay Kamakawiwo'ole. 2002. *Dismembering Lāhui: A History of the Hawaiian Nation to 1887.* Honolulu: University of Hawai'i Press.

Page, R. I. 1995. *Chronicles of the Vikings: Records, Memorials and Myths.* London: British Museum Press.

Panagariya, Arvind. 2000. "Preferential Trade Liberalization: The Traditional Theory and New Developments." *Journal of Economic Literature* 38:287–331.

Parker, Linda S. 1989. *Native American Estate: The Struggle over Indian and Hawaiian Lands.* Honolulu: University of Hawai'i Press.

Patterson, G. D. 1968. *The Tariff in the Australian Colonies, 1856–1900.* Melbourne: F. W. Cheshire.

Patterson, Wayne. 1988. *The Korean Frontier in America: Immigration to Hawaii, 1896–1910.* Honolulu: University of Hawai'i Press.

Persson, Torsten, and Guido Tabellini. 2008. "The Growth Effect of Democracy: Is It Heterogeneous and Can It Be Estimated?" In *Institutions and Economic Performance,* ed. Elhanan Helpman, 544–585. Boston: Harvard University Press.

Pierce, Richard A. 1965. *Russia's Hawaii Adventure.* Berkeley: University of California Press.

Postan, M. M. 1972. *The Medieval Economy and Society: An Economic History of Britain, 1100–1500.* Berkeley: University of California Press.

Pratt, Julius W. 1932. "The Hawaiian Revolution: A Re-interpretation." *Pacific Historical Review* 1:273–294.

Putterman, Louis, and David N. Weil. 2010. "Post-1500 Population Flows and the Long-Run Determinants of Economic Growth and Inequality." *Quarterly Journal of Economics* 125:1627–1682.

Rallu, Jean-Louis. 2008. "Pre- and Post-contact Population in Island Polynesia: Can Projections Meet Retrodictions?" In *The Growth and Collapse of Island Societies: Archaeological and Demographic Perspectives*, ed. Patrick V. Kirch and Jean-Louis Rallu. Honolulu: University of Hawai'i Press.

Ravago, Majah-Leah, James Roumasset, and Kimberly Burnett. 2008. "Resource Management for Sustainable Development of Island Economies." Working Paper no. 08-04, Department of Economics, University of Hawaii.

Rieth, Timothy M., Terry L. Hunt, Carl Lipo, and Janet M. Wilmshurst. 2011. "The 13th Century Polynesian Colonization of Hawai'i Island." *Journal of Archaeological Science* 38:2740–2749.

Roback, Jennifer. 1982. "Wages, Rents, and the Quality of Life." *Journal of Political Economy* 90:1257–1278.

Robinson, Chalfant. 1904. *A History of Two Reciprocity Treaties: The Treaty with Canada in 1854, the Treaty with the Hawaiian Islands in 1876.* New Haven, Conn.: Tuttle, Morehouse & Taylor Press.

Rosa, John P. 2014. *Local Story: The Massie-Kahahawai Case and the Culture of History.* Honolulu: University of Hawai'i Press.

Rose, Louis A. 1989a. "Urban Land Supply: Natural and Contrived Restrictions." *Journal of Urban Economics* 25:325–345.

———. 1989b. "Urban Land Supply: The Effect of Topographical Restriction on Price." *Journal of Urban Economics* 26:335–347.

Rose, Louis A., and Sumner J. La Croix. 1989. "Urban Land Price: The Extraordinary Case of Honolulu, Hawaii." *Urban Studies* 26:301–314.

Roumasset, James, and Sumner J. La Croix. 1988. "Coevolution of Property Rights and Political Order." In *Rethinking Institutional Analysis and Development*, ed. V. Ostrom, D. Feeny, and H. Picht, 315–336. San Francisco: International Center for Economic Growth.

Rowland, Donald. 1943. "Orientals and the Suffrage in Hawaii." *Pacific Historical Review* 12:11–21.

Russ, William Adam, Jr. (1959) 1992. *The Hawaiian Revolution (1893–94).* London: Associated University Presses (Selinsgrove: Susquehanna University Press).

———. (1961) 1992. *The Hawaiian Republic (1894–98), and Its Struggle to Win Annexation.* London: Associated University Presses (Selinsgrove: Susquehanna University Press).

Sahlins, Marshall, with assistance of Dorothy B. Barrère. 1992. *Historical Ethnography.* Vol. 1 of Patrick V. Kirch and Marshall Sahlins, *Anahulu: The Anthropology of History in the Kingdom of Hawaii.* Chicago: University of Chicago Press.

Sai, David Keanu. 2008. "The American Occupation of the Hawaiian Kingdom: Beginning the Transition from Occupied to Restored State." PhD diss., Department of Political Science, University of Hawai'i-Mānoa.

Saiz, Albert. 2010. "The Geographic Determinants of Housing Supply." *Quarterly Journal of Economics* 125:1253–1296.

Sandwich Islands Missions. 1834. "Answers to the Questions of the Circular of the Sandwich Islands Mission, June & July 1834." In *American Board of Commissioners for Foreign Missions Pacific Islands Missions Records, Sandwich Island Missions, Letters, etc.*, Feb. 20, 1830–Dec. 29, 1836, pt. 1. [66], vol. 4, 65–68.

Schanzenbach, Max M., and Robert H. Sitkoff. 2007. "Did Reform of Prudent Trust Investment Laws Change Trust Portfolio Allocation? *Journal of Law and Economics* 50:681–711.

Schmitt, Robert C. 1968. *Demographic Statistics of Hawaii, 1778–1965.* Honolulu: University of Hawai'i Press.

———. 1970a. "Famine Mortality in Hawaii." *Journal of Pacific History* 5:109–115.

———. 1970b. "The *Okuu*: Hawaii's Greatest Epidemic." *Hawaii Medical Journal* 29:359–364.

———. 1971. "New Estimates of the Pre-censal Population of Hawaii." *Journal of the Polynesian Society* 80:237–243.

———. 1976. "Unemployment Rates in Hawaii during the 1930s." *Hawaiian Journal of History* 10:90–101.

———. 1977. *Historical Statistics of Hawaii.* Honolulu: University Press of Hawai'i.

Searle, John E., Jr. 1886. *A Few Facts Concerning the Hawaiian Reciprocity Treaty.* Washington, D.C.: Thomas McGill & Co.

Shanks, G. Dennis. 2016. "Lethality of First Contact Dysentery Epidemics on Pacific Islands." *American Journal of Tropical Medicine and Hygiene* 95:273–277.

Sharp, Andrew. 1957. *Ancient Voyages in the Pacific.* Harmondsworth, UK: Penguin.

Shineberg, Dorothy. 1967. *They Came for Sandalwood: A Study of the Sandalwood Trade in the South-West Pacific, 1830–1865.* Carlton, Victoria: Melbourne University Press.

Shiue, Carol H. 2004. "Local Granaries and Central Government Disaster Relief: Moral Hazard and Intergovernmental Finance in Eighteenth- and Nineteenth-Century China." *Journal of Economic History* 64:100–124.

Shoemaker, James H. 1940. *Labor in the Territory of Hawaii, 1939.* Washington, D.C.: Government Printing Office.

Silva, Noenoe K. 2000. "He Kanawai E Ho'opau I Na Hula Kuolo Hawai'i: The Political Economy of Banning the Hula." *Hawaiian Journal of History* 34:29–48.

———. 2004. *Aloha Betrayed: Native Hawaiian Resistance to American Colonialism.* Durham, N. C.: Duke University Press.

Sparrow, Bartholomew H. 2006. *The Insular Cases and the Emergence of American Empire.* Lawrence: University Press of Kansas.

Spitz, Allan A. 1963. "Organization and Administration of the Hawaiian Homes Program" (working paper, Legislative Reference Bureau, Honolulu).

———. 1964. *Land Aspects of the Hawaiian Homes Program.* Report no. 1b. Honolulu: Legislative Reference Bureau.

————. 1967. "The Transplantation of American Democratic Institutions: The Case of Hawaii." *Political Science Quarterly* 82:386–398.

Spolaore, Enrico, and Romain Wacziarg. 2013. "How Deep Are the Roots of Economic Development?" *Journal of Economic Literature* 51:325–369.

Spriggs, Matthew, and Patrick Kirch. 1992. "'*Auwai, Kanawai*, and *Waiwai*: Irrigation in Kawailoa-uka." In *Anahulu: The Anthropology of History in the Kingdom of Hawaii*, vol. 2, *The Archaeology of History*, ed. Patrick Kirch, 157–164. Chicago: University of Chicago Press.

Stannard, David E. 1989. *Before the Horror: The Population of Hawai'i on the Eve of Western Contact*. Honolulu: Social Science Research Institute, University of Hawai'i.

————. 2005. *Honor Killing: Race, Rape, and Clarence Darrow's Spectacular Last Case*. New York: Penguin Books.

State of Hawaii, Department of Business, Economic Development and Tourism. 1970–2016. *State Data Book*. Honolulu: Department of Business, Economic Development and Tourism.

State of Hawaii, Department of Hawaiian Home Lands. 2015. *2014 Annual Report*. Accessed December 17, 2017. http://dhhl.hawaii.gov/wp-content/uploads/2011/11/DHHL-Annual-Report-2014-Web.pdf.

State of Hawaii, Hawaii Housing Authority. 1982. *Annual Report July 1, 1981/June 30, 1982*. Honolulu: State of Hawaii.

State of Hawaii, Legislative Reference Bureau. 1946. *Congressional Debates on Hawaiian Organic Act*. Foreword. Compiled May 1946. Honolulu: Legislative Reference Bureau.

State of Hawaii, Office of the Lt. Governor. 1969. *Housing Costs in Hawaii: Report to the Legislature of the State of Hawaii*. Honolulu: State of Hawaii.

Stauffer, Robert H. 2004. *Kahana: How the Land Was Lost*. Honolulu: University of Hawai'i Press.

Stewart, Charles S. 1830. *Journal of a Residence in the Sandwich Islands during the Years 1823, 1824, 1825*. London: H. Fisher & P. Jackson.

Stewart, Watt. 1951. *Chinese Bondage in Peru: A History of the Chinese Coolie in Peru, 1849–1874*. Durham, N.C.: Duke University Press.

Stigler, George J. 1966. *The Theory of Price*. 3rd ed. New York: Macmillan.

Stirling, Yates. 1938. *Sea Duty: The Memoirs of a Fighting Admiral*. New York: G. P. Putnam's Sons.

Survey and Marketing Services. 1976. *1975 Census Update Survey: Oahu*. Honolulu.

Surveyor General, comp. 1887. *Index of All Grants Issued By the Hawaiian Government Previous to March 31, 1886*. Honolulu.

Takaki, Ronald. 1983. *Pau Hana: Plantation Life and Labor in Hawaii*. Honolulu: University of Hawai'i Press.

Tate, Merze. 1965. *The United States and the Hawaiian Kingdom: A Political History*. New Haven: Yale University Press.

———. 1968. *Hawaii: Reciprocity or Annexation.* East Lansing: Michigan State University Press.

Taussig, Frank W. 1892. "Reciprocity." *Quarterly Journal of Economics* 7:26–39. Reprinted in Frank W. Taussig (1920), *Free Trade, the Tariff and Reciprocity* (New York: MacMillan).

———. 1914. *The Tariff History of the United States.* 6th ed. New York: G. P. Putnam's Sons, The Knickerbocker Press.

Taylor, M. Scott. 2010. "Buffalo Hunt: International Trade and the Virtual Extinction of the North American Bison." *American Economic Review* 101:3162–3195.

Taylor, William H. 1935. "The Hawaiian Sugar Industry." PhD diss., University of California-Berkeley.

Terrell, Jennifer, ed. 1988. *Von den Steinem's Marquesan Myths.* Trans. Marta Langridge. Canberra: Target Oceania/The Journal of Pacific History.

Terrell, John Edward. 2011. "Recalibrating Polynesian Prehistory." *Proceedings of the National Academy of Sciences* 108:1753–1754.

Thrum, T. G. 1905. "The Sandalwood Trade of Early Hawaii as Told by Pioneer Traders, Voyagers, and Others." *Hawaiian Annual* 31:43–74.

Trigger, Bruce. 1993. *Early Civilizations: Ancient Egypt in Context.* Cairo: American University in Cairo Press.

Truman, President Harry S. 1948. *Annual Message to Congress on the State of the Union.* January 7, 1948. Accessed December 10, 2017. https://trumanlibrary.org/whistlestop/tap/1748.htm.

Tumarkin, D. D. 1983. "Materials of M. Vasilyev's Expedition: A Valuable Source for the Study of Cultural Change and Intercultural Contacts in the Hawaiian Islands." *Pacific Studies* 6:11–32.

Tyerman, Daniel, George Bennet, James Montgomery, and London Missionary Society. 1832. *Journal of voyages and travels by the Rev. Daniel Tyerman and George Bennet, esq deputed from the London missionary society, to visit their various stations in the South sea islands, China, India, &c. between the years 1821 and 1829.* Boston: Crocker and Brewster.

Umbeck, John R. 1977. *Theory of Property Rights with Applications to the California Gold Rush.* Ames: Iowa State Press.

———. 1981. "Might Makes Rights: A Theory of the Formation and Initial Distribution of Property Rights." *Economic Inquiry* 19:38–59.

U.S. Bureau of the Census. 1923a. *Fourteenth Census of the United States Taken in the Year 1920.* Vol. 3, *Population, 1920: Composition and Characteristics of the Population by States.* Washington, D.C.: U.S. Government Printing Office.

———. 1923b. *Fourteenth Census of the United States Taken in the Year 1920.* Vol. 4, *Population, 1920: Occupations.* Washington, D.C.: U.S. Government Printing Office.

U.S. Commissioner of Labor. 1903. *Report of the U.S. Commissioner of Labor on Hawaii, 1902.* Washington, D.C.: U.S. Government Printing Office.

U.S. Congress, House of Representatives, Committee on Territories. 1946. State-hood for Hawaii: Hearings before the Subcommittee of the Committee on the Territories on H.R. 236, 79th Cong. 2d Sess., January 7–18, 1946. Washington, D.C.: U.S. Government Printing Office.

U.S. Department of Justice. 1932. *Law Enforcement in the Territory of Hawaii.* Washington, D.C.: U.S. Government Printing Office.

U.S. Department of Justice and Federal Trade Commission. 1992. *Horizontal Merger Guidelines.* April 2, 1992.

———. 2010. *Horizontal Merger Guidelines.* August 9, 2010.

U.S. Department of the Interior. 1908, 1919. *Report of the Governor of Hawaii to the Secretary of the Interior.* Washington, D.C.: U.S. Government Printing Office.

U.S. Government, Hawaiian Commission. 1899. *Report.* Washington, D.C.: U.S. Government Printing Office.

U.S. House of Representatives. 1876. Committee on Ways and Means, Report: Hawaiian Treaty. House Report no. 116, 44th Cong., 1st Sess., parts 1 and 2.

———. 1883. House Report no. 1860, 47th Cong., 2d Sess.

———. 1891. House Report no. 3422, 51st Cong., 2d Sess.

———. 1920. Proposed Amendments to the Organic Act of the Territory of Ha-waii, Hearings before the Commission on the Territories, 66th Cong., 2d Sess., February 3, 4, 5, 7, 10, 1920.

U.S. National Archives and Records Administration. 2016. *Code of Federal Regu-lations.* Title 43, Part 50. Procedures for Reestablishing a Formal Government-to-Government Relationship with the Native Hawaiian Community.

U.S. President. 1918. *Proclamations of President Woodrow Wilson, 1918.* Washing-ton, D.C.: U.S. Government Printing Office.

U.S. Senate. 1867. "Message of the President of the United States," 40th Cong., 1st Sess.

———. 1883. Senate Report 1013, 47th Cong., 2d Sess.

———. 1893a. Senate Executive Document no. 76, 52d Cong., 2d Sess.

———. 1893b. Senate Executive Document no. 77, 52d Cong., 2d Sess.

———. 1894. "The Sugar Schedule in the Tariff Bill of 1894," Senate Report no. 603, 53rd Cong., 2d Sess.

———. 1898. *Constitutions of Hawaii.* Senate Document no. 109, 55th Cong., 2d Sess.

———. 1901. Senate Document no. 231, Pt. 6, 56th Cong., 2d Sess.

———. 1932. Hearing before the Committee on Territories and Insular Affairs, United States Senate, 72d Cong., 1st Sess., on S.J. Res. 81, A Joint Resolution Providing for an Investigation of the Government of the Territory of Hawaii, and for Other Purposes.

Valeri, Valerio. 1985. *Kingship and Sacrifice: Ritual and Sacrifice in Ancient Hawaii.* Trans. Paula Wissing. Chicago: University of Chicago Press.

Van Dyke, Jon. 1992. "The Evolving Legal Relationships between the United States and its Affiliated U.S.-Flag Islands." *University of Hawaii Law Review* 14: 445–517.

———. 2008. *Who Owns the Crown Lands of Hawaii?* Honolulu: University of Hawai'i Press.

Van Tyne, Claude Halstead. (1902) 1959. *The Loyalists in the American Revolution.* Gloucester, Mass.: Peter Smith.

Vargha, Louis A. 1964. *An Economic View of Leasehold and Fee Simple Tenure of Residential Land in Hawaii.* Bulletin no. 4. Honolulu: Land Study Bureau, University of Hawaii.

Vause, M. M. 1962. "The Hawaiian Homes Commission Act, 1920: History and Analysis." Master's thesis, University of Hawaii.

Voigtländer, Nico, and Hans-Joachim Voth. 2012. "Persecution Perpetuated: The Medieval Origins of Anti-Semitic Violence in Nazi Germany." *Quarterly Journal of Economics* 127:1339–1392.

———. 2013. "The Gifts of Mars: Warfare and Europe's Early Rise to Riches." *Journal of Economic Perspectives* 27:165–186.

Wakukawa, Ernest K. 1938. *A History of the Japanese People in Hawaii.* Honolulu: Toyo Shoin.

Walpole, Mary. 2014. "Eastern Polynesia: The Linguistic Evidence Revisited." *Oceanic Linguistics* 53:256–272.

Walther, Michael. 1997. *Pearls of Pearl Harbor and the Islands of Hawaii.* Honolulu: Natural Images of Hawaii Press.

Ward, R. Gerard. 1992. "Pacific Island Land Tenure: An Overview of Practices and Issues." In *Land, Culture and Development in the Aquatic Continent*, ed. D. G. Malcolm, Jr., and Jeanne Skog. Kihei, Hawaii: Kapalua Pacific Center.

Wells, David A. 1878. *The Sugar Industry of the United States and the Tariff.* New York: Evening Post Press.

Wilcox, Carol. 1998. *Sugar Water: Hawaii's Plantation Ditches.* Honolulu: University of Hawai'i Press.

Williams, Raburn M. 1993. *The Politics of Boom and Bust in Twentieth Century America: A Macroeconomic History.* Minneapolis/St. Paul, MN: West Publishing Company.

Williamson, Claudia R., and Carrie B. Kerekes. 2011. "Securing Private Property: Formal versus Informal Institutions." *Journal of Law and Economics* 54:537–572.

Williamson, Jeffrey G. 1995. "The Evolution of Global Labor Markets since 1830: Background Evidence and Hypotheses." *Explorations in Economic History* 32:141–196.

———. 2000. "Globalization, Factor Prices and Living Standards in Asia before 1940." In *Asia Pacific Dynamism 1500–2000*, ed. A. J. H. Latham and H. Kawakatsu, 13–45. London: Routledge.

———. 2011. *Trade and Poverty: When the Third World Fell Behind.* Cambridge, Mass.: MIT Press.

Williamson, Jeffrey G., and David E. Bloom. 1998. "Demographic Transitions and Economic Miracles in Emerging Asia." *World Bank Economic Review* 12: 419–455.

Williamson, Jeffrey G., and Timothy J. Hatton. 1998. *The Age of Mass Migration: Causes and Economic Impact.* New York: Oxford University Press.

Wilmshurst, J. M., A. J. Anderson, T. F. G. Higham, and T. H. Worthy. 2008. "Dating the Late Prehistoric Dispersal of Polynesians to New Zealand using the Commensal Pacific Rat." *Proceedings of the National Academy of Sciences* 105:7676–7680.

Wilmshurst, J. M., T. L. Hunt, C. P. Lipo, and A. J. Anderson. 2011. "High-Precision Radio-Carbon Dating Shows Recent and Rapid Colonization of East Polynesia." *Proceedings of the National Academy of Sciences* 108:1815–1820.

Wittfogel, Karl August. 1957. *Oriental Despotism: A Comparative Study of Total Power.* New Haven, Conn.: Yale University Press.

Wright, Philip G. 1924. *Sugar in Relation to the Tariff.* New York: McGraw-Hill.

Wyllie, R. C. 1848. *Answers to Questions Proposed by R. C. Wyllie.* Honolulu: Department of Foreign Affairs.

Zalburg, Sanford. 1979. *A Spark Is Struck! Jack Hall & the ILWU in Hawaii.* Honolulu: University of Hawai'i Press.

Ziegler, Alan C. 2002. *Hawaiian Natural History, Ecology, and Evolution.* Honolulu, University of Hawai'i Press.

Index

A page number in *italics* refers to a figure or table.

sugar plantations, 9, 125, 139, 170, 171, 255, 256
Johnson, Lyndon, 205
Johnson, Simon, 265
Jones-Costigan Act of 1934, 193–94, 196, 197, 219
Jorgenson, Dale, 48
Judd, Gerrit P., 96, 99, 100, 116
Judd, Lawrence M., 158, 159
judicial independence, 198–99
Jussawalla, Meheroo, 264

Kaʻahumanu: crushing revolt on Kauaʻi in 1825, 93; death in 1832, 94; dismantling state religion, 81–82; expected land redistribution by, 303n49; military strength of, 85; portrait of, 83; redistributing rights to sandalwood trade, 282; sharing power after Kamehameha's death, 81; supporting literacy, 92
Kahahawai, Joseph, 158
kāhuna (prayer specialists): abolition of state religion and, 7; in basic natural state, 49; functions of, 7, 283; land redistribution by Kamehameha and, 80–81
Kakaʻalaneo, 52
Kalākaua, King: Bayonet Constitution and, 112, 133; Bayonet Rebellion and, 10; death in 1891, 136; efforts on behalf of reciprocity treaty, 119–20, 154; growing opposition to, 133; income from sugar leases on crown lands, 312n45; opposed to cession of Pearl Bay, 311n27; opposed to renewal of reciprocity treaty, 131, 133, 139; reviving Hawaiian culture, 288n15; sugar interests helping to elect, 119; U.S. military power ensuring 1874 choice of, 142
Kamakau, Samuel, 52, 54, 61, 76, 78, 79, 80, 92, 288n8
Kameʻeleihiwa, Lilikalā, 80, 149, 282
Kamehameha, King: centralized institutions established by, 162, 164, 165; consolidation of political power under, 8, 69, 70, 300n5; death of, 81; huge temple built for, 44; invading Maui, Molokaʻi, and Oʻahu, 54; invading Oʻahu and bringing disease, 298n63; kapu on harvest of pearls, 54; kapu on selling goods to foreign ships, 74, 298n50; Kauaʻi chiefs

and, 72–73; land redistribution by, 3, 8, 70–72, 80–81, 267, 282; military victory of 1795, 8, 70, 77, 88; monopoly on provisioning visiting ships, 74; portrait of, 71; property rights in sandalwood and, 78–81; sandalwood revenues invested by, 84; sandalwood trade and, 75–76, 77, 78–79, 83, 302n24; taxing ships in harbor at Oʻahu, 297n38
Kamehameha II. See Liholiho (Kamehameha II)
Kamehameha III. See Kauikeaouli, King (Kamehameha III)
Kamehameha IV, 310n21, 311n26
Kamehameha V, 129
Kamehameha Schools, 216, 227, 329n16, 340n44
kānaka maoli: defined, 6; dismantling of state religion and, 82; growing sugar on aliʻi-controlled land, 103; initially concentrated on shoreline, 29; literacy among, 92; in mature natural state, 141; opposing foreign land ownership, 99; property rights under Māhele, 335n23; prostrating themselves before aliʻi, 6
Kapena, Jonah, 92
Kauaʻi: agreement of 1810 with Kamehameha, 72–73; Kamehameha's two failed efforts to conquer, 72; possibly first island to be settled, 25; suited to small ponded taro farms, 28–29
Kauikeaouli, King (Kamehameha III): annexation crisis with Britain and, 100–101, 149; annexation treaty negotiated with U.S. in 1854 and, 310n21; bringing Western property institutions to Hawaiʻi, 149; crown lands as private property of, 96, 149–50; governmental changes instituted by, 95; land redistribution under, 3, 267, 282; pressure from Western governments on, 89; supporting literacy, 92; using U.S. help in French crisis, 116
Kaumualiʻi (alʻi nui of Kauaʻi), 72, 86
kauwa, 290n21
Kawānanakoa, Princess Abigail, 173
Kay, Peter, 264
Kekauaokalani, 81, 83–84, 86, 93
Kennedy, Anthony, 272
Kingdom of Hawaiʻi. See Mōʻī (king); monarchy